'77

'77

DENVER, THE BRONCOS, AND A COMING OF AGE

TERRY FREI

Photographs by Kenn Bisio

TAYLOR TRADE PUBLISHING
Lanham • New York • Boulder • Toronto • Plymouth, UK

Published by Taylor Trade Publishing
An imprint of The Rowman & Littlefield Publishing Group, Inc.
4501 Forbes Boulevard, Suite 200, Lanham, Maryland 20706
www.rlpgtrade.com

Estover Road, Plymouth PL6 7PY, United Kingdom

Distributed by NATIONAL BOOK NETWORK

Library of Congress Cataloging-in-Publication Data

Frei, Terry, 1955–
    '77 : Denver, the Broncos, and a coming of age / Terry Frei.
       p.   cm.
    Includes bibliographical references and index.
    ISBN-13: 978-1-58979-213-5 (cloth : alk. paper)
    ISBN-10: 1-58979-213-0 (cloth : alk. paper)
     1. Denver Broncos (Football team)—History.   2. Football—Colorado—Denver—
History.   I. Title.   II. Title: Denver, the Broncos, and a coming of age.
GV936.D37F74   2008
796.332'640978883—dc22
                                                          2007033820

∞ ™ The paper used in this publication meets the minimum requirements of American National Standard for Information Sciences—Permanence of Paper for Printed Library Materials, ANSI/NISO Z39.48–1992.

Manufactured in the United States of America.

To Helen
And to the '77 Broncos

Contents

Foreword

There is nothing quite so special in life as a "first": a first car, a first kiss, or just maybe a city's first championship. That's what the 1977 Denver Broncos represented for both Denver and the entire Rocky Mountain region.

Denver in 1977 was a far different place than what it has become today. Thirty years ago it was dealing with a complex: how are we viewed by the major cities back east? Can we be favorably compared to them? Well, Denver did have NFL, NBA, and NHL franchises. But the Broncos were in many ways symbolic of the city. They were a team that had never made the playoffs in their sixteen years. And to some, they were best known for their embarrassingly gauche vertically striped sox.

And then came 1977. A team and its town were never the same again.

In '77: Denver, the Broncos, and a Coming of Age, Terry Frei gives us a unique view of what that team and this city were like. He gives us insight into the diverse group of people that turned that team around. There were many personalities and characters, but there were two people in particular who saved or reinvented their careers.

Head Coach Red Miller was a career assistant coach. Long overdue for a promotion, he finally got an opportunity to become a head coach and wasn't about to waste it. He was the perfect choice after the controversial way John Ralston lost the job. (You will read and learn things you never knew about the "Dirty Dozen" who tried to oust him.) Red was and still is a man's man who didn't mind getting down in the trenches and letting you know how he wanted it done.

Quarterback Craig Morton took a different path. After spending his career in the spotlight in Dallas and New York, his trade to Denver in

1977 gave the veteran a final chance to maximize what football he had left. And in any number of ways he was reborn. He was a veteran who didn't make mistakes and showed his team and a town what toughness was all about and what it really was like to play hurt.

But any analysis of the '77 Broncos has to start with the Orange Crush Defense, a defense loaded with characters and led by a stalwart corps of linebackers. Randy Gradishar, Tom Jackson, Bob Swenson, and Joe Rizzo came from different places and had different personalities, but on the football field they were the "four horsemen." They worked in perfect unison. Standout defense has become almost expected in Denver, but the work of that unit of linebackers set the gold standard.

You will read about the life and times of Lyle Alzado, Barney Chavous, Rubin Carter, Haven Moses, Otis Armstrong, and Jumbo Andy Maurer and realize what an amazing story the run to the Super Bowl really was. That season put all of us in Denver, whether we covered the team or rooted for it, on the map.

This was Denver before LoDo. This was Denver before a certain other number 7 came on the scene. This was Denver before two Super Bowl rings.

This book reminds us of just how special that time was.

Ron Zappolo
News Anchor
Fox 31
Denver, Colorado

Acknowledgments

Editor Rick Rinehart of Taylor Trade has my gratitude for his continuing faith—in me, in this book, and in *Horns, Hogs, and Nixon Coming.*

The men who covered the Broncos in that era as beat writers or columnists—especially Dick Connor, Joe Sanchez, Steve Cameron, Woody Paige, and Bob Collins—did great work that holds up on microfilm. Bob and Dick both left us too soon; I salute them and their memories.

The librarians at the *Denver Post*, the Colorado Historical Society, and the Denver Public Library were tolerant and helpful.

To expand on the dedication: Most of the '77 Broncos I contacted were gracious in agreeing to talk, open up, and trust me. I can't thank them enough. I fully understand as I write this that there have been many Broncos books and more are on the way. I hope '77 vindicates the decisions of those I contacted who did consent to speak with me.

ESPN.com has been supportive of all my book projects, and hockey editor Joy Russo has been a joy to work with the last couple of years—the period in which I often had my mind back in 1977.

And thanks again to the reading and feedback committee—friends, family, and compatriots. You know who you are. Sorry about all those attachments.

Author's Note

Material from my contemporary interviews is attributed in the present tense—e.g., "says" and "recalls." Quotes obtained from archival material are attributed in the past tense, and sources are cited in the notes following the text.

—T.F.

The Young Sportswriter, a Different Denver . . . and a Player Revolt

When Red Miller took over as the Broncos' head coach, I was a grizzled veteran journalist. I had just turned 22 and had been a full-time sports writer at the *Denver Post* for a month.

It was an experiment.

A few years earlier, in Eugene—where my father, former World War II fighter pilot Jerry Frei, was the head football coach of the University of Oregon Ducks—I took a South Eugene High journalism class in the fall of my junior year. Part of the class requirement was to submit stories to the *Axe*, the school paper. Intrigued when I heard my favorite disc jockey say on the air that he would speak at a forum in downtown Eugene sponsored by the Vietnam Veterans Against the War, I attended the meeting, listened, interviewed, took notes—and turned in a story that would have been too long for the *New Yorker*. A much shorter version ran, and it was my first published newspaper story. My second was about the UO campus appearance of the former VVAW national leader, an ex-Navy man named John Kerry. The third, I think, was about the candy selection at the school store.

I had the writing bug.

A few months later, in February 1972, I moved with my family to the Denver area when my father became the Broncos' offensive line coach. He came to Denver with one of his Pacific Eight Conference competitors, John Ralston, who had guided the Stanford Indians to consecutive Rose Bowl victories, over Ohio State and Michigan. For several weeks, before my mother and sisters arrived and we moved into the home my parents had purchased in suburban Wheat Ridge, I lived with my father and the other new assistant coaches in the Broncos' official local headquarters—the Continental Denver[1] at Speer Boulevard and Interstate 25—and commuted west to attend Wheat Ridge High.

I composed a few "In Their Own Write" youth opinion columns for the local weekly, the *Wheat Ridge Sentinel*, plus opinion pieces for the WRHS paper that earned me the nickname "Rebel" from my new baseball coach, Steve Bell. By then, I was playing catcher for the Farmers and was the batterymate for, among others, a hard-throwing senior right-hander named Dave Logan.[2]

That summer, in one of our last American Legion games, my troublesome right knee gave out. After undergoing my second major knee surgery, I was in a hip-to-toe cast and was speeding through the Wheat Ridge hallways on crutches early in my senior year, regretting that I wasn't able to play football. (It was not a major—or even minor—setback for the Farmers' 1972 football fortunes.) I accepted an offer from a *Sentinel* editor who knew of my injury: I covered high school football for the *Sentinel* editions in Lakewood, Arvada, and Wheat Ridge.

I played my senior year of baseball in the spring of 1973, and then declined an invitation to go out as a walk-on at the University of Colorado to play for Buffaloes coach Irv Brown, who had a high profile nationally because of his work as a college basketball referee. I was realistic enough to know that I would have walked on and then walked right down to the bullpen, and done all my catching there. Instead, I started working part-time at the *Rocky Mountain News* as a CU freshman. At the outset, my tasks were typical of the college-age part-timer. Mostly, I answered the telephones and took results and statistics:

Caller: "Zigmandokovich 27 pass from Smith."

Me: "Spell that, please."

Caller: "S-m-i . . ."

Old-school journalism was colliding with the new technology and rep-ortorial attitudes. Veteran *News* writers, such as Chet Nelson, Manny Boody, and Leonard Cahn, could have stepped right out of *The Front Page*—the original, in black and white. The rock was Bob Collins, a pipe-smoking Iowan. He moved up from assistant sports editor to sports edi-tor, often also covered the Broncos, and held the department together. The department's unofficial auxiliary office was the nearby Denver Press Club, where *Post* folks also hung out and the congenial bartenders were willing to serve a 19-year-old *News* part-timer after work.

For the next three years, I gained invaluable experience. Using the copy desk worker's tools of the time—pencil, scissors, glue pot, *Webster's*, and a thesaurus—I edited stories and wrote headlines. I was neither disil-lusioned nor surprised to discover that there was a bookie in the back shop, among the linotype machines, trays of type, and clicking sounds as the men called "printers" put together the pages. When sent back to be the liaison between the sports department and the printers, I learned to read the type backwards and discovered—the hard way—that if I noticed transposed lines and touched the type in the page layout to point out the error, it violated 27 union-mandated rules and caused more commotion than a fire alarm.

I helped Boody with the high school sports coverage, and in the sum-mers, when I worked full 40-hour weeks, occasionally pinch-hit on beats when writers took vacations. Eventually, I was allowed to write a few features, including one on new Colorado football coach Bill Mallory and another on Tammy Beeson, a young high school girl from Eads, Colorado, who had made national headlines by going to court to chal-lenge the rule that married students couldn't play sports. She had become pregnant, married the father, had a son, and returned to school—and wanted to play basketball for the new girls' program at Eads High. Writ-ing those disparate stories—one about a hard-nosed football coach, the other about a young woman rebelling against being ostracized in a small town—convinced me that I enjoyed asking questions and listening to the answers, or otherwise learning about people, and then writing about them.

During my *News* tenure, a young writer, Woodrow Paige Jr., joined the sports department in a dual role—to cover the Denver Nuggets and write columns. He came to us from Memphis, and he represented the onset of the revolution—both in the department, and, to an extent, in Denver journalism. He was young, brash, and talented.

When I was a CU junior, my parents moved away. Dad left Ralston's staff after the '75 season to coach the offensive line for John McKay with the expansion Tampa Bay Buccaneers. Dad and McKay had been young assistant coaches together under Len Casanova at Oregon, and our families also were close, so Dad was rejoining an old buddy. My father left on good terms with Ralston, who showed he had no hard feelings when he hired my older brother, Dave, fresh out of the Army, to be the Broncos' assistant director of public relations. So I still had a family connection to the Broncos as the '76 season unfolded.

That fall, in my final semester before graduating, I decided I was going to try sportswriting as a profession for a couple of years, salt away some money, and then perhaps go to law school. The *News* didn't have a full-time job available, but Dick Connor, the assistant sports editor at the *Denver Post*, let me know they were about to add a writer, and maybe even two, and invited me to apply. Sports editor Bick Lucas hired me to cover high school sports, horse racing, and auto racing. I began my career on December 20, 1976—three days after I took my last CU final exam.

The *Post* was in an old building at 15th and California streets.[3] We were across from The Denver Dry Goods department store and the Sportsman, the greasy spoon watering hole where it didn't seem at all strange to order *huevos rancheros* and a beer on the breakfast break while working the 6 a.m.–3 p.m. shift in the office, which is what we often had to do at an afternoon paper. It was a wonderful building, with huge picture windows along the California Street side where pedestrians could stop and watch the presses rolling and the afternoon paper coming together. You half expected one of the papers to jump off the press, do a few 360-degree turns, and come to a stop in the air in the window, as in the old movie trick that lets you know that "Yanks Cop Flag!" or "Yanks Storm Beach!" I'll never forget that first look at veteran scribe Frank Haraway, who bravely overcame polio and scrambled around on his crutches, covering University of Colorado sports and his beloved baseball Denver Bears for decades. Frank was ensconced at an ancient typewriter at the window. He wore a visor and always seemed to be carefully aligning carbon paper between the sheets of paper.

More than the Denver newspaper business was in a state of flux: Denver itself was, and sports were a part of it.

Baseball had been Denver's signature game for so long, it didn't seem fair that it was the only one of the major-league sports that didn't have a franchise in town. The American pastime traditionally was big, especially in the Bottoms area, on the east side of the Valley Highway, and in heavily Italian-American North Denver, with Police Athletic League and American Legion programs and sandlot games going until it got too dark to play. The Denver Bears were the New York Yankees' Class AAA farm club in the late 1950s before switching affiliations several times in the ensuing years, and by 1977 the parent club was the Montreal Expos. Their owners were the Phipps brothers, who also were majority owners of the Broncos. Gerald had long been in construction, while Allan was an attorney who also was involved in real-estate development.

The NBA Nuggets were the most entertaining act in town, thanks to the stewardship of Carl Scheer. He was brought to Denver to revive a struggling American Basketball Association franchise, the Rockets, who played in the tiny downtown Auditorium Arena. Scheer pushed through a renaming; brought in Larry Brown, the coach he had worked with during his tenure with the since-folded Carolina Cougars; and shocked the basketball world with his signing of prized college star Bobby Jones in 1974, plus David Thompson and Marvin Webster in 1975. Dan Issel also came from the Kentucky Colonels in a 1975 trade, and the Nuggets packed the new McNichols Sports Arena, originally envisioned as the anchor for the 1976 Winter Olympics awarded to Colorado. Those Games were moved to Innsbruck because Colorado voters—following a drive led by environmentalist State Representative Richard Lamm—rejected the host's role at the polls. Some considered that a dishonorable backing out of a commitment and a black eye in the international court of public opinion we still hadn't gotten rid of in 1977. Others stood by it as a commonsense refusal to bankrupt the state and pillage the environment in a time when Olympic Games were capable of doing both.

The Nuggets raced through the 1975–76 ABA season with a 60-24 record, but came up short against the Julius Erving–led New York Nets in the playoff finals. Tiring of raids and ridiculously accelerating salaries, the NBA took in four ABA teams—the Nets, Nuggets, Indiana Pacers, and San Antonio Spurs—for the 1976–77 season, and Denver was well on its way to a division title in early '77, proving the ABA had been no soft touch.

The other McNichols tenant was the NHL Colorado Rockies. The franchise was born as the expansion Kansas City Scouts in 1974. After the money ran out in Kansas City, the Scouts were sold to Denver oilman Jack Vickers and moved to Denver for the 1976–77 season, but they were terrible on the ice and drew sparse crowds in their first NHL year.

The Broncos were the city's first major-league team, beginning play in the American Football League in 1960. Overcoming a rocky start at the gate, they became perennial sellouts even as the stadium grew. A 1967 vote rejected public funding of a new stadium, but the Phipps brothers resisted overtures from potential buyers who wanted to move the team. Instead, the Phipps brothers eventually sold voters on approving $25 million in public funding for a two-phase stadium expansion. Football capacity went from 51,706 to 63,532 for 1976, and after new movable east stands were constructed in the off-season, a sellout would be about 75,087 in 1977. The funding was tied to a limited-time seat tax on tickets.

However, John Ralston wasn't going to be around to coach in the enlarged stadium.

As coach and general manager, Ralston took the once-ragtag organization to respectability, guiding the Broncos to their first winning season (7-5-2) in 1973 and a 9-5 record in 1976. Immediately after the '76 season, Gerald Phipps—citing precedents around the league and aware of unrest in the organization—told Ralston he wouldn't be allowed to be both GM and coach. Ralston says, and others confirm, that he was given the choice of either job. "I wanted to be a coach," Ralston says from his office at San Jose State University. "I wanted to be a coach when I was 13 years old."

Phipps must have known what Ralston's answer would be, and one of the nearly overlooked aspects of the reorganization was that Phipps said that "tighter control over the operation is needed in the area of expenditures, where there is a feeling that some of the money we've spent hasn't produced the desired results." In other words, ownership had concluded that Ralston the GM was spending too much money for Ralston the coach. If Ralston had become a GM only, he might have been terrific in that role and gone down as the architect of the Broncos' turnaround. As it was, he probably *was* the architect, anyway.

Fred Gehrke, the former Rams halfback famed for painting a horn on his helmet and starting a trend, stepped up to GM from assistant GM and director of player personnel. Two days after Gehrke's promotion, on Monday, December 20, Ralston left for Montgomery, Alabama, to attend practices for the upcoming Blue-Gray game. Coincidentally, that was my first day on the job at the *Denver Post*.

A group of Broncos players gathered to talk about Ralston. With defensive end Lyle Alzado doing a lot of yelling and others joining in with more reasoned views, the meeting produced a draft of a statement essentially calling for Ralston's firing. The players at the meeting agreed they would release it at a news conference the next morning. It said, among other things: "We don't believe that it's possible to win a championship under the guidance of John Ralston. He has lost the respect of the players and we don't believe he is capable of coaching us to a championship. We deeply appreciate the tremendous support that the people of Denver have given us, and we feel that they deserve a championship team. Under the present coaching situation, we don't believe this is possible."

The number of players who wholeheartedly supported the revolt is uncertain. There also has been blurring between (a) players meeting to discuss what steps they should take and the actual crafting of the anti-Ralston statement and (b) the gathering of players in conjunction with the scheduled news conference at the Holiday Inn on Colorado Boulevard. As will become clear in subsequent pages, at least one player later listed as a member of the "Dirty Dozen" present on the day of the scheduled news conference disputes the widespread assumptions that they all (a) endorsed the original statement and (b) supported the idea that they should *publicly* express dissatisfaction with Ralston.

With that disclaimer in mind, the twelve players listed in media accounts as being at the hotel were Alzado and his fellow defensive lineman John Grant; running backs Otis Armstrong, Jon Keyworth, and Jim Kiick; linebacker Tom Jackson; offensive linemen Tommy Lyons and Carl Schaukowitch; wide receivers Haven Moses and Rick Upchurch; defensive back Billy Thompson; and receiver/punter Bill Van Heusen.[4]

Word of the imminent news conference reached Gehrke and Gerald Phipps. They showed up at the hotel before it began and met with players.

Some inferred that Gehrke and Phipps were asking them to back off, so they could fire Ralston in due time. The full news conference instead became Billy Thompson reading a far more mild statement—one so mild that, if interpreted literally, every player on the roster could have justified supporting it.

After saying the players had met with Gehrke and Phipps, the statement went on: "The players will support Fred Gehrke completely and we are looking forward to a championship season under his leadership. We also give our full support to the owners in their attempt to bring this about." Thompson said there would be no further comment. However, several of the players did informally talk with reporters, and Bob Collins's *News* story quoted Moses saying that 22 players were "verified as in agreement with what we are doing." But that was in the context of Thompson reading only the watered-down statement. Other reports said 32 players had signed off, and that seems dubious at best. Alzado later said the number was "36 or 37." That's nothing short of absurd.

The originally drafted statement, of which many copies had been made and circulated, was leaked, anyway. That did further damage to Ralston's credibility and angered some players, including Moses, who believed they all had agreed the original statement would remain their secret. It offended Phipps and probably made him determined to avoid any appearance that the players could tell ownership what to do. Plus, the kindly co-owner, who all agree was a gentleman, felt betrayed by the release of the original statement after he had been told the players would back off. In that sense, the strategy of leaking the original statement almost backfired: The move almost saved Ralston's job.

Although that original statement mentioned "the undersigned," it never was officially issued. No list of "undersigned" ever became public, so nobody had to defend their claims with names. The toned-down statement vaguely mentioned "the players." This much was clear: The firebrands in the anti-Ralston movement were Alzado, whose hatred for Ralston was irrational and bordered on the ridiculous, plus the more sensible—if highly passionate—Thompson, Jackson, and Van Heusen.

Two days later, Ralston "announced" he was staying and Gerry Phipps publicly backed him at a news conference. "Now I think it is up to those players to prove, not just to the organization, but to the people of Denver, that they can contribute in a positive way to the Broncos," Phipps said.

Ralston said he had accepted an apology from Van Heusen, who actually was pressured by ownership, was trying to save his job as a punter/backup receiver, and was subjected to a long lecture. Then Ralston made the strategic error of talking about the players as if they were Stanford sophomores. "In my 26 years of coaching and working with young people," he said, "I've learned that they are impetuous and make mistakes. Peer pressure is very strong in pro football and often accounts for some of those mistakes. I've never held it against them."

His point, valid on the surface, that it would have been better—and, by implication, more courageous—if the players had come directly to him with their complaints to talk "eyeball to eyeball" added fuel to the fire, because some players *had* approached him after the 1975 season. They came away believing Ralston had promised he would trade for a quarterback, perhaps New England's Jim Plunkett, in the wake of Charley Johnson's retirement, and that he wouldn't stick with Steve Ramsey, who inspired little faith among his teammates. Nothing happened.

After a month passed, the coach seemed to have ridden out the storm. He hadn't. There was staff unrest—and not only because Ralston had decided to make some changes among the offensive coaches, beginning by firing offensive coordinator Max Coley,[5] whose dissatisfaction with Ralston hadn't been a secret among the players. Gehrke was discovering that Ralston didn't seem to realize that in the new power structure, Gehrke was the boss and had the last say. Ralston, former college linebacker and Marine, the eternal optimist and positive thinker, and a very nice man who tended to respond to requests by making promises that were impossible to fulfill, was in denial. However slight they might have been all along, the chances of him remaining on the job for the '77 season became zero. It all added up. So trying to specify just how many players wholeheartedly—there's that word again—supported the revolt is almost irrelevant; the revolt was only part of a bigger picture.

The coach was fired coming off the best season in the history of the franchise. The announcement came on Monday, January 31, 1977.[6] Red Miller was introduced as head coach the next day.

Looking back, Ralston refuses to be bitter about the ringleaders or the revolt and he won't talk about the details. Maybe you have to know Ralston to understand that it's not disingenuous. "That's water under the bridge, Terry, honest to God," he says. "I was at fault because I was raised in the Depression, just like your dad was, and I got to doing some speaking, and of a sudden, gee, they're giving me $5,000 for a speech and I think I did too much speaking and didn't spend enough time on the coaching."

His successor was touted as the man who could take the Broncos to the next level. That's exactly what Miller did.

Red Miller was the right man, in the right place, with the right team, at the right time. Those of us in Colorado at the time got to watch and be a part of a town turning into a city. The transformation was already underway, involving forces that had nothing to do with sports. Yet, looking back, I'm convinced that never has one team, one season, one year, been such a crucial part of a market's transformation and even maturation. It doesn't mean Denver would be different than it is now if the Broncos had gone 2-12 in 1977. I'm not here to tell you that. I'm telling you if you were in Denver, you're nodding now and saying, hell, you know exactly what I mean. It was ineffable, inexplicable, and unprecedented in a Denver that was different by the time of Stanley Cup and Super Bowl championship parades 20 years later. If you weren't in Denver, I'm going to try to show you what I mean. If you never have set foot in Denver, I'm going to try to show you that teams can be champions without necessarily ending up the season with a trophy raised overhead and champagne spraying.

Never mind the way this book ends.

The '77 Broncos were champions.

I watched it all as a young reporter, just breaking into the business. I watched it as a recent transplant to Colorado who had come to love the state. I was only a couple of years from rooting for the Broncos with the passion of a Bronco coach's son; I knew some of the players through my father and I had Broncos' season tickets of my own. I was trying to reconcile all of this with knowing that I was supposed to be developing a journalist's cynicism and theoretical objectivity. My friends and neighbors and fellow Coloradans were about to get caught up in a season that ended up being about more than games, players, coaches, and wins and losses.

There is only one first time, and in this case, the first time didn't end with a victory in the final game.

That team changed Denver.

Notes

1. The old *Continental Denver* today is split into a Ramada and Knights Inn.

2. Dave went on to be one of two men (with Dave Winfield) to be drafted by NFL, NBA, and major-league baseball teams; was an All-American end at Colorado; and had a long NFL career. He is the state's top high school football coach, the Broncos' longtime radio play-by-play man and a commercial spokesman for a local bank. I always have told him he could have been a major-league outfielder if he had treated baseball as anything other than a diversion.

3. The new Hyatt Convention Center is on the former *Post* site.

4. Lyons, Schaukowitch, and Van Heusen didn't play for the Broncos in 1977.

5. Small world: Coley had been one of my father's Oregon assistants before moving to the NFL.

6. Initial reports said Ralston had been fired the previous Thursday, but the announcement was delayed at his request so he could attend a reunion of his former Utah State teams before the news broke. However, Gehrke later told Dick Connor that he made the decision on a drive that weekend with his wife and that the moves—Ralston's firing and Miller's being offered the job—all came down on Sunday, January 30.

CHAPTER 1

New Coach, New Job

Whatever I had, I had to work for.

—RED MILLER

Getting His Chance: Robert "Red" Miller

In and around Macomb, Illinois, John Samuel Miller had no tolerance for slackers, whether in the fields or under his own roof. He had left school as a young boy in nearby Colchester to work underground in the area's coal mine, and he never learned to read and write. Yet, like many of the men who started out in the mines, he took pride that his word and his handshake were as binding and trustworthy as anything that any slick lawyer might get down on paper. He told his children—the surviving eight following the deaths in infancy of twins Billy Gene and Betty Jane—that it was the way Millers would operate.

"As we were growing up, the biggest thing my dad gave me was the hard work ethic," one of the sons, Robert, recalls. "He would say, 'When you go to work and you're being paid by another guy, you work your rear end off, you be there on time, you give them a day's work—or you don't take their pay.' Hard work was his God."

Robert, born in 1927, was the youngest of Jennie Miller's surviving five sons. At home, he was called "Bo." Elsewhere, he became better known as "Red."

As he sits in his home in South Denver years later, Red calls his mother, "a beautiful woman. A saint. Talk about the glue that binds."

The family moved several times. Wherever they were, the boys jammed into one bedroom, sometimes even in one bed. The nation was in the clutches of the Great Depression. A day's work could bring a dollar, if you were lucky. John Samuel scrambled to support his family, working as a general laborer, but also doing stints as a tenant farmer. When he could get no other job, he would go back to the coal mines. "He would not go on relief," Red says. "He would not take any money from the various agencies, either."

At the dinner table, the eight children sat in order, oldest to youngest, and that's the way the food got passed around. Red, the seventh child, knew that when the tray reached him, he needed to save half for his younger sister, Pauline, the last in line. Many times, their shares weren't much.

The sons were expected to work and help support the family, but the thought never crossed their minds that they shouldn't. "In my house," Red recalls, "it was like this: 'I respect you, you respect me; don't ask me for money because I don't have to give it to you. You earn what you get every day.' That was the creed. Whatever I had, I had to work for."

Red had paper routes at age seven, shined shoes, dug ditches, worked in restaurants, and also used his bicycle, until it was stolen, to deliver flyers that advertised businesses. When he got a little older, he got a sample of what his father had been through.

"I worked one summer in the mines," Red says. "It had a vein of coal about four or four and a half feet high, so you were working on your knees down there in the coal mine every day."

He knew he never wanted to go back.

It was a wonder that Red found time to work, given his enthusiasm for sports. In the family home's yard, the school yard, or a vacant lot, the game was rough tackle football. Before long, Red, at age nine, was organizing and coaching a team. Red's team represented Macomb's Fourth Ward, and they defended the area's honor in informal games against the other three wards. No referee, no uniforms, no parents watching. Red was coach, general manager, promoter, organizer and—when blood flowed—trainer.

"I could name my position," he says, "but I was always a lineman, because I thought too many guys wanted to carry the ball and somebody had to do this. We gotta have a team! So I was always a lineman and linebacker."

Always, the poor kid from the big family stood his ground. "What trouble are you going to get in if it's Macomb, Illinois, with 8,000 people at that time?" he asks. "The only troubles I had were to establish myself. I had a lot of fistfights. They call you names, like 'red-headed wood-pecker,' but they would only call me that once because I'd challenge 'em. If they didn't back down, we'd duke it out. What helped me was that I was tough and wouldn't back down to anyone."

Along the way, he also was developing his piano talents—on his own. "My dad's people were from West Virginia, and that was bluegrass before bluegrass was born," Red says. "My dad was a guitar picker. All of my older brothers played string instruments. When I came along, I started out on steel guitar then went to the piano. I never have taken a lesson, I don't know one note from the other, but I know music in my ear. I just watched and copied and we formed a band. I liked ragtime. I can't play a million tunes, but I can play two or three in ragtime."

His first formal sports team was at Edison Junior High, and he arranged his jobs around basketball practice. There, he already showed the talent that stamped him as one of the town's best athletes. The United States was in World War II, and his oldest brother, Leonard, went into the Army and eventually survived the Battle of the Bulge. Young Red followed the news on the radio and in the papers.

In high school, Red earned 12 letters—four each in football and basketball, and two each in baseball and track—while juggling his jobs and trying to save up enough money over the summer so he didn't have to work as much during football season.

After the war ended, Leonard returned home and became a second father for Red, moving back into the family home, opening a cement block plant with brother Glade in Macomb, and hiring his own father as one of the truck drivers. "He couldn't get a license because he couldn't read the test," Red says. "There was an Illinois state senator who lived in our town, I can't remember his name, and he said, 'John, come into my office, and if you can tell me what these signs are by eyeing them, OK.' And my dad did that. He knew the shape of a stop sign, slow, yield, all the signs. So he got a truck driver's license that way."

As a senior at Macomb High in 1945–1946, Red was an all-state football player and the homecoming king. In what passed for a recruiting blitz at the time, it came down to Red choosing among three colleges—Purdue, Kansas State, and the hometown Western Illinois State Teachers College. The Purdue offer came from the owner of a bookstore in Macomb, who said if Red went to Purdue and played football, he would pay all of his college costs and expenses. (That sort of private offer from a booster was typical at the time and certainly not untoward or illegal.)

Red didn't visit Purdue, but he did ride the train to Kansas State. He didn't want to leave his parents—or, mostly, his beloved mother—and Western Illinois came through with an offer of $17.50 per quarter for tuition. Plus, he had gone to Western Illinois games as a kid and dreamed of playing for the hometown team. "I didn't have any money, so I sneaked in there," he says. "I remember the homecoming parades, too. They marched around the square and all the way to the edge of town. I followed their band all the way out to where they stopped playing and disbanded."

He decided to stay home—cutting costs by continuing to live with his parents and his oldest brother, Leonard.

"I chose to be the big boy in a little pond and it was the right choice for me," Red says.

His parents had never gone to any of his high school games. His mother couldn't drive and his father didn't understand why there was all this fuss about sports. When Red told his dad he had gotten a scholarship to go to college and play football, John Miller responded, "What's the matter with you, boy? You need to get a job." With encouragement from his brother and mother, Red decided to go to college, anyway.

He started right away, as a freshman, for the Leathernecks football team, playing as a guard and linebacker. Then, as a boxer, went to the regional Golden Gloves. "I lost my first fight," he says. "That was in the winter and I dropped out of school immediately. I thought it was such a disgrace."

In disgust, he went to work full-time at his brother's block plant. "All I did was load and unload blocks all day long, every day," he says. "I think I made $40 a week, $1 an hour. That was a lot of money for me back then. Boy, was I in shape, though!"

He went back to school in the fall and went on to be the Leathernecks' MVP the next three seasons, the Illinois Intercollegiate Athletic Conference's MVP as a sophomore, and both team captain and campus homecoming king as a senior. He also avenged his boxing loss by becoming regional Golden Gloves heavyweight champion before giving up that sport. He picked up some spare change forming a band and playing piano. "We were Red Miller and His Three Plus Two, and we played for a couple of proms," he says. "We got $5 each."

Later in his college career, he landed a coveted job working as the late-shift bartender in the local Elks Club. While going to school, his official hours were from 4 p.m. to midnight, but they often ran much longer than that.

"There were no slot machines or gambling allowed in Macomb—except in the Elks Club," Red says.

The club also had two poker tables. After the club was officially closed, Red would stay behind the bar and keep serving as long as the players tipped him a dollar an hour. It was a good deal for everyone—well, at least for the winners, who often tipped more—but it made for long nights and little sleep for the college student behind the bar.

Even after his final college football game, a 13-0 Western Illinois victory over Wheaton in the Corn Bowl following the '49 season, Red hurried back to Macomb to be able to work at the Elks Club's big dance.

He knew he wanted to be a coach. In fact, he had known it for a long time, even telling a high school counselor he wanted to be a coach in the National Football League. "He kind of snickered a little bit," Red recalls.

In the postwar years, many young men—some wartime veterans, some not—were hitting the job market at the same time, and coaching was one of the fields that didn't expand quickly. So despite his playing credentials, a diploma, and a transcript that showed a major in physical education and minors in journalism (!) and biology, Red didn't land a coaching job right away. For nearly a year after leaving Western Illinois, he continued to work at the Elks Club and wondered what it would take to break into coaching and start proving that counselor wrong.

He visited legendary Western athletic director Ray "Rock" Hanson, who had served as the school's football coach between the two world wars. As a Marine in World War I, he earned the Navy Cross, a Silver Star, and a French *Croix de Guerre*. Honoring that service, Congress gave permission for the program coached by the former Marine to adopt the Fighting Leathernecks nickname and the Marine seal and emblems. ("Our opponents," Red says with a smile, "often called us the Leatherdicks.") Hanson reentered the Marines during World War II, and when he returned to the campus he gave up coaching and became the AD only.

Hanson suggested that Red keep his job at the Elks, but help coach the Leathernecks' new junior varsity team. After a year, Hanson told Red he had lined up two job interviews for him.

"I drove up to a little town by Peoria," Miller says, "and I didn't get that job."

Next, he went to tiny Astoria, Illinois, about 24 miles from Macomb. The high school had 90 students and the coaching job had three candidates. "Lo and behold," Red says, "they called me back and offered me the job."

His annual salary was $2,700. He started in the fall of 1951, when he was 23.

"Now you won't believe this," he says, "but I taught three biology courses plus four PE courses each day. I was head football coach, head track coach, assistant basketball coach, and I ran my own boxing program. I loved it."

For his first year, he rented a room in a boarding house and then married his Macomb girlfriend, Nancy. The young couple moved on to Canton (Illinois) High School in 1953, and that's where their son, Steve, was born. Next, Red heard from the man he came to consider his mentor, Carthage College coach Art Keller.

"When he called me, I was really happy," Red recalls. "He was 30 miles from my hometown and he knew about me because I was the best football player around there and now I'm a high school coach."

In 1954, Miller signed on as the line coach and track coach. Years later, he still calls Keller "the best, most intelligent football coach I've ever worked with or been around."

"You know how many coaches we had?" he asks. "Two. You know who did all the athletic training and taping? Me. You know how we got to the games? We drove cars."

Miller liked taking players to the games because he got a mileage allowance that helped out the family finances. One week, Keller and Miller were among the five drivers taking the team to Eureka College—the alma mater of actor Ronald Reagan—for what the Carthage coaches believed was a Friday night game.

At the campus, Miller spotted a night watchman and asked how to get into the stadium and the visiting dressing room.

The watchman gave Miller a quizzical look.

"Coach," he said, "you don't play until tomorrow."

Such were the pitfalls of small-college football in those days.

"We drove home, came back the next day, kicked their ass and went back home," Miller says, smiling.

———

During Red's stay at Carthage, his second child, Lana, was born.

In early 1957, Miller got a phone call from Dr. Frank Beu, the president of Western Illinois, who was looking for a coach to succeed Wes Stevens. Red's name had been tossed into the mix, but he wasn't yet 30. Beu said he would be driving through Carthage that afternoon and asked if he could have about a half hour of Miller's time.

When he arrived, he put a strange offer on the table. The ex-Marine Hanson still was the athletic director, but was clearly winding down his career, and Beu took the lead in the coaching search.

"He says to me, 'Red, you were a hell of a player and a hell of a leader for us, and I'd love to have you as head coach, but I don't think you're ready yet.'"

Next Beu said he was considering about 20 other candidates, handed Miller a list and asked what he thought. One name jumped out. Lou Saban had been a star at Indiana and in the All-American Football Conference. He had moved up from an assistant's role to be the head coach at Northwestern in 1955, and that single 0-8-1 season was in a holding pattern before Ara Parseghian took over for '56. But Saban's name still was familiar, and he certainly looked qualified on paper—and to a young Red Miller. So that's what he told Beu.

Beu also said he was going to keep asking around and interviewing, but he hired Miller on the spot as the new coach's offensive and defensive line coach.

Saban got the head coaching job, and Miller's Western Illinois contract didn't start until the fall, so he had to coach in spring practice as a volunteer and continue to teach at Carthage. "I told Keller, and he was great about it," Miller says. "He said, 'Take off as soon as you're done with your last class and get your rear end up there every day.'"

The Leathernecks also hired a young coach, former Northwestern end Joe Collier, as an assistant. For three years, Saban, Collier, and Miller guided the Leathernecks to records of 5-4, 6-1-1, and 9-0, winning the last 15 in a row. Miller also taught golf and archery classes, and after Hanson heard he once had been a lifeguard, he informed Red he now was the school's swimming coach. "I couldn't believe it," he says. "I'd never been around competitive swimming. I bought a book and I did all right."

After that undefeated '59 season, Miller and Collier were doing some paperwork when Saban asked them to come to his office. With the door closed, he told them he was heading to talk with the ownership of the Boston franchise in the American Football League, which would begin play in the 1960 season. If he got the job, Saban said, he would want to take Miller and Collier with him and wanted to know if they were interested.

Sure, they said.

A few days later, Saban was the head coach of the Boston Patriots and offered jobs to his two college assistants. But Miller also was offered the chance to be Saban's successor at Western Illinois. His alma mater. His hometown. Head coach!

Finally, he thought of his goal—to make the NFL—and he decided that he should take the chance to get in the pro game, albeit in the "new" league. So he and his family were headed to the East Coast. Miller caught a flight to Boston and picked out a home.

It was his first time on an airplane.

At times, Miller wondered if going to the AFL was a smart career move. With the new league's 33-man rosters for 1960, Miller was an offensive line coach with his starters and only a couple of guys to back them up. The Patriots had horrible practice facilities at Boston University and also played there. Losing their final four games, the Patriots finished 5-9 in their inaugural year. In the second season, 1961, despite the addition of quarterback Babe Parilli,[1] Saban was fired after a 2-3 start and player personnel head Mike Holovak became head coach. Holovak wanted to retain both Miller and Collier, and even told Miller he could run the offense. (The title "coordinator" was just coming into common use.) Saban got the job at Buffalo for the 1962 season and recruited his former Western Illinois coaches to rejoin him. "I decided to go because I liked working under Lou better than I would like working under Holovak," Miller says.

Saban also gave Miller an important assignment: Help recruit the Canadian Football League's greatest running back, Cookie Gilchrist, for the Bills. He visited Gilchrist in Canada. The blustery Gilchrist joined the Bills and immediately was one of the league's stars, gaining 1,096 yards his first season in the league. The Bills lost their first five, but got righted. When the Bills also claimed quarterback Jack Kemp on waivers from San Diego—he had a bad finger and the Chargers failed in an attempt to rescind the waivers—that also helped considerably. So Buffalo seemed on the move, and Saban informally assured Miller he would add the offensive coordinator title. By then, that sort of title was becoming more important for résumé purposes, and Miller already was looking ahead to trying to move up. When Saban introduced him at a postseason rally as the offensive line coach and Miller asked about the promised offensive coordinator title, Saban informed him that, at least officially, his title wouldn't change.

"I knew then I was going elsewhere," Miller says.

Having no idea what he would do next, Miller quit. The next day, Denver Broncos coach Jack Faulkner called and offered Red a two-year contract—unusual for assistant coaches, who usually had one-year deals. Red and his family came to the Rockies for the first time, and Miller at times felt as if he were back in the inaugural year of the AFL. The Broncos weren't a complete joke—just close to it. The Broncos' infamous hideous brown and yellow uniforms were in the past, but the team's practice facilities adjacent to Mile High Stadium were ramshackle, as the original ownership was in the process of selling the team to the Phipps brothers, Allan and Gerald. Miller laughs when remembering the practice field. "It was tilted," he says. "The offices were in a Quonset hut, so every time I stood up, I hit my head on the curved ceiling," he says. He stayed three seasons, through 1965, working under Faulkner and then—after Faulkner was fired—Mac Speedie. The Broncos won only eight games in the three years, and although the franchise was moving toward credibility under the Phipps brothers, Red jumped at the chance to move to the NFL, joining the St. Louis Cardinals for the 1966 season. Driving to St. Louis for the first time in his new 1965 cherry-red Mustang, he thought: "I've finally made it! I'm going to the NFL!"

At St. Louis, he again was working for a team owned by brothers—Bill and "Stormy" Bidwill. Stormy had a rogue's charm to him, but Bill's penurious ways were aggravating, and in retrospect it seems amazing that the Cardinals were as competitive as they were.

All five of Miller's most frequent starting offensive linemen—Bob De-Marco, Irv Goode, Ken Gray, Ernie McMillan, and Bob Reynolds—were selected for the Pro Bowl during his five-season run. Theirs was the strongest link in an otherwise frequently weak chain, and Miller stayed through the 1970 season before moving on to the Baltimore Colts, who had just won the Super Bowl under Don McCafferty. Eventually, the staff got word that the owner, Carroll Rosenbloom, had traded franchises and acquired the Los Angeles Rams, and that air conditioning magnate Robert Irsay was buying the Colts. He rubbed the coaches and players wrong from his first meeting with the team, and Miller wasn't shocked when the entire staff was fired after the 1972 season.

By then, he had a solid reputation as an offensive coach, but there weren't many coaching changes that off-season and Miller was starting to worry when he got an offer from former Oklahoma coach Chuck Fairbanks, who was taking over the New England Patriots. Fairbanks was a defensive-minded coach who was astute enough to turn the offense over to an experienced, reliable hand, as he had done with the Sooners. So, as Miller remembers it, Fairbanks told him: "You coach the offense, you write the playbook, you use your terminology, you call every play, and I will never second-guess you."

How did that turn out?

"In four years," Miller says, "I called those plays and he never, ever second-guessed me. Not on one play."

Fairbanks later became a bit of a Colorado joke punch line—that is, "Who coached CU to two consecutive losses to Drake?"—but any attempt to get Miller to say anything negative about the taciturn coach will fail. Miller was in charge of not only an offensive line that included standouts John Hannah, Leon Gray, and Sam Adams, but he was running the offense—and becoming a bit restless. Miller felt he was ready to be a head coach in the NFL.

His final game with the Patriots, as it turned out, was a controversial 24-21 loss to the Oakland Raiders in the 1976 postseason. That game lives in infamy because of the phantom roughing-the-passer penalty on the Patriots' Ray "Sugar Bear" Hamilton that kept the Raiders alive. The referee was the caustic Ben Dreith, ironically a longtime Denver resident, and it's arguable that the call cost the Patriots a Super Bowl championship, since the Raiders went on to easily win both the AFC championship game over Pittsburgh and the Super Bowl over Minnesota. Some Patriots fans didn't get over that call until the Patriots' Super Bowl victory over St. Louis after the 2001 season. And some of them still haven't gotten over it. Neither has Red.

After the season, Miller told Fairbanks he felt he had done all he could do as a Patriots assistant—and as an assistant, period—and was going to keep his ears open more than ever before for other possibilities. Fairbanks gave him his blessing.

On about January 20, when Broncos general manager Fred Gehrke broached the possibility of Miller returning to the Broncos to be John Ralston's offensive coordinator, Miller had a succinct answer.

"No," he told Gehrke. "No more lateral moves."

Miller's phone rang after he had come home from church on January 30. As he remembers it, the caller was Gerald Phipps.[2]

"I know you turned us down as an offensive coordinator," Phipps said, "but how would you like to be head coach?"

Miller recalls that he was "so excited, it was unbelievable." He thought to himself, *Does a bear shit in the woods?*

He said yes.

Red Miller, at age 49, was the head coach of the Denver Broncos.

The year was '77.

Notes

1. Miller's quarterbacks coach with the '77 Broncos.
2. Many reports that year said Fred Gehrke's was the first voice on the line and that Gehrke made the offer. Miller doesn't recall it that way. It seems likely that the phone was passed from the owner, Phipps, to Gehrke.

CHAPTER 2

Defenders of the Realm

It was kind of like God coming to Champion.

—RANDY GRADISHAR

It All Stops Here: Randy Gradishar

Number 53, Linebacker, 6-3, 233, 4th Season, Ohio State

The phone rang in the little B&J Supermarket in the one-stoplight, steel-company township of Champion, Ohio. Randy Gradishar was there working, as he often had been ever since he was 11, because his father, Jim, and his uncle had opened the store after World War II—and when you were one of the Gradishar boys, you worked. You swept the floor, you worked the cash register, you stocked the shelves and put the price stamps on boxes, you sliced meat and cut steaks, you put out the produce, and maybe you wrote the amount of the purchase in the big black book where Jim tallied all the on-your-honor credit accounts that were the way of doing business in the small town.

Randy was a senior at Champion High, which had dismissed classes at noon that day for a teacher's workday.

The phone call was for him.

He came to the phone.

"Hey, Randy," Champion High's principal told him, "Woody Hayes is here and he wants to talk to you."

Years later in his upstairs perch at a Denver automobile dealership, Gradishar smiles as he remembers that day.

"It was kind of like God coming to Champion," he says. "I said, 'OK, I'll come down.' Woody was sitting in the principal's office."

The legendary Ohio State football coach, the Navy veteran from World War II, peppered Gradishar with questions about his future. His future, that is, in everything but football.

"He was asking me, 'Are you going to be an engineer, a doctor, a lawyer?' I was just an average C-plus student in high school, and I'm saying, 'OK, sure.' Then he says, 'What's your dad do?' I said, 'Well, he has a grocery store.' He says, 'Where's it at?' I pointed and I said, 'A couple of miles that way.' He said, 'Let's go.'"

They drove to the store and Woody Hayes strode to the back and stood with Jim Gradishar, right there among the meat slicers.

"So for the next hour," Randy recalls, "they're standing back by the meat slicers and they're talking about what Woody calls 'the Big War'—World War II. They're talking and I'm just standing there."

They had a lot to talk about, the football coach and Navy veteran and the grocer who had served in ground war on the Philippines.

Randy listened. He listened in part because when he was younger, whenever he attempted to ask his father about World War II, his father wouldn't say much—or didn't say anything at all. Jim hadn't even told his son—not then, anyway—that he had been born in a Colorado steel town, Pueblo, before his family moved to Ohio when he was about 13.

Woody Hayes said what a treat it was to meet Jim Gradishar, said his farewells all around, and left.

"Soon after, I realized—and this was an appreciation for Woody—he never mentioned my name," Randy recalls. "Some coaches would come and say, 'Hey, you'd change the direction of our team,' 'I'm going to make you a starter,' and that kind of stuff. Woody never said anything about how good I was. There was nothing about Randy, it was all the World War II stuff."

Randy had been playing football only four years. Football was huge in nearby Warren, five miles away, and certainly throughout Ohio, but in Champion, nobody played the game until ninth grade. In his senior year,

Champion had what was, for the small-town school, a terrific record—5-5. Gradishar had played basketball and baseball and done well, and in a way, he still was learning about football—playing tight end and linebacker—when his high school coach, Al Carrino, sent out film of him to coaches around the region. Actually, Randy thought of himself as a better basketball player. But in addition to Carrino's work in promoting him, a local Ohio State graduate, a car dealer, figured out this local kid was raw, but special, and touted him.

Hayes wasn't the only big-name coach who showed up in Champion. Penn State's Joe Paterno sat in the Gradishars' living room and extolled the virtues of State College. Gradishar's basketball coach, Roger Rogos, drove him to visit the Penn State campus. "My parents, God bless 'em, didn't know that was something you were supposed to do," Gradishar says. "They had dropped out in middle school and gone to work."

When Gradishar visited Columbus, Hayes took him to dinner. Randy also went to a function for recruits and gorged. "You could eat as many hot dogs as you wanted!" Gradishar says, making it clear that he thought that was great at the time. Hayes's pitch was: "Randy, I'm going to give you an opportunity." That's it. Hayes did tell Gradishar how impressed he was with his size 14½ feet. "Son," he said, "you have a pretty good foundation there."

Gradishar also visited Purdue, and years later he would gently tease Michigan's Bo Schembechler for only calling him and not visiting him. He also thought of going to Bowling Green or Kent State, but finally decided to give Ohio State a shot.

In the late summer of 1970, Randy's mother, Ann, made the 175-mile drive with him to Columbus and dropped him off. He was the guy from the little town being introduced to high school All-Americans from Cincinnati Moeller and All-State guys from the other powerhouse schools. "I was saying, 'Holy baloney, I'm all-nothing,'" he says.

The Buckeyes' freshman team played only two games, and mostly was the scout team for the heralded varsity team, which had lost one game in the previous two seasons.

"All of a sudden, I'm playing against these guys in a scrimmage, and I'm trying to prove to myself how good I was," Gradishar says. "I was playing linebacker and the guard blocked down, and all of sudden there was this big hole and I rush in there thinking I was going to sack the quarterback. I put my hands up like this"—he raises his arms—"and [John] Brockington came from somewhere and nailed me and cracked my sternum. Now trainers are out there and I have no clue of how much I'm hurt. I was out for a few days. But the theme was that the guy behind you is going to take your job. These guys are All-State and All-Americans! I was back in a day or a couple of days, strapped up and taped up. But I knew in my mind, *I can play with these guys.* That was kind of my turning point."

Years later, Woody Hayes talked about Gradishar with Shelby Strother of the *Denver Post*: "We noticed right away that he was something special. George Hill, who was the linebacker coach, told me, 'This Gradishar kid is something else,'" Hayes said. "Hell, I had eyes. I already knew that."

As the next season approached, Gradishar was running with the first defense when he suffered a broken finger at practice. "I was out for the first three weeks," he says. "Then as soon as I was able to come back and had a cast on, I played against Wisconsin."

He immediately was one of the Buckeyes' stars.

Gradishar liked playing for the gruff Hayes, who had been at Ohio State since 1951. "You kind of did it Woody's way, and back then you didn't even think about talking to anybody, whether it was military or your coach or anybody," he says. "At least I didn't. Coach, principal, parents talk to you and say to do something? That's what you do. You do it. No question. You just believed. You believed he was doing the right thing, and you look back, it was all about the ethics, the values, the character of a man as an athlete, and he wanted to help you mold into that. He demanded you give everything you can. You just had to trust that he could get it out of you."

Gradishar wasn't thinking about the NFL, at least not until he suffered a knee injury when he was clipped at the end of his 1972 junior season and heard someone say, "If it's not too bad, you can still go the NFL."

The NFL? Me?

Yes, you.

"Randy was always the best," Hayes told Strother. "His ability at recognition allowed him to move quickly. He's quick mentally. He's quick visually. He made the plays from sideline to sideline and, yes, sir, he's the best we ever had."

He had a stretched knee ligament and went to New York to be fitted with the Lenox-Hill brace, the kind originally designed for Joe Namath, and played in the Rose Bowl. He underwent surgery after the bowl game and was ready by the next season and had a strong senior year. As far as he was concerned, his knee was back to full strength, and he played in several all-star games and hooked up with a Columbus lawyer to help him negotiate his first contract.

The lawyer started checking around, and he told Gradishar he probably would go in the first half of the first round, to Chicago (picking fourth), Baltimore (fifth), or Detroit (eighth). The Colts' orthopedic physician looked at Grandishar's knee and said it was fine. "Then the Detroit Lions' trainer calls and says he's going to be in town and said to come down, he'd meet me in the training room," Gradishar recalls. "This is a couple of weeks before the draft. We're in the training room and he's doing his knee evaluation, and he pulled it out this way and he says, 'Whoa! What's wrong with that.' I said, 'Nothing.' He said, 'OK.'"

A few days later, the lawyer called and asked, "Randy, did you get hurt?"

Gradishar said no.

The lawyer said the Lions' trainer was putting out the word that his knee was shot.

Next, John Ralston called Gradishar. The Broncos were picking fourteenth. Gradishar recalls Ralston saying, "We heard that Baltimore looked at you and Detroit looked at you, but that you may be available in the first round for us."

Gradishar declined to go to Denver to be examined, saying he didn't know what the Lions had seen. (In fact, his knee was just "loose," and it had little or nothing to do with his previous injury.) Gradishar told Ralston to call Woody Hayes, and that the coach would vouch for the fact that the knee hadn't been a problem after his surgery. So Ralston did that and also talked to the Buckeyes' team orthopedic surgeon.

"I talked at great length with Woody Hayes," Ralston recalls. "I knew Woody very well because we had played against them in the Rose Bowl. Woody said, 'He'll play ten years in the National Football League and he'll be the best player you've got.' And he was right."

The Bears took defensive back Waymond Bryant at number four. The Colts took defensive end John Dutton at number five. The Lions took linebacker Ed O'Neil at number eight. The Saints even took Gradishar's teammate and fellow linebacker Rick Middleton at number thirteen. Denver was up, and all the whispers were about this linebacker having fallen out of the top ten because of his knee, and now anybody taking him high would be taking a huge risk.

Ralston did it anyway.

Gradishar was underwhelmed during his introductory visit to Denver. When he walked off the plane at Stapleton International Airport, the first person who came up to him was venerable KMGH/Channel 7 sportscaster Starr Yelland.

"He said, 'Randy, how do you like Denver?'" Gradishar recalls. "I'm thinking, *I ain't even been there yet!* I had just landed. I don't even know what I said."

The Broncos put him up at the Continental Denver, which didn't strike Gradishar as palatial. The he visited the team headquarters in Adams County, north of downtown Denver.

"You walk in and everything becomes small," Gradishar says. "There's the tiny waiting room, and within the locker area, there are weights because there isn't enough room to have a weight room. Then you go into the trainer's room and there are two little small tables and there's no space there. Then they walk you out and see the field, and it was 60 yards one way and some Astroturf over here. I asked, 'How do you guys practice?' And they said, 'Well, some days we're on this part of the 60 yards going north and south, and on Wednesday and Thursday and Friday, we use this 60-yard field.' And I get back to the hotel, and I remember the cinder block construction. And I'm thinking, *Huh, it's the NFL!*"

Gradishar didn't start immediately as a rookie, running behind veteran Ray May, and this is how much the Ohio State experience had changed the kid from Champion who had a hard time believing how good he was: He got mad.

"I think I started halfway through the season," he says. "[Defensive coordinator] Joe Collier finally let me start. It all worked out great. It's not like I knew the system or the different terminology or the things Joe was doing. But coming in, unlike college, I knew I could play in the NFL. That was a plus for me. Then I learned that, well, all those eleven guys on the other side are all really good!"

When Lyle Alzado was injured in the 1976 opener and sidelined for the season, and Collier adjusted by going to the 3-4, it didn't change Gradishar's role much, because he usually had been lined up over a gap and the guard in Denver's previous scheme. The Broncos had used four-linebacker alignments in select situations before, but in 1976 went to it almost exclusively.

The coaching change from Ralston to Red Miller didn't affect him much, either, since Collier and linebackers coach Myrel Moore still were around on the defensive side of the ball. So were his fellow linebackers—Tom Jackson and Bob Swenson on the outside, Joe Rizzo with him on the inside. They were a complementary group both off and on the field. Gradishar had a subtle sense of humor that required paying attention to "get" sometimes, but his teammates learned to look for it.

"Oh, Gradishar was the funniest human being on the face of the earth," recalls guard Tom Glassic. "But you wouldn't know it, he was so deadpan in his deliveries. He was just constantly cracking the wisecracks and putting the whole locker room in a fit. Jackson, Randy and Swenson were like a comedy team, those guys. They were like the Marx Brothers."

They weren't at all funny to their opponents.

When Gradishar first met with Miller, he was struck by some similarities to his college coach.

"He didn't say this, but it was like, 'Goddamn, this is what we're going to do. Let's go.' So I was like, 'Sure, coach, let's go!' "

Brain Trust: Joe Collier and Company

The bespectacled and professorial Joe Collier was the guru, the longtime Red Miller friend who was more than willing to remain in the background as Miller ran the show, motivated with fire and brimstone, and supervised the offense while Collier handled the defense with virtual carte blanche.

Collier was a soft-spoken Rock Island, Illinois, native who had starred for an undefeated Rock Island High team in 1949, moved on to be an All–Big Ten end at Northwestern, and then was drafted by both the New York Giants and the United States Army. He didn't get a signing bonus from the Army, but he also had no choice, and he served most of his military stint on a Pacific island wondering if the atomic-oriented projects on the next island over might be affecting him.

After his discharge, he was planning on working on the Southern Illinois staff and working toward his master's degree when he stopped in Macomb, Illinois, and ended up hearing about an open assistant coach's spot at Western Illinois. In a whirlwind sequence that would change his life, he talked about that job and took it, joining the staff with Lou Saban and Miller.

Like Miller, Collier went with Saban to the new Boston Patriots and then rejoined his former boss with the Buffalo Bills in 1962. His and Miller's paths separated after Red left the staff because of his anger with Saban over the offensive coordinator's title, and Collier remained with the Bills.

After Saban was fired, Collier was offered the head coaching position. With misgivings, he took it. He knew that was what coaches were supposed to do, but he sensed he wouldn't enjoy the day-to-day details that go with being the head coach. It took him away from his tinkering, his detail-oriented fascination with defense, and even his interaction with the players. "I didn't do a good job," he says, without embarrassment, because it wasn't anything he particularly hungered to excel at and he didn't consider it a true measure of his capability.

Under Collier, the Bills were 9-4-1 in 1966, 4-10 in '67 and 0-2 in '68, when he was fired. The next season, he rejoined Saban in Denver. The Broncos defense, with such mainstays as linemen Rich "Tombstone" Jackson and Dave Costa plus safety Billy Thompson, was the bright spot as Saban tried—and ultimately failed—to turn around the franchise. When Saban was fired early in the 1971 season and Jerry Smith finished out the year as interim head coach, Collier wondered what the future might bring, but he accepted the chance to remain under new head coach John Ralston. He had seen what vagabond existences had done to other coaches and their families, and he and Shirley Collier had three school-age children—Julie, Lisa, and Joey—who liked Denver. Collier stayed with the Broncos and his defense remained the team's major force, the face of the franchise once you got beyond running back Floyd Little.

When Ralston was ousted, on the surface it might have made sense to turn to Collier. It might have made sense, except for one thing: He didn't want any part of it. But he knew Red Miller, and Miller wanted to be a head coach. So when Miller—the fiery sort that Collier knew he never could be—came in, there wasn't much doubt that Collier would stay as defensive coordinator.

The players loved Collier in an arm's-length, intellectual sort of way. His grasp of defenses and his multilayered planning for every alternative stunned those who played for him. He preferred the four-man front, but he had fooled around with the 3-4 off and on—as several other teams had done, including the Dolphins under coordinator Bill Arnsparger. Lyle Alzado's season-ending injury in the first game of the 1976 season nudged Collier toward a deepening embrace of the 3-4 defense. It wasn't as revolutionary in appearance as it sometimes was portrayed, because it was a lot like the old college "Oklahoma" defense, a 5-2 alignment with the outside men in an upright stance and essentially playing linebacker.

But as 1976 went along, and as Collier recognized he had a complementary group of four linebackers—two draft choices and two free agents—who for some reason meshed and worked well together, he was the scientist in the laboratory, coming up with ways to make the defense even better. He remained a stickler for detail, and the mental challenges of playing for him were as daunting as the physical ones. His defense and his calls came with variables, and the men in there better damn well be able to read, to react, to remember all those "ifs" from the meetings and practices.

If they do this, you do this. But if they do this, you do this. And if . . .

To play for Collier, you had to know them all, or you'd end up standing over on the sideline, watching someone with a better memory playing.

Collier had three other holdovers working with him—Myrel Moore, defensive line coach Stan Jones, and defensive backfield coach Bob Gambold.

When he came to Denver, Ralston had hired Moore from the California staff, and Myrel was a high-energy, tireless worker whose enthusiasm and similar passion for details served him well as the linebackers coach.

"Joe Collier was incredibly encouraging," Bob Swenson says. "He was a man of very few words, but when he spoke, people listened. He didn't have to continually rebuke a guy in a meeting. All he had to do was turn and say, 'Bob Swenson, pay attention,' and that was like, 'Whoa,' and that was like a half hour of another guy ranting.

"Myrel was a maniac for detail. I've never seen a coach ever in my life turn as many stones as he would in a meeting, going over every little single thing the offense might do, and when it came to work ethic, Myrel just set the pace for everybody. As soon as we were out there it was full-speed running. He was a great coach."

Stan Jones, who coached with Collier in Denver from 1967 to 1971, returning to the Broncos for Ralston's final year, had the built-in credibility of having been a star lineman—and a pioneer of weight training in a league that previously had disdained it—in the NFL for 13 years, most of them under Bears coach George Halas. For most of his career, he was an offensive guard, but he moved over to the defensive side of the ball at the end of his playing career and did well there, too. He also had been the major proponent of drafting Lyle Alzado and had Lyle's respect, which would be important in getting the most out of the mercurial defensive end.

Defensive backfield coach Bob Gambold had been a quarterback at Washington State and then briefly an NFL player with Philadelphia and the Chicago Cardinals before getting into coaching. He was on Ralston's staff at Stanford, and then moved to the Broncos with him. That would lead to some tension with Miller, but he was on board for 1977.

The staff had a great defense to work with, a greater sum than its individual parts, and it all revolved around the four starting linebackers—Randy Gradishar, Tom Jackson, Bob Swenson, and Joe Rizzo.

"When you're talking about four linebackers, I think they were the best four-man group that I've ever seen," Red Miller says. "Each had different attributes. That was a hell of a job Myrel Moore did putting that group together, and he didn't get enough credit."

Moore says, "They probably could have played in a three-linebacker package, but it wouldn't have been what they could really do best. They worked off of each other and they had great camaraderie together. They would know each other's moves before anybody else did. They spent a lot of time on film together and talking about it, and they were so doggone quick, nobody could block them."

By '77, they were a package deal.

Free Agent: Bob Swenson
Number 51, Linebacker, 6-3, 215, 3rd Season, California

Nobody wanted him.

It was nothing personal, and certainly not a reflection on his background. Robert Swenson—and that's what he was called then—was the

quiet high school basketball coach's son in football-crazy Tracy, California, 65 miles east of San Francisco. Bill Swenson, his father, was the surrogate dad for both his players and other students at Tracy High. His mother, Ann, was the daughter of missionaries, and spoke Portuguese in addition to English because of the time she had spent in Brazil.

Robert talked just enough to get good grades in school. "I was just real shy. Very, very shy," he recalls in a coffee shop in downtown Erie, Colorado. Beneath the quiet exterior was a dreamer, a boy who dared to think of what might be. In the summers, he would lie in the backyard hammock, turn on his tiny transistor radio, and listen to the San Francisco Giants' sluggers-in-a-row of Willie Mays, Willie McCovey, Jim Ray Hart, and Orlando Cepeda, creating the game in his head. Even if the games had been on TV, this would have been better.

He was growing, but he looked more like the basketball coach's son than a potential football player in the town that had produced Nick Eddy, the Notre Dame running back who finished third in the 1966 Heisman Trophy voting to quarterbacks Steve Spurrier of Florida and Bob Griese of Purdue. Given a shot at quarterback as a Tracy High freshman, Swenson's passing was so unimpressive he was told he was a defensive lineman. And at the time, he wasn't very fast. "Slow white guy," he says, smiling. But he got better. "I tried hard and hustled a lot and we had great, great players," he says. "We were from a little town, but we won all the time."

Surely, he thought, his college plan—his dream—would work out. "I used to go to the Stanford games in high school," he says. "I loved watching Jim Plunkett and those guys walk into the stadium with the massing crowd around them, and watch the Stanford band. It seemed to me Stanford was the greatest place you could possibly go to school. I wanted to go there *so* bad."

He was going to be a Stanford Indian, and he had the grades to do it without having the athletic department pull any strings in the registrar's office.

"I made all-league, but I wasn't that good," he says. "I think they saw my dad and he was 6-3, 235. He never worked out, but he was all muscle. I think they just looked at him and his [big] feet and looked at me and my feet and figured I might fill in. I think that's why they were sending me letters and stuff."

It broke his heart when the Stanford coaching staff—John Ralston was the head coach—told him sorry, he wasn't big enough yet, not even to be projected as a contributor. (And in many cases, "not big enough" is a nice way of saying "We don't think you're going to be good enough.") He was 6-3, but only 200 pounds.

He "settled" for going to nearby California–Berkeley, planning to be an engineering major, but the Golden Bears hadn't offered him a football scholarship, either, and he was going to be a walk-on. In the fall of 1971, he settled into Norton Hall. The star athlete in the dorm was quarterback Steve Bartkowski. The resident graduate assistant was Leigh Steinberg, the future leading player agent in the NFL. A wacky student named Steve Wozniak had this racket going for anyone who asked. "Wozniak wired most of the phones so you could call anywhere long distance free," Swenson says of the cofounder of Apple Computers. "All you had to do was flip a switch and it would give busy signals to the computer while you talked to anybody in the world. He used to come and bet guys that he could call the pope. He was kind of crazy. But it was a crazy dorm. We used to have track meets in the hall, things like that."

Around them, though, the campus still was in turmoil in the early 1970s.

"There was tear gas everywhere," Swenson says. "You'd get tear gassed on the way to school. Tear gas would drift up to the stadium for practice. I remember the first quarter, the National Guard was outside the dorm windows, just surrounding it, with rifles pointed up to all the windows. There were big crowds gathering all the time. You'd walk a block to campus and a car—like a Suburban-type thing—would go down Telegraph Avenue and do a U-turn, and they'd hit a button and tear gas would come out. They'd be shooting rubber bullets. Things were going on in People's Park. It was crazy. For a guy from a small farming town, it was really something."

In football, what would become a familiar pattern was playing out.

Wait a minute—this guy can play!

As a starting defensive lineman, he had a scholarship by the time he was a sophomore, and he moved into an abandoned fraternity house with about 30 other guys. They weren't part of the Greek system, but that didn't matter. "We were Animal House before Animal House," he says.

Before his senior season, he was moved to outside linebacker. He still was Robert Swenson, but because there were so many Roberts on the roster, he was designated "Robbie" in the team nomenclature, and he hated that.

The Golden Bears, often overlooked by scouts because, well, scouts didn't like to risk inhaling tear gas, were beginning to attract attention as the previously struggling program was getting better under coach Mike White. After one spring workout, a visiting NFL coach gave Swenson a ride home. Swenson had a chance to remind the coach, the Denver Broncos' John Ralston, how much he had wanted to go to Stanford.

"I'm thinking, *You know, maybe I have a shot at the pros,*" he says.

The Bears were 7-3-1 in 1974, Swenson's senior year, and he says he had "an average year. Just average." He knew he wouldn't be a high draft choice—not like teammates Bartkowski and Chuck Muncie—but he thought *somebody* might take him. For 17 rounds, he waited, along with his roommate, Bears guard Chris Mackie.

"We're sitting around for two days and the phone never rings," Swenson says. "Well, it rings once. It's my mom."

He was devastated. Another dream down the drain. Seventeen rounds, and he wasn't taken. Ralston's Broncos even took guys like Tulane quarterback Steve Foley and Albany State kick returner Lester Sherman, but not Robert Swenson. He took the hint.

"I went out and bought a bunch of skis and a ski coat, and I was going to be a ski bum," he says.

Soon, though, he had offers to attend camps as a free agent, including one from the Broncos and one from the Los Angeles Rams. Myrel Moore, who had been a Cal assistant when Swenson was a freshman before moving to the Broncos' staff, made the Broncos' pitch on behalf of Ralston. Swenson liked Moore, so that was one reason he picked Denver. Another was that he looked at the Rams' and Broncos' roster, and figured he would have a better chance of sticking with Denver. Why? He says he noticed some of the Broncos' linebackers seemed small, including one-year veteran Tom Jackson, listed at only 5-11. Smiling at the absurdity, Swenson recalls thinking: *If I can't beat out Tom Jackson . . .*

He also was very proud of himself for talking Moore into increasing his bonus offer. "I worked an extra two hundred bucks out of him," Swenson says. "I got twelve hundred bucks. *That'll get me by for a while!*"

He says he knew the odds, but was determined to give it his best shot, and among other things, he told the Broncos he now was Bob Swenson, primarily because he didn't want to be Robbie or Rob.

"I'm 6-foot-3, I can dunk a basketball, and I'm thinking if I can't beat them out I don't deserve it," he says. "I decided to get in the greatest shape of my life. So I quit everything. I quit playing rugby and just worked out. I got in the best shape I could possibly be in and came to camp, thinking I would be cut within a week. I was just there to be cut. I knew that."

At first, he was in awe of the Broncos' high draft choices, including San Jose State defensive back Louis Wright and Miami defensive tackle Rubin Carter.

"We go to Pomona for camp and I think on the first day, we run 40-yard dashes and I do pretty well," he says. "But you've got a hundred guys there who are brought in to be fresh meat for the guys they're going to keep, and you know you're one of those guys."

He remembers feeling a bit lost as an outside linebacker, but being pleasantly surprised that he didn't feel out of place in an NFL camp.

"Remember, I only played one year of outside linebacker in college, and it was a continual growing thing. In practice, every day I'm intercepting a ball and I'm finding I can run with all these guys, even [wide receivers] Jack Dolbin and Rick Upchurch and Billy Van Heusen. At least I can run a ways with them and when they're running square-ins, I'm picking off balls. So Joe Collier starts kind of coming up to me and saying, 'I like you.' And I'm going, 'Wow, Joe Collier likes me.' And I just know that they kept bringing around a video camera and were filming me. I kept getting better and better every practice."

By then, he knew he had underestimated the other outside linebacker. "I found out that Tom Jackson might have been 5-11 but he was 6-4 in terms of what he could do," Swenson says. He adjusted his thinking about whom he needed to beat out and make the team. He focused on a fellow rookie, third-round pick Drew Mahalic from Notre Dame. "I could right away figure out that I wouldn't make it unless they cut him," Swenson says. "But I was thinking they're not going to cut high draft picks, no way, it's too embarrassing."

As the '75 exhibition season was winding down, Swenson was keeping an eye out for player personnel guru Carroll Hardy,[1] who acted as the infamous "Turk" in telling players to go to the coach's office—and bring their playbook.

"I remember sitting in that locker room and I was at the end and Drew Mahalic was sitting in front of me," he recalls. "We were at the end and Carroll Hardy came walking down that room and I knew that either I or Drew Mahalic was going to be cut. Carroll looked down at Drew and said, 'Bring your playbook.' And I was like, *Oh, I can't believe it. I've made the team.*"

He had an up-and-down rookie season in 1975. "I started a few games as a rookie and then I'd screw up and be back on the bench," he says, smiling. "Joe Collier didn't like starting any rookies, I didn't think."

The next season, with the Broncos locked into the 3-4 after Lyle Alzado's injury, Swenson was proving himself to be about as good as there was in covering or otherwise taking on tight ends. The defense's collective confidence was rising. "Tom Jackson and I would blitz, and we'd just add stuff to it. It just evolved and they kept adding schemes and after a while the offenses were so confused. They had no idea what we were doing. It just seemed like they short-listed their whole playbooks so you could predict what they were going to do."

He recalls the '76 player revolt as "amazing. . . . I didn't say anything. It was mostly Lyle [Alzado] who was doing all the talking. All I remember was a lot of guys thought he [Ralston] had lost control, [had] great vision but had lost touch with what was going on. I think he's a great man, he cast visions about the Super Bowl."

All along, though, he felt as if he were playing for Myrel Moore, the linebackers coach, and for Joe Collier. That much wouldn't change.

But not even Moore, the former California assistant, had known that Bob Swenson would be this good.

Commentator: Tom Jackson

Number 57, Linebacker, 5-11, 220, 5th Season, Louisville

He wanted to be Jim Brown. Tom—Thomas III, actually—would sit in the upper deck of Cleveland's Municipal Stadium with his father and watch the punishing and elusive Browns fullback pile up the yards. Sometimes, Tom would have to lean to be able to see around the stadium's poles, or wished he had binoculars, but it was thrilling for the kid from southeast Cleveland to be there.

It wasn't easy for Thomas Jackson Jr., Tom's father, to come up with the money for the tickets, but he knew what this meant to his son. Tom Jr. was a World War II veteran who painted water meters to support the family—wife Katie, stepdaughter Barbara, and Tom—and there wasn't much to spend after taking care of the necessities. Katie was considered one of the guiding forces of the neighborhood, often visiting and taking care of families from church when someone was sick.

Tom walked the straight and narrow, and one reason was that the one time he didn't, in stealing a bag of M&Ms, he was waiting to be struck down—or, as he would joke in his 1987 autobiography, *Blitz*, written with Woodrow Paige, for the FBI to hunt him down. He never did eat the candy.

Even then, the future sportscaster loved to talk. His teachers often sent notes home with him, telling his parents that he sometimes wouldn't heed requests to stop talking.

That didn't exactly shock them.

Already, Tom was showing promise as an organizer and leader, running his neighborhood street team, proudly representing 121st Street against the kids from the other area streets. He would go home and talk of the games with his mother, Katie, but there came a time—way too soon—when he couldn't do that anymore.

In 1964, Katie Jackson said she had a headache and needed to rest, and when she didn't get better, she went to the hospital the next day and soon died. She had suffered a stroke, and Tom was left without his mother. He was 13.

When Tom went out for the John Adams High football team, he said he wanted to be like Jim Brown and carry the ball. His problem was that he couldn't hold onto it—at least not on the two carries he had before the coaches decided he might look better on defense. That's where he stayed, though he was far from a prodigy. As a sophomore, he never suited up for a game, victimized by the 65-player limit and his coaches' unwillingness to rotate the assignment of having to watch in street clothes. That wouldn't have taken a lot of flexibility, given that only five players from a 70-man roster couldn't dress. But Tom always was one of them.

He made great strides as a junior, and in his final high school season became a bona fide star and hoped to go to Ohio State. At the time, a grocer's son, Randy Gradishar, was a junior at Champion High, less than an hour's drive away. It was clear Gradishar eventually might be big enough to measure up to the Buckeyes' standards for linebackers. But in Cleveland, it was apparent that Tom Jackson would not.

Tom was 5-10 and 185 pounds, and he was getting more scholarship offers for wrestling than he was for football. An Ohio State assistant said he had to be up-front with Tom: That just wasn't big enough. Others weren't as tape-measure conscious, and Tom was impressed when newly hired University of Louisville coach Lee Corso didn't try to bluff, instead saying that he didn't know much about the school yet, but he did know that if he could land Tom and others from Cleveland—others who didn't make Ohio State's list but were undeniably talented—he could turn around a moribund program playing in a terrible off-campus facility, Fairgrounds Stadium.

Jackson and the other freshmen, many of them from Cleveland, repeatedly dominated the varsity in scrimmages in 1969. The Cardinals lost to league champion Memphis State 69-19, and as they watched, the freshmen vowed to remember how the Tigers ran up the score. But Tom was restless because his girlfriend at the time was attending Ohio State, and he was tired of going back and forth. He considered transferring, hoping to eventually get a scholarship. Corso said he understood and would help Tom, if need be, but when he made a thunderous speech to the entire team at a meeting the next day about commitment and honor, he was challenging Tom to stay—and Tom did. While it might have been interesting to see whether or how soon he could crack the Buckeyes linebacking corps—there would have been this Gradishar fellow to contend with, among others—it almost certainly aided his development in the long run.

In Tom's three seasons, the Cardinals went 8-3-1, 6-3-1, and finally 9-1. The only loss in Tom's senior year came to Tulsa, and the Cardinals were ranked 11th in the country. He was no malcontent at Louisville: He loved Corso, so much so that he later called him "incredible" in *Blitz* and argued that the coach's offbeat tactics and showmanship meant he wasn't given enough credit—for the Cardinals' turnaround or for having method in his madness. As a senior, their linebacker made the All-Missouri Valley Conference All-Star team for the third straight season, and was the league's player of the year for the second time. Tom knew he was going to at least get a chance to play in the NFL. The Cowboys told him they would take him in the second round of the 1973 draft, but he was savvy enough to not plan to be wearing the helmet with the star on it. He still was around in the fourth round, and the Broncos took him. After getting the news, he and his roommate, Rick Howard, went to a map to figure out just exactly where the Mile High City was, and he wondered if he would be playing virtually every game in the snow. He signed for a $15,000 bonus and used much of it on a new Chevrolet Monte Carlo.

From the start, although Ralston had drafted him, Jackson was uneasy about the Broncos' coach. In his autobiography, he would say Ralston felt his biceps before his first training camp, and that clearly got the relationship off on the wrong foot. The well-meaning gesture from the Dale Carnegie devotee made Jackson feel even more like a commodity, and he interpreted Ralston's remarks about how Lyle Alzado also was a fourth-round pick—if Lyle could do it, Tom could, too—to border on condescension.

In Jackson's rookie training camp in Pomona, his knee went out when he was blocked in a Saturday drill. It didn't look good at the time, or in the next couple of days when the team orthopedist, Dr. John Leidholt, checked it out, discovered a lot of "play," and said surgery probably would be necessary. Jackson noted, "At that time—as I had found out twice, the second time after Leidholt checked me out—major surgery meant the huge cast for eight weeks." Leidholt and Jackson were leaving camp and heading for an airport in a taxi when veteran linebacker Tom Graham[2] called out that they should take another hard look at the knee before operating. As they pulled up to the airport, Jackson muttered something about how it would be nice if this were like his "old injuries."

Leidholt asked what Jackson was talking about, because he hadn't mentioned having any previous problems. Jackson said he periodically had minor issues with the knee at Louisville. "I wasn't really trying to hide it," Jackson told Dick Connor later. "It had never kept me out of a game, so I didn't really think of it. . . . I just happened to mention it on the cab ride."

This might have happened anyway, but back in Denver, Leidholt took a harder look at the knee with the revolutionary arthroscope while Jackson was under anesthesia and decided he merely had a loose knee and that surgery wasn't needed. Jackson quickly was back to full strength.

A few weeks later, he nailed star running back Floyd Little in the knee in a scrimmage. Jackson later said both John Ralston and several teammates told him it was not a good idea to hit Floyd Little in the knee, that it was not the way to secure a spot on the roster. He also said he told Alzado and Haven Moses that he was afraid of being cut. Moses laughed and told him that there was no way that was going to happen.

He was set to back up veteran Chip Myrtle when Myrtle's knee was torn asunder by a crackback block from Washington's Charley Taylor in the opening exhibition game. Jackson suddenly was a starter, and though a dislocated shoulder limited him to eight games, he showed that those who fretted that he didn't have the prototypical linebacker's size had been off-base. With speed and smarts, he more than compensated. By his second season, 1974, he was an entrenched starter and star. When the veterans were part of an NFLPA strike and picketing that year, rookies reported, and he shot water with a squirt gun at the Broncos' top draft choice—Gradishar—and called him a "scab." Randy got over it.

Jackson and Gradishar eventually became training-camp and road roommates, and Jackson discovered that beneath a calm off-the-field exterior lurked a prankster who could give T.J. a run for his money. Gradishar might sabotage the shower head, meaning water sprayed virtually everywhere except it where was supposed to go. Or Jackson would be stunned to see Gradishar dropping water from a garbage can onto teammates from the sixth-floor dormitory window.

As he became a star, Jackson seemed to be playing for Myrel Moore and Joe Collier—and not so much for Ralston. In that sense, his leadership in the revolt—he signed on after a phone call from Billy Thompson—was consistent with views he made little effort to hide. So when Red Miller came in, his weak-side outside linebacker—meaning he lined up on the side away from the tight end and often ran down the play—was being challenged to play well enough to help prove the change would make the Broncos better.

He lived up to it.

Abandoned Ship: Joe Rizzo

Number 59, Inside Linebacker, 6-1, 220, 4th Season, Merchant Marine Academy

Contrary to some of the talk about Joe Rizzo, the Broncos' inside linebacker didn't come out of nowhere.

He came from New York.

He was born in Queens and raised where collars were blue, a sarcastic sense of humor was a great help, and a lack of pretension and airs was required. When he was leaving high school, no big-name coaches came after him, and he settled on the Merchant Marine Academy in Kings Point, New York, which had the lowest profile of the five U.S. service academies.

There, as a football player, he bounced around, playing quarterback and defensive back before settling into a linebacker spot. But that didn't seem all that fortuitous at the time, considering no Merchant Marine Academy player in his right mind would be looking ahead to a pro career. The postgraduate service obligation wasn't as extensive as at the other academies, and it could be met in the reserves or the government-regulated maritime industry. Yet it wasn't known as a proving ground for NFL players.

The Broncos were intrigued and had him down as a late-round possibility for 1973, but the Buffalo Bills beat them to it, taking him in the 15th round. In the same draft, Buffalo took Joe DeLamielleure and Joe Ferguson.

Rizzo was coming off surgery on his right knee, though, and he flunked his physical and was released.

The next year, with an NFLPA strike on, teams were looking for extra bodies to be able to hold camps and also preserve options if the veterans stayed out. Carroll Hardy, then the Broncos director of scouting, gave Myrel Moore some film of Rizzo playing at the Merchant Marine Academy. "He was flying all over the field and doing all kinds of things," Moore recalls. "I said, 'If we can get this guy, let's do it.' Carroll said it probably could be for nothing or a plane ticket because he flunked the physical with them [the Bills] and we don't know what's wrong with him."

Moore called Rizzo and asked if he might be interested in giving it another shot with Denver—pending a physical. At the time, Rizzo was in San Diego. He was going to be the third officer on a new tanker heading to the Persian Gulf, but Rizzo put those plans on hold and passed his Denver physical. His knee was fine. "He had some bone spurs in his ankle, but that was really all he had," Moore says. "So we signed him."

Rizzo went to the Broncos' camp in Pomona, telling his boss he would be back soon. He wasn't. "I wanted to play pro ball," he said during camp. "I don't care for sailing too much." The veterans missed nearly a month of the camp before the NFLPA strike ended in early August, when they agreed to come back to work without a new deal. While they were out, Moore told writers that Rizzo "will be able to push a couple of vets in camp." He ended up doing more than that.

Denver kept nine linebackers to open the '74 season, and he started much of the time as a rookie. He was fast and strong, and if the Bills were paying attention, they probably were kicking themselves for not being more patient.

Understandably, Rizzo was vehemently loyal to Moore, the fiery linebackers coach who thought he was worth bringing to camp, and to Collier, who had a scheme that took advantage of him.

With Denver, he also fit right in with the cut-up nature of the linebacking corps, joking about, among other things, race. He would get on the bus, spot black teammates and say things like, "Oops, is this the black bus? Where's the boom boxes?"

The black guys would give it right back to him.

He missed the final two games of the '76 season with a broken jaw, but by the start of training camp in '77 he was recovered and ready to go. With the Broncos committed to sticking with the 3-4, he was locked in as the guy lining up with Gradishar on the inside.

Notes

1. Hardy, a former major-league baseball player and terrific all-around athlete, was the Broncos' director of player personnel. One of his claims to fame was being the only man ever to pinch-hit for Ted Williams.

2. Graham still lives in Denver. His son, Daniel, played at Colorado and became an NFL tight end with the Patriots and Broncos.

CHAPTER 3

M&M Connection

I said to myself right then and there: "This is fantastic."

—HAVEN MOSES

Prelude

As the Broncos linebackers and their teammates prepared for their first training camp under Red Miller in 1977, the Denver metro-area population was about 1.3 million, or barely half of what it would be 30 years later.

When we considered travel logistics, we talked of Arapahoe Road on the south end as if it were halfway to Colorado Springs, and anything above 104th Avenue on the north side was, well, just this side of Fort Collins.

Stapleton International Airport seemed a long way out, but we understood why it had to be.

The open spaces on the way to Boulder were sprawling and sometimes breathtaking, and we still called U.S. 36 "the Boulder Turnpike," though the tollbooths had come down several years earlier.

A peanut farmer and former Navy man, Jimmy Carter, was in his first year as president. Our U.S. senators were a pair of Democrats, upstart Gary Hart—best known as the campaign manager for presidential candidate George McGovern in 1972—and Floyd Haskell.

Our first-term governor was 41-year-old Richard Lamm, a Wisconsin native and University of Wisconsin graduate whose college roommate was Badger-football-player-turned-historian Stephen Ambrose. Lamm also was the same former "hippie lawyer"-turned-state-legislator who led the campaign to tell the world that the 1976 Winter Olympics weren't wanted in Colorado.

Denver's mayor was Bill McNichols, a venerable machine politician whose brother, Steve, previously had been governor. In 1975, he blushingly accepted the city's "decision" to name the new $10 million arena across the street from the stadium after him.

In the 11 years Miller had been gone from Denver, some things had changed, some hadn't. Mostly, it was a city waiting to happen.

Miller understandably had gone along with keeping all of Ralston's defensive coaches, but the offensive staff—which would have undergone an overhaul regardless—was new. Quarterbacks coach Babe Parilli had been out of football for a year after being the head coach of the World Football League's New York Stars and Chicago Winds. His connection to Miller dated back to when Red was a young assistant for the Boston Patriots and Parilli, the former University of Kentucky star, was the franchise's original quarterback. Backfield coach Paul Roach was coming off two years as the Packers' offensive coordinator. Receivers coach Fran Polsfoot had been with several NFL teams, including with Miller at St. Louis. Line coach Ken Gray had been an All-Pro guard under Miller at St. Louis and was a gentleman pig farmer in Texas when he heard that Miller had landed the Denver job, and then Gray called him. None of the assistants had the offensive coordinator title. The play calls would come from assistants upstairs, but would go through Miller—and his headset—and would be subject to change.

Miller's film scrutiny of the offense after his arrival confirmed the justification of the players' lack of faith in quarterback Steve Ramsey. Miller told Fred Gehrke he liked Norris Weese, the second-year scrambler from Mississippi, as a change-of-pace backup. In the Broncos' season-ending win at Chicago in '76, Weese *ran* for 120 yards, or more than a single-game total for any Denver running back that season, on only 12 carries. Originally a 1974 Rams draft choice, Weese couldn't stick with

Los Angeles and played a season with the Hawaiians in the World Football League before catching on with the Broncos as a free agent. Miller also had coached holdover backup Craig Penrose, also entering his second year, in the Senior Bowl and believed the former San Diego State passer had promise.

But Miller pushed Gehrke to check around. (Ralston says that before his firing, Ralston was lobbying to acquire Greg Landry from the Detroit Lions.) When Gehrke said Giants veteran Craig Morton, considered a bit over the hill after three disappointing seasons in New York, also might be available, Miller felt like dialing the Giants himself and handing Gehrke the phone. In early March, the Giants and Broncos swapped Ramsey for Morton.

Gehrke also signed former Heisman Trophy winner and 49ers quarterback Steve Spurrier, who had spent the '76 season going winless with the expansion Buccaneers. Morton was 34, Spurrier, 32, and it seemed likely that only one of them would stick, with Weese and Penrose virtually assured of being the backups.

With veteran cornerback Calvin Jones still suspect physically because of a knee problem, the Broncos sent a future draft choice to Cincinnati for defensive back Bernard Jackson in mid-March. Where he fit in was uncertain, because he had played both free safety and cornerback for the Bengals. Jackson had been an offensive star in college, at Washington State, where he was the Pacific Eight's leading rusher as a small yet swift tailback in 1971.

In meetings and the brief off-season camps, Miller hammered home his philosophy, and many of the players came away thinking this was a guy who would both pat on the back and praise, but also offer to take off the whistle, shed his role as coach, and settle it man-to-man. He told them, among many other things, not to bring soft drinks or munchies into meetings. With disdain, he banished one sign of that togetherness of the Ralston era that had been brought to the Broncos by linebacker Ray May. Looking back, Miller laughs about using an epithet in getting it across. "I told 'em, 'You mother————, if you hold hands with anybody in the huddle, you're out of this goddamn place and on your way, do you understand that?'"

Actually, that was fine with the Broncos.

"And in one of the first meetings," he adds, "I told them, 'You guys got a pretty good squad here, but you're missing something and I'll tell you what it is. You got your ass beat by the Oakland Raiders, that's what you're missing! I'm telling you now, you're going to beat the Oakland Raiders! I've beaten them more than they've ever beaten me with any team I've been with, and I know how to beat them!'"

Years later, cornerback Louis Wright remembers the speech vividly.

"It's the very first meeting and he had an attitude!" Wright says, laughing. "I mean, the first thing I was thinking was, *Wait a minute, wait a minute! You're supposed to be on our side.* He was saying, 'You guys, I'm gonna tell ya' . . . I mean, I'm thinking, *Give us a chance to screw up in practice and then chew our butts or something. You haven't even seen us play or practice!* But after he kind of calmed down, he was saying, 'Hey, there isn't any secret here. We're going to have to whup their ass.'"

Wright remembers Miller repeatedly driving his right fist into his left open palm, punctuating his points.

Whap!

"Number one, you gotta beat the Raiders . . ."

Whap!

"Whup their ass . . ."

Whap!

"No fancy stuff . . ."

Whap!

"The New England Patriots are a hard-nosed football team, and that's what we want to be . . ."

Whap!

"I don't care what plays we draw up, what kind of meals you eat, if you don't whup that guy's ass across from you, we just can't win!"

Whap!

Wright's fellow starting cornerback, Steve Foley, remembers the Miller speech along these lines: "So you guys haven't been able to beat the Raiders. Oh, every now and then." Suddenly, Miller was yelling. "Let me tell you where I'm coming from! I'm coming from the New England Patriots and we kicked their ass! . . . We're gonna knock their dicks in the dirt! . . . I don't care if you have to get in fights with them or whatever."

Foley says Miller "was dead serious. We took on an edge to our team that brought out an incredible confidence that we had that was waiting there, waiting to come out."

Billy Thompson laughs as he says his initial impression of Miller was as "a wild man. Very, very emotional. And he *hated* the Raiders."

The Broncos had gone 2-7-1 against the Raiders under Ralston, and had lost four in a row in the series when he was fired. In the Broncos' history, they were 6-26-2 against Oakland.

That was obscene.

Smut was a problem. Or at least we thought so. The den of iniquity was Kitty's "bookstore" on the seedy East Colfax strip to the east of the State Capitol. The vigilant state legislature had passed an antiobscenity law that went into effect on June 30, and it was a vague and dizzying mandate that could have covered anything from *Lady Chatterley's Lover* to the most hard-core pornography.

To make a point, Denver District Attorney Dale Tooley mandated a showy raid of Kitty's on the law's first day, with officers seizing copies of *Playboy, Oui, Hung Roommates,* and *Bitch Goddess*[1] as the DA obtained an injunction, calling for Kitty's to stop selling obscene materials. Tooley's point? A statewide obscenity law—one size fits all, in other words—was impractical, and definitions and standards would be better left up to each municipality. Ironically, the Playboy Club, one of downtown's top after-dark hangouts, was a three-block walk from Kitty's, in the Radisson Hotel.[2]

Illegal immigration was a problem. Or at least we thought so. In June alone, the Department of Immigration and Naturalization reported, a staggering total of 1,031 illegal immigrants were rounded up and sent back to Mexico.

A labor strike at the Coors Brewery in Golden continued, but the brewery still was making the beer that was a cult attraction because of its limited distribution. Boycotts didn't seem to be hurting the brewery or lessening its resolve.

I worked in downtown Denver, and we knew where to go and what spots to avoid, especially at night. Much of the time, we could have fired a bazooka down some of the streets and not hurt anyone after dark, even on the weekends, though we heard stories of the not-so-long-ago days when kids "dragged" 16th Street and perhaps ended up in North Denver at the Scotchman Drive-In, which by 1977 was struggling to retain business after the end of the hot-rod age. Larimer Square was safe, but going beyond 15th Street on Larimer was risky—or at least a pain—because of the skid-row ambiance and the drunks in the gutters and alleys. In fact, "Skid Row" was anything above 17th Street on Larimer, Market, and Blake. At least there were department stores downtown, though, including the Denver Dry, May D&F, and Joslin's.

I briefly pondered trying to buy a house and seriously looked at the Huron Green development in Westminster, near where I had lived in an apartment during my senior year at CU. But the prices—the cheapest was $33,200—gave me sticker shock, and then I also got the news that I had a new assignment, which would have me driving many days to a hockey practice rink in Littleton.

Sports editor Bick Lucas called me into his office and asked me what I knew about hockey. Well, during my father's years as a football coach in Oregon, he had encountered and become friends with a lot of the folks connected with the Portland Buckaroos, the longtime Western Hockey League franchise that played against teams such as the Seattle Totems, San Diego Gulls, Denver Spurs, and San Francisco Seals. I could rattle off the Buckaroos' somewhat stable roster and was convinced that high-scoring center Art Jones should have been in the Hall of Fame. We had gone to some of the Western League Spurs games after moving to Denver, and I had casually followed the Rockies in their first season in Colorado, when they had won 20 games.

That was good enough for Bick. (Actually, my saying I knew the color of the blue line might have been enough for Bick at that point.) Still only 22, I was assigned to cover the NHL's Rockies. I settled on renting half of a duplex near the University of Denver campus, an easy commute to downtown one way and to South Suburban Arena in the other. I was driving the new 1976 Pacer I had bought in Boulder as a college junior, and I saw absolutely nothing wrong with it. It looked like a fish tank on wheels. When I covered the Pike's Peak Hill Climb and asked the police officer at the bottom of the hill on time trials day if I had time to get up to the press area at Glen Cove before the road shut down, he gave me a withering look and asked: "In *that*?"

For diversion, among other things, I tried to get to at least one movie a week.

Rocky, a few months removed from an upset knockout Best Picture

Oscar at the Academy Awards following its 1976 release, still was playing in 10 theaters around the metro area.

New York, New York, directed by Martin Scorsese and starring Robert DeNiro and Liza Minnelli, opened to mixed reviews. Scorsese was taken to task for a dragging final half hour, and if he ever was going to win a Best Director Oscar, it wasn't going to be for this film.

I went to see *Slap Shot*, considering it both entertainment and a homework assignment in my new role as a hockey writer. Despite its credentials—Paul Newman starring, George Roy Hill directing, a reteaming from *Butch Cassidy and the Sundance Kid*—it was doing tepid business, and I was among an audience of about 10. We all laughed.

One of my favorite scenes was when Dickie Dunn, the Charlestown sportswriter, tries to look modest as Chiefs player-coach Reg Dunlop (Newman) reads his prose aloud in the bar.

Dunlop reads: "'To see the three Chiefs make a scoring rush, the bright colors of their jerseys flashing against the milky ice, was to see a work of art in motion.'" Then he adds: "Now, that's good writin,' Dickie."

"Aw," Dickie responds, "I was just trying to capture the spirit of the thing, Reg."

"Oh, you did," Reg says.

Ever since, I have been trying to capture the spirit of the thing.

I had read that *Slap Shot* screenwriter Nancy Dowd was the sister of Ned Dowd, who played the dreaded goon Ogie Ogilthorpe.[3] She had her brother carry around a tape recorder during his playing days in the minor leagues, and much of the movie came right out of what really happened in Johnstown and other stops on the bush-league circuit.

Perhaps five writers at every showing of *Rocky* walked out thinking if Sylvester Stallone could do it, so could they, and went straight to Waldenbooks to buy a book on screenwriting.

Slap Shot did that for me. Within a few days, I put a stack of new records on the automatic turntable, including Heart's *Little Queen* and Kansas's *Leftoverture*, and was fooling around with the opening scenes of a screenplay based on my father's crazy teams in a crazy time on the Oregon campus.[4]

Most of the malls—including Westland, Southglenn, University Hills, Villa Italia, and the cavernous Cinderella City—had a theater in the parking lot that usually got the top new releases, and most of them were showing *The Deep*. Like the earlier blockbuster *Jaws*, it was based on a Peter Benchley novel.

The other choices around the area were the star-studded marathon *A Bridge Too Far*, Woody Allen's *Annie Hall*, and *Grand Theft Auto*, the first directorial effort from Ron Howard. And the publicity tub was thumping in Denver for the imminent opening of what turned out to be the insipid *One on One*, about basketball star Robbie Benson going from a small Colorado town to Western University in Los Angeles, where he was tutored—in matters both academic and otherwise—by Annette O'Toole. Much of it was filmed at Colorado State in Fort Collins in 1976, so many Colorado residents were hoping to spot themselves among the extras in the crowd and campus scenes. In the basketball footage, former Broncos running back Bobby Anderson played the dirty-playing, cheap-shot artist villain.

The nightlife options mostly were in South Denver, including the Turn of the Century nightclub, and in adjacent Glendale. Bill Medley, fresh from (another) Righteous Brothers breakup with Bobby Hatfield, came in for a weeklong run at the Turn. At Lori's Theater in Glendale's Warehouse Restaurant, you felt as if you should be able to walk out after the show and play craps or blackjack. Fats Domino was packing the place in July, and the rest of the summer schedule included Steve Allen and Jayne Meadows, the Oak Ridge Boys, Vikki Carr, and comedian Jimmie "Dyno-mite!" Walker, who still was starring as J.J. on the sitcom *Good Times*.

Some concerts played McNichols Sports Arena, but the best venue was the Red Rocks Amphitheater near Morrison. Parking and access were a mess and hard rock acts had been all but banned after some previous problems, but tickets were on sale for the summer schedule—Carole King, Jackson Browne, Dan Fogelberg, Jimmy Buffet, and the team of Waylon Jennings and Jessi Colter. King was the most expensive, with tickets to her two-night stand going for $7.

In North Denver, dueling amusement parks were doing well that summer. Elitch Gardens, at 38th and Tennyson, was the classier of the two, dripping with history, enhanced by the Trocadero Ballroom, where famous big bands had played over the years, and the Elitch Theatre, since

1897 one of the top stops on the national summer stock circuit. In July, Lynn Redgrave starred in Neil Simon's *California Suite,* and then Keir Dullea and Rosemary Prinz drew standing ovations for Bernard Slade's *Same Time, Next Year.* Comedies tended to play far better in the low-key summer atmosphere, and the only real problem was when the members of the audience were too busy fanning themselves with the programs in the sweltering theater to pay attention to the punch lines. Because of the heat, dressing up for the theater wasn't a social requirement, so a lot of the season ticket holders made it a habit of arriving early enough to take a ride on Mister Twister, renowned by fans of such things as one of the top roller coasters in the country.

I never had the guts to try it myself.

The park's motto: "Not to See Elitch's Is Not to See Denver."

A few blocks to the west, Lakeside Amusement Park was the more blue-collar alternative. The park played host to regular auto-racing programs on Sunday nights, with drivers who worked regular jobs during the week, worked on their cars in their garages at night, and went to the track on the weekend. The grandstands were decrepit but packed, and one match in the wrong place would have caused an inferno. The same hot dogs that were okay in the amusement park somehow magically were transformed into delicacies at the track, and young drivers like my contemporary Rick Carelli—"The High Plains Drifter"—cut their racing eyeteeth on the track with a straightaway that lasted about 17 feet. Lakeside was north-side racing; Englewood Speedway, on South Sheridan Boulevard, was similar south-side racing, running weekend programs. I went to both tracks over the summer of '77, doing features on a handful of drivers.

Drag racing also was big at Bandimere Speedway in Morrison, near Red Rocks. The Bandimere family started the track in the late 1950s to augment and help promote its auto parts business, and also to provide a strip that could get the hot rodders off the back roads and where they could safely race among themselves. And by 1977, John Bandimere Jr. was the boss, and was putting on national-class and elite regional events. In advance of a big race, I wrote about local racer John Abbott, 39, who teased me about being a suburban boy from Wheat Ridge and offered me a history lesson about the old high school rivalries. "In those days," he told me of the late '50s, "South and East were the big rivals in cars and football both. The East kids had the money and the '55 Chevys."

Ah, those were the days, when you could live in the Denver area and know where all the high schools were—at least in general terms, if you couldn't drive right to them. When I had gone to Wheat Ridge, it was one of the few Jefferson County high schools in the exploding west-side suburbs that wasn't overcrowded, using trailer-style temporary classrooms, or double-shifting—or all of the above. By 1977, other new schools had opened and eased the crowding, though I wasn't quite sure how to find them.

In the 2nd Congressional District, which included Boulder and Denver's western suburbs, Democrat Tim Wirth had unseated longtime Republican congressman Don Brotzman—a former CU football captain and World War II veteran—in the Watergate backlash of 1974. Wirth appeared at one of the new schools on the southwest side of town: Columbine High School.

He held an hourlong question-and-answer session with 200 social studies students, many of them attending classes in the summer. When one student said the government should create more jobs for teenagers, Wirth responded: "OK, but how are you going to answer the kid in the back row who wants us to cut taxes? That's the biggest argument in the country right now. You two guys go outside and work it out." Afterwards, he was clearly frustrated when he reacted to *Post* education writer Art Branscombe, among the many journalists in attendance. "It's incredible to see 16 and 17 year old kids who are so bright but so closed down," Wirth said. "They put on blinders—both those on the left and on the right—so they can't see the other side of these issues."

In Denver's 1st District, Democrat Patricia Schroeder, 37, was in her fourth term after beating Republican incumbent Mike McKevitt in 1972. By 1977, she was a respected member of the powerful House Armed Services Committee, and she had fended off a challenge from Republican Don Friedman in 1976, in part because Friedman said he would support the right of NFL teams to black out television broadcasts of home games, while Schroeder was publicly aghast. She said she wouldn't vote to "deprive Denver fans of their Sunday afternoon football." In a *Denver Post* profile of Schroeder, John Boslough wrote, "One wonders whether Schroeder has ever seen a football game on television," and noted that

Schroeder is "far prettier than she appears in photographs or on television."

In her district, North Denver also was the haunt of most of the city's organized crime figures. One of the hangouts was Gaetano's Restaurant on West 38th.[5] Many Italian-Americans in the neighborhood refused to set foot in Gaetano's, believing the mob was sullying the Italian-American image in a community in which Italian-Americans provided many of the workers in the railroad and other gritty industries. However, by '77, the mob was losing its grip. Two men the papers politely labeled "gambling figures"—Clarence "Chauncey" Smaldone and Paul Villano—had been convicted of bookmaking after the feds made the case that they had run a gambling ring that took bets on NFL games from 1972 to 1974. They still hadn't gone to jail, though, and it was considered even money that they never would.

I was ruing the end of *Mary Hartman, Mary Hartman*, the soap opera satire. *Fernwood 2Night*, with Martin Mull and Fred Willard mocking the talk show format, was the limited-run summer replacement show. Host Barth Gimble (Mull) was the twin brother of Garth Gimble, who had been impaled on a Christmas tree on *Mary Hartman, Mary Hartman*. (Ouch.)

Charlie's Angels, with Farrah Fawcett-Majors (and her hair), and *Laverne and Shirley* were the top-rated shows in the rerun season, and I still was trying to figure out what the hell Cindy Williams and Penny Marshall meant in the opening credits when they sang: "Schlemiel, schlimazel, hasenpfeffer incorporated."

Periodically, I visited the Rockies' offices at McNichols Sports Arena, getting to know GM Ray Miron and other staff members. They tried to talk me into doing a story on their season ticket campaign, which featured considerable discounts on what many considered the outlandish single-game ticket prices of $5, $6.50, and $8. Miron told me the team's search for a new head coach was proceeding slowly because they wanted to make sure they got the right man, but shortly after that, Jack Vickers disclosed the real reason: He was considering selling the team to Edmonton oilman

Nelson Skalbania, who would move the franchise to his hometown, presumably to supplant the WHA's Edmonton Oilers, whether the ongoing NHL-WHA merger talks came to fruition or otherwise. "In a nutshell, I'm going to bust my tail to make the thing work here," Vickers told me.

Gee, I thought, *I might lose my first major-league beat before covering a single game.*

I was enjoying my continuing association with the racers—both of the auto and horse variety. Centennial, the horse track, was a cavernous facility at the intersection of South Federal and Belleview, near the South Platte River, and old-timers still were talking about having to recover from the devastating flood of 1965. It was a fun place for a young reporter to be and learn and watch, whether in the barns of the "back side" or in the press box on the grandstand roof. I rubbed elbows with such Runyonesque characters as *Daily Racing Form* trackman Pat Caudill, who sagely advised me after I told him I "had" the winner, but only in a mental bet: "Kid, never bet in your mind. You can only lose your mind once." The trainers and the jockeys, including the cigar-smoking Jack Keane, who always took his horses to the rear of the pack and sometimes closed and sometimes didn't, annually came to Denver from the meeting at Turf Paradise in Phoenix.

Many of the folks along the rail or in the clubhouse went straight from the afternoon races at Centennial to the evening greyhound races at Mile High Kennel Club in Commerce City. A true horseman wouldn't get caught dead at the dogs, but a lot of the gamblers liked both.

At Mile High Stadium that summer, the Bears' Frank "Moose" Ortenzio was threatening to break the franchise single-season record of 42 home runs, set in 1956 by Marv Throneberry—who had passed through Denver before joining the expansion Mets and becoming "Marvelous"—and in 1976 by Roger Freed. Nobody, and I mean nobody, mentioned altitude as a factor, either in the home runs or as a pitching alibi.

The Nuggets held a rookie camp at McNichols, and Larry Brown was high on his number-one draft choice, Anthony Roberts from Oral Roberts.

Red Miller was antsy. This was it, finally: his crack at being a head coach. He had bought a nice home, nothing extravagant, near Cherry Creek

High School, and settled in. He knew he was fortunate in the sense that this was a team on the verge, not a team that had gotten its coach fired because it was rotten. The funny thing was that he and Ralston were both rah-rah guys, but Miller had a way of making the players feel he was part of the huddle and they were all in it together.

So as the Broncos went to camp, they knew there was a new sheriff in town. Some of them knew that after essentially pushing for a coup d'etat, they were under pressure to show that Ralston's ouster was justified. That would be hanging over them all season, and it's impossible to overstate its impact. At the same time, there seemed to be no fissures caused by anti-Ralston and antirevolt positions. ("Antirevolt" didn't have to mean "pro-Ralston.") And they all knew Miller had targeted a Public Enemy Number One: the Raiders. To beat Oakland, the Broncos would need better quarterback play than they had gotten in '76, and Miller was hoping Morton would turn out to be a Raider-killer.

Off the Scrap Heap: Craig Morton

Number 7, Quarterback, 6-4, 210, 13th Season, California

Like so many other sons and daughters of World War II veterans, Craig Morton never was able to find out the whole story.

His father, Ken, served in the Army on New Guinea and the Philippines during the late stages of the Pacific fighting, and saw things he refused to talk about. Ken was a sergeant when mustered out, and he was a sergeant through battlefield promotions. Ken returned to Flint, Michigan, to a wife, Maxine, and Craig, who had been born in 1943, and he came back with horrific memories. At least, that's what Craig assumed in later years, because dragging them out of his father was impossible.

"My mom always said it affected him, that when he came home he wasn't the same guy," Craig says in his office in the University of California–Berkeley's Haas Pavilion. "He never ever talked to me about the war. Never. I found out more about his war experiences on the History Channel the last couple of years, looking at things about New Guinea. He really hated the Japanese. But as a kid you don't understand. I used to say, 'How can you hate all these people?' He really hated them. Now I see why."

This sounds familiar to me, and the coincidences are stunning. Morton played for the Broncos after my father, Jerry Frei, returned to serve a second stint as the team's offensive line coach under Dan Reeves and then moved into scouting. My father's 26th Photo Recon Squadron—the pilots flew unarmed versions of P-38 fighters over potential bombing targets to take pictures—was based in New Guinea and the Philippines, the same places where Morton's father was stationed and fought.

Yet Morton never knew that because, like his father, my father—at least for many years—just didn't talk about it.

In the late 1940s, Ken Morton decided he—and his family—needed a fresh start. They were going to move west, and they ended up in Campbell, California, near San Jose. (That sounds familiar, too: My father and my mother loaded up a car and moved from Wisconsin to Portland, Oregon, in 1949, without any job prospects.) Moving the family into a small house in Campbell, Ken found work as a glassblower in San Jose, but his demons never left.

"He always did his best, and he was very, very strict," Craig says. "I was scared to death of him. I did not cause too many problems. He did not spare the rod and I didn't like it. After a few of those things, I didn't want any more.

"He had this little trick. When the ice cream man would come by, we'd get the ice cream and put it in the icebox. He'd take the wrapper off and leave the wrapper there and you'd go get yours and it would be gone, there wouldn't be ice cream there. I did that one time and he didn't think it was funny. He beat the shit out of me. I remember my mom had to call him off, he was so upset. He had told me not to do it. So I didn't cross him too many times."

Craig otherwise had what he considers an idyllic childhood. Fruit orchards were abundant in the Campbell area, and the kids—including Craig and his younger sisters, Sharon and Sandy—had their pick, literally and figuratively. They also played outside virtually nonstop. "The house was too small and the weather was too great," Morton says.

While generally avoiding running afoul of his father, Morton became a multiple-sport standout at Campbell High School, and it seemed a toss-up whether he was a better prospect in football or baseball. He was recruited for both. From the start, he knew he was going to remain in the

Bay Area, picking between California and Stanford, but he consented to make a recruiting visit to Notre Dame.

"I just wanted to see what Notre Dame was like, and it was everything it was supposed to be," Morton says. "Daryle Lamonica was my host there. At the time it was all males and had curfew every night at 10 o'clock, and you couldn't have a car. I said, 'What do you guys do around here?' And they said, 'We hitchhike to Chicago.' Well, all my life I'd had curfew, so I wasn't about to go to college and have curfew. And it was snowing in April. So I wasn't really tempted."

Morton decided on California, instead of the closer Stanford, and didn't regret it. That made Golden Bears head coach Marv Levy happy, as well as the assistant who did most of the recruiting of Morton—Bill Walsh. Morton was on a combination football and baseball scholarship and played both sports, as a quarterback and centerfielder.

He was a major-league prospect in baseball, and he was considering not going along with the request of Cal's new football coach—Ray Willsey—to quit the baseball team during his junior season and come out for spring ball. It wasn't an ultimatum, and Willsey's reasonable view was that if Morton wanted to be a captain as a senior, he should participate in spring practices.

Morton says he thought about continuing to play baseball and hoping for a pro career there. "We had a series down at UCLA, and I said if I had a good series, I was just going to keep playing baseball and drop football," he recalls. "I played fairly well and it came to the second game of a doubleheader. In the top of the seventh—the second game always was shorter—I got up with the bases loaded. I fouled a few off. It's 3 and 2. Then I hit the ball. I said, 'Well, I guess I'm playing baseball,' because I thought it was gone.

"Then I heard a cheer and I knew it certainly wasn't for me because we were on the road and I looked up and saw the left fielder hanging over the fence with the ball. I said, 'I'm not playing baseball anymore.' That's the last time I played baseball."

The Berkeley campus was becoming notorious at the time. (The chaos and unrest would peak between his student days and Bob Swenson's tenure as a Golden Bear.)

"I was in ROTC," Morton says. "That was a tough deal. You walk around here in a uniform in those days. . . . It was a tough time but it was still a great time. The real riots happened after I left. I saw Free Speech and the Hippies and the flower children, and bare breasts. But it was a great experience."

As U.S. involvement in the Vietnam War escalated, Morton says he "didn't really know how to think. A lot of my friends went off to Vietnam and I was torn."

So as he finished up his Golden Bears career and was an All-American in 1964, Morton knew how good he had it as he prepared for an NFL career that was certain to come. The Cowboys took him in the first round of the 1965 draft, and he was introduced to the coaching ways of the taciturn Tom Landry.

"Landry was a lot like my father—very stoic, very distant, very non-communicative," Morton says. "Not one to really instill a lot of confidence. But he certainly knew football. I learned a lot of football."

Veteran Don Meredith, for whom the party never was over, was the Cowboys' starting quarterback, and Morton served an apprenticeship. By 1969, he was the starter and helped lead the Cowboys to Super Bowl IV in January 1970. As he was about to take the field, he was stunned to see the quarterbacks' faces on two huge balloons. One was a likeness of Johnny Unitas; the other of Morton. That awed Morton, who had been a Unitas fan growing up in Campbell. In that game, Morton was 12 for 26, for 126 yards, with one touchdown pass and two interceptions, and the Colts won 16-13 when Jim O'Brien kicked a 32-yard field goal with five seconds left. The way the game had been going, it wouldn't have been surprising if the Cowboys had blocked the kick and returned it for a touchdown.

"That was just such a goofy game, with interceptions, fumbles, everything—just mishaps like balls going off hands into other people's hands," Morton says. "Duane Thomas fumbled on like the 1-foot line when it could have won the game for us, and we actually recovered the ball, but they didn't give it to us. [Center] Dave Manders clearly had the ball. They changed the rule to wait until everybody was off the ball, but that cost us the Super Bowl."

After former Naval Academy quarterback Roger Staubach fulfilled his military obligation and joined the Cowboys at age 27, Morton had competition. The Cowboys considered trading Staubach, but Morton's shoulder problems at the time helped Dallas decide to stand pat. Staubach took over the starting job in 1971 and led the Cowboys to a 24-3 victory over Miami in Super Bowl VI, in January 1972. The next season, it was Staubach's turn to suffer a shoulder injury, and Morton played most of the '72 season, throwing for 2,396 yards and 15 touchdowns before Staubach came off the bench to lead Dallas to a comeback playoff victory over San Francisco. Morton backed up Staubach for most of the '73 season, and he had enough of inactivity when he still wasn't playing in the early stages of '74. At one point, the Cowboys even had tried a ridiculous shuttling of the two quarterbacks.

"I just said I don't want to do this anymore and I called [general manager] Tex Schramm and I said I'm not going to play," Morton recalls. "He started to say something and I said, 'Uh, uh, trade me.' I thought I was going to be traded to San Francisco because Dick Nolan was the coach there and he had been our defensive backfield coach at Dallas. Then at the last minute, they traded me to the Giants.

"Here I am, on a Wednesday morning, at LaGuardia Airport, with all my luggage, standing there looking up and saying, 'Are you the dumbest ass in the world or what? What have you done?' The Giants were not very good and then this guy picked me up in this old Ford station wagon and took me out to Pace University and they were practicing. I couldn't get number 14 because it was Y.A. Tittle's number, so I said, 'What you got?' and they said 15, so I said, 'Give it to me.'"

The trade was made on October 22, and on October 27, he started for the Giants *against* the Cowboys. In a 21-7 New York loss, he went 11 for 22, for 185 yards, and after four days of studying the playbook, he did an amazing job of even getting on the field.

"What was really hard was that in Dallas's offense, even was to the left. I'd been in that for nine and a half years," he says, "and I was in a new offense where even was to the right and I had a new terminology."

As Morton points out, though, the Giants' numbering system was the norm in football, and the Cowboys' was the exception—and that was because Landry was a defensive-oriented coach and essentially was looking at the offensive world from the other side of the ball. From that perspective, even *was* to his right—except it was to the offense's left.[6]

For the rest of 1974 and the two seasons following that, Morton was the much-criticized Giants starter, throwing far more interceptions (49) than touchdown passes (29). But was it any wonder? With that team, he had to try to make something happen.

"It was just a horrible, bad team, bad conditions," he says. "Great guys, but bad teams. We had fights and unrest, and it was horrible. We were just bad and the press was just unmerciful, horrible on us. Bill Arnsparger was the coach and he just didn't handle it very well at all, because they were really on him. One day he was like Captain Queeg, standing there with all the change in his pockets, running through that, and wouldn't stop. He said, 'I wonder what it takes to be a winner and I want to know what everybody thinks a winner is.' So 50, 60 guys got up and said what a winner was. What a joke."

Late in the 1976 season, after John McVay had succeeded Arnsparger as head coach, the Giants lost to the Broncos 14-13 in Mile High Stadium, in part because Denver blocked a Joe Danelo extra point. Or, as Morton puts it, "Our kicker stubbed his toe." Morton was 11 of 24 for 137 yards, with two interceptions. "I looked at Denver and I said, 'This is a great team. They just need a quarterback because their defense is really good.' Lo and behold, John McVay called me and said, 'Craig, we're sorry, we traded your rights to Denver.' I said, 'Thank you so much! Thank you kindly!'"

When Red Miller called him, the new coach didn't promise Morton the job, saying it would be an open competition. That was fine with Morton. Left unsaid was the assumption that it was Morton's job to lose, to prove that he could be the final piece in the puzzle.

By then, Morton was engaged to Susan Sirman and had become a born-again Christian. In fact, he said he picked number 7 to wear at Denver after he and Susan decided it had biblical significance.

Morton says he felt comfortable and welcome from the moment he came to Denver for a minicamp, walked into the locker room for the first time, and saw one player at the other end of the room.

Morton walked up to Lyle Alzado and put out his hand.

"Craig Morton," Morton said.

Morton says Alzado looked at him, shook his hand, and announced, "Now we'll win a championship."

Amazing Grace: Haven Moses

Number 25, Wide Receiver, 6-3, 200, 10th Season, San Diego State

For his first two years of high school, Haven Moses had bus schedules in his hand and coins—barely enough coins—in his pocket as he prepared to navigate the 15-mile trip from his family's Compton, California, home to Fermin de Lasuen Catholic High in San Pedro. The trip was from Compton, to Harbor City, to Wilmington, to San Pedro, and then back again each night, often after a sports practice. He did it because his mother, Annabelle, wanted it that way, and he did what his mother wanted.

"Centennial High School, the premier public school, was right in our backyard," Haven recalls in the living room of his downtown Denver condominium. "I used to walk by and watch Centennial practice sometimes. The Centennial Apaches!"

By high school, Haven was accustomed to the standards of the woman-run household. His father, also Haven, embittered because he couldn't find more than mostly menial jobs even after serving in the Army in World War II, degenerated into an alcohol-induced haze and eventually died when Haven was a Fermin de Lasuen senior.

The family had lost their house—at 110th Street and Avalon Boulevard to the east of the Los Angeles Coliseum—when Haven was about ten, and they also lost a bit of their sense of permanency as they moved around in South Central and Compton. It was Haven's mother; his aunt, Lillian; his grandmother, Mary; and his four younger siblings.

"Football, and really all sports, at that time was not something I thought about. I was born in 1946, a Baby Boomer, so it was the early '50s," Haven says. "The only thing I remember in terms of sports was that my grandmother, who came from Louisiana, couldn't read or write, but she could decipher the baseball box scores. It was unbelievable. She loved baseball, and that was because in Louisiana, their contact was with the old Negro League. Satchel [Paige], Josh [Gibson], she called them all by their first names."

He calls his youth "good years. I probably know more about what we didn't have, but it was a family of faith and one of those neighborhoods where if you went two blocks away and did something, you'd get a spanking. By the time you got home, they were ready to spank you again. That whole neighborhood was an extension of family. It was safe to walk around. We used to play out in the streets, especially in the summer, until the streetlights came on and that was time to high-tail it home."

He played what he could at St. Leo's School, but the official teams and programs were few. The kids played on the playground and in the neighborhood, sometimes under the auspices of the Catholic Youth Organization. "Basketball, baseball, football, kickball, dodgeball, four square, tetherball, you name it," Haven says. "My father bought me my first baseball glove and tried to get me in the little leagues. It was a three-fingered glove. I'm left-handed. It was the oddest-looking thing. I know he probably got it at a discount or something. At the time, it was the only thing he could afford. But I tried out and got cut, got kicked off two teams."

As he was approaching ninth grade, Annabelle was insistent that he wouldn't attend Centennial. "We had two Catholic schools in our area, Serra and Mount Carmel, and they were both powerhouses in sports," Haven says. "I couldn't get into either one of them. So finally, my mother found this Catholic high school in San Pedro. Brand new. Fermin de Lasuen."

When Haven began there, the all-boys school was in its second year, and had only ninth and tenth graders, gradually making the transition to a four-year school. He remembers the football coach asking of the new students, "'Who's going to play baseball?' I raised my hand. 'Who's going to play football?' I raised my hand. 'Who's going to play basketball?' I raised my hand. He looked at me and said, 'I guess we have a clown here.' I didn't know any better. I was just going to do as much as I could."

He did it all, despite his long commute. He mastered those bus schedules, but also sometimes rode with a neighbor who worked halfway to San Pedro and then hitchhiked the rest of the way. It was easier when he got his driver's license as a junior and Aunt Lillian bought him a car at one of the used lots on Slauson Avenue.

"Then I was able to recruit," he says. "I had three or four other kids from St. Leo's go with me to Fermin. That helped with gas and other things. It was a '55 Ford Fairlane, with two doors. It had been jacked up and jacked around, but it got me there. I couldn't go too fast on the freeways because it wobbled all the way."

In football, the school's fledgling program won a lower-division California Interscholastic Federation championship with its first senior class, when Haven was a junior. He was playing defensive back and running back, and he was good—not great—as a senior and was preparing to try to go to Compton Junior College when Floyd "Scrappy" Ray, the football coach at Harbor City College, approached him and his mother at the team's football banquet. Ray asked Haven if he had thought about trying to continue his football career.

Actually, he hadn't. He hadn't because nobody had asked him to.

Ray asked Haven to consider Harbor City.

"My mother said, 'What about school?' He said they'd get me enrolled and in the right classes toward my major, which I told him was going to be history. I was intrigued by the idea of continuing to play, or maybe more so the idea that somebody *wanted* me to keep playing at the next level."

He not only was on a junior college All-America team with San Francisco City College's O.J. Simpson in his first season, he became a star. In his second season, he played both ways, at cornerback and receiver. He had three touchdowns against San Diego City College, and San Diego State coach Don Coryell was there, scouting another player, but decided Moses was the big-time prospect and started going after him hard. By then, though, the USC–Harbor City pipeline was working, and Moses had all but committed to going to play for the Trojans. When a former Harbor teammate, Aztec quarterback Don Horn, tried to talk him into at least visiting San Diego State, Haven responded: "Don, I'm going to wear the cardinal and gold." And his mother was ecstatic. He would be playing close to their home and attending a high-quality school.

As a favor to Horn, he agreed to take a look in person at San Diego State. The Aztecs sent him a plane ticket for the short trip. He never had been on an airplane before, so on his scheduled departure day, by the time he figured out what he needed to do at Los Angeles International Airport, he missed his flight and went home. When he did get to San Diego the next day, he met the coaches—Coryell, Sid Hall, Joe Gibbs, Rod Dowhower, and an affable and rumpled fellow named John Madden[7]—and toured the campus. He says he just felt more comfortable and welcome there, contrasting it to when he had been at USC and noticed its stockpiled talent in the days of few limitations on scholarship numbers.

"They were down-home guys at San Diego State," he says. "SC was very pretentious. I got back and I couldn't put my finger on it. Then Coryell and Madden came to my house in Compton, and that was the thing that impressed me the most. They told my mom two things: they'd make sure I got an education and that I'd have fun. No other coach talked about that and no other coach came to my house."

So he decided to go to San Diego State, angering USC coach John McKay, who pointed out that they were both Catholic and that meant "you don't lie." Moses thought about that, but realized that his conference letter of intent with the Trojans was only for the Pacific Eight. Also, San Diego State still was playing in the NCAA's College Division.[8] He decided he had nothing to feel guilty about. (He was right.)

"Sid Hall came in his car," Moses says. "I had a '59 VW by then and we stuffed everything I had into his car and my car, and we went down I-5 to San Diego. They got me enrolled and squirreled me away from USC, and I bet the CIA couldn't have found me. My mother was heartbroken and wouldn't talk to me for about six weeks. She was bragging that her son was going to SC, and all of our family was in Southern California. I was the hottest thing in our family since the automobile and it took some time for me to get through that, but I was happy."

Within a year he was serious with his future wife, Joyce, whom he met at a campus function, and he was playing both ways for a national powerhouse small-college program that was entertaining and pioneering in the passing game. They moved into the new San Diego Stadium in 1967, drew well, and won the College Division national championship two years in a row.

He credits San Diego State sports publicist Bob "Sky" King[9] for putting "us on the map. Bob King was *good*. He got us some attention from the *L.A. Times* and other newspapers. Coryell kept saying, 'Haven, you have a chance to play pro ball,' but I had the same attitude I had in junior college and high school. It just didn't sink in. I didn't think I was doing anything other than I was supposed to do. But I was invited to the North-South game and the Senior Bowl, and my eyes were wide. I thought, *There's something to this.*"

The Buffalo Bills made him the ninth overall choice in the 1968 draft, and he went after only such players as Ron Yary, Claude Humphrey, and Larry Csonka. "I remember going back to Buffalo, and I had my California clothes on, and there were no jetways at the time, and I walked off the plane," he says. "This was late April and the sun was shining, but it was cold! They had to take me to a department store to get me a big ol' sweater, kind of a turtleneck, and it almost covered my head up. I was so cold."

After Jack Kemp was hurt in the next training camp and retired, the Bills had a succession of quarterbacks and Moses had decent, but not great, numbers as a receiver. "I couldn't throw the ball to myself," he says. "That's when I learned that every ball thrown to me, I better catch it."

When Lou Saban returned to the Bills for a second stint as head coach before the 1972 season, Moses saw trouble coming. He rebelled when, under Saban's orders, the equipment man changed his single-bar to a regular two-bar face mask and gave him conventional shoulder pads instead of his previous light pair. The equipment man returned his other equipment, but Saban had him marked down as not going along with the program.

When the Bills wouldn't let him on the field for the sixth game of the season, at Oakland, he suspected something was up, and he was traded the next day.

John Ralston acquired Moses for wide receiver Dwight Harrison, who had made himself, well, expendable. Harrison had argued with Lyle Alzado—his longtime friend and former road roommate—and was so angry that he went out to his car, retrieved a gun, and brought it into the dressing room. Harrison didn't come close to using it, but that made all concerned nervous, and everyone was breathing easier when he was banished to Buffalo.

An in-season trade made it difficult for Haven and Joyce, who just had given birth to their son, Chris, but Haven was determined to make the best of it.

"I loved Denver right away," he says. "I got here and I couldn't believe how blue the skies were and [administrative assistant] Joanne Parker came and picked me up. It had snowed two days before, but the skies were so clear and it was crisp. I never had seen clouds so white, like you could touch them."

While Joyce and Chris remained in the Buffalo area for a while, Haven lived at the infamous Continental Denver. "I'd walk over to Larimer

Square. That was the only thing going at the time, with the Café Promenade and Rathskellar."

He finished the '72 season with six touchdown catches, and he liked playing with quarterback Charley Johnson. He also moved his family to Denver and settled in. He felt he was at home after a play he remembers vividly—*an incomplete pass*—on the final play of a home exhibition against the Colts in 1973.

"Charley said, 'Haven, can you run by that guy?' He said he'd just throw it down the sideline. I mean, he was falling apart by then. But that son of a gun bought some time and he threw it down to the north end zone. I kept looking and saw the ball coming. I dived. And it went off the tips of my fingers. I didn't catch it. But they cheered. They cheered! I had dived for the ball and made the effort! In Buffalo, they would have booed. They liked me at Buffalo, but they didn't like me that much. I remember running to the locker room, and it seemed like it took forever, and there were cheers! I said to myself right then and there: *This is fantastic.* That's when I started to realize how it was here, how the people just gravitated towards you."

He had 116 catches in his first four full seasons as a Bronco, and it didn't help that quarterback Steve Ramsey was only mediocre after Johnson's retirement. But still, there was that 9-5 record in 1976—the one that led to the player meeting.

"I know they called us the Dirty Dozen, but there were only three pushing it," he says. "There was something going on that season, they didn't like Ralston. And I think there were some coaches involved, too. John wasn't a football guy per se, but he knew what he was doing, he knew personnel. He was a student of Dale Carnegie, yes, but he was introducing something new to football. Everyone thought he was rah-rah, but it was the power of positive thinking.

"So we're sitting in this [meeting] room, saying let's talk about what's going on, and we're hearing this all from one end about we need to get him out of here. I'll never forget Otis Armstrong saying, 'What are these guys talking about?' It was confusing. I do remember the last thing that was said was, 'Nothing leaves this room. Nothing leaves this room.' People were pretty adamant and B.T. [Billy Thompson] was the one sounding that charge. But it hits the papers and we're trying to figure out what happened."

Moses was one of the players who spoke that season of knowing that the Broncos had needed a new spark of leadership, but he clearly didn't like all aspects of the way it came about.

"I didn't know about Red. Knew he was an offensive line coach so I felt we would go back to being more of a running team," Moses says. "I remember we had meetings and we talked as players about whatever happens, we were still the team. We had to prove that it wasn't about us being responsible for getting rid of a coach. We had to go out and prove that we were that good of a ball team. We wanted to get rid of that other stigma about whatever happened there, getting John fired. We wanted to erase that. And Red was a motivator, a gung-ho guy, a down-in-the-trenches guy. Whoever came in, we were going to play for that coach."

Then the Broncos traded for Craig Morton. "When Craig came, I knew he had a heck of an arm and I knew he didn't have any legs, but I figured I was going to catch a few more passes," Moses says. He pauses, then adds: "I didn't anticipate what happened. I don't think either one of us saw that."

Notes

1. Amazingly, the *Post* ran all those titles.

2. In 2007, the Warwick.

3. One of the models for Ogilthorpe, Bill Goldthorpe, briefly played for the World Hockey Association's Denver Spurs in 1975.

4. It evolved into *The Witch's Season*, the greatest unpublished novel and unproduced screenplay combination of all time. (Of course, about 100,000 would-be novelists and screenwriters think the same thing about their works.)

5. For several years, the restaurant was owned by a group headed by Denver Mayor John Hickenlooper. He sold out to his partners in August 2007.

6. This would cause considerable transitional problems for holdover Broncos when Dan Reeves brought the Cowboys' offense to Denver.

7. All but Hall, who became a high-profile NFL scout, later were NFL head coaches.

8. Essentially, the forerunner of Division I-AA.

9. King later was the Denver Nuggets' publicist and a team executive.

CHAPTER 4

Campers

You could see the twinkle in his eye, like he was thinking,
Goddamn, I wish I was with you guys!

—MIKE MONTLER

Fort Collins: July 15–August 4

After five seasons of John Ralston, Red Miller was going to have a honey-
moon period under virtually any circumstances. But his passion and fire
from the start of training camp at Colorado State University in Fort Collins sold the Broncos.

"I didn't know Red from a man in the moon," nose tackle Rubin
Carter recalls. "But I know this: He came in with energy and enthusiasm
that were unbelievable. There's an old saying that the speed of the leader
is the speed of the pack. Well, you better keep up with Red Miller because
when he got to the field, he hit it running."

Beyond the attention paid to the new coach and his methods, including allowing the players to take a Popsicle break in the middle of practices, the spotlight also was on the quarterback race among Craig Morton,
Steve Spurrier, Norris Weese, and Craig Penrose.

Miller's official position was that the race was wide open and he was
noncommittal, but in truth he was rooting for Morton to step up. Miller
assigned young Joey Collier, Joe Collier's 13-year-old son, the task of

charting every pass the quarterbacks threw in anything that approached significant practice work. The four learned to take a look at Joey, and perhaps even subtly lobby.[1]

After a while, Miller didn't need to look at Joey's notes. "I knew Craig was going to be the quarterback after a couple of weeks," Miller recalls. "Remember, I stood behind Johnny Unitas for a couple of years when I was with the Colts and watched him throw the football. On a lot of throws, Morton was a better passer than people thought. If he had a good pair of legs, really good so he could run, he would have been one of the best passers ever. That's how good he was. You get behind him and you see the drop-off zone and you could see a guy who could drop it right over the linebacker, and he could do it on a dime."

Morton disputes the idea that everyone assumed he was going to be the starter. "I know the fans didn't particularly think I was going to be the quarterback," he recalls with a smile. "I remember they took a poll. [Craig] Penrose was my roommate and we were watching TV one night, and they were going around the bars and other places and asking who the quarterback should be. I think Penrose was the top choice and I got seven percent of the vote. So the fans weren't too excited."

Perhaps the fans skeptical about Morton had looked at his nearly 2-to-1 ratio of interceptions to touchdown passes in New York. But when he came to Denver, he knew what the strength of the team was, and he says he didn't even need to be told that his challenge was going to be quite different.

"What a defense!" he says. "That's one thing I knew, to play to the defense."

Miller didn't convince him of that?

"Oh, believe me," Morton says, "I was smart enough to know that. Let's play to the defense. Let's play field position. Let's not make mistakes. That was Red's whole deal. No mistakes."

———

It also became clear early in camp that Miller was intending to be his own de facto offensive line coach and also offensive coordinator. Rookie coach Ken Gray, the former All-Pro, was capable of relating to the linemen and being credible in passing along what he knew, but wasn't bothered when Miller often wandered over and joined the linemen.

When Miller wasn't around, veteran center Bobby Maples also did a lot of the instructing. Maples was one of the most universally respected players in the game, and not only because of his status as the best long snapper in the league. The former Baylor University standout—who came from Mt. Vernon, Texas, also the hometown of former Cowboys quarterback Don Meredith—had played six seasons with the Oilers and Steelers when Denver acquired him in 1972, when my father was a rookie NFL line coach. Maples immediately became one of my father's favorite players ever, and that covered a lot of territory.[2] "Mapes" even was named the Broncos' offensive MVP in 1975. By 1977, he was 34, and he had been banged up through most of 1976 and gave way in the starting lineup to veteran Phil Olsen, Merlin's younger brother, down the stretch.

Denver had another option after the Broncos acquired Boulder resident Mike Montler's rights from Buffalo on July 21 and got him out of short-lived retirement and into camp. Montler walked out for his first practice wearing the number 53 jersey the equipment staff had given him. But before practice started, they sheepishly came to him and said, oops, that's Randy Gradishar's number, and asked Montler if he would mind switching to 52. Heck, no, Montler said. He was just glad to be there.

Miller made it a habit to work the locker room after practice, patting backs, kidding around, chewing out. Early in the camp, Miller came to free-agent center Ken Brown and tried to demonstrate something about blocking technique. Brown jumped into a wrestling position, pretending he was ready to take Miller on. Next thing everyone knew, the coach and the center were rolling on the floor, and Miller was acting as if it was a high school dual meet with the team winner going down to this match. They weren't mad, they weren't fighting, and although Brown was a bit befuddled, they were just two guys rasslin'. Eventually, Miller also would wrestle a lot with backup linebacker Godwin Turk.

It was one more sign that Red was taking this *real* serious. There were plenty of others.

"That was our second year of camp at CSU, and it was still kind of new to us," Louis Wright recalls. "It was just kind of like we had this new coach, a new attitude, and everything was just new and everyone was excited. And our practices were much harder, with much more hitting."

The boys still let off some steam after hours, though.

"One night we really got rowdy and Red had to hand out fines the next day," Montler, the newest Bronco at the time, recalls. "You could see the twinkle in his eye, like he was thinking, *Goddamn, I wish I was with you guys!* You could just see him thinking, *My boys are feisty!* And he liked that."

The way defensive end Barney Chavous remembers the incident, a bunch of the players—not including him and his roommate, Rubin Carter—waited until Myrel Moore and Stan Jones made the bed checks and sneaked out for a night of carousing in Fort Collins. But the coaches doubled back, noted who was gone, and turned over the list to Miller the next morning at breakfast.

Miller addressed the players in the cafeteria. They remember that he looked at the list, pointed to the names and said, "All you guys? I ain't working you hard enough if you think you can go to bed, then go back out and go party."

Fact was, Miller had quit drinking himself—cold turkey—in early 1976, thinking perhaps it might help his chances to become a head coach. Until then, he was a conventional football social drinker, but he decided it was time to stop even that as he attempted to move up.

It wasn't lost on the players that he backed the fines up with what seemed to be a brutally long and hard practice. Chavous remembers Miller's challenge at the end of practice.

"*Now* go out and party."

With the Denver Bears drawing nearly 5,000 a game to Mile High Stadium, a decent total for Class AAA baseball, general manager Jim Burris went to the major-league All-Star Game in New York and said he was campaigning for Denver as a major-league city. "It would be nice if we had a group here making a financial push to obtain a franchise, but we don't," he said.

New York seemed a whole different world, especially to me; I already was looking forward to visiting the city for the first time during my rookie season on the Rockies' beat. But Burris was making his visit in a tough summer for the Big Apple. A lightning-caused blackout paralyzed the city for about 16 hours in mid-July, and unlike the generally smile-through-it attitude of the city in the infamous northeast power blackout in 1965 (it even spawned a terrible Doris Day–Robert Morse movie, *Where Were*

You When the Lights Went Out?), the darkness set off looting and rioting. Two weeks after the power—and, relatively speaking, order—was restored, a mysterious killer, known only as the Son of Sam, committed his sixth murder. On August 3, bombs exploded in two Manhattan office buildings. One person was killed. After what was labeled a "terrorist action" in the media, the group claiming credit warned that bombs might go off in as many as five other towers. In the ensuing panic, several major office buildings—including the World Trade Center—were evacuated and searched. The terrorist group was the FALN (Armed Forces of National Liberation). The terrorists' cause was independence for Puerto Rico.

———

Plans for new development in downtown Denver seemed to be springing up weekly, confirming the health of the oil-fueled Colorado economy. As Oxford-Anschutz Development was just finishing up the huge 40-story Anaconda Tower at 17th and Glenarm, construction was about to begin on the high-end Fairmont Hotel at 18th and Welton.[3] Meanwhile, First Hawaiian Development announced plans for an $84-million Sheraton Hotel and office complex in the block bounded by Arapahoe and Larimer, and 16th and 17th Streets. A week later, Oxford-Anschutz unveiled another skyscraper project—a $40-million twin-tower office complex at 16th and Broadway. While the Broncos still were in Fort Collins, a Calgary firm let it be known it would build another twin tower of offices and a hotel at the block between Champa and Curtis, and 18th and 19th. Then the Regional Transportation District said it was planning to turn 16th Street—the busy one-way street and part of the old "drag" pattern—into a tree-lined pedestrian mall.

I thought about the time in 1972, when my father and I were temporarily living at the Continental Denver, and I took pictures of Denver's downtown skyline to send to my friends back in Oregon. But when I looked at them later, I decided the skyline didn't look any more impressive—or big-time—than Portland's and didn't send them.

Maybe in a year or so, I'd get out the camera again.

More evidence that my new hometown was becoming big-time came at the airport: The city announced that Stapleton had become the nation's eighth busiest, behind both New York airports, plus those in Chicago, Atlanta, Los Angeles, San Francisco, and Dallas–Fort Worth. The Denver-based Frontier Airlines,[4] one of United's competitors, was doing very well for investors, with net earnings of $2.72 million in the second quarter. Two other of Stapleton's tenants, Braniff and Delta, both announced new nonstop service to Atlanta, meaning one fewer destination that involved making connections in either Chicago or Dallas.

But in Denver we couldn't get cable TV. Other cities already had been wired as cable broadcasting made the transition from enabling customers in outlying areas to get reception to giving customers in metro areas a better signal and more choices. That was especially frustrating because a handful of major cable companies—including Tele-Communications Inc. (TCI), American Television and Communications (ATC), Cablecom General Inc., and Daniels Properties, the empire of cable pioneer Bill Daniels—were based in Denver. United Cable was in the process of moving its headquarters from Tulsa to Denver. In Denver, we were told we would have to wait until the city awarded a franchise, and that the longer we had to wait, the more advanced the technology would be when we finally were wired. I kept playing with the antenna and trying to get clean-shaven and paternal anchorman Bob Palmer to stop appearing as if he had an Abe Lincoln beard.

A teenager from the eastern Colorado town of Yuma, the University of Colorado–bound Steve Jones, was getting tons of publicity as the state's latest golf phenom. Heavily favored, he lost 2 and 1 to Ken Krieger in the semifinals of the state match play tournament at Lakewood Country Club.

"I felt like Rocky out there this afternoon," Krieger said. "I kept slugging and hitting and waiting for him to go down. But he never would."

Krieger apparently had forgotten that Rocky Balboa lost.[5]

The Denver Comets pro volleyball team drew 4,652 to the Auditorium Arena for its match against the Orange County Stars. The attraction was the Stars' Wilt Chamberlain, who was surprisingly low profile in the Comets' 3-0 victory.

By then, we figured that if any league started, in any sport, Denver would get a franchise. Volleyball, team tennis, soccer . . .

Then again, that was how we got the Nuggets and Broncos.

Frances Melrose of the *Rocky Mountain News* visited a North Denver institution, Cerrone's Market, which "Ottey" and Millie Cerrone had been running for 50 years. Located on Osage Street near Mount Carmel Church, it was the type of place where the owners knew most of the customers by their first names, and the customers teased Ottey about keeping his thumb off the scale when he weighed the sausage. Ottey told Melrose of the couple's rough early days in control of the store, after the 1929 stock market crash.

"Everybody was broke and we were carrying a lot of them on credit," Ottey said. "Times got pretty rough, but we lasted it out and finally when everyone got jobs, we got paid. They nearly all paid us back."

In a world of supermarkets, the Cerrones were determined to hang on.

A few of the Broncos players pondered taking a break from camp to drive back to Denver to see blues guitarist B.B. King—and Lucille, his guitar—at his sold-out run at the Turn of the Century. But they decided that wouldn't impress Red, especially if they got delayed on the way back. It was a great summer for the "Turn": The next attraction, crooner Tony Bennett, still as popular as ever and showing no signs of slowing down, already was sold out as well.

Lana Turner, the sweater girl and famous film actress, opened at Elitch's in *Bell, Book, and Candle* but it was obvious about 10 minutes into the play that the stage wasn't her thing. The season ticket holders were hoping that the next attraction, Broadway star John Raitt in *I Do! I Do!* was going to be a lot better, and I was hoping he would bring in his daughter, Bonnie, for a hastily arranged concert beneath Mister Twister. Bonnie's version of Del Shannon's *Runaway* was the big hit on *Sweet Forgiveness*, and I was typical of a lot of her converts: After buying and liking *Sweet Forgiveness*, I ran out to Budget Records and filled in my Raitt collection.

On July 29, the Broncos put on the traditional "rookie show" in the CSU student union.

When the appointed organizers of the show—the top two draft choices, guard Steve Schindler from Boston College and tailback Rob Lytle from Michigan—playfully asked if a rookie coach shouldn't be in the show, too, Red Miller said, fine, get a piano.

"They were rookies and I was a rookie!" Miller recalls. "So I had to step up, man."

Miller put on a ragtime performance that would have impressed Scott Joplin, playing "Somebody Stole My Gal."

"You know what it did, Terry?" Red asks. "It made me a little bit more one of them."

The Broncos shook their heads about how their new coach never stopped surprising them. They also appreciated that an earlier skit in the show hadn't offended him.

In that skit, Lytle "played" Red. Ron Egloff, a rookie free-agent tight end from Wisconsin, "played" backfield coach Paul Roach.

By then, the players were familiar with the sort of comments the real Miller and Roach made during training-camp film study with the team, when they showed New England's running game from the previous season to illustrate what they wanted done.

In the playbook, the running-game series were called "flow," "plunge," "ride," and "dive."

Lytle and Egloff had their teammates in stitches as they rolled an 8-millimeter film and imitated the coaches reacting to it, talking about "flow," "plunge," "ride," and "dive."

Lytle still laughs, giving part of the spiel years later.

"Got that, Paul?" Lytle asks in a guttural voice.

The scenes on the screen, though, weren't of football games. "Miller" and "Roach" were commenting on a cheap porno film. Lytle and Egloff had gotten some help in cutting it up and splicing it back together, to fit the proper designations.

Lytle's teammates loved it and also admired his bravery. "They voted that I'd be gone the next day," he says.

But Red thought it was funny, too.

The other hit of the rookie show was rookie center Ken Brown, who did an Elvis Presley imitation, singing "Hound Dog."

In making calls around the hockey world, I came across a WHA executive who told me that if they weren't already, the Rockies should consider hiring Pat Kelly, who had done a good job in a bad situation after taking over the WHA's Birmingham Bulls in November 1976, but didn't yet have a contract for the upcoming season because of the precarious state of the Birmingham franchise. *Gee, he'd be right at home here,* I thought. And then the WHA man added that Kelly, who had been a player, a player-coach, and then a general manager–coach in the Eastern League and Southern League, was widely considered to be one of the several models for player-coach Reg Dunlop in *Slap Shot*. That was good enough for me. Kelly was on vacation in the Canadian wild, but when I ran his name by someone in the Rockies' office, I got reluctant confirmation and wrote that Kelly was at the top of the list of candidates, but that they couldn't make a move until Vickers gave the go-ahead.

Soon, I was talking to Kelly daily on the phone, developing a friendship and trying to get up the nerve to ask him how much of *Slap Shot* really was true. We both were waiting for the Rockies to make up their minds.

By late in the month, the tally for the Rockies' season ticket campaign was 2,000. It was looking as if Kelly might not have a team to coach.

Discussing his proposed compromises on Denver-area highway issues at a news conference, Governor Dick Lamm presented a railroad spike to reporters.

They got the joke.

He said he hoped the compromises on the table represented the "final chapter."

In 1975, Lamm had vehemently opposed a proposed 26-mile freeway loop, mostly through the southern end of the metro area. As Interstate 470, it would be part of the federal interstate freeway system and be constructed with federal funds. Saying it would contribute to sprawl and pollution and only encourage a Los Angeles–style reliance on the automobile, he vowed to drive "a silver stake" through the heart of the project.

In the wake of an outcry that he was an obstructionist fanatic, he slightly tempered his initial opposition and after two years of sometimes acrimonious fighting over the issue, his study committee in the summer of '77 was calling for a four-lane parkway, not a freeway. The proposal was to remove the project from the interstate system, at a significant savings, and use the remaining federal money on other road projects, such as Santa Fe Boulevard and South Kipling Street.

Looking back 30 years later in his office at the Institute for Public Policy Studies at the University of Denver, Lamm is within walking distance of Denver's new light rail line, but also not far from C-470 and E-470—which, while not parts of the interstate system and also toll roads in places, at least *look* like freeways.

"The wisdom of my action there is just now I think being played out," Lamm says. "I couldn't make people understand, and we didn't have global warming at the time, but my argument is that given the finiteness of petroleum, you don't build a modern city around the automobile. You have to start a transition. I also felt that there was no way our children were going to be able to buy the price of oil, that we had to start having foresight. I kept citing Toronto, and we had to start building the city of the future around mass transit. I handled it badly, I still am somewhat embarrassed, but I have no apologies for what I was trying to do. . . . I did not have a good sense of when to stop fighting and start compromising. It went on too long and was very distracting to my administration. It was a Pyrrhic victory because the whole intention was to start to move away from the automobile. That was my goal. And I failed."

What of the light rail?

"We could have done that! We could have done that, Terry! You know, Colorado is a wonderful place and I love it. Colorado has a public accommodations law two years after *Plessy vs. Ferguson*. We had early fair housing laws. We had early sunshine laws. This isn't a hopelessly redneck southern state. A lot of people like you and me have come here. It has so enriched the state and it's given us I think a certain progressiveness, but not when it comes to spending money. . . . When I would talk mass transit and building mass transit back then? It wasn't all that new, because we had had modest mass transit proposals before. But it was a bridge too far for Colorado."

While this was being played out, Lamm's relationship with the state legislature was turning from testy to warlike. On July 17 alone, he vetoed 7 bills, including one calling for uniform sentencing for felonies, citing inconsistencies in the law and parts of it that could backfire, bringing his total for the year to 31. That was a staggering total considering most of the 600 bills passed were routine and noncontroversial.

"I was 39 years old when I was elected and I had been successful fighting for things," Lamm says. "I had been an advocate. I did not have the wisdom enough at 39 to recognize that that's a different role. . . . One of my main platforms was to pass a severance tax on Colorado's natural resources and use the money to fund the removal of the sales tax from food. The Republicans in the Senate wouldn't even consider it, wouldn't even hold a hearing. I just got my back up. I certainly learned the famous statement that the oilcan is mightier than the sword. I look back and I think if I would have invited some of those people over to the [Governor's] Mansion for dinner, and if I would have used those normal political skills I finally developed, I sure could have saved myself a lot of headaches."

———

On July 30, amid ongoing controversies about illegal immigration and continuing deportations, and even an in-depth *Post* story about growing resentment of affirmative action, Denver police officers shot and killed two Hispanic men, Arthur Espinoza and James Hinojos, in Curtis Park, near downtown. The police said they had been called to the park because of a report that Espinoza was under the influence of drugs, and that the two men had passed a gun between them. But area residents and the Chicano community didn't buy the explanation or believe it was sufficient to explain the deaths, and protests at the park threatened to turn to violence, leading police to use tear gas to disperse the gathering.

———

The next night, Miller held court at a team barbeque and saluted the Broncos for their hard work so far. For much of the camp, Miller's mantra had been that the days of the offense-defense schism had to end, that everyone had to think as a team. One for all, all for one, all in it together, regardless of the side of the ball or the prominence of the role. He preached "Togetherness and dedication." His favorite speech was that everyone needed to build their own house, do a good job of that, and they'd have a great neighborhood.

"Red was a fireplug," recalls guard Tom Glassic. "Red was the best motivator I ever saw. Our practices were precise and everyone focused and concentrated because everything was just like that"—and at that point, Glassic snaps his fingers several times. "John Ralston's practices were guys smoking in the locker room and hanging out and nobody's paying attention. That all ended with Red. . . . But he didn't bring in that ticky-tack college crap. He treated us like we were all in it together, we all were professionals and he'd treat us that way. And we took to that."

———

Ron Zappolo, a young New England–raised sportscaster fresh from a stint with a station in Washington, DC, reported to work at KOA/Channel 4 on August 1. Thirty years later, he is one of Denver's most respected and successful television journalists ever, and is the coanchor of KDVR/ Channel 31's newscasts. "I remember going to Fort Collins that week," he says, "and introducing myself to Billy Thompson first. I was thinking to myself, *I've got a long way to go, I've got to meet everybody, but the only way to do it is to keep showing up.*"

But Zappolo only had time to make a couple of trips to Fort Collins, because with a six-game exhibition season coming up—there was some grousing about it being too long, but no change seemed on the horizon— the Broncos were set to bolt from Fort Collins, head to Denver, face the Baltimore Colts at Mile High, and practice at the team headquarters from then on. Even if they had homes in Denver, the players would stay at the Inn at the Mart, across the street from the offices and practice fields, but the collegiate period was over.

Although Miller downplayed its significance, he named Morton the starter for the Baltimore game, and the implication was clear: He was rooting for Morton in the quarterback race.

Morton was going to need a lot of help from his line, including the recently arrived center who was a veteran—in more ways than one.

From the Halls of Montezuma: Mike Montler
Number 52, Center, 6-5, 254, 9th Season, Colorado

Marine Lance Corporal Michael Montler, 20, was minding his own business, serving on Okinawa and playing football for the Marine Devil Dogs squad that kicked the hell out of other service teams in the Pacific region and made generals proud.

It was August 1964.

Then American military authorities said North Vietnamese forces had fired on two U.S. destroyers in the Gulf of Tonkin. Okinawa suddenly became so jammed with men and materiel "we wondered why the damn island didn't sink," Montler says.

A captain informed Montler that he was part of K Battery now, not a football player and recreation supervisor. "He says to me, 'In 24 or 48 hours we will be hitting a beach and there will be bodies floating in the water and there will be blood,'" Montler recalls. "He's excited about this." The captain told Montler to go down to supply and get gear and a weapon. "They had two weapons left," Montler says. "Everything else had been packed up and shipped to White Beach [the staging area]. There was a .45 and there was an M1 rifle with no firing pin it."

Well, said Montler, given the choice, he'd have to take the .45. No way, the supply man said. He insisted Montler couldn't have it because only officers and noncommissioned officers "rate" .45s. Montler tried to talk both the supply man and then his captain into letting him have the .45.

"Look," he told his captain, "you told me there would be bodies floating in the water and there would be blood in the sand! An M1 with no firing pin doesn't do me much good!"

"Only officers and NCOs . . ."

Exasperated, Montler went back and took the only weapon he could get. He went off to what might have been war with an M1 rifle without a firing pin. "I went down to White Beach and got put on a troop ship," he says. "We're in the 7th Fleet, it's huge, and everybody's speculating about what's going on. The consensus is that as soon as the election is over, [President Lyndon] Johnson will be secure in office, he can talk about how we kicked butt, and we'll be coming home. We're going back and forth between Saigon and Da Nang in the South China Sea, just floating. It's hot and humid and at night we're in blackout conditions so we have every hatch closed. After about two weeks of this, we fall out in formation."

A sergeant announced that after he read a list of names, those Marines would stay and the rest could leave. He read about 10 other names . . . and then Montler's. When the other Marines left, Montler looked around.

"It's a bunch of mostly little guys who are 115 pounds, soaking wet, and I'm 6-5 and the sergeant says: 'This is what's happening! Our troop ship is going down the Saigon River into Saigon and we're going to pick up and evacuate American civilians out of there! Because the Saigon River is fairly narrow, we need sharpshooters to patrol the banks on either side so we don't get incoming fire lobbed at us all the time as we go through.'"

Montler asked permission to speak.

"Sir," he said, "but I never have fired a rifle in my life except at boot camp."

"Well, you were rated 'expert'!"

Montler tried to explain that he had a good eye, but that his score was 221, one point beyond the "expert" threshold and that he hadn't fired a gun before or since.

"Besides, sir," he added, "I don't have a firing pin in my weapon!"

"Don't worry about it, we'll take care of it!"

The sergeant showed his newly assembled group of sharpshooters around the ship and pointed out where each would be stationed during the mission. Everyone had a spot shielded by an armor plate. All these little guys. "Except for you, Montler—you're here, at the fantail," said the sergeant.

"The only thing on a fantail is a pipe about one inch in diameter with a chain," Montler says.

His fellow marksmen now thought this was hilarious. The big guy, still without a firing pin in his rifle, is going to be in the open! They even joked that no self-respecting Viet Cong sniper would claim him as a kill after shooting him because he was so damn big. Shooting him would be too easy.

"This is one of those 'fortunately' or 'unfortunately' things," he recalls, "but by the time we were going to go down there, the Viet Cong had sunk a barge in the Saigon River so the ship couldn't maneuver without getting too close to the shore. So they canceled the trip. And I *still* didn't have a firing pin in my weapon."

A few days later, as the possibility of Americans jumping into the battles as more than advisers still loomed and tension reigned in the 7th Fleet, a cargo helicopter hovered above Montler's ship. It sent down a line, with the ring that could pull men and equipment up to the helicopter. Holding his gear, Montler climbed in it. The chopper crew pulled him up, hauled him aboard the copter, and it flew away.

Below, Marines wondered: *What the hell is that all about?*

The general was putting the football team back together.

The Montlers—James, a minimum-wage laborer at odd jobs; his wife, Frances; and their two boys—lived behind the Schottenstein's store in Columbus, Ohio. "It was the wrong side of the tracks," Mike says in his home adjacent to a golf course in Grand Junction, Colorado. "If you said you live around Schottenstein's you were shunned. Kids would say, 'You're kidding me, you live down there?' We were right down by Buckeye Steel Casting Company, too. A great percentage of the neighborhood was black. There was a small percentage of hillbillies. There was a small percentage of 'others.' I fell into the 'others' category."

Mike, the younger of the two sons, spent much of his time playing sports in the nearby city park, usually against far older boys.

"It was kind of the neighborhood thugs and hoodlums there," he says. "It wasn't like today. If you had an altercation, the worse thing you had to worry about was a black eye, not a 'shiv' or getting shot. It was like an honor amongst thieves. Besides, my mother was highly respected in the neighborhood. There were ex-cons who would say, 'Hello, Mrs. Montler,' and my mom would say, 'Isn't Lawrence the nicest boy?'"

Despite their poverty, his parents insisted their sons go to Catholic school, and Mike went to St. Mary's, which had 33 students—including Mike—in his high school graduating class. He was the star athlete, but that wasn't saying much, because St. Mary's was everyone's homecoming patsy and he seemed to have different coaches every season. His options were the traditional ones of the neighborhood.

"You went to work at Buckeye Steel Casting Company or you joined the Marine Corps," Montler says.

He and a couple of buddies joined the Marines.

"I really enjoyed boot camp at San Diego because of the discipline," he says.

He was not a model Marine. Or, on second thought, maybe he was. At Camp Pendleton, when a sergeant demanded Montler give up his seat in the crowded mess hall, Montler refused—and, after they exchanged words, they settled it in traditional Marine fashion. They went behind the mess hall and fought. "I beat up on this sergeant very good," Montler says. "He was tall and skinny. He had all the moves and none of the power."

Montler heard that the San Diego Marines' renowned football team, whose opponents annually included college teams, was holding a tryout. He hoped to be a tight end. When he showed up, he noticed that team already had two tight ends—and both had been collegiate stars.

"Well," he told himself, "I guess I'm a tackle."

He made the team, and Major Scotty Harris, the coach, liked what he saw, telling San Diego writers that this kid Montler was going to be an All-American someday.

He was so raw that in the first game, against Long Beach State, he charged downfield on a screen pass that went for a touchdown, having no idea that it was a problem—and was befuddled when officials called illegal man downfield and called the play back.

In his second season on the team, 1963, the Marines were about to play San Diego State in an annual charity game at Balboa Stadium. When the Marines took advantage of a pass interference call and scored the winning touchdown in the final seconds, a San Diego State linebacker took exception to the Marines' halfback raising his arms in celebration and cold-cocked him.

"Both benches emptied, both teams are fighting on the field, the fans come out of the stands and they're fighting—at this charity event at Balboa Stadium," Montler says.

After weeks of acrimonious debate, the Marines versus San Diego State series officially was ended.

Montler got caught with an official Marine ID that he had bought blank, then filled in to make himself 21 and a corporal. "I just wanted to meet girls and have a beer," he says. "I didn't think I'd go to Leavenworth because of it." As he was about to be court-martialed—the brass mainly were trying to get him to reveal who had sold him the real and numbered, but otherwise blank, ID—General Bruno Hochmuth,[6] a football fan, intervened and made it clear that Montler would *not* be court-martialed.

But now he was getting a "reputation." When a buddy told him he should put in for a transfer to Okinawa, where the Marines had a football team, he listened. "The guy told me, 'Oh, yeah, it's great. Cheap beer, cheap women.' He gave all the basic reasons."

Coach Harris and other officers were flabbergasted, but they approved the transfer and all went well until the Gulf of Tonkin incident. Montler went back to the Marines' Pacific football team and then joined the Marines' basketball team as a reserve for a trip to Nationalist China, among other places. Finally, he went back to the United States, killing time at Camp Lejeune, North Carolina, waiting for his discharge.

"Then there was a crisis in Santo Domingo and they started sending Marines there," Montler says. "Let's see, they're sending Marines to Vietnam and Marines to Santo Domingo. I liked the Marines, but I'm thinking this isn't good, because I might be 'extended.'[7] So I called the University of Colorado."

Montler had been hearing from CU assistant coach Chet Franklin for several years, because Franklin was in the Marine reserves and did occasional duty in San Diego and was able to scout the football team. "If you had 90 days or less to do and you enrolled to go to college, they'd discharge you," Montler says. "They enrolled me in summer school at CU. I got out of the Marines June 1 and somewhere around August 1, they extended the Marines. I had just beaten it."

He loved some things *about* Boulder—including The Sink and Tulagi, both watering holes on "The Hill"—and some of his classes, but he at least initially didn't love Boulder. He says CU coach Eddie Crowder talked him out of his plan to major in philosophy and psychology, and he ended up in the business school. He still signed up for one philosophy class, heard the professor drone on, and then went to The Sink and told owner Herb Kauvar that he had no idea what he had just heard and was ready to go back to the Marine Corps. Kauvar calmed him down and told him to use the athletic department tutors. While Montler bounced all over the map academically and never got a degree because his hours were in so many different subjects, he got good grades and even made some academic all-America lists.

He also got married. He and Suzy had a son, Brandon. He wasn't thrilled with the football program, in part because he had played in a pro-style offense in the Marines and hated lining up in a four-point "Oklahoma" stance and trying to hook defensive linemen, rather than block them. He credits legendary sports publicist Fred Casotti for making him a 1968 All-American, and wasn't enamored of his own play in the system he despised.

He was ready for pro football, and he was disappointed when the

Boston Patriots—and not the Chargers—took him in the second round of the 1969 draft. He spent four seasons with the Patriots, mostly playing guard. The funny thing was, he and Suzy decided to stay in Boulder and make it their off-season home. The Patriots still were a ragtag organization at the time, without a stadium of their own and with terrible facilities. When the Patriots hired Chuck Fairbanks away from Oklahoma, Montler considered that the last straw. A bad organization and now a "college" coach? He said he was quitting unless he was traded.

Fairbanks tried to talk him into reporting to an off-season training camp in Florida, telling Montler he remembered him from Colorado and respected him and his character and things were going to be different with the Patriots from here on . . .

Sorry, coach, said Montler. No.

"Now he's yelling at me." Montler pretends to hold a phone receiver far from his ear. "I'm holding the phone out here and saying to myself, *What happened to the Mike's-a-good-guy stuff?*"

Another irony: If Montler had reported, he would have been working with offensive coordinator Red Miller.

Montler said he was "just hanging out" when his agent, Jack Mills, called and said the Patriots had given in and traded him to Buffalo, in a multiplayer deal.

When he reported for the 1973 training camp, the Bills' equipment man handed him a number 53 jersey. Uh, said Montler, there must be some mistake. That's a center's number. No, said the equipment man; the coach says you're a center. Montler had never played the position before.

He had some rocky moments at first with head coach Lou Saban and line coach Jim Ringo, but eventually earned the starting job and played four seasons with Buffalo, blocking for O.J. Simpson. He was a member of the famed Electric Company[8] offensive line and helped Simpson break the 2,000-yard barrier in 1973.

"I don't know what to say because there's the good O.J. and the bad O.J.," Montler says. "The good O.J. was the most gracious, wonderful person you'd ever meet in your life. He gave credit to his offensive line, the whole team, the receivers who blocked, [fullback] Jim Braxton, a key part of the whole thing. He was just the greatest."

Montler was standing nearby when Simpson told NFL officials he wouldn't appear at a news conference after he passed the 2,000-yard mark in the game against the Jets at Shea Stadium. "If you don't have room for my boys," he heard Simpson say, "I can't do the interview because you don't have room for me." The Electric Company was part of the news conference.

By 1977, Montler was 33 years old. He decided he wanted a contract extension to give him some security after Ringo was named head coach. He had one year left on his deal; he wanted at least a one-year extension. "I was always in shape, I was never hurt, I always made practice, and I never threw Suzy off the balcony or had syringes in my locker," he says. "I figured Ringo, being an old center, would understand how I feel about this."

At a minicamp, he told Ringo—whom he liked—that he wouldn't play unless he got the extension. "When I said I'd go home, he said, 'You're done playing football,' and I said, 'I don't care.'"

He went back to Boulder, and he swears he considered himself retired. Yet given his Patriots experience, teams were assuming he might agree to play if he were traded.

On Monday, July 18, a lean and tan former Marine rode his bike to the Broncos camp at Fort Collins. He rode from Boulder. "That wasn't a very smart thing to do," he says, laughing. "I thought I was going to get killed before I got up there."

He watched practice and, as he must have known would happen, drew a lot of attention—including from reporters. Broncos general manager Fred Gehrke admitted he had been talking with the Bills about a possible deal for Montler for about three weeks, but he assumed the Bills were waiting to see if Montler might report to Buffalo before deciding whether to trade him. The coaches saw Montler, too, and knew he was in good enough condition to hit the ground running. Three days later, the announcement came: Apparently concluding that Montler wasn't going to back down, the Bills traded his rights to the Broncos. Denver had a new center. Or possibly a guard or a tackle.

When he returned to Fort Collins, this time as a Bronco, he drove. He wasn't going to be completely among strangers: He knew some of the Broncos, including the veteran safety who had been a Montler teammate on the College All-Star team that barely lost to Broadway Joe Namath and the Super Bowl champion Jets in the summer of 1969.

"Bronco Billy": Billy Thompson

Number 36, Strong Safety, 6-1, 201, 9th Season, Maryland State

In Greenville, South Carolina, he wasn't just "Billy." To many, including his brother and sister, and to his mother, Emma Lou, he was "June." His father, the local watch repairman, was William Thompson Senior, and young Billy was a Junior. Ergo . . . *June, where have you been?*

All the kids in his neighborhood went to the same area school. Well, except for Billy. "I went to Catholic grade school," Billy says in the Broncos' marketing offices in Invesco Stadium. "So through the seventh grade, I wore a uniform, so I had to come home to change clothes to go with my friends."

He would yank off his tie, get rid of the uniform, switch shoes, and run out and play.

"My mom wanted to know where I was and where I was going," Thompson says. "Besides, in my whole community, we didn't need the Internet back in those days. If you did something there, it beat you home. Everybody looked out for everybody. My mom took care of everybody, too, especially the older people. She always had me delivering Easter baskets, Christmas dinners, to the elderly who couldn't get out. I asked my mom, 'Why do you always want me to do it?' I never realized how good that was until years after, and I could see that those people in the community watched us, and if anything happened, they were there. Everybody knew me. I couldn't do anything. If I got in trouble, it would have to be outside my community."

By the time he reached Sterling High School—Emma Lou was OK with a public high school—he was looking up to the star athlete three years ahead of him. Everybody would say: That Jesse Jackson, what a player! "He was a great quarterback and a pretty decent basketball player," Thompson says. "He was a tall guy and he could *throw* the football. That was a huge high school and if you were the quarterback, you were known."

Thompson followed Jackson as the Sterling Tigers' multiple-sport star, even playing quarterback his senior year, in part because he was the best athlete and there was nobody else to do it. He was the captain of all three teams that year—football, basketball, and baseball—and also the student body president. He knew if he had a future in football, it wasn't as a quarterback. He was hearing from colleges, he recalls, "but I didn't have them knocking down my door, either."

He was leaning toward going to South Carolina State when he was selected to play in a high school all-star game in Columbia. He and a Sterling teammate rode the Greyhound bus down to Columbia and went through the practices, but Billy was distraught to find out that he wouldn't start. He got in the game late at quarterback—and soon was thrown out when he tossed the ball at an opponent who jumped offside and took a cheap shot at him.

"So I was sitting down on the bench and these guys came down to the front of the stands," he recalls.

Billy! Billy!

He had no idea who they were, but he knew they looked older and big. They said they wanted to talk to him after the game. Okay, said Billy.

After the game, they came in the locker room and introduced themselves. Two of them were Art Shell and Emerson Boozer. They explained that they played for Maryland State College[9]—in Princess Anne, Maryland—and wanted to take him to dinner with their coach, Roosevelt Gilliam.

That sounded good to Billy.

At dinner, Gilliam offered him a scholarship. Thompson accepted on the spot.

"I got home Sunday and I came in and told my mom, 'Mom, I committed, I'm going to Maryland State," Thompson says. "She said, 'What, are you crazy? Do you even know who these people are? Do you know anything about them?'"

Billy talked her into accepting his plan. Not long after that, the same four guys—including Shell and Boozer—stopped by the Thompson house in a beat-up station wagon to pick up Billy and head back to Princess Anne. "The baggage was on top," Billy says, laughing. "I said, 'Mama, I'll see you at Christmas.'"

At one of the first practices, Thompson was playing linebacker. "Boozer came through a hole and I hit him and lit him up!" Thompson says. "They said, 'Don't you understand? You can't hit this guy!' But that's when I made the team."

He starred for Maryland State, both as a two-time NAIA All-American in football and as a baseball outfielder and catcher who eventually turned down an offer from the Baltimore Orioles, realizing he probably would be minor-league fodder. During an injury crisis, he even had played running back in one game for Maryland State, gaining 106 yards and scoring a touchdown, but he knew that if he had a pro football future, it would be on the defensive side of the ball.

The Broncos claimed him in the third round of the 1969 draft, after taking defensive back Grady Cavness in the second round. (Denver had given up its first-rounder for quarterback Steve Tensi.) In their introductory phone call, Denver coach Lou Saban asked him if the Broncos were his favorite team. Well, no, he said truthfully, because he always had liked the Colts and the Redskins. "Lou said, 'Well, what about now?'" Thompson recalls, "and I said, 'Now you're going to go to the Super Bowl, now that you've got me.' I was just teasing."

Initially fearful about going to Denver because he thought "it was the coldest place on earth," he was impressed when defensive lineman Dave Costa picked him up and drove him around as if he were making a recruiting visit. "I met everybody and I was telling myself this was great," he recalls. "It was the cleanest place I'd been. I was used to the East Coast—Philadelphia, Baltimore, New York, with trash and clutter."

After playing against the world champion Jets for the College All-Stars, as a Mike Montler teammate and with James Marsalis at the other corner, Thompson reported to the Broncos. Joe Collier, in fact, came to the game in Chicago—a 26-24 Jets victory—and took the flight back with Thompson, who had been assured by Saban that he was locked in as the starter at corner.

"I get back and when I start to practice—and those were the days when you had so many guys in camp—I'm on the fifth team," Thompson recalls, laughing.

Eventually, he did climb up the depth chart and started as a rookie. After the 12th game, a loss at Kansas City on Thanksgiving, Saban was so mad he called a practice the next day. "Somehow I didn't set the clock or my alarm didn't go off and when I woke up, it was too late," Thompson says. "The first thing I could think of was to call Joe. I said, 'Coach, I'm not gonna lie to you, I overslept,' and he said not to worry about it."

The next day, Collier told Thompson he had talked with Saban and everything was fine. "I loved him ever since," Thompson says. "I wanted to play hard for him."

As a rookie, he became the first player in NFL history to lead the league in both kickoff and punt returns.

Thompson was entrenched at cornerback and playing well after five seasons when Collier, who had stayed on the staff after Saban's firing and John Ralston's hiring, told him he was being moved to strong safety for the 1974 season. Thompson recoiled, not liking the idea, but Collier told him it was because he would be the prime "force" man in run support and had the savvy, speed, and strength to do it. Eventually after the two of them watched hours of film, going over how to read the guard, how to read the tight end, and even pick out which one to read, the light bulb went on: Thompson got this "recognition" thing.

"After my second year at safety, I thought I was one of the top ones, and every year I was getting better," he says. "The only thing that bothered me was that we weren't scoring and a lot of times the defense was on the field a lot and was getting tired and you were giving the other teams an opportunity."

Early during Ralston's tenure, Thompson seemed to be buying into the program, even quoting some of the coach's favorite sayings—including "Whatever the mind can conceive, it can achieve"—to reporters. But he lost faith in Ralston, and he is unapologetic about his participation in the Ralston Revolt.

"I wanted to win," he says. "I hadn't been on a losing team. I'm coming from high school where we won. I'm coming from college where we won, and I'm coming to the Broncos and I'm going up against Art Shell and he's like, 'Don't worry, you guys'll have your chance.' I just wanted to beat the Raiders bad. It wasn't like I hated them, but they were too cocky and too arrogant."

He says a 17-3 '76 loss at Houston, when offensive coordinator Max Coley—who by then wasn't getting along with Ralston, anyway—was ill and Ralston couldn't step in to supervise the offense, convinced him. "We were in the game and we were dominating the game and nobody could run the offense," he says. "They were trying to get Charley Johnson[10] out of the stands to come down and help them run the offense. After that, it was embarrassing."

Thompson says Lyle Alzado had approached him as far back as the '76 training camp. "He woke me up and said, 'Ralston's gotta go.' I said, 'Why?' He said, 'Well, he was supposed to get some guy out of jail for me, and he didn't, so he's gotta go.' I said, 'Man, that's not a reason, get out of here.' "

But Thompson said other players came to him with more legitimate gripes about Ralston, and then there was the feeling that they had under-achieved in '76—and would continue to do so if Ralston stayed. He says he stuck to his end of the bargain with Gerald Phipps and Fred Gehrke after reading the toned-down statement at the news conference and say-ing he would have no further comment, and was shocked when the origi-nal no-faith manifesto hit the papers.

"Tommy [Jackson] and I go to the basketball game that night, and we're watching David Thompson. And a guy came up and said, 'Hey, guys, have you seen the early edition of the *Rocky Mountain News*?' I said no. He said, 'You guys ought to get it.' "

They left and looked at the paper. Thompson says they assured each other that they hadn't leaked the original statement, and that when Jack-son mused that they might be "shipped out," Thompson said he would be at peace if that happened. "I told Tommy that if that's what it is, I'm fine with that because I did it because I want to win," Thompson says. "That's all. I did it because I want to win and if I have to leave Colorado to do that, so be it."

He stayed. Ralston didn't.

Ironically, Thompson was playing in a secondary with a pair of cor-nerbacks who both were in Denver because of Ralston's uncanny talent-evaluating skills.

At the Corners: Louis Wright and Steve Foley

Wright: Number 20, Cornerback, 6-2, 195, 3rd Season,
     San Jose State
Foley: Number 43, Cornerback, 5-11, 189, 2nd Season,
     Tulane

In early 1975, the Broncos brought in all their choices in the recent draft for indoctrination and a minicamp. As they gathered in a meeting room, some were nervous, some self-assured.

Steve Foley, the eighth-round choice from Tulane University, hadn't planned to get a chance to play pro football, hadn't followed the draft, and was shocked to have been taken. So he had paid minimal attention, and even now he wasn't sure who the guys were around him, or who was highly touted. One thing he assumed, though, was the big guy in the fur coat who looked as if he were from quarterback central casting—or doing an imitation of Broadway Joe Namath in his prime—probably was the top pick.

Wearing jeans because he had assumed this wasn't a formal occasion, Foley was standing next to a fellow wearing a green leisure suit and tennis shoes. This fellow, quiet and seemingly nervous, had a bushy Afro hairdo and a low-key demeanor. Foley turned to him and, feeling comfortable, asked, in a thick Cajun accent, "Who's the number-one draft choice?"

The question came with the assumption that the "number-one" was the big guy in the fur coat, who—as it turned out—was Central Michigan quarterback Mike Franckowiak, a third-round pick.

Years later in his Greenwood Village office, Foley relishes recounting how self-conscious the question made the fellow next to him.

"Uh . . . uh . . . uh, I am," the young man said.

"*You* are?" responded Foley. He reached out his right hand. "I'm Steve Foley. What's your name?"

As they shook hands, the other fellow said, "I'm Louis. Louis Wright."

It was the beginning of a beautiful friendship and parallel careers for the two men.

Beep, beep!

Glover Wright was impatient, and by honking the horn in his little truck outside the house in Bakersfield, California, he let his family know it. Here he was, already having put in a full day working at the post office as a letter carrier, and he had been home, changed clothes, stepped out to the family truck, and was ready to roll.

Beep, beep!

The Wrights weren't going out to dinner.

They weren't going to a movie.

Glover and his sons—Louis, the youngest by three years, and Fred—were going to work, cutting lawns and working in yards around town. Depending on the time of year or the day of the week, that might not even be the end of it, because on many of these days, they would do the outdoor labor until the sun went down and then head to the Masonic

Temple. There, Glover's wife, Verbena, and their daughter, Patsy, would join them and they would wash dishes and clean up after functions until at least 10, maybe 11 o'clock.

One time, emboldened by something that had come up at school—and Louis figures this would have been about when he was in junior high—Louis had the temerity to mention this concept called "child labor laws."

"You gotta shut your mouth and get to work!" Glover snapped, shaking his head.

Glover and Verbena both were from the East Texas town of Gilmer, so small that often if you needed to find it on a map, you were told to look for the bigger Longview and know that if there wasn't a dot for Gilmer, it at least was nearby. Although his parents had moved to Bakersfield in 1952, Louis was born in Gilmer on January 31, 1953, because Verbena went back to Texas to be among her family when it was time to give birth.

Not only was Glover determined to make the best of being one of the first black mailmen in Bakersfield, he wasn't going to come home and rest after work, and he was going to include the rest of his family in his "other" jobs. The money was nice, but it also was to make a point. "Looking back," Louis recalls as we talk in a gym at Aurora's Mrachek Junior High, "it was a good thing because he taught us a good day's work and that a job needed to be done right and no excuses accepted. It made yourself accountable, plus you were out and being active."

But there was an out.

"He would say if you were doing sports or were doing a school activity, you were relieved of duties," Louis says, then laughs. "I did everything I could! I signed up for everything. I was constantly out for a sport. Football, basketball, track. I was in student government and anything else I could think of."

Later, when attending the huge Bakersfield High, which had nearly 4,000 students, Louis landed jobs he could do around his sports schedule through the Youth Corps—custodian work at the school or in restaurants—and his father was impressed. Louis gave up basketball after his sophomore year, concentrating on football and track, while carrying about a B average in school, often taking upper-level courses, and immersing himself in math classes. He had it all plotted out: He hoped to go to the prestigious University of Southern California, play football for the Trojans, and then become an accountant or otherwise enter the business world. He would follow Mike Garrett and O.J. Simpson and have a glorious career and go from there. There was one problem. "They didn't recruit me," Wright says. "They didn't even call me or send me a letter, so I was a little hurt."

An Arizona State University assistant coach, Joe McDonald, came from the Bakersfield neighborhood and his family still lived there. McDonald's parents knew Wright's parents and once Joe said he hoped Louis would go to ASU, it was as if it were a brokered deal among the parents. "His family, my family, everybody was saying, 'You're going to Arizona State,'" Louis recalls. "I was, 'Well, sounds good to me.'"

Frank Kush, blunt, closed-minded, acerbic, and often mean-spirited, was the head coach.[11] He had a standout freshman team that year, including running back Woody Green and quarterback Danny White. Louis Wright was a lower-profile member of that team, but he seemed to have a decent future with the Sun Devils.

Late in his freshman year, the staff told Louis he would need to stick around Tempe for the summer and attend classes. That didn't bother Wright, or at least not after he heard Woody Green and others say they were told the same thing, but had been lined up with places to live and summer jobs. So when Kush called him in for one of the individual chats he was conducting with all the scholarship players, Wright expected to hear the same things. Instead, Wright heard Kush say he needed to get his summer-school work "taken care of." Uh, Coach, what about a place to live and a job? Kush ignored that and said, "We'll see you in August."

Wright says he walked out the door thinking, *I ain't coming back here, that's for sure.* He stuck to that, going home for the summer and then enrolling at Bakersfield Junior College. "I played football," Wright says, and then catches himself. "No, I went out for football. I think they were mad at me because I didn't go up there coming out of high school and it was a tradition that everybody goes there coming out of high school. The whole season, the total number of plays I was on the field, I think, was six. Six plays! I could not believe it. I was going to quit, but I decided, Naw, I couldn't do that."

Wright, who ran the 100-, 220- and 440-yard dashes, jumped at an offer to attend San Jose State. "I figured my football days were over," he says. In the spring, after spring football practice ended, he was going through track practice when Jim Colbert, the defensive backs coach under new Spartans football coach Darryl Rogers, showed up and told Wright he was "looking for speed" and had been told Wright had played some football.

"I've been down that road," he told Colbert.

"Look," said Colbert, "come out in August for a few days. If you absolutely hate it, you'll be free to pack it in, no grudges held."

Wright gave in and went out for the football team in the fall. He didn't hate it, but he didn't take the sport by storm, either. As a football junior, he settled in as a seldom-used backup cornerback. "I thought I could have been a starter, but there was a guy who had been there the year before and that was his spot, and I was playing right corner behind him," Wright recalls.

On October 13, 1973, the Spartans traveled to Tempe to face Arizona State, and Wright spent part of the pregame warm-up period saying hello to his former freshman football teammates. "About midway through the second quarter, I'm just standing there and a coach goes, 'Wright, get in there at corner,'" he recalls. "I get in there and the very first play they throw a quick screen to the receiver and I just remember these two linemen coming at me like they were going to destroy me. Somehow I went under them and dived and made the tackle for a 4- or 5-yard loss, something like that. And I'm asking myself, *How did I do that?*"

San Jose State lost 28-3 that day, but they had a 5-4-2 season, the Spartans' best record in ages. After cracking the starting lineup, Wright missed several games with a separated shoulder—a shoulder that would trouble him for the rest of his football career. "Our last game of the season was Hawaii in Hawaii, so I determined that I *had* to make it back," he says with a laugh. "I wasn't quite 100 percent but I was close enough and made the trip to Hawaii. At that point, I really didn't have that much experience and I didn't think much about football. I had one more year of track so I didn't have to go out for spring ball that year, either."

In his senior year, with the Spartans on their way to an 8-3-1 record, Wright heard that scouts were showing up to watch him and a handful of San Jose State pro prospects, but he didn't take it all that seriously. The fashionable "cool" practice of the time was to use adhesive tape to wrap your football shoes on your feet, producing a "spat" effect. Some thought it went too far as a statement of individualism, and while Rogers didn't ban it, he didn't particularly like it. One day at practice, Wright finally gave in to the campaign of a teammate and allowed his buddy to tape Wright's shoes, and he went out on the practice field with "spats."

Several scouts were at the practice, and Rogers was fuming. He called Wright into his office after the workout.

"He said, 'I've been telling all these guys you're not into that, and you come out like that!'" Wright recalls. "That's when I first thought, *Yeah, maybe they* are *interested in me.*"

He played in several all-star games, including the Senior Bowl in Mobile, Alabama. He was on the North squad, and in the game's usual fashion, the NFL supplied the coaching staffs. John Ralston and the Broncos' staff coached the North, and Wright and his teammates—not so much looking at the game as a pro tryout camp as a reward—weren't thrilled that the coaches seemed to be taking the game and the practices seriously. "We were all ragging on the Denver Broncos' coaching staff," Wright says, laughing, and adds that he didn't get the impression that any of the Denver coaches were enamored of him as a prospect.

On January 28, 1975, Wright was shocked to hear that the Broncos had claimed him in the first round. He went 17th overall. Four other defensive backs went after him in the first round—Texas A&M's Tim Gray to St. Louis, Louisiana State's Mike Williams to San Diego, Ohio State's Neil Colzie to Oakland, and Michigan's Dave Brown to Pittsburgh. Amateur draft nuts, armed with their clippings and data, especially were outraged that the Broncos hadn't taken the far-more-heralded Colzie.

Wright took the congratulatory call from Ralston at his aunt's home in Palo Alto, but he wasn't in the mood to gush his thanks. "I might as well be going to Siberia as far as I knew," he says, laughing. "I felt like I was going to be isolated, in a faraway, inaccessible city that nobody cared about. Instead of going to L.A. or Dallas, San Diego, New York, I was going to Denver. I wasn't very happy about it, to be honest with you."

On his first trip to Denver the next week, he didn't get red-carpet treatment at the airport. "It was snowing," he says. (And, again, this story has Wright laughing at himself all the way through, given the way things turned out, both during and after his career.) "I thought, *This is torture, not only am I going to a place I don't know about, but it's cold as hell here!*

I'd never been around snow. This guy named Tiny—and he wasn't Tiny at all, he was about 500 pounds—picked me up at the airport and I remember coming through downtown to the hotel, the Continental there at Speer Boulevard. I was thinking, *We better get there because you can't be driving around in the snow!* Little did I know that you could drive in snow. All this was new to me and I'm in Denver and not liking it very much."

The next morning, he met Steve Foley.

In later years, Wright's favorite Steve Foley story was about when nearly 20 Broncos went to the New Orleans home of Foley's parents during the weeklong buildup to a certain big Bronco game in the Superdome. As they headed to the Foley home in several cabs, Wright and some others wondered how their teammate's parents—Ivan McIvor Foley and Jane Olivier Mestayer Foley—were going to handle such a mass gathering for dinner. When they got in the Foley home, they were amused to notice the dining-room table was big enough for them all. They also got a kick out of the fact that there were locks—*locks!*—on the doors of the refrigerator and freezer.

"Steve had twenty brothers and sisters," Wright says, "so this was like a *normal* dinner for his family."

That was an exaggeration. A slight one. Steve was the middle of thirteen children, part of a pack of eight Foley sons. He heard his grandparents on his mother's side speak French, and his own thick Cajun accent was—he assumed—an all-American phenomenon. His father was an accountant by training, who turned to sales, primarily as a lumber trader, to support the family. When Steve was about nine, the family moved from a rough neighborhood of New Orleans to a home Ivan had been thrilled to find.

The house was the former convent adjacent to Saint Rita of Cascia Catholic Church. The church's school, a wooden building, had burned down, and when it was rebuilt, church authorities added floors above the classrooms to house the nuns. In the early 1960s, the Foleys paid $25,000 for the former convent. Before the family moved in, Ivan—"We called him 'Ivan The Terrible,'" Steve recalls with a smile—dropped his sons off at the house one day when he went to work and told them to do what they could to clean up the convent and otherwise get it ready for the family.

The oldest son, a mischievous sort who also was by far the brightest academically of all the brothers, came up with the plan to take down the cross on the roof of the convent, not out of sacrilegious disrespect, but because it just seemed the right thing to do to end the association with the nuns.

"He decides we're going to pull this down without asking my father," Steve recalls. Like a cowboy, he lassoed the cross with a rope, pulled it tight and tied it to a car.

When the car pulled away, the cross came down—but so did part of the roof, because the base of the cross went down into the rafters.

Uh-oh, the brothers thought. *Wait'll Dad sees this.*

"That was my mom's big stick over everybody," Steve says. "'Wait until your father gets home!' We'd be, 'No, please,' and then you started to bargain. 'I'll do this, I'll do that.' But how do you keep thirteen kids in line?"

Well, sometimes you don't. Ivan got over having to make roof repairs, and the family moved into the home that came with a grotto and a little shrine the brothers decided they'd better leave alone.

Steve and some of his brothers still were young enough to attend the St. Rita School across the street. "We could hear the bell ring at school and we knew we had 30 seconds to get there," he says. "We could run out, buttoning our shirts, running, jumping inside the schoolyard, and then we just had to freeze [for roll-call]."

But that also meant they were growing up across the street from nuns whose influence still was felt—sometimes quite literally. "They'd grab you by the hair and slap you in the face, but you deserved it!" Steve says. "It never was something you didn't deserve. You never felt abused or anything because you were saying, *How stupid was I for doing something like that?*"

Steve was small for his age, but he played on the St. Rita teams and soaked up the neighborhood atmosphere. "They call it 'The Big Easy' for a reason," he says. "Everybody's pretty mellow. It was a great experience."

At Jesuit High School, he was only 5-foot-3 and 105 pounds in the ninth grade, and his brothers talked him into going out for freshman football. Or, more accurately, they ordered him to do it. Rob was three years older, about to be an All-State linebacker, and Mike, already a star, was one year ahead of Steve. Steve was the runt, and he worked in the Jesuit cafeteria to help pay his way and get extra food.

"I said, 'I'm playin' golf and I'm fishin,'" Steve recalls. "That's what I wanted to do, that was my temperament. But Robbie said, 'You're going out for football.' It was either that or take the verbal and physical abuse coming home every day. So he talked to the freshman coach [Mike Crow], who was a good friend of his, and said, 'Give him a chance.' The freshman coach said, 'Rob, I can't let Steve play, he's going to get killed!' I did get killed. But I would stick my head in there and I would tackle. I remember Mike Crow saying, 'That little bastard'll stick his head in there.'"

By the time he was a 16-year-old senior, he was a star himself, but still only 5-11 and 165 pounds. His only football scholarship offer came from Nicholls State in Thibodaux, Louisiana, and he decided to stay in New Orleans and walk on at Tulane, which was 10 blocks from the Foley home. Rob was the Green Wave's starting center and Mike was a wide receiver, and they again lobbied for coaches to give their little brother a chance. He also had the team doctor in his corner. Steve's best friend at Jesuit, Mark Olivari, was a much-recruited nose guard who had turned his back on Penn State's Joe Paterno and Oklahoma assistant Barry Switzer, among others, to stay home and attend Tulane. Olivari's girlfriend was the daughter of Dr. Ken Sayer, the Saints' and Tulane's team orthopedist, so Sayer had come to some Jesuit games. When he heard that the little quarterback wasn't offered a scholarship, the doctor and some friends told the Foleys that they were providing Steve with a private scholarship, paying his way for at least his freshman year.

Steve started for the freshman team, but still was far down the varsity depth chart in the subsequent spring practices. The coaches were exasperated because he kept scrambling—what else would he do, playing with the fifth-string line?—and not staying in the pocket, but he was catching a lot of attention, in part because of his resilience and bravery. "Guys would grab my helmet, shake my helmet, and they used to call them 'face-changers,'" Foley says. "Coaches would be screaming, 'You stay in that pocket! You *will* this and this and this!' And I would go, 'Yes, suh, I will,' but when you get back there your instincts take over. I started to just run around these guys and maybe make a first down. Pretty soon the coaches started to say, 'Well, maybe . . .' "

He had moved up a bit, but wasn't running with the first team, when an NFL head coach watched practice and was quoted in the New Orleans paper predicting: "That little number 10 is going to be your starting quarterback." The Green Wave coaches considered that an affront and unprofessional, but Foley was complimented and grateful.

The NFL coach was John Ralston of the Denver Broncos.

Steve kept growing and, at least according to the official Tulane roster, was 6-2 and 185 by his sophomore season. He was a part-time starter that year, then led the Green Wave to a 9-3 record as a junior—the Wave lost to Houston in the Bluebonnet Bowl—and a 5-0 start as a senior before he suffered a fractured ankle, ending his college career. Tulane lost all of its remaining six games. All along, he had been assuming he wasn't a pro prospect and hadn't even bothered to take part in the weighing, measuring, and running when pro scouts came through the Tulane football offices. His ankle was healed in January when he was working out and the stunning news came over a radio in the weight room: *Also, Tulane quarterback Steve Foley went in the eighth round, to the Denver Broncos.*

Ralston had remembered number 10. He had drafted Foley as a safety, although Foley hadn't played the position in college.

After Foley visited Denver and introduced himself to Louis Wright, among others, he went through the rookie workouts with the Broncos— and immediately felt overwhelmed when the coaches ran all the defensive backs, safeties included, in one-on-one drills against the wide receivers.

"They told me to get 6 yards off the ball, and I'm up against this slow guy named Rick Upchurch," Foley recalls dryly. "I'm backpedaling on my heels and your heels aren't even supposed to touch the ground. Rick was by me so fast, before I even turned, and I'm thinking, *I don't think this is going to work out well.* I could run but I had no idea of keeping a cushion or anything like that."

The Broncos knew he was a project, and probably as a safety. But the Jacksonville Express of the World Football League jumped in with a bonus offer that dwarfed the Broncos' figure—$17,000 to Denver's $7,000—plus a no-cut contract and the promise to at least *look* at him at quarterback. He signed with the Express, who looked at him at quarterback for about eighteen seconds and switched him to safety, where he was grateful to have former Kansas City Chiefs star Johnny Robinson as his position coach. Robinson was patient and taught him a lot about the mental and physical challenges of playing defensive back, and Foley to this day views his WFL stay as an invaluable transitional step. The problem was that the WFL folded 11 games into the 1975 season.

Meanwhile, Louis Wright's rookie 1975 season with the Broncos was a mixed bag. In the next-to-last exhibition game at San Francisco, he recalls, "I was making this tackle and the guy was down and all of a sudden Joe Rizzo comes flying in and whacks me on the leg and tears some ligaments and some stuff in my ankle and I don't play for over a month."

He recovered gradually, and Joe Collier gently broke the news to him before the fourth game of the regular season. He was starting at Pittsburgh in what turned out to be a 20-9 loss to the defending world champions. Lynn Swann. Jon Stallworth. Terry Bradshaw. And how did he do? "I got annihilated," Wright says. "Swann caught two touchdown passes on me in what seemed like a matter of seconds. One was cover-two [zone] with me and B.T. [Billy Thompson], but it was me because I lost the ball and didn't turn fast enough. The other one was straight man-to-man and he went by me. I was thinking, *Whoa, these guys are serious.* I remember B.T. telling me, 'You're OK, you're OK.' I was thinking, *Why are you lying to me like that? I am not OK! I'm killing the team!*"

Wright settled down, started the rest of his rookie season, and proved the Ralston staff's faith in him wasn't folly.

Foley signed with the Broncos for the 1976 season and showed in workouts that he now knew what he was doing as a defensive back. He practiced at both free safety, where he was listed behind John Rowser, and at corner, where he was behind veteran Calvin Jones, and he was frustrated because he wasn't playing early in the season. The consensus view was that he was the Broncos' free safety of the future.

Jones, though, suffered a knee injury halfway through the season, and Foley was pressed into the starting lineup at the corner for the final six games, opposite Wright. He had two interceptions against San Diego,

and he had faced up to the challenge of knowing—and this would be a pattern—that teams would go after him instead of Wright. Foley understood why. "He'd probably be embarrassed, but I learned most of my technique from studying Louis Wright," Foley says. "I'd study how he shifted his weight. He was so quick and agile for a guy 6-3, 200 pounds. His straight-out speed and his acceleration both were phenomenal. His quickness and agility and drive were just incredible. I could mimic his movements. I'd just watch him and in my mind I'd have it etched and I could see myself in his body doing the same things."

For his part, Wright says he "felt good" about his play in his second pro season and was more comfortable, but also shared the view of many teammates that their 9-5 record was underachievement. However, he didn't go along with the view that it was Ralston's fault. He was marrying his longtime girlfriend, Vicki, in California the next month, and he and roommate Rubin Carter—they were living in an apartment in southeast Denver—left town the morning after the season-closing victory at Chicago.

In January, Wright was in San Jose when his mother called him from Bakersfield, telling him a teammate—and Wright isn't 100 percent sure whether his mom said it was Lyle Alzado or Billy Thompson—was looking for him. He remembers a buddy hearing about something going on in Denver and asking him about it, and he figured the phone call had something to do with it. But he says he never talked with his teammates before the word broke weeks later that Ralston was out.

"I didn't even know why they were firing him," Wright says. "Nobody mentioned anything during the season. That happened after the season was over. I had no clue. I kind of liked Ralston. Some of his staff I didn't think were working totally in his best interest, but he was a nice guy, always positive, always kind of pushed you to another level, never degrading. I liked Ralston and if I had been there and if it had come up I think I would have said, 'I don't think that's the right thing to do.' But the biggest thing was I was too young. I was here to play football."

The rebels did find Steve Foley, who told the player who called him—Foley won't disclose which one of the anti-Ralston militants it was—that he wouldn't go along.

"He said, 'We want you to sign a petition to have the coach fired,' and I went, 'You're out of your mind,'" Foley says. "This guy [Ralston] gave me my shot to play pro football, drafted me personally, and I liked him. I said, 'There's no way.' I didn't sign anything. When Red came in, I'm sure he asked, 'Who the heck signed this, what guys are these?'[12] I thought John Ralston was an incredible assessor of talent. He assembled that whole team. Red was the motivator, the guy who gave us the confidence that we could beat the Oakland Raiders."

As the '77 season and more meetings with the Raiders approached, Louis and Vicki Wright settled into an apartment. Wright was the unquestioned starter, increasingly comfortable in Denver. He even had figured out it was possible to drive in the snow.

Using $12,000 of the $13,000 he had left from his Jacksonville signing bonus, Foley had made a down payment on a triplex. He also seemed to have secured a long-term spot on the roster, and the only question was whether he would play cornerback or safety.

Notes

1. In 2007, "Joey" Collier goes by Joel and is the New England Patriots' secondary coach.

2. And Maples stayed that way. When Jerry Frei died in 2001, one of the pictures on his den wall was of him with Maples during a Denver game.

3. In 2007, the former Fairmont is the Grand Hyatt.

4. A different entity than the modern-era Frontier Airlines.

5. Steve Jones won the U.S. Open in 1996, at age 37.

6. In 1967, General Hochmuth was the commander of the 3rd Marine Division when a helicopter transporting him burst into flames and went down in Vietnam. He and four others were killed.

7. Essentially, not being allowed to leave the Marines in times of crisis.

8. Joining Reggie McKenzie, Joe DeLamielleure, Dave Foley, and Donnie Green.

9. Maryland State became Maryland-Eastern Shore.

10. Charley Johnson was the Broncos' former quarterback, who was retired and living in Houston.

11. More than any person, Frank Kush was responsible for John Elway ending up with the Broncos. Elway's father, Jack, so despised Kush and his methods that the Elways were adamant that John didn't want to play for Kush, then the coach of the Baltimore Colts, who drafted the phenom quarterback out of Stanford. It was the family's disdain for Kush, and not any lack of regard for the city of

Baltimore, that caused the Elways to use John's baseball alternative as leverage to force a trade.

12. Most came to believe that Billy Van Heusen, as a punter, was made the scapegoat for the rebellion and his ouster was a reminder to the players that while the more talented ones were allowed to stick around, they were not going to be running the asylum.

CHAPTER 5

Runners

I'm going to get you a car like mine! I'm going to get you a Lincoln.

—ELVIS PRESLEY

Exhibitions: August 5–20

Friday, August 5 vs. Baltimore Colts, Mile High Stadium
Saturday, August 13 vs. St. Louis Cardinals, Mile High Stadium
Saturday, August 20 at Atlanta Falcons

In the exhibition opener, the Broncos beat the Colts 14-8 before only 40,059 at Mile High Stadium. Because the two home exhibitions weren't tied to the season ticket package, fans could wait to the last minute to decide whether to go—and many did. However, the ticket windows had such long lines, many gave up and went home rather than wait.

They didn't miss much of a game.

Craig Morton and the first-team offense initially were ineffective before coming out of the game in the second quarter and seemed done for the night when the Colts led 6-0 at the half. But Red Miller surprised many by putting Morton back in at the start of the third quarter, and he threw a 51-yard touchdown pass to fullback Lonnie Perrin before retiring for the night. Craig Penrose's 14-yard TD pass to Rick Upchurch ended up the game-winner.

The game also was the debut of the Pony Express, the new cheerleading dance team that replaced the more sedate and traditionally dressed—traditionally dressed, as in costumes that would have passed muster with vice principals and nuns—Bronco Belles. On the morning of the game, the *Rocky Mountain News* ran a picture of Pony Express members Linda Ebert of Broomfield and Diahann Miller of Denver modeling the new uniforms, and they caused quite a stir.

My brother, Dave, the second-year assistant public relations director under the terrific Bob Peck, had pushed for the concept. He recalls that one of his first assignments when joining the Broncos staff in 1976 was to judge the Bronco Belles tryouts. "For the 16 positions that year, I think we had 24 girls try out," he says from his office at the Westminster Kennel Club in New York, where he is the longtime analyst on the WKC Dog Show telecast and also serves as the organization's director of communications. "Overall, it was a nice group. At the end of '76, we were talking with the Channel 9 people and got talking with a woman who was their promotions person. I said, 'You know, we'd like to do a little more with our cheerleaders.' It was happening other places around the league, so it wasn't an original idea, but I said we'd like to—well, I'd hate to use the word 'upgrade,' but that's probably what it was—do a little something with it." Dave asked if Channel 9 might sponsor and promote the new group, and the television station jumped on it. "They got Bob Mackie to design the costumes. They also advertised the tryouts on TV, and we had 200 girls try out."

So when the Broncos played their first home game, albeit a noncounting one, the fans who showed up saw a much bigger group of women, all dressed in cowgirl outfits featuring fringes, tassels, and boots that would have passed muster with Cher, one of Mackie's other clients.

Some traditionalists among the longtime fan base argued that there was no need to add a sideshow. But most didn't seem to mind, including the infamous regulars in the South Stands, the freestanding structure behind one end zone that housed the Broncos game-day locker room. The South Stands traditionally were the home of the most rowdy fans in the stadium, and their most famous stunt was enthusiastically throwing snowballs at the Kansas City Chiefs, causing coach Hank Stram to order onside kicks with the Chiefs far ahead to keep his team away from the fans at that end. But in 1977, there was some concern that the stadium expansion meant many of the South Stand regulars had "upgraded" their seats to other parts of the stadium, possibly leading to a new and more gentrified crowd in the end zone.

They needn't have worried.

Going after the upstart Budget Records, the heavyweight Target was running a big record sale. It was open to debate about whether the acts would turn out to be short-lived on the music scene, but for $4.99 or less, we could stock up on the new releases from Crosby, Stills and Nash (minus Young again); the Steve Miller Band; Bob Seger; Peter Frampton; James Taylor; Ted Nugent; Barbra Streisand; Heart; KISS; Foreigner; the Bay City Rollers; Fleetwood Mac; Shaun Cassidy; and Marvin Gaye.

Jimmy Carter's Colorado campaign chairman, former three-term state representative Wellington Webb of Denver, was named the principal regional official for the Department of Health, Education and Welfare. Webb, respected for having written and sponsored the state's first bill to ban discrimination against the handicapped, also had been rumored to be in line for jobs in Washington, but he said that he and his wife, Wilma, had cooled on that possibility after their children announced they didn't want to move. He bristled at the suggestion that the appointment was a blatant political payoff from the Carter forces. "I'm the most qualified, and the major point in my getting the job wasn't my ethnicity or heading the campaign—although that didn't hurt," he said. As a state legislator, Webb had walked out of Governor Lamm's 1975 inauguration, protesting the lack of any black appointees in Lamm's cabinet.[1]

The Broncos were upset over the turf conditions at Mile High Stadium, and the problems weren't solely attributable to the Bears' baseball season. In fact, Bears GM Jim Burris was even angrier, and he and Denver head of parks and recreation Joe Ciancio publicly blasted young concert impresario Barry Fey for not taking enough care of the precious field during a June 26 stadium rock concert. The war of words escalated over the next week, with new *Post* sports columnist Steve "Candid" Cameron especially having fun going back and forth between the camps. It reached a crescendo with this salvo from Fey, who soon would become a close Cameron friend: "Ciancio has always been against us. He's just anti-youth. And Burris, I called him a blackmailer when he wanted so much money for one date last year. He's not a blackmailer. He's a bleeping extortionist." Fey said he paid for the damages to the field, but repairs weren't made. Ciancio conceded that, but said there hadn't been time to start from scratch, which is what would have been required to get the field back in top-flight condition.

Cameron, a colorful and voluble 30-something writer, had joined the *Post* as sports columnist in July. It was an obvious competitive reaction to the wild popularity of the *News*'s Woodrow Paige Jr.

Woody was both writing columns and, after moving over from the Nuggets beat, covering the Broncos. At the *Post*, we were reacting to Woody by making Dick Connor, the longtime Broncos beat writer and assistant sports editor who had been so instrumental in my hiring, a full-time columnist and part-time feature writer, and teaming him in the columnist role with the caustic Cameron, who was fresh off a magazine-writing stint in Kansas City.

Woody wore glasses, and had long hair and a beard.

Cameron wore glasses, and had long hair, in a bushy style, and a beard.

They both were cordial, funny, and more than willing to mentor younger writers. Woody had been friendly and helpful when I was at the *News*. Cameron had spent a brief time as the public relations director of the Rockies' forerunner, the Kansas City Scouts; he knew hockey and a lot of men in it, so he was a great help to me. For the next year or so, we were running mates, and I had the headaches and occasional hangovers to prove it.

One of our strengths at the *Post* was that Cameron and Connor were complementary. Connor was thoughtful, a terrific writer, and knew everyone in town. Cameron fired away, off the top of his head. He also was the fastest writer I've ever seen. He would write his column in no longer than a half hour, sliding sheets into the portable typewriter and writing completely in a flow-of-thought style that meant he never ripped a sheet out of the carriage, crumpled it up, tossed it aside, and started over. (I did that all the time.) Speed was of the essence for us only on

Saturday nights, because the *Post* at the time still was an afternoon paper on all days except Sunday, but Steve always wrote as if his deadline was imminent and he needed to beat last call somewhere.

As a columnist, Paige had the advantage—and disadvantage—of having to be with the Broncos virtually every day. Cameron spread out his subject matter more, but he was diving into the Broncos, too. Connor was brilliant and thoughtful, an essayist who gave his readers credit for intelligence.

They were finding plenty to write about.

———

A headline in the August 9 *Rocky Mountain News* was ominous: "Police Say Bomb Try Could Herald Terrorism."

An organization called the New World Liberation Front had taken credit in a call to the paper for placing a bomb at a Coors distributorship in Aurora, Timberline Distributors. The pipe bomb hadn't gone off, but that didn't quiet fears that violence might be a problem as the Coors labor strike continued. The NWLF also had claimed credit for placing similar pipe bombs at two California distributors, part of at least 44 bombings the organization had said it was responsible for. Though the brewery workers' union in subsequent days would denounce the attempted bombing, there were fears the strike was taking a violent turn.

———

I took great interest in a vote by the Wheat Ridge City Council on an Oklahoma City company's plan to put a Bavarian Village–style complex of a shopping center, offices, and townhomes on the land abutting Crown Lake across the street from my alma mater, Wheat Ridge High. For years, as development and progress encircled it, the land had remained a family farm, and the joke on the new kid in 1972 was to tell me to be careful when retrieving batting-practice foul balls from the farmland, because the owner had been known to shoot salt pellets at trespassers. Five years later, the farm was history. By a 3-3 vote, the development plan was tabled, in what would become an increasingly rare defeat for "progress." A total of 5,500 area residents—including many of my friends still living in Wheat Ridge and their families—had signed petitions against the development. The attorney for the company told Karen Newman of the *Rocky Mountain*

News that "something" would be done with the property. "We're going to use that ground. It's just a matter of time."

I applauded and wondered what would happen to the property.[2]

During film study at the Broncos' offices, Lyle Alzado took offense to a Miller comment about a play, got up, and punched a wall. Alzado meant business when he punched anything or anyone. He put a hole in the wall.

Miller didn't react, but when the film was over and the lights came on, he told Alzado that the wall from then on was going to be designated the Lyle Alzado Wall. Alzado, the coach said, could do anything to that wall he wanted. It was going to be his outlet.

It would not be the only hole he would punch in the wall that year.

The deaths of Arthur Espinoza and James Hinojos in Curtis Park the previous month still bothered Hispanic leaders, who since had led a march on police headquarters to protest and also demand more representation on the force. Frank Moya of the *News* found several people who had been at a picnic in the park that day and who questioned whether the officers needed to shoot the two men, and whether they had been warned to drop the gun. Moya wrote that autopsies showed that Hinojos was shot six times and Espinoza once, and that both men had been drunk. "They just lit 'em up," swimming-pool volunteer Dino Castro told Moya.

Crusade for Justice leader Rodolfo "Corky" Gonzales, a former top professional boxer I would encounter when covering boxing matches he promoted at the Crusade's school, Escuela Tlatelolco, was irate that the police records of the men shot by the police had been released in what seemed—at least to him—to be an attempt to justify the shootings. "The *Rocky Mountain News* editor waved a gun around the other night, but nobody shot him," he said of troubled editor Michael Balfe Howard, who—it would turn out—had a serious cocaine problem. In the previous week, Howard was arrested in the early morning hours in Denver's Trader Vic's restaurant after he and a friend got into an argument with another patron, and he was accused of showing his .44-caliber pistol and then scuffling with police officers called to the restaurant. He was charged with carrying a concealed weapon, flourishing a weapon, and interfering with police.

We still could shake our head about how much worse it was in troubled New York. It turned out that a woman knifed to death in a nationally notorious random attack in a subway station, Claudia Curfman Castellana, was a former Denver resident and George Washington High School graduate who had moved to New York to study for a master's degree and liked it so much, she stayed and became a teacher. Her father was a Denver physician, and a memorial service for her was held at Montview Presbyterian Church.

A parking ticket turned out to be the big break in the Son of Sam case. Traced because he had received a citation for parking too close to a fire hydrant near one of the murder scenes, postal worker David Berkowitz announced to a police officer who approached him and asked his identity as he got into his car outside his Yonkers apartment building: "I'm Son of Sam. Okay, you've got me." He had killed six, wounded seven, and terrorized an entire city, claiming to be ordered to kill by the voices of a 6,000-year-old man and of a neighbor named Sam.

In Denver, John Raitt was in mid-run of *I Do! I Do!* at Elitch's. In the wake of reviews that said the show, only 12 years after its Broadway run, was painfully dated, he argued that it was the sort of material audiences wanted in this age. "There are going to be a lot of people who aren't going to want to see *A Chorus Line*," he said. "They want to go down to see shows like *Shenandoah* and *I Do! I Do!* It has to do with where we're going in our national moral structure, which has changed. You can see the difference between the last two blackouts in New York. The behavior of people has changed. I think people are looking for grassroots shows; that's why Carter was elected." Reading that, I doubted if Bonnie would have completely agreed with her father. Lighthearted fare was continuing to play well at the movies, though. *Smokey and the Bandit* was getting withering reviews, but filling the theaters.

United States Supreme Court Justice Byron "Whizzer" White was a guest at a Broncos' midweek practice, and he made a point of saying hello to Lyle Alzado. At CU in the 1930s, Whizzer had been student body president, Phi Beta Kappa, and an All-American football player, and then he went on to a brilliant career with the Detroit Lions.

A month earlier, the indefatigable Alzado had been named the winner of the Whizzer White Award as the NFL's man of the year, which annually went to the NFL player judged to have done the best work in the community.

At the downtown Auditorium Arena, Nick Bockwinkel outwrestled Pedro Morales to claim—ahem—the World Heavyweight Championship. The wrestling shows were weekend staples at the little arena, usually drawing big crowds, and fans who didn't seem to care that there were about 114 World Heavyweight Champions on various circuits around the country, some of them winning matches after foiling villains who pulled dreaded foreign objects out of their boots as everyone in the building spotted them except the blind referee. The cards had wrestlers short and tall, skinny and fat, masked and should-have-been-masked. Their "supplements" were cheeseburgers and acting lessons.

Miller said Norris Weese and Steve Spurrier would split the work at quarterback against the Cardinals, and Spurrier was indignant that the reporters—and virtually everyone else—were considering him running fourth on the depth chart at that point. "Where do you guys get that stuff?" he asked. "You see me go fourth in the practice rotation, so you assume I'm last in the rankings. I go last because the other guys like to go first." He added, "I came here to make the team and that's what I intend to do. I've said all along that I'm not a practice quarterback."

On five Jim Turner field goals, the Broncos beat the Cardinals 15-7 on August 13. Weese was 3 for 7, for only 44 yards, and Spurrier didn't do much to jump up the depth chart, completing 8 of 15 for 113 yards.

With all due respect to Buddy Holly, Ritchie Valens, and the Big Bopper—and the Don McLean song that saluted them—the music died on August 16, 1977.

Elvis Presley, the inspiration for Ken Brown's rookie-show imitation, died in Memphis at age 42.

At Holy Family Catholic Church in North Denver, a saddened Father Raymond Jones[3] disclosed that the next Sunday's 9:30 a.m. mass would be said in Presley's honor. He told of Elvis attending the funeral mass for Denver police officer Eugene Kennedy at Holy Family the previous year. For nine years, Presley had been a friend of Eugene Kennedy's older brother, Denver Police Captain Jerry Kennedy, a 20-year veteran of the force who also headed both the DPD's vice squad and the security detail at Broncos games. Eventually, reporters tracked down a stunned Jerry Kennedy for his comments, and he said he had spoken with Presley on the phone about two weeks earlier.

Jerry Kennedy was a Denver native, the son of Irish immigrant parents who had moved to Denver from Philadelphia before he was born. A graduate of Holy Family High, he was Old Denver, and he and Denver Police Detective Ron Pietrafeso became honorary members of the Presley entourage.

"I met him in 1968," Kennedy recalls. "He came here for a concert at the Coliseum and took the 10th floor at the Radisson. He wanted police officers on the floor to keep the interlopers out of there, so I supplied a half-dozen officers up there, including myself. We were in his living quarters, basically, because he had the whole floor, and he came wandering out, talking, and we hit it off. Joe Esposito was his business manager and he and Pietrafeso hit it off, and I hit it off with Elvis. He liked to tell jokes and he liked to hear them. He had his Memphis Mafia with him and we got along with those guys, too. A couple of years later, we did the same thing at the Hilton downtown and cemented the friendship. He came out and rode with us."

It was a long-distance friendship, and Kennedy wasn't fooling himself about that. But he made several visits to Graceland at Presley's invitation, and also went to Nevada for some of his shows. "He'd often call me in the middle of the night, because he had his hours all messed up," Kennedy says. "The guy never really saw any normal people. He liked cops. He liked them down in Memphis and he said he had thought about becoming a policeman when he was about 19, and he'd been in the military. Basically, it was stories and good times and laughs, and the normality of new friends he could feel comfortable with was what he liked."

In January 1976, Presley came to Denver on a whim to celebrate his 41st birthday, and announced to Kennedy and Pietrafeso that they were part of a group heading to Vail on a Trailways bus. He would be staying in a house at the base of a ski run, and Kennedy and Pietrafeso took time off from work and joined the Presley group for about 10 days. "We tried to be good hosts and picked up his people as they came into Stapleton and brought them back up and got them ski outfits and this and that," Kennedy recalls.

It was during that visit that Kennedy's brother passed away, and Presley went and visited his family and attended the funeral, wearing a police uniform and sitting among the Kennedy brothers' fellow officers.

Kennedy says that as the visit was coming to an end, Presley asked him what kind of car he drove. A little Audi, Kennedy said. "He said, 'I'm going to get you a car like mine! I'm going to get you a Lincoln.' I said, 'Oh, no you're not.' He said, 'Yeah, I am. I appreciate everything you did for me and my people here.'" Kennedy says that when he continued to balk, Presley insisted, saying, "You gave me a flashlight, and I can afford to get you a car." Kennedy adds: "About that time, Ron walked in, and Elvis said, 'Ron, I'm going to give you a Lincoln, too,' and Ron said, 'I'd rather have a Cadillac.' Elvis said OK, but he looked at me and said, 'Tell you, Captain, you're getting the best car. I've had 'em all—Mercedes, Rolls, and Cadillacs, and the Lincolns are the best cars.' But it wasn't just me."

Presley ended up buying Lincolns for Kennedy and police medical coordinator Dr. Gerald Starkey, and Cadillacs for Pietrafeso and Sergeant Robert Cantwell. They made a prearranged nocturnal visit to a Denver dealership, and Presley offered to buy Kennedy a Rolls-Royce on the showroom floor instead of the blue Lincoln Continental Mark VI he had reserved over the phone.

"He told me, 'Damn, when my dad gets these checks, he's probably going to shit,'" Kennedy says.

(The city's ethics board eventually allowed the police officers to keep the cars, ruling they had come because of off-duty work outside the Denver jurisdiction.)

A few days later during the same visit, KOA/Channel 4 daytime news anchor Don Kinney joked on the air about what kind of car he would pick and Presley, watching the broadcast, called and offered Kinney a car, too. Kinney thought it was a prank, but finally was convinced it really was Presley and received a Cadillac.

Several weeks later, Presley brought Kennedy and Pietrafeso to Memphis for a visit and at one point in the Graceland living room, they were talking with Elvis and members of his entourage about the famous King's Gold Loaf sandwich at the Colorado Mine Company in Glendale, also a hangout for the Broncos players. The sandwich was made with a loaf of Italian bread, bacon, peanut butter, and grape jelly, and it went for $49.95. Elvis had it after one of his Denver concerts and always remembered it. He announced they were making a road trip, and soon they were in the air on his plane, the *Lisa Marie*. They landed in Denver at 1:40 a.m., and Mine Company owners Buck and Cindy Scott were waiting with a huge order of to-go King's Gold Loaf sandwiches for Elvis, Kennedy, Pietrafeso, and all the other passengers.

They ate on the plane and then they went back to Memphis.

After Presley died, Kennedy went to Memphis for the funeral and was considered part of the official entourage at Graceland, at Esposito's behest. "We saw Elvis laying in state in there, in his music room," Kennedy says. "I felt like we were friends, but we weren't family and we tried not to get in the way. I remember we were standing in front of the house at Graceland as they brought him out the door, and a big branch fell off a dogwood tree I was standing by. It seemed kind of ominous. We were in the funeral procession, and we came home the next day."

At the time, reporters asked Kennedy if he had any suspicions that Presley had drug problems. Kennedy said no. Ultimately, it became clear that at least an abuse of prescription drugs played a significant role in Presley's death. "He certainly never indicated to me he was using drugs, but I know that he chose the times you saw him," Kennedy says. "He decided when he was going to see you. Those times that we did see him were of his choosing and at those times, there was never any indication that he was using drugs."

Kennedy's church, Holy Family, went ahead with the mass said for Presley that weekend. It was six blocks to the north of Elitch's in a neighborhood in transition, with many Hispanic immigrants moving in among many Italian-American families. But Spanish was being heard more often in the neighborhood and even at the church. It wasn't an issue at the church's high school, but bilingual programs were becoming more common in the public schools in the area. Funding, though, was being threatened, because Denver Public Schools officials were told on a trip to Washington, DC, that federal monies—$728,500 in the previous school year had funded programs at 11 grade schools and 4 secondary schools—might disappear in the next cycle. Many Italian-Americans couldn't understand the need for the programs in the first place, since their parents and grandparents often had spoken Italian in the home, but didn't consider it the government's obligation to provide Italian translation or bilingual instruction. Two weeks later, the Denver Board of Education—despite heated dissent from board member Naomi Bradford, whose argument was that most of the students in the programs already spoke some English and should be taught in that language—voted to allocate $637,102 to keep the bilingual programs going.

In hot and humid Atlanta on August 20, the Broncos beat the Falcons 10-2—yes, 10-2—and Atlanta's only points came when Spurrier was tackled in the end zone. Denver's touchdown was on a 38-yard pass from Craig Penrose to Riley Odoms. Morton had been in the game enough to go 6 for 14, for 62 yards, but Miller didn't seem to be concerned that his presumed number one hadn't looked all that good so far. In the postmortems over the next few days, though, he admitted he had hoped the offense would have shown more progress after three games.

At the time, the Broncos' top ball-carrying threat was trying to become accustomed to a downgraded role in Miller's system.

Preacher's Son: Otis Armstrong

Number 24, Running Back, 5-10½, 196, 5th Season, Purdue

Otis Armstrong had his first stomach surgery when he was 19 months old. His intestines were all twisted and fouled up, and at first, the doctors couldn't make them right. So as he grew up, he knew the stomachaches were coming at times both inevitable—such as when he defied his mother and ate a couple of Almond Joys and maybe a Snickers—and unpredictable.

When Otis was about five and still not the picture of good health, he nonetheless could run—and run fast. He and a buddy, Darryl, lived four houses apart on the same block in the Lawndale neighborhood of Chicago. At stake was the claim to be the fastest kid on the block. They picked out a crack on the sidewalk as the starting line.

"No cheating!" Otis said, over and over.

Little Darryl didn't need to cheat. He always won. Until one day, Otis talked his mother into buying him new sneakers. Chuck Taylor All-Stars. When Otis finally won, Darryl was flabbergasted. "How'd you do that?" he asked.

Otis smiled, pulled up his pant leg and pointed down.

"New shoes," he said.

Darryl Stingley laughed.

Although Otis's family moved a short distance away, he and Darryl would remain friends.

Otis's stepfather, Frank McCall, was a popular Baptist preacher. "That meant I had to go to church quite a bit," Otis says over lunch in a Denver restaurant. Reverend McCall, it seemed, didn't believe in sparing the rod with the eight children in the household. "We got 'whuppins' back in those days," Otis remembers, without a trace of bitterness. "You'd get one from Mom, and then you get 'whupped' when your dad got home, too—and it would be the double whammy."

They lived near Comiskey Park, and Otis and his friends picked up spare change by washing cars while fans were at the White Sox games. "Every time there was a home run, fireworks would go off, so we got to see fireworks a lot," he says.

Because of his stomach problems, his mother opposed him playing sports, especially football, any thought of which was taboo. As a result, Otis had too much spare time. He got those "whuppins" regularly. "Everybody in the neighborhood expected a lot more from you, and we couldn't get into trouble," he says. "If I got in trouble, everybody knew about it. 'The preacher's son!' But I was hanging around with the wrong guys. I was with guys who were stealing bikes, shoplifting—kids' stuff. When I got to eighth grade, I decided to go in a different direction. I was tired of my mom coming to the police station to pick me up."

His older brother, Curtis, came up with another solution at Farragut High. *Hey, Otis, we promised that our brothers would go out for the freshman football team.* The implication was that Curtis would be in trouble with the coaches if Otis didn't turn out. Curtis knew how quick and talented Otis was, and he told his little brother he would be a great football player. Otis didn't believe that, wasn't all that excited about going out, but he did. Because of his stomach problems, his mother was aghast, but he stuck to it, even getting accustomed to his originally issued leather helmet. "I wasn't good at the beginning because I had to learn how to block and tackle and all that," he says. "Just being fast isn't going to get it done all the time."

He caught on fast, though, and by the time he was a Farragut senior— riding the city bus to school for 10 cents or walking the couple of miles—he was one of the top running backs in Illinois and a highly sought college prospect. He still was having the stomachaches, but he was keeping them quiet, especially from the recruiters.

Otis visited Wisconsin and enjoyed meeting athletic director Elroy Hirsch, who had gotten his nickname, "Crazylegs," for heroics in a Badgers' 1942 game at Soldier Field against the Great Lakes Naval Station. Otis knew that Purdue coach Jack Mollenkopf, like a lot of college coaches, was recruiting both him and a John Marshall High star—Darryl Stingley.

When recruiters came to see Otis, he often called Darryl after they left. "They're on the way over," he would say. Soon Darryl would call back and say, "Yeah, they're here."

They both picked Purdue, and a lot of Otis's friends told him he was crazy, because surely he couldn't beat out Stingley, one of the nation's top recruits. But Otis wanted to stay close to home, and he loved East Lafayette when he visited. "Athletes don't run from competition," he says.

Armstrong arrived on campus first, and he asked for Stingley as his roommate. "Two days later," Armstrong says, "he was standing there in the door with his suitcases."

They both played tailback on the freshman team, but they didn't let that affect their friendship. At least not at first.

"We used to get into wrestling matches in the dorm, flopping all over the place, and we'd really go at it," Armstrong says. "That's the way he was, competitive at everything. We were like two little boys, I guess. And we joked around a lot. We'd laugh so hard we'd end up on the floor."

In spring ball, the Boilermaker staff moved Stingley to wide receiver.

Otis was fifth on the tailback depth chart, so it wasn't as if he was handed the job instead. "Actually, he didn't talk to me for a couple of weeks," Armstrong says. "Once he started doing really well out there at wide receiver, he started to talk more and I think he started to like it."

Their friendship preserved, they moved to an off-campus apartment together as sophomores. "We rode our bikes every day, we never walked," Armstrong says. "We thought it was a good idea to keep our legs strong, plus it helped us get to practice faster, because our last class was on the other side of campus. We had to get to practice and get taped up and get ready to go. Those bikes were a godsend."

Both had big sophomore years. Otis was the starting tailback, gained over 1,000 yards, and was a bona fide Big Ten star. Every once in a while, a former Purdue star running back—Henry "Hank" Stram—showed up to watch practice.

Armstrong hadn't been able to hide his stomach issues, though. "The pain was unbelievable sometimes," he says. "I got sick one time the day before a game and I'd get so weak, but I'd fight through it. I thought I was going to have to live like that the rest of my life."

Doctors at Purdue told him they could fix the problems, but he was resisting surgery. The doctors told him they'd give him "three strikes." By that, they meant the third time he had a major problem and had to seek help, they would operate. "I went to the emergency room," he says. "Strike one. I went to the emergency room again. Strike two. The third time I was on spring break and I was in Chicago. I got sick there, and the people in the emergency room there said, 'Let's call your school, your team!' I said no, no! I was sick for two days and in the hospital and I was trying to keep it quiet. But then my sister said, 'I'm calling your coach!'"

Purdue coach Bob DeMoss, Mollenkopf's successor, showed up. "They had an entourage come and get me out of that hospital," Otis says. "University cars pulled up to the hospital. They didn't even sign papers or anything. They wheeled me out, put me on the elevator and they took me down and put me in a car and we were on the way. They operated on me within hours."

Surgeons removed much of his intestines and rearranged what remained. It would make him better long term, but short term, he lost 40 pounds and still was weak when his junior season opened. Not knowing whether Armstrong would be able to play that fall, Purdue coaches moved Stingley back to halfback, and he and Armstrong ended up together in a wishbone backfield at the start of their junior season in 1971.

"We ran it for four games," Armstrong says. "I remember the coach pulling that screen down like we were going to watch some tape, but first he said, 'We're going to change our offense. Otis, you're back at tailback; Darryl, you're going back to wide receiver.'"

Armstrong adds, "That's the only season I didn't gain 1,000 yards. I wasn't strong enough."

Full strength as a senior, he took great pleasure in winning the *Chicago Tribune*'s Silver Football as the Big Ten's most valuable player. (I showed Otis a picture of Wisconsin star Dave Schreiner receiving the Silver Football in 1942, in *Third Down and a War to Go*. "That's it!" Otis exclaimed. Marine Lieutenant Dave Schreiner was killed in action in 1945, in the final hours of the Battle of Okinawa.)

The night before the 1973 draft, he saw a television report at home saying he would be a Chicago Bear the next day. Bears coach Abe Gibron called and told him the same thing. He remembered what a lot of his football friends, both at Purdue and elsewhere, told him: *The team that says it's going to draft you won't be the team that drafts you*. He didn't know why, but he felt compelled to drive back to East Lafayette and wait there during the draft.

The next day, the Bears took defensive lineman Wally Chambers with the 8th overall pick and the Broncos claimed Otis with the 9th choice. Stingley went 19th, to the New England Patriots. Armstrong hadn't spoken with the Broncos, and here he was, taking a call from John Ralston and hearing the coach and general manager tell him that he was on a speakerphone hookup with a bunch of reporters listening in. Otis decided he should bluff.

"He asked me what I thought about being a Denver Bronco," Armstrong says. "I said, 'I'm excited, I can't wait to get to Denver,' and all that, but I didn't know anything about Denver! So I went to the travel agency in the student union about an hour after that and got some booklets. They showed the skiing and they had a picture of Floyd Little. And I'm thinking what do they want with a running back like me if they have Floyd Little? I didn't get it. I didn't think that was going to work because they have Floyd Little and I'm going to unseat him?"

He didn't, at least not at first. "My first year, I only carried the ball 26 times. I wasn't very happy."

Little still was going to be the workhorse starter in 1974. It seemed as if Otis would have plenty of time to watch from the sideline, and perhaps work on his world championship imitation of Muhammad Ali, which never failed to break up his teammates. "We traded away Joe Dawkins, the number-one fullback," Armstrong says. "Bobby Anderson breaks his ankle one week before the season, and we were all wondering what we were going to do about a fullback. I didn't even think about me. We had [Jon] Keyworth; that's his position, he's next in line. Ralston called me in the office and I thought it was something I did in a game. I was trying to think of what I had done. Did I say something to a coach? I sit down and I'm nervous and everything. He says, 'The reason I got you here is because I want you to start at fullback on Sunday.' I was like, 'Fullback?' 'Yeah, fullback.' I said I never had played fullback in my life! I couldn't believe it. I was excited that I was going to be in the game, but ..."

The Broncos opened against the Los Angeles Rams, and the Broncos' new fullback had some problems. "Merlin Olsen nearly took my head off," Otis says. "I had to fill in when the guard pulls and chop down Merlin Olsen. He ran right over me and they laughed in the film study. They laughed! I said, 'That didn't feel so good, either.'"

But he stuck with it—and Ralston stuck with him. Each week, he and Darryl Stingley were comparing notes on the phone.

"Halfway through the season, I was the leading fullback in the league in rushing—and in headaches," Armstrong says. "Here comes another surprise, we're playing the Colts in Baltimore and Mike Curtis tags Floyd and knocks him out. He was on the field for 10 minutes. Now they put me back at tailback and brought in Keyworth, which I thought they should have done eight weeks before that—instead of me. The first game back, I'm rusty and we're playing the Chiefs on *Monday Night Football* and Willie Lanier had a field day with me. I had forgotten how to read from the 'I,' and I was reading horrible. I had to get used to being that far back again."

Still, he finished with an amazing—under the circumstances—1,407 yards and a terrific 5.3-yards-per-carry average.

Little still was with the team the next season, and Armstrong had an injury-plagued year, first going out with torn rib cartilage and then suffering a ruptured hamstring against the Steelers. "I was running a sweep and my hamstring popped," he says. "Everybody said, 'It looked like you got shot.' I look at the tape and I hate to see it. They brought out a stretcher. My hamstring was like blubber. About a week later, they sent me to California to see the Lakers' orthopedic guy, Dr. [Robert] Kerlan, and then they sent me to see a guy in Oklahoma City. They all told me I was through for the season."

Little retired that off-season. Armstrong ran for 1,008 yards in 1976 and signed a new contract after the season and seemed entrenched as Little's long-term successor, destined to be in the Colorado travel brochures for years.

He says Lyle Alzado and Billy Thompson kept calling, asking him to be a good teammate and show up at the Holiday Inn for the meeting to talk about Ralston. "Oh, every time I think about that, my teammates used me that day," he says, looking back. "They *used* me. I had just signed a new contract. I had no problems with Ralston. He was good to me." He says when Alzado and Thompson asked him why he wasn't at the meeting, he responded: "I'm not there for a reason." Yet he gave in and went. "When I picked up newspapers, it was like I was leading the revolt."

When Red Miller was hired, there were two ways for Armstrong—or any running back—to look at it. The former offensive line coach loved to run the ball, and run it until he couldn't get away with running it any more. But he also believed in rotating ball-carrying responsibilities, and giving bonus points for blocking ability—even to the tailbacks. In 1976, the Patriots had used five backs, and none gained 1,000 yards. In light of that, the Patriots' team rushing total of 2,948 yards—the fifth-best total in league history to that point—was nothing short of astounding.

Armstrong went to the team offices on the day of the 1977 draft and actually liked it when Denver selected a lineman, Steve Schindler, with its first pick. He says he was having coffee and joking around with the assistant coaches—either on draft day or shortly thereafter on another visit—when Miller called him into his office. "He said, 'We're going to use you a little different.' I said, 'What do you mean, use me a little different?' He said, 'We're going to give you some rest, we're going to rest you more.' I said, 'I'm fine, coach, I'm fine!' He said, 'No, we're going to rest you.' We all know what happened."

Still the starter and still the best-known running back, Armstrong no longer was going to be the workhorse.

Clothier: Rob Lytle
Number 41, Running Back, 5-11, 195, 2nd Season, Michigan

As a Navy lieutenant, William Lytle witnessed General Douglas MacArthur's wading ashore at Leyte in October 1944. In fact, Lytle was part of the maneuvering, as all made sure that the famous general wouldn't get too wet as he stepped into the water. Water up to his knees in the pictures of him fulfilling his famous vow—"I shall return"—would be okay; getting in over his head would not.

A few years later, if Bill Lytle were the dramatic sort, he could have said the same thing in Fremont, Ohio. After the war, he eventually rejoined the family business, running the downtown clothing store that had been in the Lytle family for several generations, since Isaac Lytle opened it in the 1880s. His equity was purchased with sweat, and both his father and uncle still were partners.

By the 1960s, Bill was determined to hang on. Even in a small town—and Fremont was a small town—family-run stores, featuring high-quality goods and service, were endangered. Shopping patterns and preferences were changing, and the options were drives to larger Sandusky, 25 miles to the east, or Toledo, 40 miles northwest.

Rob, the youngest of the three Lytle children, worked in the store, too, his duties adjusting for his age. He cleaned up, restocked shelves, put on price tags, helped sell during sidewalk sales. "Most of it was learning it from the ground up," Rob says from his desk in Fremont's Old Fort Bank.

Otherwise, he was busy with sports, swimming competitively in age-group AAU programs, and playing both on the sandlots and in formal competition. He had speed in his genes, since Bill Lytle for years held several sprint records at Bowling Green State University, set just before he went off to war.

"When you're a little kid and they ask, 'What do you want to be when you grow up?' and kids would say 'fireman, policeman, president,' I said, 'No, I'm going to be a professional football player,'" Rob says. "I still remember my dad bringing me home a football when I was five."

By the time he was in Fremont Ross High School, playing for the Little Giants, Rob was taking a bit more active interest in the store, but it was apparent he would be heading off to college soon.

And heading off to college just about anywhere he wanted.

Rob and Bob Brudzinski were cocaptains of the 1972 Fremont Ross team that went 9-1 and was a Buckeye Conference cochampion. Lytle rushed for 1,253 yards as a senior. The tugs on both Lytle and Brudzinski came from all over, and retired Ross coach Mal Mackey—still a legend in Fremont—hoped to steer them to Purdue, where Mackey's brother Red had been athletic director. (And where the basketball arena was renamed in Red's honor in 1972.)

Ohio State wanted them, too, but Woody Hayes apparently never got around to talking with Bill Lytle about the war. Among others, Lytle early on said no to Southern California's John McKay and Oklahoma's Barry Switzer.

Rob narrowed the field to Ohio State, Purdue, Michigan, Notre Dame, and Alabama, but he confessed to Crimson Tide coach Bear Bryant that he was leaning toward playing close enough to home so his parents could watch him.

Lytle remembers Bryant responding: "Son, you come down here, your parents can come down here every weekend. I'll make sure of that."

(Ah, the good old days . . .)

"But he understood," Rob says. "The funny thing was, he made a comment to me, 'So Notre Dame, huh? That Ara [Parseghian] is a great man.' But then he said, 'I'll be quite honest with ya', I don't think he's going to last your four years. If you're talking to him, ask him point blank.' "[4]

Finally, it was Ohio State versus Michigan. Hayes versus his close friend Bo Schembechler. Brudzinski chose Ohio State, Lytle chose Michigan, and the teammates would go head-to-head for the next four seasons.

"I loved Woody, but there was something about Bo," Lytle says. "Bear even called me and said, 'Which one you going to?' I said Michigan, and he said, 'That's good, I had Bo coaching for me in an all-star game and that's a good boy, you'll do well there.' "

What was it about Bo?

"He looks at me and says, 'You're not going to be any greater than you are right now, you can't get any greater than what you are.' But he says, 'When you sign with Michigan, you'll be the eighth-team tailback and whatever you do from that point is going to be an accomplishment for you. I have the firmest feeling that you *can* be the greatest running back that ever came out of Michigan.' That's what he told me."

Lytle laughs.

"He lied to me. A guy quit, so I was the seventh-team tailback."

The rivalry was storied, but not as ballyhooed as it is now, so Lytle says that talk over the years of him taking a lot of heat for choosing Michigan over Ohio State was exaggerated.

"One guy did come right down to the store and told my father he'd never shop in the store again," Lytle says. "My father looked at him and said, 'Well, I hope you're kidding, but if you're not, are you even a graduate of Ohio State?' The guy said no. I guess he was a turnpike alum."

At Michigan, Rob ran indoor track for two seasons, but otherwise concentrated on football and played both fullback and tailback for Schembechler. "I loved the school and that was the biggest thing I took away from the experience—well, that and Bo," he says. "His integrity was above everything. If he said something, that's the way it was. Like or dislike it, he told you how he felt, and you never had guessing games with him.

"He was a taskmaster. He believed in doing things the right way. He had a great sense of humor and was a lot of fun, but he seemed to know when to turn it on and off. He said there's a time to work and a time to play. When it's work time there is absolutely no screwing around. He was true to his word and to me you can't ask for anything more than that."

As a senior, Lytle ran for 1,402 yards; finished third in the Heisman Trophy voting, behind Pittsburgh's Tony Dorsett and USC's Ricky Bell; and was a consensus first-team All-American. The Wolverines went 1-2-1 against the Buckeyes in Lytle's tenure, but the win was in his senior season and he scored Michigan's touchdown in the 14-6 Rose Bowl loss to USC on January 1, 1977.

On draft day—in May, after the NFL finally moved the draft back to the spring—Lytle waited. And waited. And waited. By early in the afternoon, he hadn't heard anything, so, assuming that the draft must have been in the fifth round or so, he left his apartment and went to work out—and work off some of his disappointment. One of his roommates chased him down and told him to get back to the apartment, that the Denver Broncos had called.

So he called and Red Miller soon was on the line, all excited and saying Lytle needed to come to Denver the next day.

"I had to ask, 'Well, why do you want to fly me out?' He said, 'Well, we think we have a nice pick here.' I said, 'That's very gracious . . . but what round are we in?' He said, 'Well, we picked you with the 45th pick, 2nd round.' I said, "Ohhhhhhhhhh.' He started laughing. He was very nice. I said, 'Well, I guess I'll see you tomorrow.'"

When Miller spoke with Lytle in a conference call on a speakerphone before letting reporters ask questions, the Broncos coach told Lytle: "Bo Schembechler says you're the best running back he's ever coached."

Lytle responded: "Aw, you know what his initials spell—B.S."

The choice helped illustrate Miller's offensive philosophy. That day, he and special teams coach Marv Braden, who had been on the Michigan State staff before joining the Broncos, raved that Lytle was as influential without the ball—as a blocker—as he was with it.

Fred Gehrke's assistant, Bill Goldy, picked up Lytle at the airport and took a slight detour, giving him a quick look at Mile High Stadium from the nearby Interstate 25. The stadium would be newly expanded for 1977, Goldy told Lytle. He would be playing in front of full houses, in front of more fans than he ever had played in front of before, Goldy said.

Lytle, who had played in front of over 100,000 fans at Michigan Stadium, said in wonderment, "Really!" He says he thought: *It doesn't look that big, it must really go down a long ways.*

Then it hit Goldy: This kid was from *Michigan.* "He was kind of embarrassed," Lytle says.

At the Broncos' headquarters, he got another awakening. "They had that cluster office, and I don't know how they had room for anything," he says. "And there's no weight room. They had an area with some weights, but it was in the locker room. I can remember looking at this and going, *My god, is this pro football?* But, really, it didn't make any difference to me. I just wanted to play pro football."

As a high school player, he had known of Otis Armstrong's play at Purdue and even considered going to East Lafayette and succeeding him as the Boilermakers' tailback. Lytle and Tracy Rauch were married in June, and when Lytle came to camp the next month, he quickly developed a kinship with Armstrong, one in which Tracy and Yvonne Armstrong would become friends as well.

But even in the early stages of the exhibition season, Armstrong and Lytle were beginning to get the impression that sharing the tailback duty would leave them both frustrated at times.

Lytle says, "Bo even used to say that I was the worst back for the first five plays of a game, until I got myself knocked around enough to get myself into the flow of things. So that was the hardest thing for me."

He pauses.

"But we worked it out."

Notes

1. Wellington Webb was Denver's mayor from 1991 to 2003.
2. The land across from Wheat Ridge High now is the Crown Lake Park recreational area and refuge.
3. Father Jones became Monsignor Jones, vicar general of the archdiocese.
4. Ara Parseghian retired after the 1974 season.

CHAPTER 6

United Front

We were always willing to give ourselves up for each other.

—BARNEY CHAVOUS

Yet More Exhibitions: August 21–September 10

Sunday, August 28 at Philadelphia Eagles
Friday, September 2 at Seattle Seahawks
Saturday, September 10 at San Francisco 49ers

Assuming Craig Morton and Steve Spurrier both couldn't be on the roster, and that they knew it, we were getting the impression that the veteran quarterbacks were bitter rivals.

Looking back, Morton says he actually got along fine with Spurrier. "He was an intense guy and very, very cocky," Morton says. "He was very smart. I felt competitive with all of [the quarterbacks]. It just seemed like he was going to be the odd man out. As smart as he was, his fundamentals were very average and his arm strength was minimal."

———

Movie star Van Johnson followed John Raitt to Elitch's, appearing in *Send Me No Flowers*, the final production of the summer season. He proclaimed in publicity interviews that he loved to come to Denver because he could stay at the Brown Palace Hotel—following, among others, presidents and the Beatles—and wander through Larimer Square. Presumably, someone had told him not to wander too far up Larimer Street from there—or to be prepared to step over the drunks. But Johnson had a lot of company downtown that week, mostly delegates to the national American Legion convention. Another star, Danny Thomas, was honored at the convention for his humanitarian work in founding St. Jude's Children's Hospital. "We have to teach our young children that it's not unsophisticated to be patriotic," he told the Legionnaires. "We have to protect our kids from the dirty bastards who are trying to destroy our country from within." That said, he joked about being one of the few entertainers who refused to use blue language on stage. "They say the meek shall inherit the earth," he said. "That's Lawrence Welk and me." Flamboyant rock star Alice Cooper was playing McNichols a few days later, but I doubted that any of the Legionnaires or Thomas planned to stick around to catch the concert.

On Sunday, August 28, both Spurrier, who started, and Weese were productive in a 28-24 loss at Philadelphia. Spurrier was 7 for 10, for 95 yards and Weese, who brought the Broncos back for two late touchdowns and took them on a threatening drive that came up short in the final minutes, was 12 of 22 for 160 yards. The problem for Spurrier was that if the Broncos were going to have a relatively immobile veteran quarterback, Morton was displaying the much stronger arm.

The major loss in the game was that starting offensive tackle Bill Bain suffered torn knee ligaments and would have to undergo surgery and be out for the season. The Broncos were in trouble up front, and it seemed as if they might have to switch one of the veteran centers, Bobby Maples or Mike Montler, or guard Paul Howard to tackle.

On Tuesday, Miller did what he had said he wanted to be able to do going into the final two exhibition games: He named a starting quarterback. He said Craig Morton was his number one. Spurrier was waived. The announcement was extraordinary: Miller had the three surviving quarterbacks attend his press session, too. At the time, Morton said he was "very happy," and added: "We've all got to get together and win a championship." He said he, Penrose, and Weese "all do things differently.

We can all be effective. My ego is not going to be shattered if I get taken out of a game. The object is to win."

That same day, the Rockies officially named Pat Kelly their coach in a news conference at McNichols. It was enjoyable to finally meet him in person. I asked him a lot of questions, but not whether he hoped to sign *Slap Shot*'s Hanson Brothers.

———

As the Broncos prepared for a Friday night exhibition game, Dick Connor caught up with John Ralston, who was going to work the game as an analyst on Seattle television. He still was living in Denver and he said of the Broncos: "I notice a very positive mental attitude among them. I'm happy they have it. I was criticized for that."

He refused to go into details, but he made it clear that he felt he had been undercut, presumably by ownership and the front office. "I've been a whipping boy in some respects," he told Connor. "You expect that. But there's nobody except my wife I will tell everything about what happened. Everybody was critical of the players. I am not. They were symptoms, not the disease." (Thirty years later, as you've seen, he still takes the same stand with me.)

Ralston's touching story—he admitted he had broken down and cried when the shock of being fired wore off—was on the top of the *Post* sports section, played ahead of the stories on Bears clinching an American Association West Division title with a 4-0 win over Wichita, behind the shut-out pitching of Larry Landreth; the much-touted Nuggets number-one draft choice, center-forward Tom LaGarde of North Carolina, signing with Denver; and unheralded rookie punter Bucky Dilts beating out veteran Herman "Thunderfoot" Weaver. Weaver was cut, along with Elvis impersonator Ken Brown. The next day, the Broncos moved to fill the hole at tackle left by Bill Bain's injury, acquiring veteran Andy Maurer from the 49ers for a draft choice. He wasn't going to report until after the game at Seattle, after Denver made some more cuts.

On Friday night, September 2, in the dark Kingdome, the Broncos improved to 4-1 in the exhibition season, beating the second-year expansion Seahawks 27-10. Morton completed the first drive with a touchdown pass to rookie tight end Ron Egloff, and Lonnie Perrin and Rob Lytle ran for the other TDs. The offense wasn't especially impressive, but Seattle turnovers—three interceptions and a fumble—had helped give the Broncos great field position.

At fullback, Miller was committed to giving both Lonnie Perrin and Jon Keyworth work. Perrin, a Washington, DC, native, was a fifth-round pick from Illinois in 1976, the final draft of the Ralston era. He was especially valuable because—as another straight-on, square-toed-shoe holdout—he handled the kickoff duties, taking some of the heat off reliable field-goal kicker Jim Turner.

The other fullback, Keyworth, had played several positions at Colorado and was a Redskins 1974 draft choice. That was notable because it was during the reign of George "The Future Is Now" Allen, who believed draft choices weren't worth the hassle and traded off most of them before Washington had the chance to use any of them to take players. Keyworth was the Redskins' first choice in 1974—but he went in the *sixth* round! After being sent along to the Broncos, he established himself as a versatile back, gaining 1,448 yards in three years under Ralston and also catching 76 passes.

Denver still was getting used to the idea of having dancing cheerleaders on the sideline, but the Pony Express members—wearing white boots and cowboy hats and a lot of Bob Mackie fringes—were becoming celebrity ambassadors for the Broncos. They gathered in the KMGH/Channel 7 parking lot during Jerry Lewis's 12th Labor Day Muscular Dystrophy Telethon to collect donations from motorists, and the local pledge total was $921,000. Channel 7 still was basking in the glory of being back on the top of the newscast ratings, and KBTV/Channel 9 was responding, announcing plans to bring in a Cleveland-based NBC correspondent as a coanchor and team him with holdover Ed Sardella. The new anchor, the young hotshot coming in from Cleveland, was Mike Landess.[1]

Maurer started practicing with the Broncos, and the left tackle job was his to lose. The joke on the Broncos was that he never had played tackle before. He was a journeyman who had started at guard for the Vikings in a Super Bowl, and Denver just figured that as a veteran lineman, he must have played both guard and tackle—and Maurer didn't attempt to dispel that assumption.

On his first day of practice, he worked so hard it angered Lyle Alzado, and the two men promptly got in a fight. Miller liked that kind of scrappiness and it probably helped Maurer, but he hadn't been that calculating.

"He tried to convince me he was all-world and I proved to him and the rest of the team that I can play," Maurer remembers. "It was a typical practice and he was a typical prima donna and prima donnas don't like to get hit. I had to learn the position, though, and I had to treat it like a scrimmage every day. He kept yelling at me and I kept yelling at him and he kept yelling at me and finally I told him, 'If you don't want to work, just get off the field. Put in your backup and get out of here.'"

After practice, Maurer confided in Alzado.

He recalls telling the Broncos' star end that he needed to learn how to play tackle "quick," adding, "You're the best there is and if I can learn to play tackle against you, I'm gonna be fine."

Maurer says, "After that we were friends and we worked our butts off for half the year and then we went to the choreographed dances you do. I had a lot to learn and Lyle knew all the tricks."

By the end of the week, Maurer was confessing to reporters that he never had played *left* tackle. It was our fault if we inferred that he had played tackle at all.

Denver had a champion: The Bears had roared back to win the final four games of the American Association championship series and take the Class AAA league's title 4-2.

With the baseball season over, the city crew finally was able to move Mile High Stadium's new three-tiered east stands in from the baseball position to the football position. That sounded simple, but nobody was 100 percent sure that the newfangled system—the stands slid on runways filled with water—was going to work. With "Anchors Aweigh" blaring on the stadium's public-address system, and with about 3,000 fans watching a Broncos public practice, the stands indeed moved 145 feet into place. If that hadn't worked, many fans—including many new season ticket holders—would have been wise to bring binoculars.

At the *Post*, we still were getting used to having Steve Cameron and Dick Connor as the tag-team columnists, having longtime high school sports expert Joseph Sanchez taking over the Broncos beat, and having me on the hockey beat. Michael Knisley, fresh from getting his master's degree from CU, had joined the staff and was ticketed to cover the high schools. Because we both were blond and looked enough alike to be brothers, Knisley and I were dubbed "the Bobbsey Twins."[2] We had a bunch of part-time writers, several of them schoolteachers, but we were about to lose our ace, Neal Rubin, who was attending the University of Northern Colorado and about to start full-time work at the *Greeley Tribune*.[3] Even after he joined the Greeley paper, he was a frequent running mate of the Bobbsey Twins and Cameron.

The college football season opened for most teams on September 10. Denver at times could be apathetic about the college game, and it seemed more so every year as the population was more heavily tilted toward natives of other states who moved in and retained their original collegiate loyalties. But many Denver residents made the drive to Boulder for Colorado games, to Fort Collins for Colorado State games, and even some to the Air Force Academy grounds north of Colorado Springs for Falcons games. On Saturday, CU—under fourth-year coach Bill Mallory—beat Stanford 27-21, with the Buffs' Jeff Knapple staging an entertaining passing duel with Guy Benjamin; CSU beat Pacific 20-3; and Air Force, beginning Ben Martin's 20th season as head coach, suffered through a scoreless tie at Wyoming.

Miller was trying to install and encourage a mindset, so he was unapologetic about going against nice-guy coaching convention in Saturday night's final exhibition game, a 20-0 shutout of the 49ers at Candlestick Park. San Francisco coach Ken Meyer, also in his first season, was so irate that the Broncos still were throwing the ball late when leading 13-0, rather than just letting the clock roll and let both teams get off the field and start pointing for the regular-season opener, he charged across the field after the game finally ended and directed an angry middle-finger salute at Miller. Bronco assistant coaches and players had to keep the yelling head coaches separated, and they looked like a couple of hockey coaches screaming at each other on the benches after an on-ice brawl.

It was one more reminder: This wasn't some hand-holding, tea-sipping social hour. This was football, and the Broncos' defense had looked impressive on a night both teams used regulars for most of the game. The Denver touchdowns came on Morton's 5-yard pass to Riley Odoms and Randy Gradishar's 70-yard interception return for a touch-down, and the defense looked primed for the regular season.

"Barnyard": Barney Chavous

Number 79, Defensive End, 6-3, 252, 5th Season, South Carolina State

As he was being raised in the 1950s and 1960s, Barney Chavous Jr. didn't need to look very hard to explore his heritage. The family cemetery, with graves of at least seven generations, was just down the road from the Chavous farm near Aiken, South Carolina.

Aiken was across the Savannah River from Augusta, Georgia, and these were the days when it would have been unimaginable that a Tiger Woods—or any other black man—someday could stride down the Augusta National fairways, eyeing his next shot and preparing to don a green jacket.

On his father's side of the family, though, there were white ancestors and riches and land—lots of land, dating back to colonial days. The Chavous family still had a lot of it, farming and living a comfortable existence outside town. Ask Barney if he worked on the farm as a kid, and the response is a hearty laugh. "Did I?" he asks from his home in Aiken. "I drove tractors. I planted and picked cotton. I hoed cotton. I helped harvest. I helped with the cattle and hogs."

On his mother Mary's side, his great-grandmother had been a slave, living on the Hammond family estate, which at the time of the Civil War belonged to former South Carolina governor and U.S. Senator James Henry Hammond, a proslavery firebrand. Barney says members of his mother's family, the Larks, had both African and American Indian heritages, and they continued to live on the Hammond estate after the end of slavery. Barney's grandfather, Harry Lark, was one of the supervisors on the estate before it was sold and became a wildlife refuge. By then, Harry Lark had been given part of the estate, and that land also still is in the family.

Barney says that the area's ingrained discrimination—this was Strom Thurmond's home territory, after all—"never really affected us because we had land. We had a refuge where we could always go to separate us from that."

Still, they could go to Augusta to experience it.

"I remember going to places where if you wanted a hot dog, you had to go to the back window," Barney says. "'Colored' in the back, and same kind of thing with the restrooms. In the '50s and '60s, on Broad Street, the main street, blacks couldn't go in the theaters. They had another theater on Ninth Street, where James Brown grew up, for blacks. You could go to that theater if you were black. That's how it was. But we had people in our family who looked so much like whites they could actually go in the theaters and nobody would even know it."

The Chavous men were not just farmers, but also tinkerers and innovators. Barney's grandfather, Oscar, was an engineer who designed a hydraulic pump that made digging water wells easier. Barney's father, Barney Sr., was a double threat, with an automobile repair garage that doubled as the site of an outdoor barbeque restaurant on the weekends.

"One Fourth of July, when I was 8 or 9 or 10, we must have cooked fifty hogs," Barney Jr. says. "We had these hogs on the pit, and it was just lined up with nothing but these hogs from end to end, and people would come up and buy whole hogs off the pit."

Then the men would play baseball behind the garage. Barney Sr. was a top-notch pitcher, perhaps past his prime by then, but willing to keep playing and hear people say, "He could have played in the big leagues, if . . ." One of young Barney's uncles had been a star catcher and had gotten an offer from the Yankees organization, and the speculation was that it could have been because he could "pass" for being white.

"I wanted to be like Daddy," Barney Jr. says. "I wanted to be a pitcher. I wasn't as good as he was, though. I wasn't as good as my uncle, but I was a pretty good baseball player. I didn't even think about football."

When he was starting his senior year at Aiken's Schofield High School, Barney was considered an athlete—but mostly a weightman in track and field and a basketball player who was known for going swimming, bike riding, and boating in his spare time. The football program was terrible and underfunded, and a lot of the top athletes—Barney, for example—didn't even play.

A new and energetic coach, William Clyburn, came into the Schofield lunchroom and hunted down the athletes who weren't playing. He approached Barney and told him, "You're a good athlete and you might be able to get a football scholarship to go to college."

Barney pointed out that to get some spending money, he—a high school senior—worked for the school as the bus driver on the route that passed the Chavous place. He got $140 a month and got to take the bus home. "I wanted to be independent, to have some money in my pocket," Barney recalls. "I did it so I could take a girl out and buy her a hamburger."

Well, Clyburn said, Barney probably would need to give that up, but . . .

"I don't even know why," Barney says, "but I said, 'OK, I'll give it a try.'"

He gave up the bus-driving job and reported to practice.

"The first day they put me in front of William Key and another young man," Barney says. William Key happened to be the brother of Odessa Key, the girl Barney had a crush on and wouldn't mind buying a hamburger (and eventually would marry). "They made it the old two-on-one, 'Oklahoma' drill, and Coach Clyburn told me, 'Tell you what I want you to do—split these guys and hold your ground and be in a position to make the tackle.' These guys came up on me and I just split them and took my hands and pushed them out of the way."

He asked himself: *How'd I do that?*

He decided he liked this football deal, and he played both defensive line and linebacker for Schofield. But he had got started so late, he was overlooked by college coaches, even by those who were willing to go hard after black players in the late 1960s. South Carolina State quarterback Johnny Jones, though, was assigned to do his student teaching at Schofield, and he came across Barney and asked the coaches about him.

Then he told Barney, "I hear you're a pretty good football player."

Barney replied, "I don't know whether I'm good or not."

Jones pitched Chavous to South Carolina State coach Oiree Banks. By then, Barney had taken back his bus-driving job—"The guy who had been driving had a wreck or something," he recalls—and when he pulled up to the front of the school one day, someone frantically gave him the message that Banks wanted him to call. Chavous and Banks agreed they would meet and talk when Barney attended the state track meet at South Carolina State, in Orangeburg.

Clyburn, who also had checked with the Schofield coaches, offered Barney a full football scholarship. This was barely a year after three South Carolina State students—Sam Hammond, Delano Middleton, and Henry Smith—were shot and killed by South Carolina Highway Patrol officers during a disturbance tied to a February 1968 protest of the segregation of Orangeburg's All Star Bowling Lanes. Chavous, unfazed, showed up in Orangeburg in the fall of '69 and began football workouts.

"I didn't have the sense enough to realize the first to get there got good equipment," he says, laughing. "I got terrible shoes. I got a blister on my foot, and it wasn't long before we had a scrimmage. Freshmen against the varsity. I had a blister and I couldn't really do anything, but I said, *Man, I'm going to play*. I walked out there with one cleated shoe and one sneaker on. The linebackers coach didn't want to be bothered with me. James Carson was the defensive line coach, and he came up to me."

(At this point, I had to break in and tell Barney that I had met James Carson when I did a *Sporting News* story at Jackson State, where Carson was coaching by then.)

"Well," Chavous says, continuing, "James Carson says, and you know how he talks, 'Y-y-y-y-you want to play football, do you?' I was supposed to be a linebacker, but he put me in at defensive end—one sneaker, one cleated shoe—and I destroyed that guy in front of me. Carson came to me the next day, and he said, 'Uh, I think you're going to be all right.'"

He started all three years and made several All-America teams. By the time he was a senior, Broncos scouting guru Carroll Hardy was showing up periodically to watch him. He played in a handful of all-star games and was impressive, but on draft day in January 1973, he didn't change his routine—he went to his student-teaching assignment at Holly Hill High School.

"We got out about 2:30 and when I went back to Orangeburg, the dean at the dormitory said, 'Hey, you have a message over there, look at the board!'" he says.

There, pinned to the board, was a note that told him to call "Fred Gehrke of the Denver Broncos," and listed a phone number.

Gehrke, then the assistant GM, told him congratulations, the Broncos had drafted him in the second round. He passed the phone to John Ralston, who talked some more, then passed the phone to defensive line coach Doc Urich, who said he was excited to have Chavous and would come down to Orangeburg to meet him.

This also was about the time Otis Armstrong, the first pick, was picking up the Colorado travel brochures from the Purdue student union. Chavous went to a map instead.

Later, he says, "I went from Augusta to Chicago, and got on the plane to Denver for minicamp. There was this guy back there with his big hat on, in his Super Fly outfit."

Chavous remembers the conversation this way:

"What's your name?"

"Otis Armstrong."

"You got drafted by Denver!"

"Yeah, I did."

"I'm Barney Chavous."

"Hey, you got drafted by Denver too!"

They went to Denver together.

Chavous started right away, as Urich had all but promised, and was best known at first as a run stopper before developing into a fearsome pass rusher as well. By his fourth season, 1976, he led Denver in sacks, with eight and a half, after Lyle Alzado was sidelined for the season after suffering a knee injury in the season opener. Because the switch to the three-man front went so well the rest of the season, and the Broncos were committed to stick with it, Alzado was going to move from tackle to end in 1977.

Chavous loved Alzado, but he says that when he was asked to stay for the meeting at the Holiday Inn, he decided to leave town. "That was one of the worst things at the time," he says, "but it ended up being one of the better things, I know. But I didn't think that was the right thing to do. If you're loyal to somebody, you should stay loyal to them. There were some other things involved, and I don't want to get into those things."

Joe Collier was making it clear that he was planning to implement a rotation to keep the starters fresh, putting in another three-man unit—

ends Paul Smith, in his tenth season, and rookie Brison Manor plus fifth-year nose tackle John Grant—every third series. As it turned out, Alzado chafed at that, but Chavous liked the plan, primarily—again—because of loyalty. Smith had been the Broncos' star defensive tackle in the old four-man alignment in the early 1970s, and made the Pro Bowl in 1972 and '73, but injuries had slowed him down and he would be playing end in the three-man front.

"When you have a player like Paul Smith, and that's who would come in for me, I wanted him to play," Chavous says. "I wanted Paul to be in there. That's the type of thing I keep talking about with this team. We thought about each other. Paul was a great football player, and we didn't lose anything, really. To me, Paul was one of the best football players I ever had seen until the injuries had started setting in. So I just loved to see Smitty go in there. I loved to see him make a sack. I loved to see him make a play. And all that did was encourage me. Okay, he did that, now let me go out there and try to do something."

With Alzado back and the three-man starting set obvious, a chemistry kicked into high gear. Even the three personalities were complementary.

"Rubin and Lyle were talented individuals, and I had some talent, too. But I guess the thing that made us good was we worked together," Chavous says. "Sometimes we had to get on Lyle about, 'Hey, Lyle, forget about Lyle right now and let's try to win this football game!' And he would always respond. We were always willing to give ourselves up for each other."

On the Nose: Rubin Carter
Number 68, Nose Tackle, 6-0, 256, 3rd Season, Miami

For about two years, when he was perhaps four and five, little Rubin Carter went into the fields with his parents, Charlie and Susie Mae, who in tough times for the family had turned to traveling up and down the East Coast as farm workers.

"You name it, we picked it," Rubin says from his office at Florida A&M University in Tallahassee. "Tomatoes, strawberries, blueberries, zucchini, squash, watermelons."

How did he do?

"I ate more than I picked," he recalls, laughing.

He turns serious.

"It certainly was a humbling experience. My parents were very strong willed and my mother had a tremendous faith through all the adversity we had to go through as a family."

Rubin was the youngest of eight children, but most were off on their own by then. The next youngest, Charles Jr., was both his buddy and his bully as they scraped along. At least the Carters had better conditions than many farm labor families, because one farmer they worked for—a man named Abby in Salisbury, Maryland—for several years let them use a house on his property as their base, and they considered it home. "Everybody else had to live in chicken coops where chickens were raised," Rubin says. When they traveled to find other work during slack times in Salisbury, the housing was in ramshackle barracks. They usually ended up working in Florida during the winters, and Rubin had been born in Pompano Beach in December 1952.

Finally, though, the Carters decided that the two youngest sons—Charles Jr. and Rubin—needed some stability, and they were determined to remain based in Salisbury. Rubin was attending a Salisbury elementary school when his father, picking mangoes, suffered a fatal heart attack.

Rubin was devastated.

Susie Mae and her two sons moved to Fort Lauderdale, to be near Rubin's sister, Ossie Belle Williams, and her family. They didn't move into a beach house or a shoreline condo. They were in government project housing. They got some money and food from the government, and also from the older Carter children. "That's how we survived," Rubin says. "Government cheese, the government, and the grace of God to make ends meet."

His older brother Johnny had a job in a Pompano Beach steel mill. For three straight summers, beginning when he was 14, Rubin went with Johnny to the mill and did odd jobs. He was working with adults. During the school years, he scrambled to find part-time work, helping support the family.

He didn't go out for school sports until the ninth grade, and that was the basketball team. "I was very, very competitive," he recalls, "but I found that basketball was not my sport because I fouled out in the first five minutes."

During his sophomore year at Stranahan High School, Rubin tried basketball again. One of the school's assistant football coaches saw Rubin's rough-and-tumble brand of hoops and was intrigued. "He said,

'You know something, son, you might need to come out for football.' I had never played football but I thought it sounded like a good idea, and I wanted to get permission from my mother to make sure it would be okay. She was concerned about injuries, like any other mother. She didn't want her baby to get hurt—and her baby was 6-foot-1, 225 pounds in the tenth grade. But she was fine with it."

So he went out for football, and in Florida—even then—that meant going through twenty days of spring practices, which were his crash course in the sport. "I found something I could really love," he says. "You could run and hit and express yourself on the football field. I remember the first day I put on pads. They had a young offensive lineman on the other side in 'nutcracker' drill, with two bags on either side and a running back behind him. So he came at me and I hit him and he hit me, and the running back tried to run between these two bags. Well, I grabbed him by the face mask and threw him down. We all know that's illegal, but I found out I loved football that day."

Still, he needed to bring money home, so he arranged a way he still could make practice every day. His schedule for the rest of his high school career, at least during football, was classes, study hall, practice, and then a few hours of work at the school as a janitor. "I cleaned the same class-rooms where I had been all day long," he says. "It made me appreciate everything more. I told those students to stop throwing things on the floors because I had to clean them up later."

He threw himself into football. If that wasn't going to be his avenue to a better life, something was going to be. He knew that much. "Having grown up where I did in the government projects, with people getting killed probably once every two weeks and seeing all the drug usage, I knew I didn't want all those negatives," he says. "I wanted to do something positive. Having older brothers and sisters, you have the opportunity to see their lives and see some good things and see some other things that make you say, 'I'm not going to do that.' I told myself, *I'm going to do some things with my life and make something of myself and put some footprints in the sand.*"

It took him a while to get the hang of football, but once he did, he was a highly sought prospect as a senior. By then, Susie Mae Carter had been diagnosed with cancer. Rubin admits most of his college recruiting trips—places as disparate as Southern Illinois and Louisiana State—were larks, taken in part because he had never been on an airplane before. It wasn't surprising when he agreed to become a University of Miami Hurricane. "I needed to be able to see my mother when I could and at the same time, I could get home to eat that fried chicken and eat that apple pie," he says.

The Miami program had been integrated for only four years when Carter arrived on campus in 1971. Early in his freshman year, he was in the football office, looking at the pictures of former All-Americans on the wall.

All the players in the pictures were white.

"I didn't lack for confidence," he says. "I made a bold statement to the secretary—her name was Pat—that 'this is where I want you to hang my picture someday.' She almost fell out of her chair laughing at this snotty-nosed, bratty kid who never has played a down of big-time football."

That spring, his mother died.

"I was able to overcome it with a strong faith and a strong belief that all things work together for good, and there had to be purpose in my life," Carter says. "But it was very difficult. At one point, I even entertained the thought of leaving school. I started questioning a lot of things about the decision I made to even go there."

After the coaching staff, especially defensive line coach Harold Allen, went above and beyond the call of duty to provide support—and remember, he had yet to play a down of varsity football—he was appreciative and filed away the memory about the role coaches could play in mentoring young men.

He was a renowned defensive tackle by his junior year. In 1973, the Hurricanes were playing at Alabama and went to a movie the night before the game. The competitive Carter was offended when the Crimson Tide coincidentally came to the same theater and movie and tried to be social. One of the players in the recently integrated Alabama program was Sylvester Croom, who in later years would become a close Carter friend.[4]

"Hey, where's Rubin Carter?" one of the Alabama players asked.

"You'll see him tomorrow," groused Rubin Carter.

He had 22 unassisted tackles and assists the next day, but the Crimson Tide won 43-13.

Despite missing the Hurricanes' final five games in 1974 because of a broken foot, Carter was a United Press International and Kodak All-American. He had hoped to win the Outland Trophy as the nation's best lineman and had dreamed of being on a Bob Hope Special when the comedian annually introduced the *Look* magazine All-American team. "I was going to shake hands with Bob Hope!" he says. But Carter didn't make that team or win the Outland. He got to do something that gave him almost as much pleasure. He walked into the Miami football office and hung his picture among the All-Americans.

Pat still was the football office secretary, and she gave him a big hug.

Although he recovered quickly enough to play in all-star games, he didn't go in the draft until the fifth round. He didn't fit the computer prototype of the defensive lineman of the time, when anyone much shorter than Ed "Too Tall" Jones could be "Too Short." The Broncos had been fooling around with three-man fronts, though using it full-time was a ways off. Denver thought Rubin could play tackle in a four-man front anyway.

"I just said wherever I go I'll show them the type of player I'll be," he says. "But I didn't even know where Denver was at first. I might as well have been going to Canada. But they assured me it was a young team, an up-and-coming team."

That was the crucial draft crop, the one with top pick Louis Wright, the safety who showed up for the minicamp in that green leisure suit. "I wanted to know, 'Where does this cat shop?'" Carter says with a laugh.

Rubin was a part-time starter as a rookie, then full-time in '76, when the switch to the three-man front put him at nose tackle.

Carter—who, like his roommate, Wright, had taken off the day after the '76 season ended—didn't like the way Ralston's firing unfolded. "I did not sign off on the petition," he says. "I wasn't into that. I wanted to play football. I knew the kind of person Coach Ralston was and I knew he had a great impact on building the success of the Denver Broncos. He had an eye for talent, a tremendous eye. I also think what people don't talk about enough is that he was good at evaluating character, which I think is important. He drafted not only good players, he drafted good people at the same time. His management style was his demise because he really trusted the people around him."

At the time, Carter was engaged to Karen Hammond, whom he would marry in June 1977. In another small-world coincidence, he had discovered that her brother, Sam, was one of the three South Carolina State students shot and killed by state highway patrol officers during the 1968 protests in Orangeburg—a year before Barney Chavous arrived on campus.

"You don't hear about those as much as the shootings at Kent State," Carter says.

That spring, a couple of months before his wedding, he had another crisis. Attending an off-campus fraternity reunion at Miami, he was driving a friend back to campus when he suddenly felt strange. He never had any memory of what happened next. Suddenly, he was out of the car and in a rage. NFL security and police later confirmed that Carter, who didn't even drink alcohol, had been slipped something—a "mickey"—in a Coca-Cola. Officially, campus police arrested him, but a university official subsequently explained that it was a legal technicality. "It took four football players to subdue him," the official said. "To admit him to the hospital, you must have an accompanying charge. When we arrived, he was banging his head against cars, trees, signs, and buildings, and was bleeding profusely." In the ensuing days, comments from teammates and former teammates that he was the *last* guy in the world they would expect to be involved with drugs were so genuine, they couldn't have been feigned. The head of campus police said an investigation confirmed that something had been slipped in Carter's Coke when he was in the bathroom, and an NFL investigation later concurred. In fact, the NFL investigator, Charlie Jackson, the league's assistant director of security, ended up calling Carter "one of the highlights of this league as a person."

A sports world accustomed to excuses and truth dodging could tell that Carter had been the victim of a sick joke.

He ended up hospitalized for several days and praying with, among others, Chavous, who had come down to see him when he heard the news. University president Henry King Stanford also visited him and publicly backed him as "a fine young man."

"That was probably one of the worst times of my life," Carter says. "Someone maybe was a little bit jealous. All that made me much more leery of being around people and I went into a real shell after that."

That was one more reason he was so different than the man next to him. No, not Chavous, but the very, very complex Lyle Alzado.

In the Clearing Stands a Boxer: Lyle Alzado

Number 77, Defensive End, 6-3, 260, 7th Season, Yankton College

With Lyle Alzado, it all depended on your timing.

You might get the Lyle Alzado with the biggest heart in the National Football League, a hulk of a man who could have tears dripping down his cheeks as he walked out of a room at Children's Hospital, or have kids in a classroom spellbound when he tried to scare them straight or coax them into raising their grades.

You might get the Lyle Alzado with the explosive, violent temper and the inability to forgive.

You might not only get different Lyle Alzados, you might get stories and interpretations of his past that could change from day to day, week to week, year to year, writer to writer. The most extensive interviews he ever did were those that produced *Mile High: The Story of Lyle Alzado and the Amazing Denver Broncos.* Alzado is listed as the author, with collaborator Paul Zimmerman, and the publisher insisted on rushing it into print early in 1978. It comes off as mostly raw transcriptions of interviews, with quotation marks around much of the text with little transitional narrative or exposition. As long as that is conceded, it did—and still does—shed some light on the subject.

Lyle Martin Alzado.

Some things seemed incontrovertible. His mother, Martha Sokolow Alzado, was Jewish with a Russian family background. His father, Maurice Alzado, was Italian-Spanish. Lyle was the second oldest of five children, and he had two brothers and two sisters. Although some newspaper stories later would say he spent part of his childhood in Harlem, that apparently isn't correct, and the most common version was that he spent his first ten years in the Brownsville section of Brooklyn and then moved to the Cedarhurst section of Long Island.

In his book, Lyle said that his father wasn't around much, but when he was, he was abusive of Lyle's mother and often was drunk. Lyle said that his father put him in boxing gloves when he was about eight and tried to teach him to fight, delivering punches to his son as part of the lesson. He said his father had claimed to be a successful boxer at one point in his life, but that Maurice didn't provide many details or evidence.

Lyle said he began fighting—and fighting a lot—in grade school, especially after other kids made fun of his limited and threadbare wardrobe, and that he knocked a kid named Massoni unconscious. He said he never was religious, and he apparently didn't fear lightning striking him down after he was caught stealing money from coats while the family attended services at the temple in Cedarhurst.

Alzado said that when his mother at one point left Maurice, Lyle ended up brawling with his father because Maurice followed Martha home and seemed to be on the verge of threatening her. Lyle said police came and tossed Maurice in jail, but that his father saw to it that Lyle was charged with assault, too. Lyle said he was stabbed several times, the first when he was caught flirting with a roughneck's girlfriend in a Rockaway bar—long before Lyle was 21, of course—and began carrying a straight-edge razor himself. He seemed to have used it.

At some point in there, Maurice left the family—for good.

At Lawrence High School, Lyle said, he at least showed up for classes most of the time, but was an indifferent and unsuccessful student. On the football field, playing for coach Jack Martilotta, he was a terror and a star.

"Our nickname was the Golden Tornadoes," he told Dick Connor when Connor shadowed Alzado for a day in the spring of 1977. "Other teams were afraid—literally, they were afraid—to come in to play us. They didn't want to. We'd break 'em up. We won the championship. Now a lot of those guys are in jail. I know one, he was a 9.6 sprinter. He's not doin' nothing. 'Just layin' back, drinkin' wine and feelin' fine,' he tells me."

There were several different versions of how he ended up playing for Yankton College in South Dakota. Occasionally in later years, he made it sound as if he made a calculated decision to seek out a small college. But in his book, he acknowledged that his grades were a problem for major programs, and that when one of his high school coaches funneled him toward New Mexico State, the Aggies eventually rejected him. In his book, Lyle said he assumed they had both checked his grades and discovered that he had spent "a couple of nights" in jail.

He ended up at Kilgore Junior College in Tyler, Texas. He said Kilgore tried him at wingback, didn't like him there, and told him he wasn't wanted. When he returned to Long Island, Lyle said, he and Martilotta looked through his letters from college programs and the high school coach jumped on Yankton as a viable alternative and announced Lyle would go to Yankton.

In 1973, however, he told the *Denver Post*'s Jim Graham: "I wanted to go real badly to New Mexico State but I didn't have the grades. But I was more afraid of getting lost and not having the opportunity to establish myself as a football player and an individual than anything, so I chose Yankton."

Yankton worked out for him. It was there, he would say later, that he began using steroids in a successful attempt to bulk up and reach the NFL, and he was an all-league choice twice in the Tri-State Conference. He told Graham he was the regional Golden Gloves heavyweight champion, too, and that he beat future heavyweight contender Ron Stander in the finals in Omaha. He haunted the weight room, and there was no doubting either his determination or the development of his affinity for working with handicapped children, which he said began with a chance encounter with a group of children in the Yankton gym.

Stan Jones, then in his first stint as the Broncos' defensive line coach, had car trouble on a scouting trip—the assistant coaches also scouted at the time—and wound up killing time at Montana Tech in Butte, Montana.[5] He asked to look at game film, and he found himself increasingly enamored of a Tech opposing player in the Copper Bowl—Yankton College's number 80. That was Lyle Alzado, and while it would be wrong to portray this as the Broncos being the only team that had any knowledge of him, Jones pushed for Denver to draft him and was peeved when the Broncos didn't take him in the second round. (Alzado told Graham that the Cowboys and Saints both told him they would take him in the first or second round.) The Broncos didn't have another choice until the fourth round, but Alzado still was there.

"I remember when the draft was—January 24, 1971," Alzado told Dick Connor. "It started at 9 a.m. . . . I got up at 5 that morning and went over to the athletic director's office and never left. I sat there all day. At 4 that afternoon, I was still in the same chair when the phone rang. It was Lou Saban. He said, 'Lyle, you are now a Bronco.' I was so happy I knocked the projector off a table running out. I broke the door. It was the happiest moment of my life."

Martilotta, his high school coach, joined him in Denver for his first visit. That summer, Alzado was pressed into the starting lineup as a rookie when veteran Pete Duranko suffered a torn knee ligament in an exhibition game. He had a good year and returned to Yankton to finish up work for his degree in special education and met Sharon Pike, who would become Sharon Alzado in May 1975.

Saban was fired during that '71 season, and Alzado professed to like Ralston for at least one season. In fact, this is what he told Jim Graham in 1973: "John Ralston is the finest thing that ever happened to me. He taught me how to win in football and in life. When I sit in that locker room before a game and he tells us there is no way we can get beat, my eye seems to catch his, and he kind of tells me without saying anything, 'You're the best in the world. Now go out and prove it.' "

The relationship obviously soured. Alzado was unhappy as soon as 1975. He said in his book that Ralston "double-crossed" him when he asked permission to leave training camp "one year" to troubleshoot some financial matters—implying some of his family members had written checks he needed to cover. He said Ralston told him to stay, that the coach would have it all taken care of. Alzado said Ralston did nothing.

In the first game of the 1976 season, playing tackle at Cincinnati, Alzado suffered a season-ending knee injury when a Bengal fell on his leg. Actually, it wasn't only the first game. It was the first *play*. He underwent major surgery and did a slow boil as he saw the Broncos go through that mixed-bag 9-5 season, believing both that Ralston was in over his head and that the coach had betrayed him.

Then he was by far the most outspoken player in the postseason revolt. In his book, he said: "I was in the Dirty Dozen. We've been called everything. I don't care. We had to do what we felt was necessary. We just couldn't relate to [Ralston] as a head coach. People told me, 'Get out of town.' Some players didn't like it. Fine. I'm my own man. I stood for what I believed. It was hard to do. To say the least, I knew I was gone if he had stayed. I asked Fred [Gehrke] to try and work out a deal for me."

Next, he listed the Dirty Dozen.

In addition to himself, he identified Billy Thompson, Bill Van Heusen, Paul Smith, Tom Jackson, Riley Odoms, Otis Armstrong, Rick Upchurch, Louis Wright, Tommy Lyons, Mike Current, and Haven Moses. There are at least a couple of problems with that list. Current, a former Bronco, had played the 1976 season with the *Tampa Bay Buccaneers*. Wright, of course, was a Ralston loyalist who wasn't even in town at the time. Plus, neither Smith nor Odoms was listed in the original media reports as being among the twelve at the Holiday Inn. Alzado seems to have replaced four men listed in media accounts—John Grant, Jon Keyworth, Jim Kiick, and Carl Schaukowitch—with Smith, Odoms, Current, and Wright. That was one more piece of evidence that Alzado's world often didn't coincide with reality.

He also put the number of players who signed off on the original petition as "36 or 37." That's absurd. And he lamely said that one player—whom the follow-up text to that section identified as Van Heusen—left a copy of the original petition behind, perhaps deliberately, for a reporter to discover. Actually, that original petition was leaked by more than one player.

In the book, Alzado explained that the beginning of his falling-out with Ralston came at training camp in 1972, when, he said, the new Ralston staff had forced star defensive end Rich Jackson to scrimmage on a knee too soon after surgery and all but ruined him. But a year later, he was telling Jim Graham that Ralston was the "finest thing" that ever happened to him? One way or another, he was being disingenuous.

And then there is Billy Thompson's remembrance—which might or might not coincide with the training-camp crisis referred to in *Mile High*—about Alzado telling him he was mad at Ralston for not getting an Alzado buddy out of jail.

He did get around to saying in his book, "In some ways, Coach Ralston was a good man. He just wasn't a good coach. It's as simple as that."

That's harsh, but a lot of his more reasonable teammates shared that opinion. But Alzado's eventual enmity for Ralston seems to have been far from that "simple."

Forget all of that for a second.

Lyle Alzado was a terrific football player in his prime, though his teammates later would joke that many of his credited "assists" came for falling on the pile and they believed that his self-promotion wore a little thin. But his fire could be spotted from the third deck. Or felt on the other end of the defensive line.

"He was so competitive," says Barney Chavous. "I remember one time we were playing the Raiders and the Raiders were beating the devil out of us. He would get frustrated. He didn't want anyone beating him at anything. That's the competitive side of him. Art [Shell] was holding Lyle and Lyle turned around and kicked him. The official threw a flag. Fifteen yards. Art went back to the huddle laughing, because he had gotten what he wanted out of Lyle. He wanted Lyle to lose his cool.

"So Rubin [Carter] went to Lyle. He said, 'Lyle, you can't do that, you see him over there laughing?' And a light went off in Lyle's head. He looked at me and he said, 'He got me, Barney, he got me.' I said, 'That was the whole point! You can't let them get to you like that.' From that point on, Lyle played a good game. But Lyle was so emotional about things."

Carter says, "He had that New York mentality where he'd try to take you into a corner and beat you to a pulp. And we needed that as a football team."

Tackle Claudie Minor spent part of his career working against Alzado in practice.

"Lyle was complex and intense," Minor says. "He liked to be the king of the mountain and liked for younger folks to be subordinate, and when I came in, I wasn't having it. He and I used each other to kind of get the practice going. I would make comments that he didn't like. When the offense and defense come together, whether it was 9-on-7 or whatever, if it's defensive day, I have to turn my burner down to five-eighths. And he's supposed to go 75 percent.

"Well, I was taught to go full speed all the time, that's how you avoid getting hurt. I missed two games in my career. He didn't like that, but that's just the way I practiced, I practiced full speed. So it made us both better, we just had to fight a lot along the way. But know what? When I'd be at my folks' house in Pomona, he'd come up from L.A. and we'd go out to dinner. We were friends off the field."

Alzado often would come into the dressing room—whether at halftime or after the game—and go off.

"I just thought he was crazy," says Billy Thompson. "He'd come in and go off, and start yelling and screaming and banging on the lockers and say we had to get going. I'd say, 'Lyle, I'm already at 100 percent.' He'd say, 'Oh, I'm not talking about you.'"

Away from the field?

When it came to working with children—handicapped, sick, otherwise challenged—there never has been and never will be anyone in a Broncos uniform more praiseworthy than Lyle Alzado. He didn't mind the cameras or reporters recording it, but his passion was not phony. He went to hospitals, to schools, to Special Olympics, to benefits, to darned near anywhere anyone asked him to go, as long as it was about kids. That day Dick Connor shadowed him in early 1977, as he continued to rehabilitate his knee, he went to a school in Brighton and to Children's Hospital. He won too many humanitarian and man of the year awards to fit on a mantle, and he deserved them.

Alzado attended many functions with Governor Dick Lamm, and Lamm says although they weren't bosom buddies, they developed enough of a friendship to run together "four or five" times.

"One of my security officers would set it up," Lamm recalls. "I really did enjoy Lyle. He really was a unique human being. But he was *so* competitive. We'd be running along, and there would be sort of an imaginary finish line. Nobody's racing. But he just *had* to beat me."

His dark side remained largely hidden.

Notes

1. In 2007, Mike Landess is the coanchor on Channel 7's news.

2. "The Bobbsey Twins" was the name of the Knisley-Frei two-man Whiffleball team, winner of the 1979 Colorado Whiffleball Federation's (motto: *Better Living Through Plastic*) state tournament in the backyard of Colorado High School Athletic Association executive Bob Ottewill.

3. Neal Rubin went from Greeley to Las Vegas to Detroit, and he is the longtime and popular columnist for the *Detroit News*. He also writes the comic strip *Gil Thorp*.

4. In 2007, Sylvester Croom is the head coach at Mississippi State University.

5. Part of the lore, often repeated, was that Stan Jones was stranded in Yankton. That's not correct.

CHAPTER 7

Paving the Way

I didn't come here to sing.

—CLAUDIE MINOR

From the Gate: September 11–25

Sunday, September 18 vs. St. Louis Cardinals, Mile High Stadium
Sunday September 25 vs. Buffalo Bills, Mile High Stadium

On his Monday night coach's show—*The Broncos with Red Miller*, hosted by affable KBTV/Channel 9 sportscaster Lynn Sanner—Red Miller tended to be relentlessly positive. But he at least acknowledged there and everywhere else that the injury to Bill Bain and the shuffling in the offensive line meant he hadn't been able to get his starters in place and have them all playing together in the final two or three exhibition games.

With teams about to make difficult final cuts, the Broncos made another deal, acquiring second-year running back Jim Jensen from the Cowboys for a 1979 draft choice. Miller and the Patriots staff had coached him in the Senior Bowl, and Red jumped at the chance to get a versatile backup and special teams player. Denver's final cuts were running backs Jim Kiick, the former Larry Csonka running mate with the undefeated 1972 Dolphins, and Mike Franckowiak, the number-three draft choice in 1975 who had been converted from quarterback to fullback; tight end Boyd Brown; and tackle Harvey Goodman. Goodman's departure was a clear sign that Miller was committed to at least opening the season with Maurer at left tackle.

Rookie linebacker Rob Nairne, an undrafted free agent from Oregon State, was one of the surprises, making the roster and joining veteran Godwin Turk and second-year man Larry Evans as the backups to the Big Four. In the defensive backfield, rookie free agent Larry Riley from Salem College was still around, and he and the other two reserve defensive backs—veteran Randy Poltl and second-year man Chris Pane—would be important on special teams. Providing further evidence that the rookie-show skit didn't offend Miller, rookie free agent Ron Egloff was going to be Riley Odoms's backup at tight end.

The Rockies still had sold only 2,300 season tickets, and I was wondering if Vickers regretted not selling—or simply hadn't gotten a bona fide offer. He called a news conference at his Vickers Energy Corporation offices, in an upper floor of one of the downtown skyscrapers, to pump the season ticket campaign. Later in the week, GM Ray Miron told me that he had reached an agreement with Harold Ballard, the irascible, profane, and penny-pinching owner of the Toronto Maple Leafs, to get first crack at players who couldn't make the Toronto roster in training camp and might have to be farmed out—and paid—if nobody would take them off the Leafs' hands.

I was new on the beat, but I didn't think they had to do that in Montreal.

Senator Gary Hart was embarrassed, but also proud, because a recent *Washington Post* story portraying the Senate as a rich men's club had disclosed that he was one of only five senators whose net worth was below $50,000. There was no monkey business there.

Denver heavyweight Ron Lyle, who had started his boxing career after serving prison time for involuntary manslaughter, lost to Muhammad Ali in 1975 and George Foreman in 1976, but neither did anything to diminish his reputation. In fact, his action-filled, fifth-round knockout loss to Foreman was considered an instant classic.

On a September 14 nationally televised *Night with the Heavyweights* card at Caesars Palace that also featured Larry Holmes and Ken Norton fighting soft touches, Lyle won a disputed and roundly booed decision over Stan Ward of Sacramento. It seemed to hurt him more than his defeats against Ali, who in 1977 again was the champion, and Foreman.

Another Denver heavyweight, the portly LeRoy Jones, won a decision over Greg Johnson in the opening fight of the night. He was undefeated, but unheralded, and yet promoter Don King seemed intent on building him into a contender—at least enough of one to warrant a title shot.[1]

September 16, and not Cinco de Mayo, is Mexican Independence Day, and banner- and sign-carrying marchers commemorated the 1977 holiday by starting at three sites—West High School, Columbus Park, and Curtis Park—before converging at the State Capitol. The rally got heated, with speakers criticizing the Denver Police for the recent shootings in Curtis Park and the city's response, and Corky Gonzales excoriated what he called the "Atlantic Ocean wetbacks." Nita Rodriguez of the Raza Association of Media Advocates ripped Channel 7, Channel 9, and both newspapers, saying the "media is downgrading us."

In Boulder, Rosalie Martinez, the state's director of bilingual and bicultural education, reacted to criticism of the programs in her speech to a luncheon feting Hispanic Heritage Week. "The child should be taught in the language he understands best," she declared. "If I gave my entire speech in Spanish, you would turn me off. That's what happens to a child confronted with English alone."

An annual controversy was bubbling over, with residents around Mile High Stadium complaining that Broncos fans were inconsiderate on game day. But it promised to get even more ugly this time because the stadium expansion didn't come with additional on-site parking. "We can't park in front of our own homes," said Fred Trounce. "We haven't even been able to park in our own driveways. The people throw beer cans and trash all over people's lawns." Mary Bustillos, who also lived in the neighborhood, said fans often reacted to requests not to park in certain spots by calling residents "spics" and treating them "like garbage." Residents were planning to pass out flyers to fans, declaring, "If the city won't stop fans from parking in Jeff Park, we will." If the Broncos played defense that aggressively, they would be in good shape.

Irv Moss covered Air Force, but he had to go in for knee surgery, so I temporarily took over the Falcons football beat for a couple of weeks, wedging it in while I prepared for the Rockies' training camp. Falcons coach Ben Martin was facing some pressure in his 20th season because some were wondering if it might be time for him to gracefully step aside after doing such a terrific job getting the program off the ground. When I visited the academy early in the week to introduce myself, the word broke that the Los Angeles City Council had approved funding for a delegation to visit the United States Olympic Committee offices in Colorado Springs to lobby to be designated the official U.S. candidate to host the 1984 Summer Olympics. Even in Los Angeles, the bid was facing considerable skepticism: The Olympics had been an economic disaster for Montreal in 1976, something that caused many to grudgingly concede that Lamm's drive to reject the Winter Olympics had been prudent. L.A. couldn't afford a North American reprise, and how could we subject the rest of the world to that traffic?[2]

The *Post* began an eight-part series on Denver's role as an energy capital, posing the question of how the area would cope with the potential for exponential growth, caused in part by many connected to the oil industry moving to the Denver area. "The future of Denver is untold, unbounded and unlimited," billionaire Marvin Davis told reporter Carl Miller in his office in his Metrobank Building downtown. "Energywise, this is the future of the United States. . . . I see the greatest future in the world for Denver, and for the energy business."

In the piece, Dick Lamm again said Denver couldn't turn into another Los Angeles. "Each city has only one moment in history to decide whether it will create urban sprawl or accept the challenge to do something exciting and different," Lamm said. "Los Angeles had only one opportunity, and it failed." Lamm argued for core development in Denver, rather than suburban sprawl.

On Saturday, I saw California beat Air Force 24-14 in Berkeley. It was my first visit to the onetime radical hotbed—well, the still-radical hotbed— and I walked around and explored People's Park and the once-occupied Sproul Hall, site of the original Free Speech movement sit-ins. I swore I still could hear Joan Baez singing. I remembered picking up imported copies of the *Berkeley Barb* in Eugene, reading them, and knowing that as open-minded as my parents were, I'd have an easier time explaining *Playboy* than the radical newspaper's ranting profanity.

Those days of protest and anger were long behind us. And as near as I could tell, nobody protested the Falcons' appearance in Berkeley—or even saw anything ironic about it.

Meanwhile, in Boulder, Jeff Knapple threw for 278 yards in CU's 42-0 win over Kent State.

On Sunday, the Broncos completely shut down the Cardinals' big-play offense, but nobody in the Denver camp was doing cartwheels over an ugly 7-0 victory in the opener. The only touchdown came on Otis Armstrong's 10-yard run in the third quarter. Rob Lytle says the score should have been worse. "It was probably the most boring game and thank God we had a great defense," he says. "I was embarrassed because we had a huge hole and I could have gone 40 yards for a touchdown—and I tripped over Tom Glassic's foot. I made 12 yards but it should have been a touchdown."

Late in the game, the defense stopped the Cardinals on the Denver 7.

"That was like a defining moment, that we could win our first game 7-0," Randy Gradishar recalls.

The Nuggets also opened training camp under Larry Brown on Monday at the Air Force Academy. Brown also made it clear to the players in a team meeting that he didn't want to be blindsided by reports of team dissension, as he had been the season before.

(Hmmm, the player dissension hadn't cost him his job.)

"Every team has problems and I feel it is easier for eleven players to adjust to the coaches rather than have the coaches adjust to one player," Brown told longtime Nuggets beat writer Ralph Moore of the *Post.* "I told them this in our meeting, that they are to come to me to work things out, that there is nothing here we can't solve."

At the Rockies' camp in Littleton, rookie defenseman Barry Beck—the top overall choice in the '77 NHL draft—was looking every bit as good as advertised. The Rockies were pushing the party line that with young star forwards Wilf Paiement, whose father had wrestled bears at carnivals and who played with his father's spirit, and Paul Gardner, plus Beck, they had a bright future. It made perfect sense. If they showed patience.

Miller still was trying to accelerate the meshing of the offensive line. During a practice that week, the coach tried to demonstrate a point while working with tackle Claudie Minor. Minor's helmet struck Miller in the head, and a torrent of blood was running down his face. The coach acted as if nothing happened and when Minor pointed it out, Miller told him to ignore it, too.

But it was hard to ignore the John Hannah rumors. Hannah, the Patriots' all-pro tackle, who loved Miller, had walked out of camp—along with guard Leon Gray—and was holding out. Both had contracts but were unhappy with them. Hannah had asked to be traded to Denver or Tampa Bay, but the interconference trading deadline was past, so the AFC Broncos were the major possibility—if the Patriots traded him. Miller had even joked that when he called Chuck Fairbanks, the Patriots' head coach had greeted Miller with, "What'll you give me for him?"

The Patriots had filed a grievance, seeking to force Gray and Hannah to return, and they said they were determined to keep both. If it came down to a trade, it was obvious the Broncos would be first in line, and the speculation was that New England would seek at least Otis Armstrong—and perhaps more. Meanwhile, Hannah was sitting at home, at his farm in Alabama, faced with choosing between doing chores or watching the season's new television shows, including a stinker the nation's critics were blasting even before the first episode was shown. *The Love Boat* seemed destined to be a shipwreck.

With the Bills coming up, Dick Connor caught up with Buffalo's star running back on the telephone. O.J. Simpson had turned 30, and he was assuming his career was winding down. "There are times when I'm filling out a form or something I'll put down 'actor' under occupation, but I'm still a football player," Simpson said. "I know football has been responsible for a majority of the positive things that have ever happened to me." A few days earlier, he had been on a television movie of the week, starring with Elizabeth Montgomery. The movie's title: *A Killing Affair*. Montgomery and Simpson were police detectives, investigating several grisly murders.

On Saturday, CU routed New Mexico 42-7, CSU picked on Northern Colorado 48-10, and Air Force kicked Pacific 15-13.

An easy 26-6 home victory over Simpson and the Bills pushed the Broncos to 2-0. O.J.'s longest run of the day was 10 yards, and he gained only 43 yards on 15 carries, apparently showing the effects of a sprained ankle that hampered his cutback ability. Asked about Denver's linebackers afterward, he said, "Oooh, bad dudes."

Buffalo's only score came on a fumble return for a touchdown, so the Broncos defense still hadn't given up any points.

Morton threw only eight times as the Broncos controlled the ball and put the game away with a six-minute drive in the third quarter.

Some fans booed Armstrong, the subject of the trade speculation, during the pregame introductions, in part because he had pulled up on one run against St. Louis the previous week. But against the Bills, he was the best running back on the field, getting 96 yards on 20 carries. "According to the newspapers, that game was going to be my last game in the orange!" Armstrong recalls, chortling. "I scored a touchdown and should have had it one play earlier because I broke away and got tackled on the 1-yard line. But they gave me the ball the next play and I just dived over."

Armstrong wasn't trying to hide his disappointment with most likely facing a season of carrying the ball far less than in the past, and he—and everyone else—knew that if Miller had to give him up to get a top-flight lineman, he would do it. Nothing personal against Armstrong, but the former offensive line coach thought the men up front were the foundation.

If Otis stayed, he would be running behind that patched-together offensive line. At least right guard Paul Howard, the fifth-year pro from

Brigham Young, seemed to be fully recovered after missing the entire 1976 season with a back injury. Mike Montler, the old Marine, was fitting in at center, and the other three starters were a disparate group. One, Tom Glassic, played with toy soldiers and studied Napoleon. One, Claudie Minor, was a reflective young father who read to his infant daughter for an hour every night and already was thinking of how he might start transitioning to the business world and be able to walk away from the violence of the game. And the other, the recently acquired Andy Maurer, was a good old boy from the Oregon woods.

Junkyard Dog: Claudie Minor

Number 71, Right Tackle, 6-4, 282, 4th Season, San Diego State

One day in Pomona, 30 miles east of Los Angeles, a flatbed Salvation Army truck rolled slowly through a tough neighborhood. The men on the flatbed were playing Santa Claus, tossing out toys to the kids who gathered along the street. One of the men spotted Claudie Minor Jr., at age six or so already far bigger than most of the kids his age. Picking up an old donated football, the man decided: *That kid can use this.* He tossed it, and for a future tackle, Claudie showed good hands, snatching it out of the air.

Claudie came to love that football like a blanket, like a teddy bear, like a first baseball glove. He had fooled around with the sport before, but now it was a passion. Mostly unsuccessfully, he begged to be allowed to play with the older boys in the neighborhood and when they said no, he would sit and watch, crying. By then, his parents had been divorced about a year, and his father was raising him. But they lived next door to his father's parents, who had moved to Pomona in 1941, eventually tearing down an old house, then overseeing the construction of a new home for themselves and a duplex next door. That's where Claudie Jr. was raised, and though it wasn't a life of luxury, the family was comfortable.

Claudie Sr. put together his own small construction, salvage, and mechanic businesses. Whatever was called for at the moment, he did it. Later, young Claudie would watch *Sanford and Son*, the Red Foxx sitcom about the Los Angeles junkyard, and smile at some of the scenes that rang bells. Claudie Sr. made it clear to the boys that they were expected to work, especially if they wanted to have their own money to spend.

"My first job was selling the *Los Angeles Herald Examiner* for 10 cents apiece at the L.A. County Fair," Claudie says in his office in downtown Denver. "I figured out that I would find someone who was inebriated, and he would give me $20 or $10 for the papers, and I'd go to the fair on that for the rest of the day."

When the Minor sons, young Claudie and Curtis, were older, Claudie Sr. would dispatch them to a lot. "We used to tear down houses with sledgehammers and crowbars," Claudie Jr. says. "We cleaned each and every brick and extracted the copper." In later years, Claudie joked that his late father had been "an environmentalist because he was recycling lumber and bricks and other things."

Claudie got to begin playing in pads in junior high, and he helped his school win the local championship three straight years. He wore baseball shoes with rubber spikes until he couldn't fit in them any longer. In his sophomore year at Pomona's Gary Village High School, Claudie already was 6-foot-2 and 245 pounds, and he started out wearing street shoes. The coaches saw that and found him a pair of decrepit high-top football shoes. Claudie nursed them through his career, but only barely. When he was a 6-foot-5, 315-pound senior, one of the sockets for a spike had worn through the sole. So Claudie sliced out that socket, and played with a hole in the bottom of his shoe.

After his final high school game, while still on the field, Claudie ceremoniously took off the shoes. "I left them on the 50-yard line," he says. The next fall, he enrolled at Mt. San Antonio College in nearby Walnut, and he played on the defensive line as a freshman for the two-year community college. But when he dropped out after the football season, his career—and love affair with the sport—seemed to be over. "I was in love, broke, and I needed to buy a pair of shoes and a car, so I went to work for a glass company," Claudie says.

He loaded the formed glass onto pallets. It was hard work, which he didn't mind, but he realized it wasn't an avenue to a career. His Mt. SAC coaches checked around, and the staff at California Lutheran in Thousand Oaks said, sure, they would give him a shot on the defensive line. After he already had moved into a Cal Lutheran dormitory and was preparing for the upcoming 1970 fall practice, the coaches came to him with bad news: His Mt. San Antonio transcripts showed all Fs for his final term. Claudie hadn't officially dropped out. Thinking it didn't matter because he was done with school, he just stopped going to class.

He was angry and embarrassed, in part because his friends and family members had given him a sendoff party as he left for Thousand Oaks. His father said he would come and get Claudie the next weekend, and the Cal Lutheran staff said he could stay for a few more days. In the interim, he watched the Dallas Cowboys going through the final stages of their training camp at Cal Lutheran, and even discovered it was easy to pretend to be one of them and go through the chow lines with them at the cafeteria. "I was amazed by how much food was made available to them," he says. He also told himself those guys were human, certainly no bigger than he was, and he could play with them. Someday.

Temporarily, he went back to work for another glass company. San Diego State's coaching staff, including Don Coryell, was recruiting one of Claudie's high school buddies, Garland Chandler, and Chandler mentioned they should take a look at Claudie, too. They did, and were intrigued, and as the word got around that Minor hadn't committed to any school, some other coaching staffs got in touch with him.

"I hadn't flown and I didn't want to go on any recruiting trips, so I figured I'd just drive down to San Diego," Minor says. "Then when I visited with Don Coryell, he said he didn't need any defensive linemen, so I said I'll play offensive line like the defensive tackle spot—aggressive. And he seemed to like that."

It took some work to clear up his Mt. SAC transcripts and get him in school, but Claudie was eager to give football and school another chance. At the time, Haven Moses had been gone from San Diego State a couple of years and was one of the many pros held up as examples cited to the Aztec players.

Minor and Chandler were SDSU roommates, with all the perks afforded football players. That meant their college costs were paid, but that was it. "I couldn't rub two nickels together," Minor says.

Hot cars? Chandler's father cosigned for a loan, and the two roommates had a 1967 Chevy Impala, agreeing to split the $150 monthly payment. When they were done with all their other expenses, Claudie recalls, "we had about $10 a month each to live off of."

Soon, he was a mainstay on the Aztecs' offensive line. "I had sweet feet and I always committed to lift weights and run," he says. "When I got to San Diego State I was 321 pounds, but when I found out what the opportunities were, I lost 40 pounds. I was lifting weights and had 10 percent body fat."

He loved playing for Coryell.

"You look at him on TV, and he seems gruff, but inside, he's just a sweet guy," Minor says. "He'd cry at banquets. We called him 'The Duck' because he has this lisp, but he was a sweet man and had talented people around him. Jim Hanifan[3] was my offensive line coach when I was first there."

John Ralston and the Broncos claimed him in the third round of the 1974 draft. Shortly after Claudie took the call from the Broncos, the Aztecs' other tackle called him to congratulate him. And as Minor did with all calls that day, he answered it with: "Po' no mo'." Decades later, that teammate still calls Minor "Po' No Mo'."

Shortly after the draft, Minor took an orientation trip to Denver and the Broncos' headquarters. He met Broncos linebacker Tom Graham and also Denver's number-one choice from that draft, Randy Gradishar. Minor and Gradishar had been teammates in a college all-star game at Lubbock, Texas, where their coach was Oklahoma's Barry Switzer, so they told each other it was funny how things could turn out.

Something else struck Minor on his tour. "I couldn't believe how ugly the uniforms were," he says. No, this wasn't a case of him spotting the franchise's infamous original brown uniforms, either. He didn't like orange and blue. Minor had played in red and black at San Diego State. "Of all the places I could be drafted, I had to go to the place with blue shoes and orange jerseys," he says, smiling. "Blue helmets. The shoes were blue and orange. Nobody wears that on the streets."

Minor pauses, and then adds, "But I grew to love the colors and cherish them."

After he signed with the Broncos, he got to go home for Denver's six-week training camp at Cal Poly–Pomona. Because of the NFLPA strike that ended with the union's capitulation, the rookies got more work than usual in '74 camps and my father, Claudie's offensive line coach, paid close attention to him. In Minor's rookie season, he would be protecting veteran Charley Johnson, who had a doctorate in engineering and had undergone so many knee surgeries, he was about as mobile as a typical guy making a living with a slide rule.

The first exhibition game, with the veterans still on strike, was against the New York Jets in Denver. Minor wasn't around for the finish.

"In the second quarter," he recalls, "I drove whoever I was blocking into the linebacker late in the play. The linebacker started cussing and barking at me, and he and I went at it toe to toe. We both got kicked out and as that linebacker was walking off the field, he was flipping off the South Stands. I couldn't believe it."

Minors laughs, because the Jets linebacker, Godwin Turk, later became a Broncos teammate, including in '77.

After the strike ended, the team returned to Denver, and the veterans tried to make up for lost time in hazing the rookies.

At lunch at a hotel near the team's training facility, the vets told the rookies to sing their school fight songs. It was a time-honored tradition, and Gradishar and Tennessee State's Carl Wafer, the second-round pick that year, honored it, singing.

"When it came to me, I continued to eat," Minor says. "I said, 'I didn't come here to sing; I came here to take somebody's job.' So the veterans started instigating. They were saying, 'We got a rough rookie here,' and they were going to sic Lyle Alzado on me."

Minor stood up and started to take off his watch. Ralston, amazed, jumped in and headed off trouble. It was the beginning of that strange relationship between Minor and Alzado, who could have fierce battles on the field in practice, but managed to be friends away from it. "We fought at every practice for three years," Minor says.

Getting thrown in as a rookie turned out to be a positive for Minor, an amazingly quick study. In the next-to-last game, he was matched up with the Oilers' fearsome defensive end Elvin Bethea, who was excited about getting a crack at a rookie.

Before the game began, Bethea asked Minor: "Does your mother know you're out here with me today?"

"I said something profane and not profound to make him think I was a barker," Minor says. "On the first play, I had to deliver a hit and then go get the safety. When I hit him, I put everything I could into it, and I hit something in his face and his face was bloodied up. I ran like hell to go get the safety because I assumed he was right behind me. As I walked back to the huddle, I saw him wiping off his face, and he didn't say anything then. But it was a war the rest of the game. He left the game in the third quarter, but he told [Broncos tackle] Mike Current that I was the best rookie he had ever played against. From a Hall of Famer, I appreciated that."

One of the pleasures of the job was blocking for Floyd Little, who was nearing the end of the line in his long and underappreciated career with the Broncos. In the Broncos' final home game of the '75 season, the writing was on the wall that it would be Little's last game in Denver. Late in the game, with Denver leading, Johnson called a screen pass, and Minor remembers Little announcing in the huddle: "If you all block, this is a touchdown."

Minor's reaction?

"I was thinking, *OK, I'm going to give it to you, baby.*"

Little signed off on his Mile High Stadium career by turning the innocent-looking screen into a marvelous 67-yard touchdown play.

Claudie and Vicki were married in June of 1976. At first, they remained in San Diego in the off-season, where Minor taught a mind and body control class, dealing with many heroin addicts, at San Diego Community Hospital. After the '76 season, Claudie and Vicki decided to move to Denver and make it their year-round home. Already, the energy industry fascinated him, and he was determined to explore using some of the money he was socking away to get into some aspect of the business at some point.

He instantly respected Red Miller, but he wasn't a participant in the anti-Ralston mutiny.

"John was good for me," Minor says. "He drafted me. He put me amongst a group of guys I've grown to love and love to this day. So what might I say bad about him? Nothing. Did there need to be changes? Some places, absolutely. We were a good team. There were other things internally that needed to be fixed, not necessarily John."

When Miller arrived, the longtime NFL offensive line coach discovered that he had an entrenched starter at right tackle.

"Napoleon": Tom Glassic
Number 62, Left Guard, 6-2, 254, 2nd Year, Virginia

Tom Glassic's grandfather, Joseph, was a coal miner, as had been other males in the family tree. Joseph's hacking cough was testimony to the hard work and maltreatment of the workers as he told his grandson of the old days, and he died of black lung disease shortly after Tom graduated from high school. "He slowly suffocated," Tom says in his rustic home in the mountains west of Denver.

Theirs was a three-generation household in Elizabeth, New Jersey. Tom's mother left the family when Tom was eight. Tom and his sister, plus their father, John, moved in with Tom's grandparents. John was a truck dispatcher, grateful to have escaped the mining tradition.

Young Tom was tall and lanky when, at age 12, he tried to join the local Police Athletic League football team. Already his rebellious streak and reluctance to blindly respect authority showed.

"They put us through this horrendous workout," he says. "They were all cops. They were all Vince Lombardi mentality type guys, yelling and screaming at little kids. Boy, it was rough. And the second day they came out with a scale and weighed us in and that's when I found out there was a weight limit. You had to be under 115 pounds. I was 12 and I was 135 pounds and there was no fat on me, either. A cop came up to me and said, 'You're too big, get out of here, beat it.' He didn't say, 'I'm sorry son, you're too big, you can't play, you're too big for these kids, you'll kill 'em.' It was just 'Beat it.' So my first experience with football was very negative."

When he got to high school, he had no intention of going out for the team. But his freshman homeroom teacher also happened to be the freshman football coach and on the first day of class, before he had even taken roll, he spotted the 215-pound kid.

"You. What's your name?"

"Tom Glassic."

"Stand up."

Glassic pulled himself out of his chair.

"Be at the field house after school."

Years later, Tom laughs. "It wasn't, 'If you want to play football be at the field house after school,'" he says. "I was too intimidated not to go. So I went and that's how my career started."

His high school career was injury plagued. He suffered broken fingers that ninth-grade year and played only two games. In the first scrimmage the next year, he was clipped. His femur snapped all the way through.

"Everybody told me, 'That's it, you're not going to play football;

you're not going to play sports. You'll walk with a limp the rest of your life.' But it healed. So then the next year, when I was a junior, I blew out my knee."

He managed to make it through his entire senior season healthy, and with such a late start, he got only two "afterthought" scholarship offers from Virginia and Rutgers, and South Carolina jumped in even later. He decided to go to Virginia, and immediately loved Charlottesville and the campus. "It's more like England than anyplace in the country," he says. "It was very stately."

His freshman season, 1972, was the first after the NCAA passed the rule allowing freshmen to play on the varsity. Glassic was a starter by halfway through his freshman season—and started every game the rest of his college career.

"We were a horrible team," he recalls, laughing. "We were 4-7, 4-7, 4-7, and 1-10. And the 1-10 was because we came from behind to go ahead of VMI by one point, 24-23, and they drove down and missed a field goal at the end. That's how we avoided a winless season."

The Virginia coach was the rough-edged Sonny Randle, a former St. Louis Cardinals receiver.

"We didn't get along at all," Glassic says.

Intrigued by his studies of Napoleon in history courses, Glassic got more serious about his longtime hobby of collecting toy soldiers. "I took all the ROTC military history courses with all the military guys, too," he recalls. "That's when I started painting [the toy soldiers], and the kitchen table always was covered with troops. We had four guys to an apartment. I got the other guys into it; we were playing war games on the table, all the Napoleonic battles. A company made these little boxes of figures, they came with 48 figures, and you could get a whole regiment of guys out of one box, a squadron of cavalry, or a whole battery of artillery."

His admiration for Napoleon cut against the grain.

"Napoleon was the first to award medals to anyone other than officers," Glassic says. "He awarded the Legion of Honor to award actual private soldiers who had distinguished themselves. No one had ever done that before. He was the first to take care of wounded veterans. Before that, you were on your own. He was the first one to take care of the widows and children of dead soldiers. Nobody had ever done that before. This guy, he was incredible! And it went beyond military personnel. The whole legal system is based upon the Napoleonic code. The reason you were able to find my address today was because of Napoleon. He instituted a numbering system for buildings on streets—odd numbers on one side, even on the other."

So why is Napoleon generally not positively portrayed?

"Especially for anything written from the British or English point of view, he was the ogre," Glassic says. "History's all perspective."

The reflective guard with the toy soldiers on his table was planning on becoming an English teacher. The NFL? He wasn't counting on it.

"They were telling me I would be drafted in the fifth to eighth round because we were 1-10," he says. "Sonny Randle and I hated each other and he told all the scouts I was a discipline problem. But my line coach, Joe Mark, and I got along well, and maybe that helped."

On the day of the 1976 draft, most of the attention in Charlottesville was on quarterback Scott Gardner, who had shown enough talent playing for a bad team to be projected as an early round choice. Gardner and Glassic lived in the same apartment building, Glassic directly below the quarterback. A local television crew was in Gardner's apartment.

"All the guys on the team were in his apartment, waiting for the call, and I'm down below waiting for the call, too," Glassic says. "The guys say, 'When Scott gets his call, we'll come down.' I was sitting there and Scott kept getting calls, but they were from his friends. And then I get the call from John Ralston, saying I'm the Broncos' number-one pick. I'm flabbergasted. I ran out on the balcony and said, 'Hey guys, hey guys! Denver first round! No shit!'"

Gardner didn't go until the draft's second day, to Buffalo in the eighth round.

Glassic signed what for then was a fairly standard contract for a late first-rounder. He got a $75,000 bonus and agreed to a rookie season salary of $35,000.

"Are you kidding me?" he asks. "I was a millionaire! I was doing the Ralph Kramden. 'I'm rich! I'm rich!'"[4]

At one of the minicamps, Glassic caused a bit of a sensation during the physical testing when he wasn't able to do a pull-up. "I'm asking, 'I know the college game is different than the pro game, but do you guys have a play where I have to do a pull-up? If you've got one, I'll work on it.'"

He and another Broncos draftee, quarterback Craig Penrose, reported to play for the College All-Stars against the NFL champion Steelers in Chicago. As it turned out, the 1976 game was the final one of the long series. Retired Notre Dame coach Ara Parseghian was the All-Stars' head coach, and renowned offensive mind Sid Gillman coached the line. If Glassic had his way, they would have spent the entire practices letting Gillman reminisce.

"Oh, the stories!" Glassic recalls. "And then he'd say, 'I'd love to keep you guys, we'd kick everybody's ass!'"

In the game at Soldier Field, the Steelers were leading 24-0 in the third quarter when the skies opened.

"The rain was coming down so hard you couldn't see the middle of the field," Glassic says. "The lightning came down and zipped right by [Steelers tight end] Bennie Cunningham's shoulder pads. He looked at me and I looked at him and we looked at each other and I ran in and he ran in and everyone else followed us. They called off the game and that was the last of the Chicago All-Star game."

The next day, the Broncos were playing the Lions in the Hall of Fame Game at Canton, Ohio, and Penrose and Glassic got there just in time to go in the locker room at halftime.

Glassic was wide-eyed.

"It was the most amazing thing I ever saw in my life in football," he says. "Here are the coaches diagramming stuff, rookies over here, veterans out doing their own stuff." A couple of the veterans were smoking cigarettes. "I'm thinking, *I have arrived! This is professional football! This is how it should be, guys are drinking Cokes and kicking back, and they're bullshitting and laughing.* My halftimes in college, I got Sonny Randle crying and throwing things and everybody's cowering because we're behind because we're so bad. He was threatening us with death and starvation."

After the team returned to Denver from Canton, Glassic rode a bus with a couple of other rookies to Fort Collins for the continuation of training camp at CSU.

"I didn't know where to go," Glassic recalls. "The rookies took off and I was by myself with my bag. Nobody greeted me, nobody told me anything. I just started wandering around. I found an assistant trainer who let me into somebody's room and I stayed there for a night. That's how they treated the number-one draft pick in 1976. That was my status. 'Tom who?'"

Glassic started every game that 1976 season, but had trouble keeping his weight up. "By the end of that first season, I was 240, 238, 237 pounds," he says. "You know they had weekly weigh-ins? You're fined $25 a pound for being overweight. Well, I'm fined $25 for being under-weight! So I filled my pockets with change. I'm having guys coming up from behind me and pulling me down, holding my shoulders, to help me on the scale, and they're saying, 'What are you weighing today, Glass Man?' And I'm putting stuff around my neck, like five-pound, two-and-a-half-pound weights, to save a few bucks."

Glassic says he wasn't even asked to help kick out Ralston.

"It was ridiculous," he recalls. "I had no idea what was going on. I heard all these rumors and then I heard that John Ralston was fired through a players' revolt and that didn't make any sense to me. How could that happen? He was the guy who drafted me. He saw something other scouts and other teams didn't see. And I looked at it like I'd had a good rookie year, but that means nothing now. It's a new guy."

Shortly after the Miller regime took over, the Broncos used a first-round pick in 1977 to take Boston College guard Steve Schindler. Glassic remembers thinking, *Thanks for the vote of confidence!*

One of the first times he was on the practice field at a minicamp as the head coach, Miller approached Glassic.

"You don't talk much," he said. "But . . ."

He left it there.

Glassic quickly realized that Miller meant it as a compliment. And before long, he loved Red.

"Logger": Andy Maurer
Number 74, Left Tackle, 6-3, 265, 9th Season, Oregon

When the Broncos acquired Maurer from the 49ers, he brought back memories for my brother, Dave, and me. Andy had played for our father at Oregon—as a Fightin' Duck, and we were familiar with the basics of his out-of-the-wilderness story . . . and with a droll sense of humor some misinterpreted. In fact, the brief stories in both papers made it sound as if the Broncos had acquired a career malcontent.

That wasn't true.

Andy came from near the tiny mountain town of Prospect in south-west Oregon, 45 miles from Medford. Prospect was a gas-station stop on the way to the stunning Crater Lake. "We didn't have a stop light. But we had a stop *sign*," Andy says from his home in Medford.

Ray, his father, was a logger who would go to work in the forest while his kids—Andy plus his four brothers and one sister—walked the mile into town to go to school.

"Our social interaction was a bunch of boys in the woods shooting birds and fishing and building and chopping wood, all the things you do to survive in the wilderness," Andy recalls. "You'd spend all the time getting ready for the winter, make it through the winter, and then go another year."

Every once in a while, his mother, Mahala, loaded up the kids in the car and drove to Medford. To them, it was like New York City. "We dressed up like it was a special occasion and bought bread and potatoes and went back up in the mountains," Andy says. "Or when mom shopped, we'd go to the Criterion Theater and away we go to see a movie. Mom would get done shopping and we'd go back home."

It was a big day in Prospect when the technology progressed enough for Medford's Channel 5 to reach the mountain town. That was their first and only TV station, and Andy got to see some 49ers games, but he never dreamed of playing pro football. That was life on Mars, as far as he was concerned.

The Maurer boys became the foundation of the Prospect High teams for years. Prospect had an eight-man football program. "We only had twelve or thirteen guys on the whole team," Andy says. He was the rare player on that level to get scholarship offers from both Oregon and Oregon State. He selected Oregon just as Len Casanova was about to retire as head coach to become athletic director and Jerry Frei was promoted to replace him.

"I didn't have a clue," Maurer says. "I had a drive that I didn't want to live in Prospect all my life. But none of the recruiting stuff made any sense to me. When I went to Oregon State, they put me up in Beta House, and I slept on a sleeping porch with a bunch of other guys. Now I had just come from home where I'm sleeping with all my little brothers, and that wasn't very interesting to me.

"I went to Oregon and they put me with a kid from Pendleton in a room, just him and me. We made some popcorn and had a beer in the dorm and that made more sense to me. Then I sat down with the scholarship offers in my living room and the Oregon State one said room and board and tuition. The Oregon scholarship had room, board, tuition, and compulsory fees. To this day, I don't have a clue what a compulsory fee is, but it sounded like more at Oregon. So I signed."

He walked onto the Eugene campus at a crazy time,[5] and it was a bit dizzying for the kid from Prospect. "I went to a liberal school and came out more conservative," he says. "People go to Oregon State, a conservative school, and they come out more liberal. All I know is what they were teaching and a lot of the stuff they were doing didn't make any sense to me."

In the spring of his freshman year, he was playing fullback in the Ducks' game against the Oregon alumni when he drew the assignment of blocking San Francisco 49ers linebacker Dave Wilcox. *This guy had played on the TV in Prospect!* "I went and hit him as hard as I could and he knocked me back and split my eye open and knocked my helmet off," Maurer recalls. "He just killed me. I knew he was a pro, and it showed me that I never would play any more than this, so I might as well relax and enjoy. I never had any drive or goal to do anything with the pros because I knew I couldn't play."

Actually, he could, and he had a solid career for the Ducks, playing fullback, slotback,[6] and, ultimately, tight end. For a big guy, he could move. He briefly balked when my father asked him to think about whether he wanted to learn the plays at tight end as well in the spring of 1969. Then at the first practice, Maurer saw another slotback candidate, a sophomore-to-be in the time when freshmen couldn't play for the varsity, run his first pattern as Andy was in line behind him, waiting his turn.

"This kid ran down, put a move on the cornerback, caught the ball and spiked it as he went across the goal line," he says. "It was really impressive. I saw that and I didn't know who this kid was, so I went over to Jerry and said, 'I need some film about this tight end position.'"

The "kid" was Bobby Moore—soon to change his name to Ahmad Rashad.

As a senior, Maurer turned into a bona fide, pro tight-end prospect, catching many of the passes that weren't thrown to Bobby Moore or wide receiver Bob Newland.[7]

On draft day, the Baltimore Colts called and told Maurer they were about to use their third-round pick to take him, and that he would start out as the peerless John Mackey's backup. One slot before the Colts could do that, though, the Atlanta Falcons—who were coached by former Oregon quarterback Norm Van Brocklin—took Maurer . . . and as a guard. He got over his shock, learned the position, and was with the Falcons for four seasons.

"Van Brocklin and I kind of saw eye to eye for a while, and he was a legend, but he was crazy," Maurer says. "He was a controlling, dynamic leader and I admired him because he was a Duck. We talked a lot about fishing. But it came down to that his antics were destroying the football team."

Maurer was the Falcons' assistant player representative during the '74 player strike, and Van Brocklin didn't like that, either. He traded Maurer to New Orleans. "I hated that," Maurer says. "We were losing and I was about ready to pack it up because this football is dumb and stupid. But Alan Page was beating everybody up in practice at Minnesota because he went so hard."

Vikings coach Bud Grant remembered that Maurer had done all right against Page while with the Falcons, and Grant traded for Andy—mainly, Maurer says, so he could go hard with Page in practice "and keep Alan off [Fran] Tarkenton."

He even got to start at left guard for the Vikings in a 16-6 loss to Pittsburgh in Super Bowl IX, in January 1975. He came down with a severe staph infection in his foot in the off-season and had foot surgery. "I worked hard in training camp," he says, "but the club gets you almost well enough so you don't have a workmen's comp claim, and they release you."

The 49ers, though, signed him to fill in for the injured Woody Peoples. But Peoples was back for '77, the 49ers were going to cut Maurer, the Broncos needed a lineman, and voilà . . .

"Denver called and asked, 'Can you play left tackle?' I said sure, I had moved around."

He *hadn't* played tackle?

"Heavens no, I never had played tackle," he says. "But it can't be that hard. Human beings can play it and I'm a human being, so let's go."

That's how the unflappable, adaptable, tough, and extremely-athletic-for-his-size guy from the tiny Oregon logging country got a chance to be the Broncos' starting left tackle in '77.

Still Unbeaten: September 26–October 9

Sunday, October 2 at Seattle Seahawks
Sunday, October 9 vs. Kansas City Chiefs, Mile High Stadium

How strange was this?

During the week leading up to the Seattle game, the Broncos practiced a goofy fake field goal play—one in which holder Norris Weese rolled right and surveyed his options, even considering throwing back to the left to kicker Jim Turner.

It served two purposes. Throwing a pass to Turner, even in practice, allowed the players to break into good-natured laughter and teasing, but also underscored that it could be something to pull out of the bag of tricks somewhere down the line.

With the Republican Party determined to cut into the Democrat dominance of the Colorado congressional delegation, some GOP powers rejoiced when former astronaut Jack Swigert, a Denver native, onetime CU football player, and former combat fighter pilot in Korea, announced on September 26 that he was seeking the nomination for the U.S. Senate in 1978. Swigert was a glamorous candidate because of his Colorado ties, but even more so because he was the command module pilot on the *Apollo 13* mission to the moon when an oxygen tank explosion made it doubtful the three astronauts would be able to return to the earth safely. But in an amazing display of ingenuity, poise, and teamwork with the NASA engineers, the astronauts beat the odds and made it back alive. It all seemed right out of a Hollywood script.[8] Reporters covering the Swigert announcement in Denver had a hard time getting taxis for the rides back to the offices, though. A strike against Yellow Cab, the dominant service in the area, was in its sixth day.

During the monumental 30-7 regular-season road victory against the Raiders, Randy Gradishar checks in with defensive linemen Barney Chavous (79) and Rubin Carter.

Raiders coach John Madden tries to rally the troops—to no avail—during Oakland's home-field loss to the Broncos.

"You see, it was like this . . ." Broncos kicker Jim Turner tells reporters about his touchdown catch on the fake field goal at Oakland.

One of the few bumps in the road was the Broncos' first regular-season loss, a 24-14 defeat at the hands of the Raiders on October 30. Late in the game, Craig Morton confers with quarterbacks coach Babe Parilli and Red Miller, while tailback Rob Lytle (41) and offensive line coach Ken Gray listen.

Otis Armstrong, who spent much of the season adjusting to a downgraded role in Red Miller's system, is stopped against the Raiders.

Against the Raiders, "Bronco Billy" Billy Thompson (36) and Bernard Jackson (29) team up to break up a Ken Stabler pass.

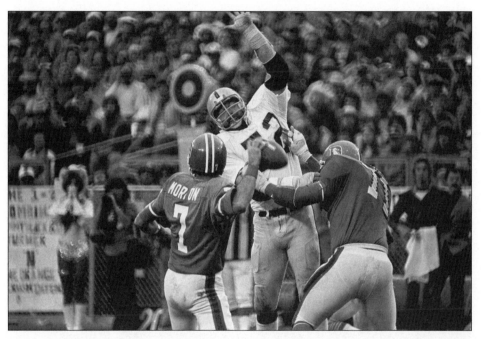

In the three games against the Raiders, Claudie Minor (71) did a good job of keeping Oakland defensive end John Matuszak (72) off Craig Morton, here about to get off another pass.

On the sideline, Louis Wright and Tom Jackson watch the clock during the final stages of the home-field loss to Oakland.

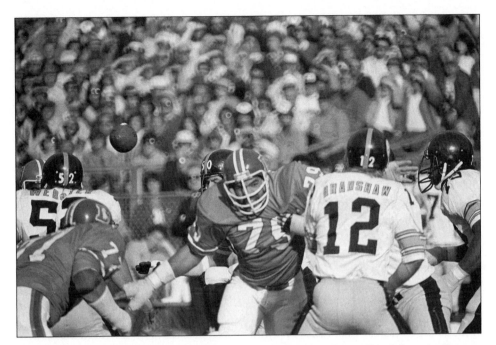

Barney Chavous (79) closes in on Steelers quarterback Terry Bradshaw in the Broncos' 21-7 victory over the Steelers on November 6 in Denver.

Rick Upchurch had only one of his record eight career touchdown punt returns in the '77 season—an 87-yarder against the Steelers—but remained a game-breaking threat as both a return man and receiver.

Red Miller made it clear from the start that he wasn't a huge fan of the Steelers, and especially their defensive line play. In this sequence after the regular-season win over the Steelers, Miller has a few choice words for Pittsburgh assistant coach George Perles; he still is grim-faced as he shakes hands with Pittsburgh head coach Chuck Noll. It foreshadowed Miller's angry challenges of both Perles and Noll at halftime of the AFC division playoff game the next month, a few minutes after Mean Joe Greene punched Denver guard Paul Howard in the stomach.

In the Broncos' 17-9 victory over the Chargers on December 11, Lyle Alzado (77) and Rubin Carter (68) are about to sandwich Chargers quarterback Dan Fouts after he gets a pass away.

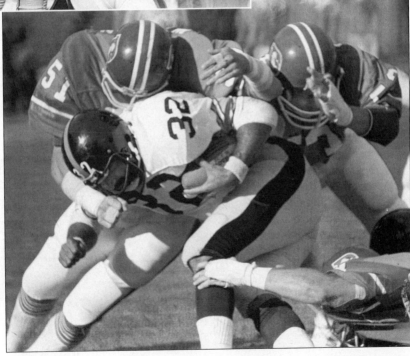

In the Steelers' two games at Mile High Stadium, one in the regular season and one in the playoffs, Pittsburgh's Franco Harris ran for 174 yards—but it took 51 carries. Here, Bob Swenson (51) and Randy Gradishar make the tackle in the AFC division playoff game.

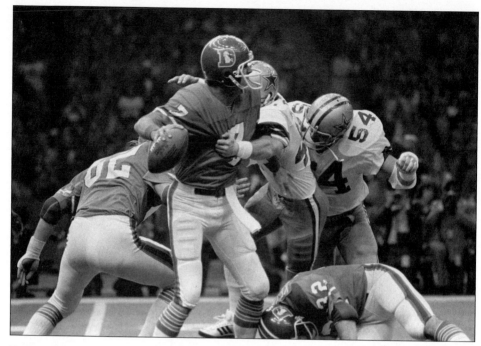

Dallas defensive tackle Randy White pressures Craig Morton as he tries to get off a pass in the Super Bowl. White harassed the Broncos quarterback all night— or at least until Morton left the game in the third quarter.

With Broncos free safety Bernard Jackson (29) covering him, Cowboys wide receiver Butch Johnson makes a diving catch of a Roger Staubach pass in the end zone during the third quarter of the Super Bowl.

After Johnson rolls to his feet minus the football, Broncos cornerback Steve Foley makes a pointed argument that Johnson didn't maintain control of the ball. The official's upraised arms signal the touchdown call—and he didn't change his mind.

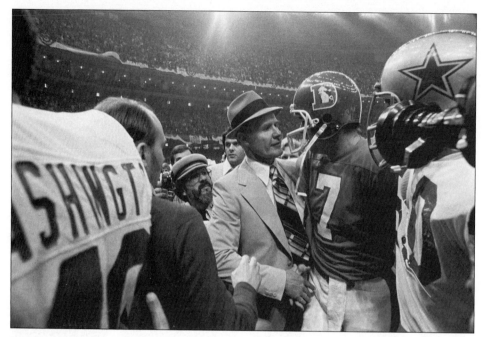

Dallas coach Tom Landry almost cracked a smile as he spoke with his former quarterback, Craig Morton, following the Cowboys' Super Bowl victory.

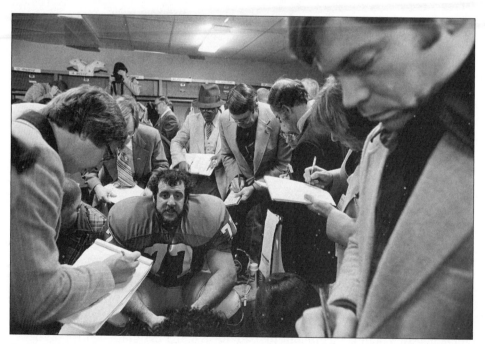

A somber Lyle Alzado is making no move to get out of his uniform and head to the showers as he speaks to reporters following the Super Bowl.

In a public forum at a church in the Capitol Hill neighborhood to the east of downtown, Mayor Bill McNichols was defiant when some residents bitterly denounced what they considered his abominable support of speed-encouraging one-way streets in the area and growth in the city, period. "People are going to continue to move here," the mayor said. "In Russia, they can and do control where they want people to be, but we don't do that here. The growth of the five-county metropolitan area is phenomenal and will continue to be so."

The feisty mayor also was asked if he would appoint gays to the Committee on Community Relations. He said that as far as he knew, he might already have done so. "I sure as hell never asked anybody that question," he said.

The huge and fancy Westminster Mall opened to great fanfare on September 29 with a ribbon cutting utilizing the famous $10,000 Zales diamond scissors. It didn't seem any different than the other new malls, but it did fill a need in the northwest suburban corridor.

On this and every Wednesday during the season, a varying pool of Bronco players gathered for Bible study and fellowship. The regulars included Randy Gradishar, Steve Foley, Rubin Carter, and Barney Chavous.

Less than a month removed from another Labor Day Muscular Dystrophy Telethon, Jerry Lewis roared into town for his run at the Turn of the Century and was his irascible self in promotional interviews. The *Post*'s Barry Morrison, among others, marveled at his energy at the ancient age of 51. "Most people can't work a 20-hour day," Lewis told Morrison. "Doctors have told me it isn't humanly possible to do it. The secret to it is this. The only way you can survive is if you want to do something intensely enough. Then you can get the power of 20 men."

Lewis's competition on Wednesday night, at least with those willing to drive to Boulder, was singer-songwriter Billy Joel, four years removed from his smash-hit "Piano Man." He was appearing at Macky Auditorium on the CU campus, in the same building that housed the CU Journalism School. He sounded as if he didn't mind the smaller venue. "I've met the big stars, and they're only in it for the money," he told *Post* writer Grant Tyson. "I'm in it 'cause it's the only thing I do. I don't know what else I could do besides write songs."

In Nuggets camp, Larry Brown's major concern was trying to find a backup center for Dan Issel in the wake of the off-season trading that brought in guards Brian Taylor and Bobby Wilkerson and shipped out Marvin "The Human Eraser" Webster. The Nuggets still hoped that their top draft choice, Tom LaGarde from North Carolina, would recover from spring knee surgery and be full strength on opening night. Every once in a while, we raised eyebrows about the Nuggets' obvious preference for players who came from either Dean Smith's program at North Carolina or the state's other schools. But the Nuggets quieted some of that concern, cutting Monte Towe, the 5-foot-5 guard who had played with David Thompson at North Carolina State and who at times seemed to have been signed and be around mainly because of his friendship with the team's star. Brown admitted he found cutting Towe difficult, in part because he had been an undersized guard himself.

Miller was open about his continuing interest in exploring a possible trade for the Patriots' disgruntled John Hannah. On Thursday, September 29, the league's grievance committee ruled that Hannah and Leon Gray had binding contracts and would have to report or go on the retired list. Hannah said he would have to decide whether to report or retire. Miller said he probably would at least contact the Patriots to check into Hannah's situation—and, presumably, his availability.

The next day, after Miller publicly said he indeed had talked with Chuck Fairbanks about Hannah and Gray, GM Fred Gehrke issued a statement that, in stilted and formal wording that read as if someone else had written it or it came with a gun to his head, emphasized that the Broncos respected the league grievance committee's ruling. Gehrke said Denver hoped they would return to the Patriots' fold and that the Broncos had "absolutely no interest" in a trade until or unless Hannah reported.

An eventual trade didn't seem impossible. But it seemed more likely that the Broncos would have to make do with the line it had. With a status quo roster, Miller's other options would have been to consider giving more time to one or more of the reserve linemen—Bobby Maples, who clearly was winding down his career; Glenn "Lumpy" Hyde, a former WFL player whose work ethic and sense of humor made him one of the most popular guys on the team; and rookie Steve Schindler, the number-one draft choice who didn't seem ready for a starting role.

Many of the players that night watched the NBC telecast of Muhammad Ali's 15-round decision over Earnie Shavers—the man Ali dubbed "The Acorn"—in Madison Square Garden. Ali started slowly, but closed the fight with a flourish, easily winning the final round to remove any doubt that he would get the decision.

He still was *The Champ.*

A group of Chicano state legislators blasted Governor Lamm for the selection process and his actual choice of a successor to Raul Rodriguez, director of the Department of Regulatory Agencies. Lamm appointed Denver attorney Gail Knapper to the position, and the legislators were angry that there no longer were any Chicano department directors in the Lamm administration. His point at the time was that it was wrong to label specific positions "minority positions" and dictate that minorities must replace minorities. Looking back, he says, "That's always a tough problem. I can understand their viewpoint. . . . Raul Rodriguez was terrific. I really do think that one of the difficulties in being a Democractic governor is that you do have to punch all these tickets, and you have to do it simultaneously. I had a black lieutenant governor, George Brown, and Wellington Webb picketed my [1975] inauguration. Again, I don't resent that, I understand what he was saying, but it's really hard to put together a competent cabinet when you have all the gender and ethnic issues."

Despite his liberal reputation and leanings, Lamm didn't pander.

In Boulder, anger, violence, and chaos at a student government—officially, the University of Colorado Student Union (UCSU)—executive council meeting on September 29 kindled memories of the Vietnam War era. Student body copresident Dan Caplis, a junior political science major from the Chicago area who was planning to attend law school, sponsored a controversial bill to allow individual students to decide whether part of their $93-a-semester student fees would be passed on to various campus organizations. When the other two copresidents vetoed the bill after it passed the student legislature, Caplis resigned the presidency to be an advocate of the bill and lead the campaign to override the veto.

The measure involved only $1.60 per student. If implemented, students could use a "negative checkoff" on the fees card at registration to dictate that the $1.60 go to a fund for the University Memorial Center, the health center, and the recreation center—rather than to the 38 student groups, many of them for minorities, designated to receive student fees. (There were a total of 109 recognized student groups, so far from a majority were receiving funding from student fees.)

As the bill was pending, Caplis repeatedly tried to explain his stand. He said he wasn't being intolerant, but wanted to give students freedom of choice about whether to contribute to the specified student organizations—especially those involved in political actions—and fire a preemptive strike against a movement in the state legislature to ban such mandatory student fees.

Caplis today is an attorney and prominent talk show host on Denver's KHOW radio. Looking back, Caplis says, "The state legislature was going to act, so this was an effort to give students the choice that I thought they should have, but at the same time try to make sure the groups could survive. The key to EC-4 was that you wouldn't get your money back if you opted out of funding the groups, but it would go to the fund that would benefit other campus facilities. But if you truly as a matter of conscience objected to your money being used to fund these political groups, you had the appropriate out. But if it was just a matter of saving a couple of bucks, no, that incentive wasn't there for you."

The possibility of giving students that negative checkoff option rankled, horrified, and angered previously funded student groups who felt as if the donations should be automatic. The opposition was led by the Boulder Student Coalition, which represented 13 student groups— including Boulder Gay Liberation, an American Indian organization called Oyate, Women's Liberation Caucus, National Lawyers' Guild, Farm

Labor Task Force, Migrant Action Program, United Mexican-American Students, and New American Movement. "I really thought having the groups on campus was to everyone's advantage and that's why I wanted to strike that balance," Caplis says. "I think what had the state legislature fired up was that some of those groups were very high profile and extremely radical."

At a previous meeting of the executive council in the UMC ballroom, Caplis says, it became apparent after the bill's first reading that there might be enough support to override the veto, and some supporters in the audience gave a hint of what their reaction might be if the measure was actually passed. "All of a sudden there was this spontaneous outrage, and I remember at that meeting getting chased through the building and actually hiding in a storeroom upstairs in the UMC," he says. The bill's opponents ran ads in the *Colorado Daily* as the final reading approached, calling for students to mobilize in opposition to the bill and advertising a meeting to rally and strategize. Caplis says he attended that meeting in the Fine Arts building, attempting to explain his position. "The room is absolutely packed with the opponents, and I just walked through the back door. And everybody in the room freezes. I'll never forget this: One brave member of UMAS walked to the back of the room, shook my hand and walked me up to the front of the room so I could talk to the group. That was such a classy gesture." He also points out—as he did then—that he had picketed Jewel markets in Chicago in support of the United Farm Workers. "I wanted to make it clear that this measure was to help them, but not to hurt them, and that it wasn't what some of their violent, radical leaders were telling them," Caplis says.

At the Thursday night meeting, the executive council voted to override the veto and the measure—officially called EC-4—was enacted. As it became clear what the sentiment was and what the vote would be, some advocate students in the audience attempted to intimidate members of the executive council. "There were a handful of people in those groups who were hard-core, front-core radical tacticians from the late '60s and early '70s," Caplis says. "Most of the kids in the groups were more normal and not intent on violence, but unfortunately, a few too many of the others got in there."

Caplis says he twice left the meeting room to call campus police, saying officers should be dispatched to the meeting, because it might turn violent. He says he was walking back into the room after his second call when it was apparent to him the final vote had been taken, and EC-4 had won. He says he knew this because he heard a woman screaming and because "all hell's broken loose" in the ballroom. He says he realized the woman was a friend and EC-4 supporter, Cassie Perlmutter. "Things are being thrown and there's screaming and people are pushing and shoving executive council members," he says. "It's just a mob scene and I get to Cassie and I wrap my arms around her and am starting to lead her to the back door of the ballroom. As I'm doing this, I'm just seeing these guys pummeling people in the ballroom."

And then his lights went out.

"I was clocked," he says.

He lost consciousness and later was admitted to Wardenburg Health Center, where he stayed several days and was treated for a concussion.

He recalls waking up the next morning, looking out the window, and seeing police cars all over the place.

The Buffs' football team didn't have as much trouble on Saturday at West Point, beating Army 31-0. CSU also improved to 4-0, routing Utah 46-7 at Fort Collins, and there were office debates going on about whether the Rams could give the Buffaloes a good game—or if they would be overmatched. But since the Buffs and Rams hadn't played since 1958, we wouldn't find out the answer to that on the field.

I remained on the Air Force beat temporarily, and I—and a lot of others—were starting to wonder whether the '77 team was going to be one of Ben Martin's worst when I saw the Falcons lose 30-3 to Georgia Tech at Atlanta. They were 1-2-1, and the one win was the squeaker over Pacific. The AFA campus, traditionally the most sedate in the state, also was in the midst of a controversy after a Friday morning raid of 12 dormitory rooms and the seizure of unspecified amounts of marijuana. Academy spokesman Colonel John Price subsequently confirmed that nine cadets had been implicated and that it was part of an ongoing investigation of possible drug use at the school.

And, yes, the Broncos were undefeated, too, though a lackluster 24-13 win over the second-season Seahawks at Seattle on October 2 didn't exactly turn a lot of heads. But Miller bristled at the notion that style points should be involved. "Enough is whatever it takes to win the game, and that's all we're really interested in," Red told reporters after the game.

Morton was 12 for 21, for 177 yards, with his 47-yard touchdown pass to Rob Lytle in the third quarter giving the Broncos a 17-7 lead, and the veteran quarterback went 1 yard on a sneak for Denver's final touchdown. Otis Armstrong managed only 29 yards on 11 carries, while Lonnie Perrin had 55 yards on 14 rushes. But because Morton had plenty of time to throw and nobody else had particularly stood out, the Broncos awarded the game ball collectively to the starting offensive linemen.

Especially because of Morton's lack of mobility, the men up front would be one of the keys all season, even more so than expected, and Miller wasn't above massaging them. By midweek, he went on the record, saying he had given up on attempting to trade for John Hannah, who had caved in and reported to the Patriots. Miller also said he had decided against moving guard Paul Howard out to tackle to supplant Andy Maurer.

Years later, Maurer laughs about it all, saying he knows the Broncos always seemed to be looking for his successor that season. "Craig was busted up by then, and we looked at it like they had worked hard to teach us how to hold and all that stuff, so we had to make sure nobody touches Craig. Hey, we all knew that. They brought Craig in and we were winning. It wasn't complicated to figure out who our bread and butter was. We're just linemen and *we* can figure that out. So, yeah, we did everything we could. I was the left tackle and in a few games he found out that I was pretty trustworthy because I'd grab 'em by whatever I could get my hand on because I was not about to let 'em hit the quarterback. We became friends really fast when he found out he could trust me."

Up at CU, the debates turned to what really happened at the student government executive council meeting the previous week. Nobody seemed to be able to agree.

At one news conference, members of the Boulder Student Coalition decried media coverage of the EC-4 vote melee and claimed Caplis hadn't ever been in danger of being seriously hurt. Student Don Holstrom was the group's spokesman, and he conceded that "emotions flared and several isolated, spontaneous and uncontrolled incidents resulted." He claimed that Caplis was "one of the main sparks" of the riot. Regardless, university police officials said they were considering filing charges, ranging from felony menacing to assault, in the wake of the incident.

The next day, three UCSU officers said the coalition's version of the events was absurd and that the violence was disgraceful. They said the council would be willing to press charges against the rioters. Caplis was said to be in Chicago.

Caplis says he first had gone to Copper Mountain for a respite, but had gotten a call from police telling him that he might have been followed. "I remember sleeping that night with a huge butcher knife in my hand," he says. "The thought was to hide out up there until the danger cooled off." Instead, he headed home to Chicago for about a week.

Rob Lytle isn't certain of the timing, but he believes this happened in the middle of a week after the Broncos' third or fourth game.

He and his wife, Tracy, were living in an Aurora apartment. He headed to the car to go to practice and couldn't find the car in the parking lot. The Lytles had only the one car—a Camaro.

"I went back in and said, 'Tracy, did you do something with the car last night?' She said, 'No, you had it.' I said, 'Well, where did I park it?' The last thing in my mind was that someone would steal it. It wasn't that great of a car."

Indeed, it was stolen.

"They never did find it," Lytle says. "The cops said those were cars that could be easily stripped and sold for parts real quick, that they can come in and chop them up."

At the time, he wasn't sweating the car as much as he was getting to the practice facility. He knew his teammates who lived in the area already had headed to the team headquarters. "I ended up getting a neighbor guy to take me," Lytle says. "He actually felt sorry for me. I thought sure I was going to get fined because I was half an hour late."

Welcome to the NFL, kid.

On Saturday, the CU football team improved to 5-0, with tailback James Mayberry running for 250 yards on 24 carries in a 29-13 victory over

Oklahoma State and the highly touted running back from Colorado Springs, Terry Miller. CSU went on the road and beat Texas–El Paso 40-31 to take sole possession of first place in the Western Athletic Conference. Air Force fell to 1-3-1 with a 10-7 loss at Ben Martin's alma mater, Navy, and losing in any intraservice matchup didn't go over well with the AFA brass.

––––––––––

Governor Lamm jogged in his second annual Governor's Cup 10,000-meter run from southeast Denver to the State Capitol. The event commemorated National Jogging Day. An astonishing turnout—800 contestants!—had led to a few traffic tie-ups and complaining phone calls to Denver police from residents. The race wasn't considered competitive, but the winner was CU medical student Sandy Sandoval.

Lamm at the time noted, "This is the best country to get sick in, but the poorest to stay well in."

Years later, I ask him what he meant by that.

"That we spent the least amount of money, made the least amount of effort, and had the least amount of public education on helping people keep healthy," Lamm says. "And that we spent a disproportionate amount on curing people. That separation certainly hasn't changed."

After reflecting for a moment, Lamm adds, "I also spent a lot of time trying to make sure that people knew they didn't have to do a 10K to be healthy. Just put out their cigarette and walk around the block a couple of times. I always had certain mixed emotions about the 10K. I did that because I was a runner and I loved that and that's me. But I tried very hard not to get it confused with the idea that you had to be a runner to be healthy. If people would moderate their alcohol, stop smoking, and walk around the block a little bit, the health statistics would be phenomenally better."

––––––––––

The Broncos shared the front page of the sports section with the Yankees, who closed out the Kansas City Royals with a 5-3 victory on the road in the American League Championship Series and advanced to face the Dodgers in the World Series. That cagey Billy Martin hadn't even started

Reggie Jackson, who had come in late in the game as the designated hitter to deliver an RBI single.

————

In their first major test of legitimacy, the Broncos passed with flying colors against Kansas City on October 9, whipping the Chiefs 23-7. They led 16-0 at halftime and 23-0 after three quarters and coasted. The defense was dominant, limiting the Chiefs to 166 yards of total offense and getting six Chiefs turnovers. Bob Swenson was the defensive standout, grading out to 12 tackles and six assists—a performance that caused Kansas City coach Paul Wiggin to call Miller on Monday and say it was the best strong-side linebacking performance Wiggin had ever seen, and the Associated Press later named him the NFL defensive player of the week.

The Denver touchdowns came on short Otis Armstrong and Craig Morton runs, and Jim Turner had three field goals. Armstrong still wasn't in high gear, gaining only 29 yards against the Chiefs, while fullback Jon Keyworth was the leading rusher, with 59 yards. Morton again didn't have to throw the ball much, was well protected, and went 13 for 21, for 189 yards.

It was a laugher, an ass-kicking and a rout, and longtime Denver fans—who still missed being able to hate and heckle former Chiefs coach Hank Stram, who had moved on to New Orleans—were pinching themselves. In this rivalry, the routs traditionally had gone the other way. The Chiefs had looked inept and disorganized, having 10 and 12 men on the field for punts. "I can remember looking across at their side and thinking, *That's the way we used to be,*" Lyle Alzado said. "Frustrated, hurt, not knowing what to do."

After the game, many of the Broncos retired to the Colorado Mine Company, the Glendale hangout owned by Cindy and Buck Scott that had the Fool's Gold Loaf sandwich Elvis Presley had loved so much.

It also was famous for huge cuts of prime rib, a young and affluent clientele, and increasingly—especially after Elvis left the building for good—for playing host to the Bronco players. Some players were regulars during the week, but after games even the married guys showed up with their wives to be with teammates and watch replays of the games or, more often, to watch *Monday Night Football* there together.

"Yeah, I used to go there, it was right around the corner from where

I lived," recalls Tom Glassic. "It was a riot. I never experienced anything like that before. Walk in there and everything was free, you just tipped the waitresses. It was like a players' lounge."

Young women knew it was the place to be seen, too, especially if they wanted to latch onto someone famous for a night. Or maybe a few nights. If the Mine Company was overflowing, customers could head to the nearby alternatives—discotheques Mr. Lucky's, the Sportspage, Nantucket Landing, and the Lift, plus restaurants Victoria Station, Maxwell's, the Library, Bull and Bush, or Cork 'N Cleaver. There was some concern that the disco craze was slowing down, but at least for the moment, all the places were at least surviving. Glendale had the least stringent liquor license procedures in the metro area, and the tiny enclave had 34 licensed establishments. Within the city limits, there were only 26 single-family homes, and residents otherwise lived in apartment buildings and one trailer park. The first-choice destination for most of the visitors was the Mine Company.

"The married guys went there, too, but they had to behave themselves," recalls Louis Wright, who was a newlywed in 1977. "You had to have the discipline to say 'No, no, no, I'm not looking over there.' And '77 was the year when the Mine Company went to there," he says, raising his hand and drawing a line over his head. "Everybody wanted to get in and it became more exclusive. Before that, anybody could get in at any time, but it became so popular. It was whatever we wanted, free, no charge, and that became the unofficial Bronco headquarters. But in those days, you could go to the Mine Company with everybody around town, players and everybody, drinking, partying, and nobody went to the newspaper the next day and said, 'Hey, I saw Louis Wright and he had a beer and he was trying to.' . . . It was a family. Now, you do that today, it will be on the Internet tomorrow. It was just a different era. I didn't drink during the season. A lot of guys did, but I just couldn't do it."

Morton remembers the Mine Company as only one of the most visible examples of a city embracing the team. It also could happen on the other side of town, when many Bronco players made it a habit of going to the Zang Brewing Company—at Interstate 25 and 23rd Avenue, a short drive from the Broncos' headquarters and near Mile High Stadium—after practice on Fridays to eat hamburgers.

"You could walk into any place and people would stand up and give you applause and you would sign autographs for as long as anybody wanted you to," Morton says. "Nobody thought we were better than the fans. It was just a great love relationship between the city and the team. It could never happen again."

After the win over the Chiefs, the other division rival was coming up. The Raiders.

The Broncos would do anything to try to win it.

Including throwing to a kicker, if need be.

Notes

1. I owe LeRoy Jones. King matched him in a 1979 title fight with Larry Holmes at Caesars Palace, and it was the first of many championship fights I have covered over the years. You've heard writers say high-profile championship fights have the most electric atmospheres of any events they've covered? It's inexplicable and sometimes it doesn't even make sense. It's also true.

2. When the '84 Olympics indeed were in Los Angeles, I covered them and was in Southern California for a month. They succeeded and saved the Olympics only because organizer Peter Ueberroth came up with the system of recruiting sponsors to offset costs.

3. Jim Hanifan later was a longtime NFL offensive line coach who also served as head coach of the Cardinals and Raiders.

4. In one of the classic 39 *Honeymooners* episodes, Ralph Kramden—so wonderfully portrayed by Jackie Gleason—responds in that fashion after hearing in a reading of a will that he has inherited "my fortune." "Fortune" turned out to be the name of the bird owned by the little old lady Ralph used to help board his bus.

5. The basis for *The Witch's Season*.

6. A hybrid position in the Oregon offense that meant the player on any one play could be a slotback, H-back, or flanker.

7. By 1977, both Rashad and Newland were entrenched NFL receivers.

8. Kevin Bacon portrayed Swigert in the acclaimed 1995 movie.

CHAPTER 8

Raiders, Raiders

God bless Norris, he threw it right on the money.

—JIM TURNER

"Ol' Hightops": Jim Turner

Number 15, Placekicker, 6-2, 205, 14th Season, Utah State

The C&H Sugar processing and refinery plant was in Crockett, the town on the north end of the San Francisco Bay area. Bethel and Bayard Turner, husband and wife, both put in their 25 years of work there, and their long hours often left their five children—including Jim, the youngest and self-professed "runt" of the group—on their own.

At the park down the street, Jim recalls, "I'd play over the line, kickball, softball, football, anything. Or I'd go fishing down at the bay and catch striped bass."

Later, during spring breaks and in the summers, in advance of automation at the plant, the "runt" went to C&H, too, and worked in the warehouse, lifting and moving 100-pound sacks for eight hours a day.

Geez, is this vacation ever going to end?

But as he got older, it was apparent sports might be a possible escape. He was the star athlete at John Swett Union High in Crockett, and recruiting coaches offered him plenty of choices—from the University of California–Berkeley to the northwest trio of Oregon, Oregon State, and

Washington State. Then the Cal assistant coach recruiting him got the head position at Utah State in Logan, Utah, and kept recruiting Turner. That coach, John Ralston, was an effective salesman, Turner loved Logan in his first visit, and he decided to take the advice of his older brother, Jack.

Jack's stand was that Jim was coming from a high school with an entire student body of 438, and that Berkeley might be overwhelming. "As I look back now," Jim says in his home in Arvada, "he was right. I couldn't have had a better situation than at Utah State because it was a great little school, and because of the friendliness of the people, and the beauty of Logan."

Under Ralston at Utah State, Turner had a solid—if unspectacular— career as a quarterback. "I was adequate," he says. "The year I left Bill Munson took over and he was a number-one draft choice of the Rams. My future never was going to be as a starting quarterback, not in the pros. In college I was a good leader."

He kicked at Utah State because one day Ralston was desperate and asked if anyone had ever done it before. Turner had in high school. Barely. "In high school, I only attempted two field goals in four years," he says. "In college, I only attempted three. So in that eight-year span, I had only attempted five field goals."

Drafted and cut by the Washington Redskins in 1963, Turner returned to Crockett, and then received a call from New York Jets executive George Sauer Sr., inviting him to be on the team bench when the Jets played an exhibition game at Oakland. He accepted and after the game did some kicking on the field in what amounted to a tryout. He ended up signing a contract for the next season, and he took over the Jets' kicking job after they sent defensive tackle/kicker Dick Guesman to the Broncos as part of a nine-player deal.

"Weeb Ewbank had worked with [Lou] Groza with the Browns," Turner says of the Jets coach, "so I had a master for a teacher. I kicked and punted and kicked off."

Turner says the Jets' signing of Broadway Joe Namath for the 1965 season "made it exciting. He was great. You couldn't ask for a better teammate. He was absolutely a great guy and a leader and tougher than nails. Everytime somebody took a cheap shot at him he just laughed and got up."

At Ewbank's suggestion, Turner tried wearing high-tops in his second year, 1965—and never took them off, so to speak.

After kicking three field goals in the Jets' historic 16-7 victory over the Colts in Super Bowl III, in January 1969, Turner yelled during the locker room celebration: "Welcome to the AFL!"

"Curt Gowdy said it's the single greatest athletic event ever because it saved the merger," Turner says. "Vince Lombardi was sitting in the stands and he saw we kicked Baltimore's ass like a drum and he said, 'They're legitimate.' The merger had been agreed upon but wasn't going to happen because the NFL hated what they called the pitch-and-catch league."

Turner had 34 field goals that 1968 season, and it was recognized as a pro football record. He missed only 12 attempts, and his longest field goal was 49 yards. The straight-on kicker wearing the square-toed shoe wasn't a boomer, but was the most reliable field-goal man in the game. Ewbank was stingy and gave the impression he believed a kicker was an interchangeable minor part, and Turner made it clear he was unhappy and asked to be traded.

Eventually, in early 1971, he was sent to the Broncos for soccer-style kicker Bobby Howfield.

"Was it disappointing?" he asks. "I knew it was coming, I just didn't know where it was coming to. I had played in Denver before, but you know that when you play somewhere, you don't get to see the city. When I got traded here and visited, I called my wife—she and my daughters were in California—and I said, 'I think I found a place we really want to live in and will love.'"

He and Mary Kay had a house built in Arvada, and moved in during 1973. He was one of the NFL's straight-on kicking holdouts for a team that gradually was improving. "You have to realize I'm coming from a Super Bowl team with Namath and [George] Sauer and [Don] Maynard, [Emerson] Boozer and [Matt] Snell. When I got out here, we had a good bunch of guys, but we weren't going to go to any playoffs."

After his former college coach, Ralston, came in, the upswing began, and one of the highlights was Turner's last-second field goal that pulled out a 23-23 tie with the Raiders in 1973, on Denver's first *Monday Night Football* appearance.

"I can't honestly say Ralston was a good pro coach, but he might be the best personnel man I've met," Turner says. "He did the same thing at Utah State, brought in the best personnel, and I think Carroll Hardy has to be given some credit, working in there in the personnel. John had set the base of a damn fine team."

Turner says of the revolt: "I thought it was totally unfair that the insane asylum would make the decision about a coach. The guys didn't like me for my statements afterward. I just said this is ridiculous. I never said John was a good coach. I just said the inmates do not run the asylum and I still believe that today."

(Here is what Turner told Bob Collins of the *Rocky Mountain News* two days after the players' meeting: "I've always looked upon Ralston as a friend, although I've had my differences with him. But this was a power play. I never was contacted by the people in the group before their meeting. I contacted them after it was held and told them that it was none of their business what Mr. Phipps did, that the boss was the boss. Many of their gripes were being taken care of by the reorganization. Ralston's coaching was not in question. The question was, 'Who is in charge, Mr. Phipps or the players?' John had helped some of them in personal, serious problems, and then they turned on him.")

If Turner got the ball through the uprights, nobody would hold a grudge. In the off-season, Turner again went to local school fields and practiced, with Mary Kay as his holder and his daughters as the ball shaggers. In the Turner home, practice was a family outing.

It was obvious from the start that under Miller, Turner might become even more important than before, because the Broncos were destined to play it close to the vest offensively, try to avoid turnovers and mistakes—and accept field goals. In the first four games in '77, he had kicked six field goals, the longest of 48 yards.

The old guy in the high-tops was going to continue trotting out there a lot.

In Their House: October 10–16

Sunday, October 16 at Oakland Raiders

On the Monday of Raiders week, with the undefeated teams set for a Sunday showdown at Oakland, the Broncos gathered for their usual team meeting in the racquetball court at the team headquarters. The weekly protocol was that Red Miller would make a brief speech about the week and opponent ahead, and then the team would break into positional meetings.

Mike Montler, among others, vividly remembers this one as being different.

"Generally, the chairs were set up so they were facing the front and there was a podium there," Montler says. "This time the seats were turned facing the side wall and there was a platform that had the projector on it. There was a reel of film and there couldn't have been that much film on the reel."

With two fingertips squeezed together, Montler shows how thin the film was on the reel.

"Red comes in with the entourage of assistant coaches and works his way up to where the projector was, and the rest of the guys lean against the wall. Red really never said anything. There's stunned silence and we're thinking, *What's going on here? Who died? This is different.*"

Montler reconstructs the rest of the scene this way.

Miller looked over at the assistant coaches and said, sharply, "Lights."

The room went pitch black.

Miller turned on the projector and rolled the film.

It was maybe 30 plays, at the most.

He stopped some of the plays with the coach's "clicker," reversed the film, then showed them again. The sequence of plays were illegal hits, cheap shots, dirty play—all collected from games Miller had coached against the Raiders over a span of about eight years, most of them when he was with the Patriots.

One of the clips showed Raiders linebacker Phil Villapiano's forearm to the face of Patriots tight end Russ Francis in the 1976 playoff game, which left Francis with a broken nose.

Miller hadn't said a word.

Finally, he was through.

"Lights!" he barked.

The lights came on.

Starting slowly, Miller said, "I want to tell you what I like about the Oakland Raiders." He began picking up steam. "I don't like a *$#@ thing about them!" Now, he was snarling and spitting it out. "I don't *$#@

like their colors. I don't *$#@ like their stadium. I don't *$#@ like their fans. I don't like a *$#@ thing about them."

He paused.

"Now, go to your meetings," he said, and walked out of the room.

Montler laughs.

"Right at that point," he says, "we could have gotten on a Greyhound with our own money and gone out and kicked their ass. I think we probably were higher then than we were for the game."

Asked about the scene, Miller says he wanted "to get my team to know that, hey, when you play the Oakland Raiders, you have to beat them at their style. That doesn't mean dirty hitting, but hitting all day long, and 1, 2, 3, 4, 5, and as many as 11, if you can get them all in, on a tackle."

Billy Thompson, second in Denver seniority only to Paul Smith at the time, had gone 2-13-1 against the Raiders in his eight previous seasons. He remembers Miller wearing a T-shirt that week imploring the Broncos to "kick their asses or something like that, but for me it didn't take any of that. I already was keyed up for the Raiders. I had played them more than anybody. I had lost to them more than anybody. So for me, there was no extra motivation needed."

Dan Caplis returned to Boulder and held a news conference of his own. He said he didn't know who had hit him or remember much about being attacked, but he offered to meet again with the groups that opposed EC-4 to make peace.[1]

Looking back, Caplis says the experience "taught me to stand up for what you believe, and that it's the best feeling in the world when you do that."

His news conference had an on-campus competitor for attention on Monday: Buffaloes football coach Bill Mallory said that despite CU's number-three national ranking, his team wasn't playing all that well offensively. "We've got to become more consistent," he groused.

With Mallory, you got both the good and the bad. Eddie Crowder's successor as the CU head coach, Mallory came from Miami of Ohio and was a Woody Hayes devotee. The Buffs' passing game especially was unimaginative and behind the times. When I was working at the *News* in college, and I was allowed to do the Mallory profile after he was hired, and when he went on at length about how important it was to him that his players graduate, I called the Miami admissions office and a nice woman looked up the seniors on his last few teams and determined that, indeed, a stunning number of them had left with diplomas. He also insisted on the institution of a "football dormitory," a concept that seemed out of place in the Boulder atmosphere, and I thought all along that it mitigated one of CU's recruiting advantages—which was that the Buffaloes often landed star players who wanted an eclectic academic and campus experience and didn't want to live, breathe, and sleep football. But in Sam Archibald's investigative journalism class, I walked around outside Brackett Hall, the football dorm, wrote down and traced license numbers and couldn't find any evidence of players driving cars registered to boosters. In previous years, CU had been notorious for the football program's "close" relationship with Continental Airlines founder Robert Six, with the players often getting summer jobs and some of the perks that go with airline employment. As NCAA rules tightened, that became verboten, but I was wondering whether Mallory would have wanted any part of such an arrangement, anyway.

Late in the week, Miller banned the media from watching practice, virtually unprecedented in Broncos history. "I was just kind of disturbed about having so many [media] guys out there today," he told the scribes. "You couldn't turn around without somebody sticking a camera in your face. It's bound to hurt your concentration."

Miller practiced all week as if Raiders mogul Al Davis had rented a hotel room at the nearby Inn at the Mart and had a telescope trained on the Broncos' practice field. Which, of course, might have been the case. That's why the Broncos two weeks earlier had practiced the trick play they might pull out of the bag—sometime.

One of the key matchups in the Raiders-Broncos rivalry was Bob Swenson taking on Raiders tight end Dave Casper. Because he always lined up on the strong side, Swenson in effect followed Casper to his side of the formation, and the Bronco linebacker's job was to keep Casper from having a free run off the line of scrimmage into a pattern. Swenson, both big and fast, was up to the task.

The Broncos viewed this one as a huge test of both their confidence and their ability, though at times they had a hard time admitting it—even to themselves. "It was kind of like, *Yeah, yeah, yeah, you guys are good, but you haven't played the Raiders yet!*" recalls Louis Wright. "And in your mind, even though you want to portray this confident persona, deep down you're thinking—at least I was—it *is* the Raiders. And out there. So I was a little concerned, actually."

The Nuggets had stumbled through the exhibition season, and the major issue was whether the stringent terms of the merger with the NBA were going to have a delayed negative effect on the franchise. The ABA teams hadn't been allowed to participate in the 1976 draft or even the dispersal draft of the players on ABA franchises that weren't accepted in the merger, and neither the Nuggets nor any of the other "new" teams were going to get a piece of the league's television money until the 1980–81 season.

(That wasn't a merger; it was a surrender.)

Both GM Carl Scheer and coach Larry Brown—the latter of whom still looked as if he could be a college sophomore walking out of a history class—were candid that the team's ownership was cash-strapped, despite impressive attendance. The team had nearly three dozen partners, but no one big hitter, and it was amazing the franchise had managed to sign and keep David Thompson. But with Thompson, Dan Issel, and Bobby Jones, the core of the standout final ABA Nuggets teams remained.

The NHL schedule was roughly parallel to the NBA's, so the Rockies also were opening the same week. And already, the first-year beat writer was tiring of hearing the view that the reason the franchise seemed in danger of extinction—already, after only one season—was that Denver—sniff—wasn't "a hockey city" because it hadn't immediately filled the McNichols Arena seats for a rotten product.

Here's what I wrote in the October 11, 1977, *Post*:

But what is "a hockey city," anyway?

If that mysterious phrase means a place where all a team has to do to draw well is set up shop, announce when and where the games are and say the magic word—HOCKEY!—then there isn't "a hockey city" outside of Canada and a couple of U.S. entries in the NHL. . . .

It's no secret this is probably the make-or-break season for major-league *hockey here. Rockies majority owner Jack Vickers is one of the richest men in the state, but his team lost about $2.7 million last year, almost the $3 million he expected to lose in the first three years.*

He probably won't put up with that kind of red ink for long.

I was figuring out what Steve Cameron meant when he said that I was going to discover that NHL executives were the sort of men who loved to wear tuxedoes to every function, major and minor, and throw up on them by the end of the night. At that point, as I would discover, the major NHL marketing move—at least in the "established" markets where the league routinely routed the NBA franchises at the box office—was to make sure the beer taps worked.

Late in the week, copies of the October 17 issue of *Sports Illustrated* began showing up in mailboxes and on newsstands.

Broncos nose tackle Rubin Carter was on the cover. He was in his stance, facing the camera as if it was the opposing center.

The cover tease for the story promised: "THE CASE FOR THE 3-4 DEFENSE."

Joe Marshall's story pointed out: "Seven NFL teams now use the 3-4 as their primary defense, and a dozen others go into it in specific situations. Oakland won the Super Bowl with the 3-4 last season. Of the seven 3-4 teams, Oakland, Denver, Houston and Miami all shut out their opponents in their opening games, and Philadelphia allowed only a field goal."

Yes, some of the Broncos—and certainly many of their fans—laughed nervously about the alleged *Sports Illustrated* "cover jinx."

Senator Gary Hart spoke to an American Bar Association group in downtown Denver and said that the nation—politicians included—was failing to come to grips with the energy crisis. "We have failed to challenge the people we represent . . . to adopt a realistic standard of living, a standard based on the overriding common good, rather than immediate personal comfort." He called for increased emphasis on developing sources of solar energy and wind generation of power. The goal, of course, was to wean the nation of its reliance on oil as soon as possible.

I wasn't there for Hart's speech, but I wondered if he had a bigger crowd than the Rockies' on opening night. Only 4,806 showed up at McNichols to see Vancouver score twice in the third period to pull out a 4-4 tie.

The state's previously glorious college football season hit a brick wall Saturday, when CU had to settle for a 17-17 tie with Kansas at Folsom Field as CSU was embarrassed 63-17 by Brigham Young in Fort Collins. Marc Wilson threw seven touchdown passes for BYU. The ugly Air Force season continued, with Arizona State drilling the Falcons 37-14 at the academy.

A couple of hours before the game in Oakland, an anxious Bob Swenson decided to take a walk.

What he came across astounded him.

Red Miller, who had bitter memories of referee Ben Dreith's crucial and perhaps history-changing roughing-the-passer penalty against the Patriots in the playoff game against the Raiders in the same stadium the previous season, was confronting the men in striped shirts.

"The Raiders were this incredibly talented team and it really did seem like the referees gave them a lot of leeway," Swenson says. "They just got away with stuff. They had a couple of guys back there like [Jack] Tatum and George Atkinson who did some things, and there was some holding, and it always seemed that the referees kind of looked the other way or just kind of had the attitude of 'they're the champs.'

"So I come around the corner and there's Red, he's just lighting into, chewing out the referees. He's saying, 'You guys call this game straight and if you don't, I will be in your face!' He's dressing these guys down before the game! And I was like, *Wow!* Red knew there was something at stake, big time, and he wanted a fair, even field. That was classic Red right there. He knew something was up, something was special."

Says Miller: "I was up for that game. Once in a while, you have to get their attention, you know. I guess that was my way of doing it."

The Broncos got *everyone's* attention that day.

They beat the Raiders 30-7, largely because Ken Stabler threw seven interceptions, three to Joe Rizzo.

Craig Morton remembers wondering if Stabler had been out too late the night before. "He just kept throwing them and I was marveling," Morton says. "*This guy's amazing; he won't stop!* He just kept throwing it to us."

Plus, there was the bizarre-looking, backbreaking touchdown pass from holder Norris Weese to Jim Turner.

Tom Jackson, in addition to covering backs out of the backfield and making tackles, devoted his energy to unleashing disdainful broadsides in the direction of the Oakland bench, including coach John Madden. After recovering a fumble late in the game near the sideline, Jackson got up, waved the ball, and spotted Madden a few feet away. "It's all over, fat man!" he yelled. He would explain later, including in his autobiography, that he meant the Raiders' domination and intimidation of the Broncos was over.[2]

Denver got away with leaving Steve Foley in the starting lineup, though he was nursing a bad calf muscle.

"I was way off the ball because I couldn't run," Foley recalls. He says his calf "has swelled up and, really, they could have picked on me all day long if they had known that."

Joe Collier decided to take the risk, at least at the start of the game.

"Joe said, 'If you can line up, it would be better than putting a new corner in there," Foley says. "I said, 'I'll try.' But I never got threatened. . . . But Joe was right. I played off a few more yards, especially on Cliff Branch, and we just started getting interceptions and we thrashed them. That set the tone because what Red was saying was true. We were playing like Red thought we could, and then you really start believing in yourself."

The Broncos were leading 14-7 late in the first half when they lined up for what would have been a Turner 42-yard attempt on a fourth down from the Oakland 25. Weese, the scrambling backup quarterback, admitted he had been "startled" by the call. It was the play they had practiced a couple of weeks earlier—a fake with tight end Riley Odoms as the first option, which was fairly conventional; but with Turner, the old man in black high-tops, as the secondary receiver along the sideline.

"It was one of those trick things you put in your bag, and never would I have thought they'd call it," Turner says. "The Raiders are so undisciplined that who in the world would think to cover a 37-year-old kicker."

Turner remembers special-teams coach Marv Braden approaching Miller and saying, "Red, this is the time."

Turner adds, "Red didn't want to do it and he growled a little bit. But we went in and did it."

Weese took the snap, rolled right, looked at Odoms, and then looked back to the left, where Turner was running along. Alone. The pass hit Turner in stride at about the Raiders' 15 and he trotted into the end zone. Within seconds, the Broncos' lead was 21-7.

The rout was on.

Although the myth was popularized that Turner was the primary receiver on the play, he wasn't. Odoms was. "If he'd been wide open for the first down, I'd have taken it," Weese said in the visiting dressing room. "But he had all kinds of guys around him, so I looked back over to the left and there was this wide-open space with nobody in it but Jim Turner. There he was, just chugging along."

Weese said Turner was so open, it put a lot of pressure on the passer.

"I was really scared I would overthrow him," Weese said. "He wasn't exactly flying out there, you know." (We knew.) "I wasn't sure how much to lead him with the pass. He's about as fast as I am."

Years later, Billy Thompson smiles when he thinks about that play. "It took Jim Turner *forever* to get in the end zone," he says. "Ol' Hightops!"

Recalls Turner: "They followed Riley Odoms, they followed Norris, they followed Randy Gradishar. They all went to our right. I went to the left and thank God there was nobody near me. I had scored so many times in high school. I think I was the second-leading scorer in the state of California my junior and senior year, so the scoring didn't bother me. It was the catching and running. I think [radio play-by-play man] Bob Martin mentioned something like I was running with a sundial, and Norris said he'd never thrown to a guy so slow. God bless Norris, he threw it right on the money." He laughs. "It was a big play and sometimes it aggravates me that I kicked 304 field goals in my career and that's all they want to talk about, that play."

Gradishar was the wing blocker on the right side. "I wanted to make sure I got that outside wing guy sucked in enough, so when Norris pulled out to the right, he'd have enough opportunity to throw the ball," he says.

The Raiders had taken a 7-0 lead early before the Broncos roared back, getting a 10-yard TD pass from Morton to Odoms and Lonnie Perrin's 16-yard scoring run. Perrin's run was one of the rare times when the tailback was leading the fullback.

Lytle remembers saying to someone that if Atkinson "is out there on force and I get a shot at him I'm going to take him out." He adds, "He came up and was not expecting it, and I just dropped down and got into his tight pads and he went down. Lonnie just walked into the end zone."

The Broncos finished off the rout with Wright's 18-yard interception return for another score and a 32-yard Turner field goal.

The most amazing aspect of the game? Well, in addition to the fact that Jim Turner caught a TD pass?

The Broncos, who scored 30 points, had only eight first downs.

Otis Armstrong, who had carried only 12 times for 24 yards as fullbacks Jon Keyworth and Perrin combined for 63 yards, remembers how quickly the Raiders deserted their sideline. "We had to use the same tunnel, and when we went over there, all of their headphones were in the mud," Armstrong says. "They didn't want to see us. They were embarrassed. In their own stadium."

"It wasn't that we beat the Raiders," Barney Chavous remembers. "It was the *way* we beat the Raiders. They're supposed to be the intimidators. We beat them physically. Nobody was supposed to be more physical than the Raiders. Then when they beat you, they just step on you and embarrass you. We did all that to them, on their field. We beat them the way they beat people, and that was the most exciting part of it. We beat them their style."

On the NBC broadcast, sage play-by-play man Curt Gowdy, the voice of American sports and *The American Sportsman*, mused that Sunday "has to be the greatest day in the history of the Denver franchise."

Up to that point, it was.

Haven Moses, who didn't have a catch in the game, remembers it as a "hurdle. To the fans, almost, it was a championship game. The Raiders had always kicked our butts. I think the fans were ready for the season to end right there because we finally beat 'em. But we knew that it was just the tip of the iceberg."

Years later, Miller calls that game "the turning point of the whole year," and says his postgame speech emphasized the clearing of a mental hurdle.

"We beat the Super Bowl winner in their house!" he recalls telling his team. "And now, gentlemen, if we can play like that and hold together, we're going to be fine."

Billy Thompson recalls it as being crucial "from the psychological point of view. You can say you're good, but until you prove it, it doesn't mean anything. After that game, it was the first time they were saying, 'Uh-oh, we're going to have to deal with them.'"

Working the dressing room for KOA/Channel 4, Ron Zappolo noticed a sudden difference. He says, "It was the first time where players were coming up and—well, I don't want to say they had a chip on their shoulders—looking at you and saying, 'Hey, we're not just the Broncos anymore, this is a pretty good football team.' And I remember a couple of guys coming by on the plane—we flew with them then—and saying things like, 'This is not just a good month, we're really a good football team.'"

Denver was 5-0 and not just on top of the division, but on top of the world. A crowd estimated at 10,000 was waiting when the team's chartered flight arrived at Stapleton International Airport.

The players walked up a stairway from the ground level and into the concourse where the fans waited and, despite a makeshift restraining gate that didn't do much good, mobbed the Broncos.

"I think that's when people knew we were for real," Morton recalls. "There were thousands and thousands of people there. Boy, that's a confidence builder."

Rematch: October 17–30

Sunday, October 23 at Cincinnati Bengals
Sunday, October 30 vs. Oakland Raiders, Mile High Stadium

Such things couldn't be immediately measured, but Denver television executives with axes on both sides of the head-to-head Sunday afternoon matchup agreed that the Broncos-Raiders game had drawn far more viewers than the Dodgers-Yankees World Series game, both in Denver and in the Rocky Mountain region. Charles Leasure, general manager of KBTV/Channel 9, which carried the World Series game, estimated that 60 to 70 percent of the area's audience was watching football on KOA/

Channel 4 instead. He took the defeat philosophically, because he too had caught Broncomania, and let it be known that he had called ABC honchos in New York early Monday morning and began lobbying for the *Monday Night Football* crew—especially that cad Howard Cosell—to pay more attention to the Broncos, especially when showing the highlights of the Sunday games at halftime as Cosell rattled off largely impromptu narration.

This was a big deal.

The Broncos no longer were ragamuffins.

The rest of the nation, by God, should be told that, and with more than some offhand reference or an 11-second clip at the end of the local newscast sports segments that were a measure of national stature and acceptance.

If your highlights weren't going to be shown on *Monday Night Football*, where the hell else would someone in Poughkeepsie catch them and be further convinced that this team in the Rockies—actually, we were at the foot of the Rockies, but most of the nation thought we needed cross-country skis to get to work and school three months of the year—deserved some credit and love?

Come to think of it, why weren't the Broncos on *Monday Night Football* at all in 1977?

As silly as it was, a lot of folks blamed Howard Cosell.

In the early weeks of the season, Broncos fans' paranoia picked up steam, and Gerry Brown, the manager of Sweetwater, a pub on Hampden Avenue, came up with a terrific publicity stunt. Customers at Sweetwater were given a raffle ticket, and the winner got to toss a brick through a used television screen during the *Monday Night Football* telecast.

The national media thought this was hilarious, and a story on the gambit even was in the October 24 issue of *Time*, which hit the streets and mailboxes a few days after the blowout victory over the Raiders.

(Flash forward to October 1978. When *MNF* came to Denver for a Broncos-Bears game, Channel 9 put on a huge luncheon at the Brown Palace on the day of the game. Cosell embarrassed himself and everyone in the audience with an incredible harangue, referring to Sweetwater as a "fleabag joint of a bar" and going on at length about it being a symptom of overemphasis on sports, excoriating "my own industry" for publicizing the stunt, and implying that if he had his way, *Monday Night Football* never would be back in Denver again. Of course, that overemphasis on sports had made Howard Cosell very wealthy.)

Turner himself had to get up early on the Tuesday after the Raiders game and make an appearance on the *Today Show*.

The night before, when Miller was leaving the KBTV building after his television show, an elderly woman in a wheelchair was waiting for him. She presented him with an orange afghan she had knitted. He also remembers her telling him to go undefeated.

Randy Gradishar says Miller preached about not letting the win get to the Broncos. And it sounded familiar. "Red, like with Woody [Hayes], didn't let you get a big head," Gradishar says. "It wasn't like, 'You guys are getting real good here' and you start reading the newspapers and stuff. I know Red was part of all that excitement, but with him and most of the staff, it was, 'OK, we've won this game, let's move on.'"

From here on, there would be no Sunday afternoon competition from baseball for attention and viewers. On Tuesday night, Reggie Jackson had three homers in the Yankees' championship-clinching 8-4 victory over the Dodgers in Game 6 of the World Series at Yankee Stadium. It capped Jackson's first season with the Yankees after he signed as a free agent and left Oakland, in a freedom-of-movement concept that we still were getting used to.

I was on the road with the Rockies, getting my first look at one of the sport's famed arenas, Maple Leaf Gardens in Toronto, after Colorado opened the season with back-to-back ties. I was in such awe at being in Toronto, I brought a camera with me, rode the mass transit Dick Lamm wanted us to copy, and wandered the ancient building's halls during the Rockies' practice, peering at the black-and-white pictures documenting the Maple Leafs' deep roots and traditions.

Pat Kelly, the first-year coach who had taken so long to reach the NHL, told me about his most recent visit to the building as a player or coach. He was a defenseman for junior hockey's St. Catharines Teepees, playing against the Toronto Marlboros, the team owned by the Leafs. A riot broke out on the ice. "Everyone had a partner in the fighting, but I happened to notice one fan leaning over the boards grabbing one of our guys," Kelly recalled. "I snuck along the boards and punched this guy out. He turned out to be Stafford Smythe."

Smythe, who was running the Marlboros, was the son of the legendary Conn Smythe, the long-time Maple Leafs majority owner and general manager.

"After he got back up," Kelly said, "he called for the cops to throw me out of his building. But they didn't. He didn't get a second chance at me. He was quoted as saying afterward, 'If I could have gotten at Kelly, I would have flattened him.' The sportswriter's quote back then was that probably put me in about as much fear as the blonde in the fourth row."

The Rockies lost to the Maple Leafs 5-4, and Kelly was convinced that referee Andy Van Hellemond had shafted his team by calling Barry Beck for holding Toronto's Borje Salming in the third period and putting the Leafs on the power play that produced Ian Turnbull's game-winning goal.

"If there was water out there," Kelly fumed of Salming, "he would have got a 9 for a high dive."

More and more, I felt that talking to Pat was what it would have been like talking to *Slap Shot*'s Reggie Dunlop if he eventually had gotten a crack at NHL coaching.

The Nuggets waived veteran forward Byron Beck, who had been with the team since its founding as the American Basketball Association's Denver Rockets. He wasn't all that distraught, because his major goal had been to make it through at least one NBA season after the merger. Beck had made it through the seriocomic days of the upstart league, and there already was some talk about retiring his number—40.

An era was over.

Without Beck, the Nuggets whipped the Milwaukee Bucks on Wednesday, 123-115, getting 36 points from David Thompson, plus 21 points and a career-high eight assists from Dan Issel. The Bucks' young coach, Don Nelson, the former Celtic, lamented how the Bucks blew a fourth-quarter lead.

Everyone who traveled often—as I was just beginning to do—winced on Thursday when a 29-year-old man, Thomas Michael Hannan, hijacked a Frontier Airlines Boeing 737 about to depart from Grand Island, Nebraska, and head to Denver. Hannan had a sawed-off shotgun and demanded a friend's release from prison and $3 million. With 15 hostages, including the crew and Denver-based pilot Jay Curtis, aboard, the plane flew to Kansas City and then Atlanta, where Hannan's friend was in custody. In Atlanta, he allowed 13 of the hostages to leave the plane and shot himself in the head.

It was about 10 years after the height of the hijacking-to-Cuba craze, and 6 years after "D.B. Cooper's" hijacking for $200,000 in ransom and his bailout from the Northwest Orient plane in the Pacific Northwest. That case still was unsolved.

Cooper had claimed to have a bomb. This was more chilling: How could someone just storm onto a plane with a sawed-off shotgun?

We knew all those stats about how private plane travel was even safer than commercial flights, and now the lesser chances of hijacking seemed to confirm that. But rock music lost more stars on Thursday, when a twin-engine plane carrying the band Lynyrd Skynyrd crashed in Mississippi, killing lead singer Ronnie Van Zant and five others. The band was headed to a date in Baton Rogue, Louisiana.

Bob Swenson had bought and moved into a new house in Englewood, and he took in teammates Chris Pane, the defensive back and special teams ace, and backup receiver John Schultz as housemates. Married teammates Craig Penrose and Paul Howard lived nearby, and the word was getting around to neighborhood residents that Broncos were in their midst.

As the season progressed, Swenson recalls, it "got crazy. I used to have food left on my doorstep. Whole dinners." He laughs and adds, "I hadn't put the sod in the yard, though, and we were all young, and the weeds were growing all over. Someone left a note saying, 'Use some of that Bronco money to buy a lawnmower!'"

The Brown Cloud was getting worse. There were days when especially a drive into downtown from the east side of the metro area could be an ugly sight, with the pollution visible and shoved up against the mountains, making it look as if you were about to walk into a smoke-filled room—and inhale. An official of the Denver Air Pollution Control Commission, Dr. John Cobb, told a conference at—appropriately enough—the Brown Palace that it was going to get worse, in part because Detroit automakers had convinced the federal government they didn't have the capability to make cars that could meet specific high-altitude emissions standards.

"Clearly it hasn't yet gotten so bad that people have been gasping in the streets and dying of respiratory distress," Cobb told the conference attendees. "But episodes of this kind are possible in Denver if we don't take necessary precautions."

Sister Gerard Mary, the nun in charge of the Little Sisters of the Poor at the Mullen Home in North Denver, was very offended at a newspaper reference to the Broncos' early schedule including teams that couldn't stop the Little Sisters of the Poor. She wrote the *Post*, complaining about the insensitivity, but also confiding that the Sisters had been forced to fold their team. "Our players found out how much some of the other players were making [so] they asked to become free agents," she wrote. "Our Superiors frowned on this, and the Little Sisters have returned to their primary duty, caring for the elderly poor."

The day the Broncos left for Cincinnati, President Carter arrived in Denver and met with Dick Lamm and eight other western state governors, and also participated in a public forum on his much-criticized water policy, which included the scuttling of water projects previously approved. "I want to make clear from the very beginning that there absolutely will be no federal preemption of state or private prerogatives in the use or management of water," Carter told the forum.

Lamm, who butted heads with the White House often on the issue, at the time gave Carter credit for "political and personal courage" in coming to Denver to face the music. And looking back, Lamm acknowledges he was "very schizophrenic" on the issue. "I certainly recognized that the president had a point. But no Colorado governor is going to voluntarily give up a whole bunch of water projects. Carter was right. Some of those were not cost-effective and should not have been built." Lamm says his goal in the dealings with Carter were to work out "some accommodation. . . . Just don't take them completely off the table, but give us a chance to reallocate that money. I recognized even at the time that he was 'righter' than I was. I really did. I couldn't say that."

This was only one of several meetings Lamm, often with other western governors, had with Carter in 1977.

"I think the western governors all had a great affection for President Carter," Lamm says. "He was such a decent, well-meaning human being. . . . We were very appreciative that he took the time to come out and listen to the problems of the west. I really felt that he sincerely tried to better understand what water means to us out here, and that we lived in a semiarid desert. I remember telling him that we could go a hundred miles from where we were meeting and see tracks of wagon wheels from the Oregon Trail that were laid down in the 1840s. And I said that if that were in Plains, Georgia, that would be green within three weeks, there would be no permanent ruts. I think that was an eye-opener for him. . . . I don't think he was fully aware that storage of water was so important, that we get our precipitation disproportionately over the winter and when it runs off, what we don't capture, we can't use."

Lamm's other public position, stated after one meeting at the White House, was to "urge Coloradans to become aware of an emerging pattern of using the West for energy production to the derogation of our agricultural role. We have to form coalitions in our own state and with other states. We have to flex our collective muscle. I don't want our Western way of life sacrificed in the energy crisis."

He says all of this involved much more than water.

"In oil shale, back in 1977, I was told at one time to get ready for half a million people to come to northwest Colorado," Lamm says. "And *then* somebody came along and said, no, 700,000. There were numbers that were hard to get your mind around, how we were going to expand the infrastructure—the roads, the sewers, the schools, the water systems. One of the proudest things of my governorship is that we didn't succumb to the siren songs of the oil companies, who said, 'Oh, just do nothing but bond the infrastructure.' We really worked hard with the locals to get them to understand that the history of the West was filled with a lot of hopes that never were realized, that they come in and develop your resources and leave."[3]

Carter's appearance also drew about 400 protesters to the downtown hotel, and they gathered outside, signaling their concerns on administration policies on such issues as the Panama Canal treaty, which was pending in the U.S. Senate; abortion; immigration laws; and calling attention to the ongoing strike at Coors and the proposed Equal Rights Amendment.

That afternoon, Nebraska whipped CU for the 15th time in 16 seasons, romping 33-15 in Lincoln behind 172 rushing yards from an alleged walk-on tailback, I.M. Hipp. (The Huskers had imaginative ways of getting around scholarship restrictions.)

That night, the Rockies finally won, beating the Chicago Black Hawks 3-0 at McNichols, behind veteran goalie Doug Favell's 18th career shutout. The crowd of 5,953 was boisterous in its salute of Favell, the onetime star at Philadelphia who was winding down his career. "I can thank Mr. Favell for that one," Pat Kelly said after his first win as an NHL coach.

The Broncos took a workmanlike 24-13 victory at Cincinnati to improve to 6-0.

The big play was an 81-yard touchdown pass from Craig Morton to wide receiver Jack Dolbin that pulled the Broncos out of a 10-10 tie late in the second quarter.

"We got in the huddle and they think we're going to run out the clock," Dolbin recalls. "Tommy Casanova is the safety and I forget who the corner was. I knew I could beat the corner and I didn't know if I could get behind Tommy Casanova because I knew he'd be playing pretty deep, but we ran a play-action, a 90-go. Craig always called me 'Doc.'"

By then they had developed a verbal signal for this kind of play—"Be Alert, Doc," or a variation thereof—and Morton gave it to the man studying to be a chiropractor.

"So I ran my pass pattern and looked around and, gee whiz, the ball was almost in my ear," Dolbin says. "Eighty-one yards, touchdown."

Tom Jackson missed the game with a strained hamstring, and backup

Larry Evans played well. Louis Wright kept playing, but he suffered a dislocated shoulder that had to be popped back in. Jim Jensen scored the final touchdown while he filled in at fullback for Jon Keyworth, who went out with a sprained knee. Glenn Hyde came on at tackle for Andy Maurer, who departed with a bruised knee. After Morton suffered a bruised knee, too, Craig Penrose came on and directed that final drive.

Before leaving, Morton was 5 for 10, for 108 yards, and Penrose came on to go 4 for 5, for 47 yards, and his 17-yard bootleg was the key in the final drive that put the game away.

The consensus was that the run of injuries wasn't a coincidence: Riverfront Stadium's artificial turf was as hard as cement. In a way, the injuries—and the response of the reserves—helped build a feeling that this was a team of destiny.

After the game, Miller was signing autographs for fans when the team buses pulled away from the stadium. Officials on each bus thought the coach was on the other one. Two fans—Miller could only identify them as "Mr. and Mrs. Fahey"—gave him a ride to the airport, and he managed to make it onto the plane before it left.

The players loved it, yelling when he came aboard the plane that he needed to go to the back and pay his fine to the hastily summoned kangaroo court.

He gave the players a smile and a thumbs-up.

The injury news was palatable, with only Maurer ruled out for the upcoming rematch with the Raiders at Mile High Stadium. Though he didn't announce it and this wouldn't become apparent until game time, Miller made the surprising decision to move rookie Steve Schindler, the first-round draft choice from Boston College, from guard out to start in Maurer's spot at left tackle.

The Rockies' record was 1-2-3 after they came from behind to tie the Boston Bruins, 4-4, before another small crowd in Denver. Dick Connor joined me at the game, and his column the next morning caught up with Bruins center Peter McNab,[4] the former University of Denver star who had been raised in San Diego, where his father was general manager of the minor-league San Diego Gulls. He had played high school football and baseball and, in fact, came to DU on a baseball scholarship. And hockey? "We played one game a week and practiced one time a week," he told Connor. "It was a little bandbox, outdoor rink in a shopping center. There were palm trees in spitting distance, and we used to pick out shoppers as they'd walk past in the shopping mall, and flip the puck at them." He walked on to play hockey at DU for Murray Armstrong.

The *Post*'s politics writer, Todd Phipers,[5] noted that "some public relations wizard" had come up with the idea of calling the Broncos' defense the "Orange Crush."

That unnamed "wizard" was my brother, Dave. Years later, he acknowledges—as he always has—that the first to toss out the name for the Denver defense was Woody Paige of the *Rocky Mountain News*—in 1976. But the name didn't catch on or take off. At that point, Dave even broached the subject with his friend, Joe Iacino, who had the local Royal Crown Cola distributorship. One of Royal Crown's products was Orange Crush. "I was playing golf with Joe, and I said, 'Joe, next year if we can get this team going, maybe we can play with that a little bit,'" Dave says. "Joe said, 'God, I'd love to do something.'

"When we got off to that good start in '77, we were sort of wandering around in the office one day, and [defensive line coach] Stan Jones said something like, 'We need some kind of nickname like the Purple People Eaters or the Doomsday Defense.' And I said, 'Well, what about the Orange Crush?' It wasn't an original thought, but it wasn't really out there at the moment. Stan said, 'Yeah, that sounds pretty good,' and we just sort of started using it and playing with it."

It wasn't a complicated written agreement. It was a sure-go-ahead handshake and nod. Iacino agreed to go along with it all. Orange Crush even issued commemorative cans featuring Broncos players and staff members.

"I came down on the field after one of the home games and I had a nice white sweater on with an Orange Crush label on it," Dave says. "God, people were jumping out of the stands, saying, 'I want one of those, I want one of those.' And for the next game, I had a bunch of Orange Crush T-shirts I was spreading around all over the place. So everybody kind of latched onto it, and we started writing about it and using it, and the media picked up on it and it went from there."

Orange Crush Defense T-shirts, sweatshirts, and windbreakers—marketed, mainly through Joslin's department store, by concert promoter Joe Fernandez—became the rage. Joslin's took out full-page ads for the gear in the papers, and despite the high prices—$7 for a T-shirt!—they flew off the tables. What better gear to wear, whether at the stadium for the rematch against the still-once-beaten Raiders, or in front of the television? And the soft drink itself? Iacino that week said the usual Orange Crush sales figure for a week was 7,500 cases. During the week of the Raiders game, Iacino expected the number to be 100,000. "We can't get it out fast enough," Iacino said. "Our backs are against the wall. We've got everybody working overtime. We'll keep working 'til Saturday, but we have to let everybody off on Sunday to see the game."

About this time, Billy Thompson realized the Denver area, including his Green Mountain neighborhood in Lakewood, was taking fanaticism to a new level. "I was driving down the road and people were honking at me and going, 'Ahhhhhh!'" (He pantomimes a driver taking his hands off the wheel.) "They had an orange arrow painted all the way up to my house. People had signed my garage door and I had oranges in my mailbox with crepe paper all around it."

Getting in the spirit, Governor Lamm proclaimed Sunday, the day of the game against the Raiders, Orange Crush Day. Denver police captain Jerry Kennedy, Elvis's buddy, rejected the suggestion that he should prepare for the worst, having police dogs waiting on the field to protect, among other things, the goalposts.

For the first time ever, a significant contingent of national writers had notified the Broncos they were coming in for a *Denver* game. My brother, single at the time, chided his boss, PR director Bob Peck, for refusing a credential and press box seat from *Playboy*. Dave's theory: The magazine might send one of its, um, models. Some of the reporters Peck did credential were from New York, and they were determined to chronicle how Morton so quickly had been transformed from a perceived and much-heckled flop in New York with the Giants to the hero of Denver. (At least they would be able to get a taxi from the airport; Yellow Cab settled its strike after 38 days.)

In the middle of the week, KOA/Channel 4 sportscaster Ron Zappolo was standing outside the locker room building before practice when Tom Jackson emerged.

"Tom said, 'What's up?,'" Zappolo recalls. "I said, 'I don't know, it's Wednesday, I need a good story today, and I've really got nothing.' Tom said, 'You need a good story? Turn that camera on.' I said, 'OK.' He said, 'I'm about to do my Ken Stabler imitation. Are you ready? Are you rolling?' And then he did the most remarkable impression of Ken Stabler. He came out in that high, squeaky voice, called the signals, and then backpedaled. He looked just like Stabler. He said, 'Is that good enough for you?'"

***

This kind of got lost in the Orange Crush mania, but 2nd District Congressman Tim Wirth chided President Carter for what the congressman termed a "ridiculous" administration proposal to prohibit the illegal immigration of Mexican workers, an issue that mostly involved farm workers. Speaking to the Chicano Democratic Congress at one of Denver's top hotels, the Regency[6] on the north side, Wirth declared: "We must hear from the farmers who are most affected, Chicano-Latino citizens of the United States whose rights and dignity may be affected, and from the undocumented aliens themselves to determine exactly why they are here and the forces that drove them to our country in the first place."

As issues go, illegal immigration wasn't anything close to having a hot button.

***

Coloradans were hoping the Broncos didn't follow CU and CSU's lead. The Buffaloes, recently the number-three team in the country with a 5-0 record, fell 24-14 to Missouri in Boulder and were 5-2-1. CU coach Bill Mallory wasn't winning style points, either, with his silly policy that players couldn't talk to reporters after losses. I liked and respected Mallory, but again wondered if his inflexibility and old-school ways were a good fit for the Boulder campus. In Laramie, Wyoming won the Border War against CSU, 29-13.

Well, this much we knew: The Broncos weren't going to duplicate the 1973 Miami Dolphins' undefeated season.

Oakland, up 24-0 in the fourth quarter and dominating the game every bit as much as that score indicated, beat the Broncos 24-14 and pulled back into a first-place tie in the AFC West. The Raiders had 200 yards rushing, and the Broncos clearly missed Tom Jackson, out with a pulled hamstring.

At the halfway point, both the Broncos and Raiders were 6-1.

"We're not ashamed of anything," Miller told reporters. "We lost to a strong, strong team. I think maybe we'll meet them again. At least I hope so."

The backbreaker was Clarence Davis's 8-yard run for a touchdown in the third quarter after the Raiders recovered Jim Jensen's fumble at the Broncos' 15. Denver made it respectable with the two late touchdowns—an 11-yard Morton-to-Dolbin pass and Otis Armstrong's 1-yard run—but that didn't erase much of the sting. Morton was sacked eight times. Part of that was protection breakdown, but some of it was due to Raiders' coverage and Morton's sensible willingness to eat the ball rather than take the sort of risks Miller wanted him to avoid.

The upside? More than ever before, the stadium was a sea of orange. Broncomania had taken off.

Notes

1. In 1978, after CU student government abandoned the tri-executive model, Dan Caplis would be elected student body president.

2. There has been considerable confusion about this incident, in part because Steve Foley and others have talked about another Jackson-Madden confrontation in a game at Denver, after Jackson drilled Clarence Davis after the Raiders running back caught a swing pass along the sideline. "Tommy hit him head on and he knocked Clarence Davis out cold," Foley says. "You heard the helmets hit in the whole stadium. . . . Tommy runs over to the sideline and gets right in Madden's face and says, 'How do you like that, fat man?' He's screaming at the top of his lungs, 'How do you like that, fat man?' I'm pulling him away, thinking there's going to be a fight and they're not going to take this."

3. After essentially building Parachute, Colorado, for example, Exxon pulled out. But the area wasn't stuck with significant bonded indebtedness.

4. Peter McNab has been the Avalanche's television analyst since the team arrived in Denver in 1995.

5. Todd Phipers eventually became a *Post* sports writer before he died, too young, of cancer.

6. In 2007, the Regency is student housing for the Auraria campus.

CHAPTER 9

Rebounding and Receiving

Our quarterback was Jimmy "The King" Corcoran—and
he named himself, by the way.

—JACK DOLBIN

"Tadpole": Rick Upchurch
Number 80, Wide Receiver/Returner, 5-10, 170, 3rd Season, Minnesota

As he lived with his grandparents, Louis and Beatrice Lindsay, on the
little country farm outside Toledo, young Rick Upchurch had chores to
do when he came home from elementary school. Most involved garden-
ing. "You know how some people talk to the animals?" he asks on the
phone from Mesquite, Nevada. "I talked to the plants."

Beatrice always talked about a higher purpose. "She was the spiritual
person of our family," Rick says. "She lived and died Jesus Christ and
that's what she taught us. And she was the comforter." It was unfathom-
able for Rick when Beatrice was diagnosed with cancer and died when he
was in the fifth grade. How could that be fair? "I went into a depression,"
he says. "I wouldn't talk. I wouldn't do anything."

Louis Lindsay told him to snap out of it, that Beatrice wouldn't have
liked his lingering melancholy. Finally, he emerged from his funk, but

not soon enough to salvage his school year, and he was told he would need to repeat the fifth grade.

Louis continued to go to work at the Standard Oil refinery. Just as Rick was beginning to get involved in sports and looking like one of the potential stars of the area, Louis also died. Rick was fifteen. Officially, he was going to be living with his mother in Toledo, but he didn't get along with her, he didn't want to change schools, and he says he simply remained in Louis Lindsay's house—by himself. "I decided that I wanted to stay in that house because I didn't like to go into the inner city," he says. "Every time I went into the inner city, there was trouble there. I decided that's not what I wanted to do."

He went to school and played sports, worked at Burger King, and did his homework when he could wedge it in. The Garrett family across the street kept their eye on him, and he knew if he got out of line, somebody would report that this high school kid was living alone.

Rick had been playing against, but had developed a friendship with, a kid named Roddy Boldon. "He went to one school and I went to another, and we would be in competition against each other in all sports, and pushed each other," Upchurch says. Roddy's parents owned one of the largest dry-cleaning businesses in Toledo. He knew what was going on, and he sensed what would happen if somebody forced Rick to go live with his mother, and he also knew the temptations Rick would face if he continued to live alone.

"I was determined to make it, but then it got to the point where it got real tough," Rick says. "I had some options. Some of my friends were making big money, and they were doing some things that weren't the best things and I could have taken those options. Roddy was the one who said, 'That ain't going to happen, you're not going to get caught up into the crazy stuff,' so he talked with his mom and dad and asked if I could move in with them."

Rick moved in with the Boldons, and the parents of another friend, Gerry Warner, were a second set of pseudoparents. So as Rick starred in every sport he tried, especially in football and track, he had plenty of mentors, and they all agreed that the first thing he needed to do was get his academic act together and get on track to become eligible for an opportunity in major-college football.

The Boldons and Warners—Howard and Marge—talked with the college coaches who liked Rick, including coaches on the staff at Iowa and Purdue. The coaches recommended that he take a GED exam to make up for his lost year of school—that repeated fifth-grade year—and go to junior college right away because he wouldn't have been eligible to play another year of high school football, anyway. He was funneled to Indian Hills Community College in Centerville, Iowa, with the understanding that if he did well enough, both on the field and in the classroom, he probably would end up at one of the Big Ten programs, but that nothing was guaranteed—on either side.

"I'd never been on an airplane, and I'm looking out the window and I'm crying," Rick recalls. When he arrived in Centerville, for several weeks he hardly said a word and stayed to himself. All the black kids that were there were from Chicago and Miami down in Florida, or places like Steubenville and Pittsburgh.

"I'd sit off in my room by myself and I didn't communicate with a whole lot of people. Those guys were hanging out and I finally broke down and dropped my guard and started making friends. My first friend was from St. Louis, David Moore, and he grabbed me by the hand and he worked with me and introduced me to the guys. There were a lot of guys who said, 'Rick, you have to come out of your stupor and you have to start making friends because you're going to be part of this football team.'"

He was a junior college All-America running back, and that meant the offers flowed in, both from coaches looking for a quick fix and also from successful programs. Ohio State even made an overture, but Rick sensed it was halfhearted. The Buckeyes staff, including Woody Hayes, seemed to be saying if he went to Columbus, fine; if he didn't, fine. He signed conference letters of intent with Nebraska and Florida, and came very close to committing to go to Lincoln. But then he took a trip to the University of Minnesota campus in Minneapolis.

"I saw that one big tall building, the IDS Building there, and that's when I said, 'I'm coming to Minneapolis.' Plus, Marian Boldon, she was with me on my visit, and they talked about education big time. So she decided for me, that's where I was going to go. But I thought so, too."

Marian even signed his letter of intent as his guardian. "She wasn't official, but she made herself official," Upchurch says with a laugh. "A lot of people didn't mess with her."

Immediately eligible to play for the Cal Stoll–coached Gophers as a junior in 1973, Upchurch's first game for the Gophers was against Ohio State—and star linebacker Randy Gradishar—in Columbus. "The first time I took a kickoff," Upchurch recalls, "I got hit and the ball went about 15 feet in the air, and then there was another collision. They said, 'Welcome to the Big Ten.'"

He laughs and notes, "Randy wasn't involved in that one, but he was always in my face that day, that's for sure."

The Buckeyes squeezed out a 56-7 win.

Minnesota was 7-4 that season, and then gave the Buckeyes a tougher time in the '74 opener, losing 34-19 at home, when Upchurch had a big game and Hayes, he recalls, shook his hand afterwards and told him, "Young man, you're one of the best running backs in the country."

He says he knew all along he probably wouldn't be able to take the pounding of playing running back in the NFL, so he wasn't disillusioned when he was listed as a wide receiver and kick returner as the draft approached. He hoped to go to the Vikings, Chiefs (his favorite team), or the Steelers to be close to home.

He says that when the phone call came, the first words he heard were, "You're going to the Mile High City!"

He didn't know what that meant.

He hadn't gone until the fourth round, after the Broncos had taken Louis Wright, defensive end Charlie Smith of North Carolina, Mike Franckowiak, Drew Mahalic, and defensive back Steve Taylor of Georgia Tech; and before they claimed Rubin Carter and Steve Foley.

In his first-ever regular season game, against his formerly beloved Chiefs, he caught a pass for a 90-yard touchdown, scored on an end-around, and racked up 286 yards in total yardage. I was in the stands because my father still was the offensive line coach, and I thought I remembered all about Upchurch's electrifying performance.

"The first time I touched the ball, though, I got my helmet cracked," he says.

I confess I don't remember that.

"I do," Upchurch says, laughing. "Floyd Little and I were back returning kickoffs, and the first time I got the ball, I got hit and my helmet got cracked and boy, my lip got busted. And then Haven [Moses] ended up getting hit, shattered his face mask and his teeth were in his hands. This was intimidating stuff."

He fully admits he was raw as a wide receiver as he alternated with Jack Dolbin. "Haven Moses, Riley Odoms, and Billy Thompson helped me out tremendously," Upchurch says. "Billy was teaching me what defensive backs like to do against receivers, and Haven and Riley were talking to me about being under control."

In later years, Upchurch repeatedly would praise John Ralston as a person, but he admits he went along with the revolt's leaders. "I was still just a young ballplayer and a team player, and what the elder statesmen were saying and doing, well, I said, 'Whatever you guys think is right.' You don't want to see anyone lose his job, especially the person who got you into the game. He always was a nice man to me."

He likens Red Miller, with whom he would be close in later years, especially after retirement, to "cayenne pepper."

With the Broncos at 6-1 at the halfway point, it was obvious that Miller indeed had spiced things up.

"Doc": Jack Dolbin

Number 82, Wide Receiver, 5-10, 180, 3rd Season, Wake Forest

The trucks roared past Jack Dolbin's house in Pottsville about every 20 minutes. This was the coal country of central Pennsylvania, and the anthracite mine was a short walk away. "At the end of the day, my friends and I would go up and look in awe at this huge hole in the ground, with the railroad tracks going down there, and see the guys with dirty faces walking out," Dolbin recalls from his office in Pottsville.

The buddies in the town of about 30,000 were a diverse group. Dick Yuengling's family owned the local brewery, the oldest in the country. Others were the sons of the local bookmaker, a cop, and the five-and-dime store manager. Jack actually was a Junior, the son of the local chiropractor and part of a well-known family in the area.

Jack's grandfather, Donald, at one time had been the coholder of the world record in the 100-yard dash. "Back in those days," Jack says, "they timed in fifths of seconds. In the last year of my grandfather's life, he knew he was sick, and he asked me what I wanted, and I said all I really wanted was his scrapbook. So he willed it to me. And he gave me his gold medal from the Middle Atlantic championships."

The times in those clippings always had awed the grandson.

"He ran the 100 in nine and three-fifths seconds," Dolbin says. "And he ran the 220 in twenty and three-fifths. Those were on dirt tracks and they didn't have starting blocks, and the shoes were not like they were today, and of course the training was different."

After leaving Penn State, Donald found work with the state of Pennsylvania as a potato inspector, but then became a chiropractor. Donald's son, Jack Sr., also ran at Penn State, but had some other business to attend to before following his father into chiropractic.

Jack Sr. was a radio operator in the U.S. Navy Signal Corps during World War II. "He often told of the experience where the submarine dropped him and his platoon off at Apo Island to set up a radar station, to monitor Japanese ship movements in preparation for what turned out to be the Battle of Leyte Gulf," Jack Jr. recalls.

Dolbin says his father was stationed at, among other places, Biak Island. Hearing that, I say that's where my father was when he flew his first combat missions. "They might even have known each other," Dolbins says. But, of course, none of this came up when Dolbin played with the Broncos while my father was the offensive line coach. That's just the way it was.

Ultimately, the World War II veteran became a chiropractor, too, surviving in the blue-collar town where work-related pains were as much a part of the way of life as the coal-darkened faces. His son also was a natural athlete, the fastest kid in town.

"We played sports all the time," Jack says. "We would play tackle football during the football season, baseball during baseball season, sandlot pickup games. And in basketball season we had an alley behind our house where we put up a rim on the tree and we'd just shoot all the time. We used to box in my backyard, and we'd fight over who was going to be Floyd Patterson and who was going to be Sonny Liston and stuff like that."

At Pottsville High, he was such a star running back, a virtual who's-who of college football recruited him, including Notre Dame and Penn State. He narrowed the field to Syracuse, Wake Forest, and Miami before his father made it known to all that he—and not Jack Jr.—would make the decision.

Jack visited Syracuse twice and met the Orangemen's about-to-graduate running back, Floyd Little. In fact, coach Ben Schwartzwalder dispatched Little for one trip to visit Dolbin. Wake Forest assistant coach Joe Madden was assigned the duty of courting Dolbin, and he quickly figured out the most astute strategy.

"He and my dad would go out drinking every night," Dolbin recalls. "They both liked Scotch."

On the national letter of intent day, Madden—no relation to John—was in Dolbin's kitchen. Schwartzwalder was in the living room. Jack himself was "upstairs hiding in my bedroom, when my dad came in with the Wake Forest contract and said, 'Sign it.'"

Jack did, and he didn't regret his choice. "I loved the Wake Forest campus and the small-school atmosphere," he says. He had an injury-marred career at running back for the Deacons, and the head coach—Bill Tate—was fired after Jack's junior season.

"Cal Stoll from the Michigan State staff got the head job and I went in to see him," Dolbin says. "I told him I wanted to play professional football, and he said, 'Well, then, you can't play running back. You can be a wide receiver or a defensive back,' but he said, 'You can't be a running back because you can't block linebackers on a blitz.'"

(Yes, that's the same Cal Stoll who would move to Minnesota and coach Rick Upchurch.)

If Dolbin had heeded Stoll's implied advice, as it turned out, he might have made the NFL sooner. But Dolbin stayed at running back, and he played only three games as a senior because of a broken ankle and a broken hand. But he was the holder of the school records in the 100 and 220, so his speed was documented. After he went undrafted, he got some free-agent offers, but he didn't sense a lot of enthusiasm from the NFL teams. Next, he got a call from Ronnie Waller, a former NFL player who was coaching the Atlantic Football League's Pottstown Firebirds. "He said, 'Give me a year and I'll teach you how to play wide receiver,'" Dolbin says.

He agreed to play for the Firebirds in 1970 for a $500 bonus, $300 a week, plus $300 more each time the team won three games in a row.

"Really, it was a terrific experience," he says. "Our quarterback was

Jimmy 'The King' Corcoran—and he named himself, by the way. Ronnie Waller took me under his wing and taught me how to run pass patterns. He had a house at Bethany Beach, Delaware, right in between John Unitas, Jimmy Corcoran, and Harland Svare, who was with the Chargers at the time.

"Another guy, Ronnie Holliday, and I stayed with Ron Waller. I remember laying on the beach listening to Ronnie [Waller], Harland Svare, and John Unitas argue about offensive football, and Corcoran would just look at the girls. At night, we'd go out to a little league field and I would catch 100 balls every night from Jim Corcoran. He was a legend in his own mind, but when you got him away from the spotlight he was really a pretty good guy, and he had a terrific arm."

When the season started, Dolbin lived with his new wife, Jane, in an apartment near Pottsville and worked during the day as a laborer with a homebuilder. That season culminated with the league championship game in Hartford, and the Firebirds beat the Hartford Knights to win the title. "We were supposed to host the game but we couldn't sell tickets," Dolbin says. "Hartford had a stadium that sat 15,000 and they sold it out. We went up the night before the game and ran into a huge blizzard. There was probably a foot of snow in Hartford that night. The field was frozen, you couldn't get any traction, so Ronnie Waller said, 'Listen—take your cleats off. Underneath those cleats you have those little screws like a track spike.'

"So we took the spikes off. We were actually digging into the ice with those little screws and every time we got tackled the guy who tackled us was wondering why his arm was all cut up. We beat Hartford pretty bad that day and we got the trophy. We had to sell 20 tickets to the team banquet to get a ring. I think I sold 5 and bought 15. So I got my championship ring—which I still have."

The Firebirds folded. He was working as a life insurance salesman in Newark, Delaware—"I was the worst salesman in the world," he says—when another semipro team, the Schuylkill Coal Crackers, signed him for $100 a game. Jack was the Seaboard Football League MVP in 1971.

"Twice a week I would drive 218 miles round trip to Frankville, Pennsylvania, to practice, and then on the weekends I would drive to the game instead of taking their bus, because I was closer to most of the teams they played," Jack says. His brother, Cameron, was a defensive back, making

$35 a week. The Coal Crackers lost only one game and won the league title.

After that season, the Giants offered him a free-agent contract and even brought him to New York to talk over the details. But in the team offices, when he insisted on getting $2,500 upfront, the Giants balked, and he didn't sign. Instead, he enrolled in chiropractic school in Chicago, intending to give up the sport and follow his grandfather and father into the business.

When the World Football League was getting off the ground in 1974, one of the Chicago Fire's officials had seen Dolbin play for the Coal Crackers and invited him to attend a tryout. Dolbin remembers that there were 168 players that day in Soldier Field, that he ran a 4.25 in the 40-yard dash, and that he was one of only two players in the group signed.

"Every other year I played football I had fun, but not with the WFL," he says. "The WFL was a lot of wind but not a lot of rain. A lot of promises were made that were never kept."

Still, he had 54 catches for 942 yards and seven touchdowns with the Fire. After the season, he still needed to work as he attended chiropractic school and settled into an off-season job. "I was chasing shoplifters at J.C. Penney," Dolbin says with a laugh. "At 4.25, I could catch shoplifters."

Then John Ralston called him, offering a tryout with Denver. Dolbin was noncommittal, and other teams checked in with similar tryout offers. The Fire had folded and the WFL, which would last only half a season longer, was on its last legs. Fire assistant coach Steve Tensi, the much-maligned former Broncos quarterback, vouched for the city and the organization, so Dolbin agreed to come to camp with Denver in 1975.

Against all odds, he made the team. Veteran Gene Washington was cut.

He didn't mind sharing time with Rick Upchurch. As it turned out, they often were the messengers, and they would continue that role under Red Miller, with Dolbin listed as the starter because he was in for the first play of each possession.

"When I was in Pottstown we were riding a bus from Pottstown to Orlando to play a football game," he says. "Now I'm sitting in Denver, or riding a 727 to Seattle and staying in a five-star hotel? I would have done anything and I did do anything."

Not surprisingly, he was open about his support of Ralston in the revolt. "I thought John Ralston was a good coach and a good person," he says. "I have this loyalty thing."

After Miller was hired, the new coach asked Dolbin to come to Denver to meet him and talk, and Dolbin and Haven Moses were in the offices at the same time.

"I remember sitting there with Haven, and we looked at the stats from New England the year before," Dolbin says. "Their two leading receivers, Randy Vataha and Darryl Stingley, each caught about 30 balls. We looked at each other and we were saying, 'Geez, we're going to be doing a lot of blocking.'"

But there still were opportunities for the receivers to be game-breakers.

Back on Track: October 31–November 13

Sunday, November 6 vs. Pittsburgh Steelers, Mile High Stadium

Sunday, November 13 at San Diego Chargers

With the Steelers coming up after the crushing loss to the Raiders, Red Miller wasn't going to abide any of this talk that Oakland had "exposed" the Broncos, showing that the way to beat them was to play conservatively—a difficult task for go-for-broke Ken Stabler—and avoid making mistakes and turnovers. The theory going around was that it would force the Denver offense to beat you straight up.

Miller defiantly said that if teams tried that approach the rest of the way, "they better have the muscle to back it up, and I can only think of a couple of teams who do." Under questioning, he said he meant Oakland and New England.

If Bronco fans wanted a diversion from the gloom and doom, they had the option to attend one of the Friday night sneak previews of an upcoming football movie—*Semi-Tough*, based on the Dan Jenkins novel, and starring Burt Reynolds and singer Kris Kristofferson. The huge ad told us: "Billy Clyde Puckett led the league in scoring last year . . . after the game."

Rocker Ted Nugent played McNichols Sports Arena on Halloween, and moments before he went on stage, he told "Dr. G" Brown, the *Post*'s rock critic, that he loved Colorado. "I go hunting every year out in Grand Junction, and I'm gonna move here someday soon and take over the mountains. I'm loaded, so I'm just getting ready to set up a real nice spread out here." But he emphasized that he didn't foresee making it a retreat that would take him off the road. "Kids don't change on me," he told Brown. "They still want primal rock 'n roll energy and that's what I give 'em. Ol' Ted's gonna go until he drops in his tracks, and that might never happen."

Myrel Moore wanted to take advantage of the matchup. Of course, the Broncos linebackers weren't going to be going up against the Steelers linebackers—Jack Ham, Jack Lambert, and Loren Towes—but Moore still looked at it as a head-to-head battle.

"Those backers of mine were always getting beaten out for the Pro Bowl by those Pittsburgh guys," he recalls. "I made a long and detailed effort to make sure they knew who they were playing, and this was their chance to make sure they wouldn't get beat out again and get into the Pro Bowl."

There was mixed news in Denver's advancement on the cultural and arts front. The Denver Symphony Orchestra's bitter strike continued, with no settlement in sight and concerts continuing to be canceled, yet the city reached an agreement with the Denver Center for the Performing Arts to lease and manage the concert hall that was scheduled to open in March 1978 in the new arts complex. That was significant for those of us at the *Post* because DCPA chairman Donald Seawell also was the titular head of the newspaper, and the suspicion always was that if there were any corners cut at the *Post*, one of the reasons might be to maximize support of Seawell's first love, the new world-class arts complex. A walk through the proposed galleria outside the concert hall alone was going to prove that Denver was no cow town.

Also, the word broke that the Denver Urban Renewal Authority had approved Writer Corporation's plan to build Writer Square, a complex of offices and apartments a short walk away from the DCPA. It would go up on a block that not so long ago was considered the hub of skid row.

The New York Rangers, with star center Phil Esposito, were coming to town, raising the question of whether a majority of the fans in McNichols Sports Arena for the game against the Rockies would be rooting for the visitors. We already had plenty of New York transplants who retained their loyalties. I got in touch with Rangers coach Jean-Guy Talbot, who had coached the minor-league and World Hockey Association's Denver Spurs, and he asked me a question before the interview started: "How's attendance?"

Not great, but when the Rockies got two goals from Paul Gardner and one from Wilf Paiement, two of their three young stars, and beat the Rangers 6-2 in front of 6,465, they had a five-game unbeaten streak, were 4-2-3 for the season, and were headed for the cover of *The Hockey News* as the young season's biggest surprise. The *Post* headline proclaimed that the Rangers had been victims of an "Avalanche of Goals." Avalanche? That seemed a strange hockey term.

The Nuggets, meanwhile, were Dr. Jekyll and Mr. Hyde, with a 4-4 record after losing at Buffalo and falling to 0-4 on the road before they finally knocked off the Tom Heinsohn–coached Celtics in the Boston Garden. General manager Red Auerbach didn't light up a cigar, but he must have been steaming about the loss to the former ABA team and the 30 points from David Thompson, who had spurned the NBA and helped make the merger necessary.

Early in the week, the pollution level got so high that officials took the extraordinary step of saying anyone with heart and respiratory problems should stay indoors, if possible. Environmental Protection Agency and Colorado Department of Health officials met with Dick Lamm, and the governor assured them—and told the public—that, if necessary, he would use the powers given him under the Air Pollution Control Act, passed in 1970. If it came to it, he could shut down the city, ordering the closure of everything except stores that sold food, drugs, and surgical supplies. At a news conference on the roof of a downtown building, Lamm pointed to the sky and said: "That cloud out there is a killer."

Looking back, he says he was starting to believe there was some hope. "I had a very fascinating meeting with the Health Department, and they showed me the statistics about the new engines versus the old one," he says. "When I was doing that press conference, I knew that the seeds of a partial correction were being planted. That was every time people got rid of their old car and bought a new car, it would improve the situation. We knew that no matter how fast this area was growing, new automobiles would give us an advantage on this problem."

Did that cause him to moderate his antigrowth, anti-automobile stand?

"I think 'antigrowth' is the way my position is perceived, and certainly it's not wrong," he says. "But it depends on whether you're talking about population growth or economic growth. *Now* I'm very concerned about economic growth because I think economic growth ties to global warming, but back in those times, I tried very hard to make people understand that economic growth and population growth are not Siamese twins. The planning issues were important to me, and the growth versus no-growth as I look back on it was another distraction. As I look back on this, Terry, I feel that I had a good and valuable sense of the future, but that I stepped on my own parade. After the Olympics, I was the *enfant terrible* with the business community. I had no idea how much the business community ultimately wanted to work with the Colorado governor. I considered them enemies because they had spent money against me in the campaign. Come on, I had been in the legislature for eight years; I shouldn't have been that dumb. I should have gone down to the Chamber of Commerce right from the start. When I finally did wake up, I found they were very cooperative. They wanted what was best for the state.

"But this growth versus no-growth? What I was most interested in was planning. What I really wanted was some better planning."

Air Force's 31-6 loss at home to academy rival Army dropped the Falcons to 1-7-1, and Ben Martin refused to address the issue of whether he would be back to coach in the remaining year of his contract.

CU and CSU got back on the winning track, though, with the Buffs upsetting Earle Bruce's Iowa State Cyclones 12-7 on the road to get to 6-2-1, and CSU was 7-2 after the Rams shocked Western Athletic Conference rival Arizona 35-14 in Tucson. That clinched a third consecutive winning season under Sark Arslanian.

A temporary footbridge across the South Platte River, linking the Auraria campus to Mile High Stadium, was supposed to have eased the parking and traffic problems in the stadium neighborhood, but protesters wanted to make sure Mayor Bill McNichols knew they didn't believe it had helped. On the morning of the game against the Steelers, they gathered outside a house near downtown, thinking it was McNichols's, but they were two blocks off, and by the time they discovered their mistake, McNichols had left home and avoided a confrontation. Their biggest beef now was that the mayor allegedly told them that issuing preferential parking stickers for those in the neighborhood, which would have prevented fans from parking there, was "un-American."

The Broncos signaled that they weren't about to fall apart with a 21-7 victory over the Steelers. They never were in trouble, not after they went 65 yards in 11 plays on their second possession, with Rob Lytle scoring from 1 yard out, and then Rick Upchurch returned a punt 87 yards for a touchdown, still in the first quarter. Upchurch hauled in the punt on the first bounce at the 13, cut left, and found open spaces down the left side of the field.

Haven Moses made a diving catch of a Morton pass for a 20-yard TD in the second quarter, and it was 21-0 at halftime. Then the Broncos let the air out of the ball, and Morton ended up throwing the ball only 12 times for the game, completing 5 for 101 yards. They dared the Steelers to score, and they couldn't. The Broncos had the best linebacking unit on the field.[1] And it also helped that punter Bucky Dilts had a terrific game, averaging 44.6 yards and nailing one for 63 yards.

After his terrific 1976 season, when he returned four punts for touchdowns, it was the first time Upchurch was a game-breaker in '77. "It seemed like they wouldn't even kick it to me that year," he recalls. "They're kicking it out of bounds or something."

But that changed against the Steelers, usually one of the top special-team squads in the league. His 167 yards on five returns were a single-game team record.

Craig Penrose came in to mop up, and maybe the day's biggest surprise was that Morton hadn't gone to the dressing room at that point, showered, and headed to the airport. After the game, he apologized for leaving the reporters in the lurch, saying he needed to get to Stapleton because he had "an important date to make."

He was getting married to Susan Sirman in Dallas the next day, and needed to catch a flight to Dallas to make the rehearsal and rehearsal dinner.

Years later, Morton says he and Susan "had said we'd wait and get married after the Super Bowl. I'd said it at the start of the year, and of course it was a joke. Then it was, 'Why not enjoy this [season] here?' so we just decided to do it. It was an unbelievable wedding. She really pulled it off well, but we had to get right back. The wedding was Monday, and then we came back Tuesday morning." He smiles. "So that was kind of, uh, unusual."

The Rockies' low attendance was continuing to draw criticism. I already was noting that reporters from the Canadian cities or New York, for example, couldn't understand why the NHL wasn't an automatic sellout from Day One in Denver. I was also starting to learn one of the NHL rules: Attendance in Detroit was rotten for a terrible team, but that was because the fans in that "Original Six" city were discerning and wouldn't patronize a bad product. Attendance in Colorado, a "new" market, was rotten for a terrible team, and that was because it was a "bad" hockey market. NHL Players Association head Alan Eagleson told the *Toronto Star* that the Rockies and Cleveland Barons might not even make it through the season and made it clear he didn't think that would be a bad thing. It all was a curious position for a union leader to take: Rooting for the loss of jobs.[2] Later in the week, Rockies owner Jack Vickers told me the Rockies were "going to finish the year in Denver. Not only are we going to finish the season, we are going to be here for years to come."

Pistol Pete packed 'em in.

The Nuggets drew a near sellout as they held the NBA's leading scorer, Pete Maravich, to 10 points in a 115-112 victory over the New Orleans Jazz. "It's just a matter of making it tough, [making] him work for everything he gets," said guard Brian Taylor, best known for his defensive prowess. *Post* readers of the game story possibly spotted a headline on the same page that said "O.J. Simpson's First Taste of Knife Termed Successful."

Despite the image that presented—what did he do, lick the knife?—it actually referred to the Bills running back undergoing minor surgery because of cartilage damage in his right knee.

Next up for the Broncos: San Diego. Red Miller, meanwhile, figuratively was knocking on wood. The Broncos were having good luck avoiding major injuries, and not only was he hoping it would continue, he was hoping it was a sign of one of those seasons when the planets aligned. His biggest concern remained the thin offensive line, and the Broncos released Jim Kiick for the second time and picked up journeyman tackle Hank Allison on waivers from St. Louis.

Patti Page and crooner Vic Damone made brief stands at the Turn of the Century, but there still were those on the west side who didn't think it was necessary to venture that far for their nights on the town and simply periodically checked in with the top local group—the Lawmen, who were regulars at Taylor's Supper Club on West Colfax. The new movies out were *Heroes*, a drama about a Vietnam veteran that was proving its star, Henry Winkler, was capable of more than being TV's Fonzie; the chilling *Looking for Mr. Goodbar* with Diane Keaton; *Julia*, with Jane Fonda and Vanessa Redgrave; and *Oh, God!* with George Burns and John Denver. But the symphony still wasn't an entertainment option. Dick Lamm called both sides in the Denver Symphony Orchestra dispute and tried to broker a settlement. He didn't even come close, he admitted. It seemed he might have been better off trying to make peace between consumer advocate Ralph Nader and Congresswoman Pat Schroeder, who was fuming after Nader stopped in Denver and accused her of "selling out" and pandering to special interests when she said she would vote against the latest attempt to create a consumer protection agency because the bill had become so flawed. Schroeder, who had been elected in part because she seemed outside the sphere of special-interest influence, said Nader was guilty of "consumer fraud."

Gerald Phipps did announce that the Broncos' official ownership group—Empire Sports—was donating $10,000 to a new Symphony Survival Fund, started during the negotiations as a potential supplemental fund for the musicians if a settlement was reached. He noted that the tax on orchestra tickets went toward the bonds that financed the voter-approved expansion of Mile High Stadium.

Lamm and Mayor McNichols also were headed to Scottsdale, Arizona, where they would pitch Denver as a possible major-league baseball city. This was quite a change from the summer, when Bears GM Jim Burris didn't have any civic company at the major-league All-Star Game. They returned saying they had attempted to make it clear Denver was ready for major-league baseball.

"Bill McNichols was the chief mourner of the 1976 Olympics," Lamm says. "Bill McNichols just couldn't believe that this state would elect this long-haired punk kid. I *really* tried to work with him and he tried to work with me. He really did. I think he disliked me intensely until the end. We were a couple of politicians put on a journey together, but what I remember about that trip didn't have anything to do with the baseball issue, but the awkwardness of being with Bill McNichols. . . . He was a very conventional thinker and a better politician than I was, by a long shot. It was just always stilted to be with him."

On Thursday, November 10, Ben Martin and Air Force officials decided to quiet the speculation, ease the pressure, and confirm that the coach would step down at the end of the season. Martin said he had made the decision in August. So when I had covered the Falcons early in the season, I had been watching a lame duck working on the sidelines, although he didn't want that out yet. "Service academy football is cyclical," he told a news conference. "You can't judge it by looking at just the past season or the year before that. It's a bigger concept and you have to judge it over a longer period of time."

By that standard, or virtually any other, he was a winner. On Saturday, the Falcons carried him off the field after they closed out their home season with a 34-28 victory over lowly Vanderbilt. CU, meanwhile, was blown out 52-14 at Oklahoma, with running backs Kenny King, Elvis

Peacock, and Billy Sims combining for 225 yards rushing. CSU's 21-21 tie with West Texas State at Canyon, Texas, was almost as embarrassing.

We had an upset. Apparently jump-started by Lamm's intervention and his making the Governor's Mansion available as the site for marathon negotiating sessions—in this case, while he was in Arizona—musicians and the symphony finally reached a settlement on Sunday morning, November 13. The catch was that the survival fund had to reach $500,000 or the musicians could pull out of the agreement.

If the deal held up, it might provide some PR points for Lamm, who had Republicans lining up to challenge him in 1978. Lakewood mayor Jim Richey became the fifth announced candidate for the GOP nomination the same day the symphony settlement was announced. Richey quibbled with Lamm's policies, saying the state shouldn't attempt to stop growth, but manage it sensibly.

If the GOP had its way, I-470 wouldn't be some silly parkway, but a full-fledged loop freeway.

The M&M Connection was buzzing.

Trailing 14-3, the Broncos got two Morton-to-Moses touchdown passes—the first a 33-yarder in the third quarter, the second with only 96 seconds remaining on a fourth down from the Chargers' 8—to knock off San Diego 17-14 in Jack Murphy Stadium.

Moses had nearly 40 friends and family members watching him in the same stadium where he played for San Diego State, and it all left him ecstatic. On the fourth-down play, Morton stepped up, bought time, and went to Moses at the back of the end zone.

"No time-outs left, one play left, and a field goal wasn't going to do anything," Moses remembers. "I remember coming all the way from the left side and he didn't hit me until the far corner of the right side. That meant I had a long way to run. I swear to God, he must have had this much space."

At that point, Moses holds two fingers about an inch apart.

"I saw the defensive back coming off Rick [Upchurch] and there was a guy chasing me, so there wasn't a lot of space between," he continues.

"I don't know how Craig got the ball in there, to tell you the truth. But what I remember was that it stuck. I mean I looked down, and it stuck. And I kept running."

Looking back, Morton calls it "an amazing play." And he confides that it was improvisation.

"They had all these plays, and I just said, 'Here's what we're going to do. Riley [Odoms], you're going to do an out and up. They will bite on Riley and I'll look over that way. Haven, just go and find a hole and we'll see what happens.'"

It was almost as if he had told Moses to cut at the oak tree in the park, or drew up the play in the playground gravel.

"Riley got covered a little bit," Morton says. "I just saw a little flash and threw it as fast as I could, and Haven caught it and that was it. I got good protection and Haven just got into a hole."

The Broncos shut out the Chargers in the second half, and James Harris—the starter while Dan Fouts was holding out—was only 13 for 31, for 166 yards. Morton came through in the clutch, but he otherwise had an off day, going 12 for 32, for 149 yards.

Denver was 8-1.

By then, it was obvious that Morton and Moses had tuned in to the same wavelength.

"He was one of the great people I had ever known," Morton says. "Haven had a certain ability—and you don't find this very often, and he was exceptional at it—of being able to see exactly what I saw from his angle. It was very easy to adjust and the things we did personally worked, and we didn't let the coaches know. Why argue?"

The coaches couldn't argue with success.

"Judge": Riley Odoms
Number 88, Tight End, 6-4, 230, 6th Season, Houston

Damn.

Because I was at Wheat Ridge's baseball practice, I missed the news conference at my temporary home, the Continental Denver.

Within 24 hours of his arrival in town, University of Houston tight end Riley Odoms had signed a Broncos contract and met reporters poolside at the hotel on February 28, 1972.

Odoms already had impressed my father, the offensive line coach, and the other Bronco staffers with his determination to succeed. He was the first-ever draft choice of the John Ralston regime, the fifth overall choice that year.

Odoms might have gone even higher if he had given the right answer to the St. Louis Cardinals, who called and asked what he thought of playing defensive end. Not much, said Odoms, who liked the idea of catching passes and blocking, and not of chasing down passers or trying to stop the run. The irony was that the Cardinals then used the fourth pick to take projected receiver Bobby Moore, that former slotback and running back under my father at Oregon. If the Cardinals had taken Odoms, perhaps without asking him about playing defense, it was virtually certain that the Broncos would have taken Moore—soon to be Ahmad Rashad. At the time, the Broncos were in sore need of wide receivers to compete with Jerry Simmons and Dwight Harrison. In fact, Denver was being second-guessed for not taking one of the wide receivers who ended up going later in the round—Jackson State's Jerome Barkum, Auburn's Terry Beasley, or Villanova's Mike Siani. Plus, the Broncos at the time already had a good veteran tight end, Bill Masters.

But this was Ralston's way of proving that he believed in a formula about first-round draft choices: If a potential number-one choice isn't good enough to be contending for, or be in, the Pro Bowl after his second season, he isn't good enough to draft. Again and again in subsequent years, he and his staff paid little heed to positional needs in making high picks, and used that Pro Bowl yardstick in both judging them before the draft and in looking back and deciding if they had made the right pick.

Ralston felt Odoms fit that standard.

A Corpus Christi, Texas, native, Odoms was a great all-around athlete who had played freshman basketball in one of the country's top collegiate programs at Houston, but then focused on football. He was no gazelle, and there was some fretting going on about whether he would be susceptible to adding too much weight, but he still had been fast enough to play flanker at the outset of his college career.

That day in Denver, while Broncos assistant GM Fred Gehrke was taking all of about four hours to negotiate a contract with Odoms's agent, Clifford Paul, Odoms—who had been told to wait at the hotel—arrived in a cab at the Broncos offices and asked to look at highlight films. He seemed so anxious to get going; perhaps his agreement to a contract so soon shouldn't have been a surprise.

"I want to live here, and I love being on a team that is building," he told reporters, including Dick Connor, at poolside that day. "That's what happened at the University of Houston. You are proud of it, maybe more proud you've been in on it from the building stage and then see it succeed. I watched your highlight film this afternoon. I was very impressed, especially with the defense. Defense is what makes a ball club, and you're just a step away from being a top team on offense, too. You've got good backs and some beautiful players."

Someone asked him to identify his "objective."

"I want to be respected as a player," he said that day. "To do that, you've got to perform on the field. My aim is to make rookie of the year. I feel I can make it if I apply myself."

Instead, he alternated with Masters that first season and had only 21 catches for 320 yards and one touchdown. But he took charge of the position in his second season. Yes, he even made the Pro Bowl then, beginning a run of four appearances in six years. He averaged 42 catches from 1973 to 1975, and in Ralston's final year, 1976, he had a broken thumb for part of the season and was limited to 30 receptions. But his blocking was always respected, and that got him a lot of marks from Red Miller, the old offensive line coach taking over for '77.

Miller was horrified when he saw Odoms—by then known to one and all in the Broncos world as the "Judge"—at the first minicamp. Odoms had played the season before at 245 pounds. At the minicamp, he was down to 215. That wouldn't do, certainly not with Miller expecting to play conservative football and play to the strengths of his defense. Odoms was ordered to get back to 230 for training camp.

As the Broncos came to the homestretch of the '77 schedule, he was back at that weight, and although this would remain under the radar, he was leading the team in receptions and seemed destined to stay that way. The wide receivers were making big catches, both in terms of yardage and impact, but Odoms was the reliable hand, producing the kinds of gains that prolong drives and open up the field.

Even more important to Miller, Odoms was doing a good job of blocking.

Notes

1. The Broncos linebackers were better on that day or any other day, which is another reason it is absurd that Hamm and Lambert went in the Hall of Fame in their first years of eligibility and none of the Denver linebackers have been inducted.

2. Alan Eagleson eventually went to prison for bilking his union.

CHAPTER 10

Standing Their Ground

They can't go inside again, can they?

—JOE COLLIER

First and Goal from the 1: November 14–27

Sunday, November 20 at Kansas City Chiefs
Sunday, November 27 vs. Baltimore Colts, Mile High Stadium

Facing the date with the Chiefs on the road, Red Miller made no attempt to conceal from reporters that Craig Morton was banged up and playing hurt. After all, he knew Morton was better off than the two quarterbacks who had suffered serious injuries over the weekend—the Packers' Lynn Dickey, who had a broken leg, and the Vikings' Fran Tarkenton, who had a fractured ankle and thumb. Morton didn't talk to reporters, but Miller passed along that the quarterback had told him "it was going to be a 12-hour whirlpool day."

Morton wouldn't be completely healthy for the rest of the season. When he wasn't at practice Wednesday, the Broncos said he had a stomach ailment and had to visit an emergency room for treatment. There was better news at running back, though, since Jon Keyworth was expected to play against the Chiefs after missing three games with a knee injury.

It was starting to look as if CU was going to have a player revolt of its own. Quarterback Jeff Knapple, demoted to second team, walked off the practice field Tuesday and Bill Mallory—fresh from a heated confrontation with some questioning fans at a Monday booster group meeting—made it clear he wouldn't take back the quarterback.

The Brown brothers—Larry and Herb—had a reunion Tuesday night at McNichols Sports Arena. The Larry-coached Nuggets, behind David Thompson's 33 points, beat the Herb-coached Detroit Pistons 123-113.

The next night, the largest hockey crowd in state history—a near full house of 15,206—watched the Rockies fall 4-1 to the defending Stanley Cup champions, the Montreal Canadiens.

The fans came for two reasons: To see Guy Lafleur and the best team in hockey. And to wholeheartedly participate in the Rockies' "Beer Night."

Beer went for 10 cents a cup.

Promoter Barry Fey didn't dare try the same promotion on Thursday night at the arena. KISS, inexplicably the most successful rock group in America, played McNichols a week before the release of its latest album, *Alive II*.

Finally, the Nuggets were back on Friday, beating their old ABA rival, San Antonio, 105-94. Scoring wizard George Gervin had only 22 points for the Spurs, who were hampered because three players were out with injuries. One of them was a young guard from North Carolina, George Karl. The losing coach, former Nuggets assistant Doug Moe, wasn't fuming, considering the Spurs had played hard while shorthanded and had come in with five straight victories.[1]

Jesse Owens, the 1936 Summer Olympics hero, stopped in to visit a class at Walnut Hills Elementary, responding to an invitation students sent him when they read he would be in town to attend a Brotherhood Dinner put on by the National Conference of Christians and Jews.

The inevitable question: When he was competing and winning in Berlin, how did he feel about Adolf Hitler?

"I saw him every day, but I had no confrontations with him," Owens told the children. "He didn't shake my hand or talk to me. I wasn't concerned because I wasn't running against him. He would come into the stadium every day at 1:30 and 100,000 people would stand up. They would raise their arms and yell, 'Heil, Hitler!' It was eerie and you were worried."

He told the children about his friendship with German runner Lutz Long, who took a considerable risk when he hugged Owens in front of the full stadium—and the führer. He said he stayed in touch with Long until Germany invaded Poland, then later heard he had died. But after the war, he met Long's wife and daughter, stayed in touch, and even was the best man at Long's son's wedding.

What advice did he have for kids?

"I want you to learn what it is like to be on a team," he said. "Everyone is responsible for the success of a team."

He sounded like Red Miller.

After a 10-year run at the Radisson Hotel, the Playboy Club closed. The bunnies were given 24 hours' notice. The managers told the bunnies they would be thrown a farewell party soon, but their purses were searched when they left to make sure they weren't trying to escape with their costumes.

The number of Playboy Clubs in the country was down to 13, from a high of 21.

Mallory quieted some of the criticism when the Buffaloes got 174 yards on the ground from James Mayberry and won 23-0 on Saturday—but the cynics noted it was only against one of the dregs of the college game, Kansas State. The Buffaloes finished 7-3-1, and there was no bowl bid in the offing.

Behind 16 tackles from star defensive tackle Mike Bell, CSU shocked 12th-ranked Arizona State to get to 8-2-1, and Notre Dame showed no mercy in Ben Martin's final game, rolling 49-0 in South Bend.

That night, the Rockies showed why they had promise for the future—if they stuck around—as their young star forwards, Wilf Paiement and Paul Gardner, combined for five goals in a 7-2 win over the Cleveland Barons.

On Sunday, November 20, Louis Wright wouldn't give up.

He kept chasing the Chiefs' Raymond Burks.

This came with the Chiefs trailing 14-7 late in the game after a 23-yard touchdown pass from Craig Morton to Haven Moses broke the 7-7 tie with 4:29 left.

On the subsequent Chiefs possession, on a fourth-and-17 from their own 47, the Chiefs went into punt formation. The Broncos were mindful of the possibility of a fake. Give the Chiefs credit, though: They tried something imaginative, snapping the ball to upback Mark Bailey, who then slipped it to the speedy Burks, who took off and made it to the right sideline.

"I kept thinking, *Somebody will get him, somebody will get him*," Wright recalls. "Finally, it hit me that he's about to score and this is my last chance. I dived and got his foot, and he tripped and was down on the 1."

Looking back, Billy Thompson calls it "one of the greatest plays I've ever seen in a football game. And nobody ever remembers it! I'm on the sideline watching this in horror. First guy misses him and I'm not too upset. Second guy misses him, third guy misses him. Now, all of a sudden, I'm concerned. But Louis ran all the way across the field and dives at the end and clips him on the ankle, and he goes down. We think the guy scores."

The Broncos defenders not on the punt team came back on the field, and Wright joined them in the huddle as the Arrowhead Stadium crowd cheered.

"Well, from the sideline you couldn't really tell if he had scored or not," Wright says, "so the defense came running on the field and when the ref spotted the ball and we're in the huddle, and Bob Swenson and Bernard Jackson are saying, 'Let's block the kick, let's block the kick!' I was trying to tell them it's not a kick, that they have the ball and a first down! Now Randy wasn't calling the defense, because he thinks there's no defense to call because it's an extra point. I'm still *trying* to tell everyone it's *not* an extra point."

Exasperated, Wright grabbed Swenson and made him look at the scoreboard, which still said 14-7.

The Broncos still had a chance to hold 'em!

Thompson remembers putting his hand out into the middle of the huddle, palm down. An instant later, 10 hands were on top of his. They were going to stop the Chiefs.

Four plays later, Denver had completed a classic game-saving goal line stand. Gradishar penetrated and stopped two running plays, as Gradishar did time and time again on the goal line in his career. It was the trademark of both Gradishar and the defense overall. "The defensive coaches really emphasized that, particularly Myrel [Moore] and Joe [Collier]," he says. "I remember when we got down there, Tommy's yelling and screaming, like he does, 'Hey, guys, let's go, we gotta hold 'em here!' I tried to do this as often as I could, but after we broke the huddle and we're in short yardage, I mentioned to Lyle and Barney and Rubin, and even to Rizzo and Swenson, 'Just stay low, just stay low!'"

Gradishar emphasizes his goal line prowess was part of a team effort.

"All they were doing was creating a stalemate or pushing them back a half step and they have no place to go," Gradishar says. "So my success was because of those six or eight guys, however many there were down there on any play, stalemating it. Sure, there was some instinct there and judgment from film study, like here's their favorite play. . . . It's not rocket science. Part of it's luck and part of it's flying over the top. I could keep flying over the top, but if those guys aren't penetrating, it wouldn't work."

With the other Broncos staying low and penetrating, Gradishar moved up and made the stops on both of the first two plays, plunges by Ed Podolak and Bailey.

On the sideline, Collier turned to Moore. "They can't go inside again, can they?" he asked. Moore agreed. They wouldn't. Collier sent in "double out," a call that looped Tom Jackson and Swenson outside, and Jackson nailed Walter White on a tight end reverse for a 6-yard loss. On fourth down, Chiefs quarterback Mike Livingston tried to hit Henry Marshall in the back of the end zone, but the pass fell incomplete.

Only 25 seconds remained in the game.

As the defense came off the field, celebrating, other players were down on their hands and knees, fanning their arms up and down, "bowing down" to the defense. One of them was Haven Moses. "That was one of the most fantastic stands I've ever seen in the game of football," he says. "You actually moved an opponent back until it was fourth-and-seven, and stop them right there? We knew right then and there how good we were."

Thompson calls it "the greatest four-play series, on the road, in a hostile environment."

Swenson recalls: "Our short-yardage defense was low, submarine everybody, and nobody could figure out what we were doing. And Joe was so smart, he would kind of know. I remember them trying to run two inside and everybody's pinching, and then Joe Collier is going, 'If the other coach runs three in a row he's going to look like an idiot and he's going to get fired.' It looks like we know the play twice in a row. So they say okay, they'll do the opposite, and we do the opposite and run right into them again. They don't score and we walk off the field like: 'You're not going to score on us.' By then, we didn't think *anyone* could score on us. You were *not* going to score on us."

When that series comes up, Rubin Carter says something similar about how it epitomized the defense's attitude.

"We were a no-matter-what kind of defense," he says. "No matter what happens, no matter what happens with the offense, no matter what happens with special teams, they're not going to get in our end zone. We were very territorial. We were young pups and we were marking our territory. *You're not coming in here.*"

The Broncos ran out the clock to go to 9-1.

Many of the Broncos said the first victory over the Raiders was the confirmation; many others believe it was the game at Kansas City. "I remember thinking it was such a small play, but that might have been my greatest play ever," Wright says. "Good things were starting to happen to us. The gods were with us."

Otis Armstrong ran for 120 yards for the Broncos. An aching Morton was only 8 for 18, for 125 yards, but that included the game-winning TD pass to Moses.

Denver was shorthanded defensively after Lyle Alzado got tossed out of the game late in the first half for punching Chiefs tackle Jim Nicholson after the Chiefs' touchdown. It was so blatant, it almost looked as if Alzado, the one-time Golden Gloves boxer, thought he was trying to knock out Muhammad Ali. Unfortunately for the Chiefs, the official just assumed Alzado couldn't have done that without provocation and tossed Nicholson out of the game, too. The Chiefs already had lost their other starting tackle, Matt Herkenhoff, in the first half with a pulled groin muscle, so it was a makeshift offensive line trying to block on the goal line in the final minutes.

The gods . . .

"You've heard of a Cloud-Nine game?" asks Barney Chavous. "That was a Cloud-Ten game."

The NFL gave the Broncos the go-ahead to mail out playoff ticket applications to season ticket holders. Considering the Broncos never had been in a playoff game, much less had one at home, it was a new experience. It even seemed a bit presumptuous, considering the Broncos still had two home games—including one on the upcoming Sunday against Bert Jones, Lydell Mitchell, and the once-beaten Baltimore Colts—and four games overall remaining in the regular season. When fans opened the letters and saw the figures, the Broncos could fend off any complaints with the truth: The league set the prices. For the first round, the tickets (including the 10 percent seat tax that helped fund the stadium expansion) went for $9.90, $12.10, and $22, while they were $12.10, $15.40, and $26.40 for a possible AFC championship game. The fans had to show faith. They had to pay for both games, subject to a credit for next season if one or both of the games didn't come off.

We were joking that Red Miller wouldn't even say the word "playoffs." Dick Connor noted that the farthest Red would go was to say "something good at the end." The team's office personnel, though, had to look ahead, and my brother was among those in the provisional planning meetings about hosting a playoff game or two at Mile High Stadium.

Growth continued, and some agreed with Governor Lamm that it was out of control. The superintendent of the overcrowded and overwhelmed Cherry Creek School District, Dr. Richard Koeppe, in a report pretty much begged the Arapahoe County commissioners to "slow down the growth rate to give the district a chance to look ahead, to breathe, to pay off some of its debts." The Colorado Highway Commission, over-whelmed by requests for construction permits from developers who wanted to go ahead with projects tied to the construction of the proposed C-470, despite its downgrade from a freeway to a parkway, declared a moratorium on the issuance of permits.

Jon Keyworth was hoping the growth signaled success for his latest venture—he and partner John Nowlen opened the High Chaparral, a Littleton restaurant.

Big-league baseball was coming!

Oakland A's owner Charlie Finley revealed in Chicago on the day after Thanksgiving that he had met the previous week with an, ahem, unnamed potential buyer of his American League team who would want to move it to Denver if the deal went through.

Finley let it be known that California Angels president Red Patterson had helped arrange the meeting between the prospective buyer, a Patter-son friend who lived in Southern California, and Finley. However, the plot thickened Friday night when Frank Haraway of the *Post* reached Patterson, who was irate that Finley had disclosed the meeting. Patterson claimed it had been only preliminary in nature—and leaving us to infer that ol' Charlie was playing games again, perhaps trying to improve his bargaining position with another potential buyer, Robert Moody, who hoped to move the franchise to New Orleans.

Even Patterson pointed out that the Athletics had a 10-year lease at the Oakland Coliseum that might prove difficult to break.

Within a few days, the news broke that the prospective buyer was Denver oilman Marvin Davis, who had a home in Southern California—the same Marvin Davis who a few weeks earlier had been so upbeat about the energy industry boom.

Larry Brown got tossed in the first half of the Nuggets' first sellout of the season, which turned out to be a 136-123 victory over the Indiana Pacers. He charged out onto the court, his hair and tie flying, to unload on referee Tommy Nuñez about the game getting so physical, it was out of

hand. "It was like a hockey game where at the end of each period, you clean off the ice," Brown said after the game.

———

On November 27, the Broncos got to 10-1—the league's best record—with their 27-13 victory over the Colts. It came the way they had become accustomed to winning: Morton threw only 14 times, completing 8, but 2 were for touchdowns—a 41-yarder to Rick Upchurch and a 19-yarder to Jack Dolbin. Andy Maurer, back in the lineup at left tackle, had his best game of the season, neutralizing the Colts' John Dutton.

Billy Thompson's interception set up the first touchdown. Then, with the Colts trailing only 14-13 and driving, Tom Jackson broke it open, intercepting a Bert Jones pass intended for Don McCauley in the flat and returning it 73 yards for a touchdown, and then tossing the football into the South Stands.

"I had all the gears open," Jackson said after the game. "When I hit that end zone, I felt like a million dollars." He also talked about how he had dropped the ball while running for an apparent touchdown after a late-game interception against the Chargers two weeks earlier, and how he received an obscene letter from what most likely was a disgruntled gambler, upset because the Broncos hadn't covered the spread. "The first thing that came to my mind was *Don't drop the ball, stupid,*" he said. "I tucked it away safely and made sure of it, then I turned on that blazing 5.2 speed to the goal. . . . I hope that man writes me a letter this week."

He said he didn't mind that he would be fined for throwing the ball into the stands.

"I just thought that something like that might happen only once, so I knew when I did it that I didn't care about a hundred bucks," he said. "That ball had to go to the fans."

After Louis Wright got another interception of a Jones pass, Morton added the final touchdown, running for 6 yards in a move that probably made Red Miller *very* nervous.

Bert Jones threw 46 times for the Colts and while the yardage, 252 yards, seemed impressive, that took 27 completions—and 20 of them were dumpoffs to backs Lydell Mitchell and McCauley. The Broncos didn't break and also came up with three interceptions.

Denver had three games left.

During the final minutes of the Broncos-Colts game, Richard Savage; his sister, Doris Deitz; and a friend, Gilbert Lopez, walked into North Denver's Arabian Bar, four blocks down Navajo Street from Mount Carmel Church. They put some coins in the jukebox and began playing music. That didn't please two men and a woman who already had been in the bar for a while and were watching the Broncos game. Savage was told in colorful terms to knock it off, that the music was competing with the Broncos telecast.

After some repartee, one of the Bronco fans yanked the jukebox plug out of the wall, heating up the disagreement, and all six ended up in an alley behind the bar. Soon gunfire was heard. Savage, 41, was shot in the stomach. He was taken to Denver General Hospital and died within minutes. Lopez was seriously wounded, also in the stomach. Deitz was shot in the buttocks.

The bartender told a *Rocky Mountain News* reporter that all six involved were Arabian regulars.

Red Miller, GM Fred Gehrke, and their wives went to dinner at Emerson Street East. When they walked in, heads turned and many clapped. A man presented Miller with an Indian rug with the Broncos logo on it.

"Gee, thanks," said Miller.

Down the Stretch: November 28–December 18

Sunday, December 4 at Houston Oilers
Sunday, December 11 vs. San Diego Chargers, Mile High Stadium
Sunday, December 18 at Dallas Cowboys

Broncos ticket manager Gail Stuckey was finding that season ticket holders didn't understand why they had to buy tickets to two home playoff games if they responded to the playoff application mailed to them. "This is the only way we can make certain we distribute the tickets if we're the home team," Stuckey told Dick Connor. He also said the Broncos were getting many fans asking to join the waiting list for season tickets, which already had 5,000 names on it despite 55 straight sellouts and no promise of when they would be able to buy tickets.

The stadium expansion hadn't met the demand, even before the '77 Broncos took off.

Stuckey also disclosed that the Broncos would have an allotment of 10,000 tickets if Denver made the Super Bowl, and they would be distributed on the basis of season ticket holders' priority numbers.

That seemed rather undemocratic.

At his Monday news conference, Red Miller wanted to focus on the Sunday game at Houston, and nothing else. "We've got three more games," he said, "and then we go from there—wherever that is."

In fact, Miller had refused to attend another organizational playoff planning meeting that morning.

Denver budget director Ted Hammond, meanwhile, told Mayor Bill McNichols and the City Council at a meeting that he already had budgeted $40,000 to cover the costs of hosting two playoff games at Mile High Stadium. The city would make at least $200,000 on the games, but Hammond was showing faith.

One Broncos fan was so mad about missing the September 18 regular-season opener against St. Louis, she sued, and on Tuesday, a Denver County judge awarded more than she sought in the suit.

Helen Harris was awarded $62.88. Yes, sixty-two dollars and eighty-eight cents.

"We're number one!" she said as she exited the courtroom.

She had sued out of principle, because RTD had been overwhelmed on the day of the opener and hadn't been able to handle all the fans who wanted to ride the bus from the Aurora Mall to the stadium. After waiting for an hour, she went home and watched the game on television, and she was especially upset because the stadium expansion had enabled her to get off the waiting list and obtain season tickets for '77.

She had asked for $31.50, the cost of two season bus tickets, and $13.20 for the cost of her two game tickets that day. The judge made RTD pay her another $18.18 for court costs.

It was premature to get in line for major-league baseball tickets. Early in the week, the latest was that a rival group inquiring into purchasing the Oakland A's franchise from Charlie Finley included Bill Cosby, Redd Foxx, Curtis Mayfield, George Foreman, and Don King. Then Marvin Davis revealed he had made tentative inquiries about a lease for the team at Mile High Stadium and didn't like what he had heard. Mayor McNichols made it sound like he believed it was all posturing. "I don't think that the lease would hold it up," McNichols told the *Post*'s Frank Haraway. "But if it does, it will have to be hung up."

Some candidate names finally hit the papers as Air Force continued the search to replace Ben Martin.

One was Bill Parcells, a young Texas Tech assistant coach touted as a defensive genius. His major competition seemed to be two offensive coordinators—California's Roger Theder and Wisconsin's Mike Stock.

The guard was changing, and not just in coaching. Veteran KMGH/Channel 7 sportscaster Starr Yelland, 62, was angry about being replaced on the 5 p.m. and 10 p.m. weekday newscasts and being shunted to the weekends. His replacement was Dan Ryan, 26, and Yelland would refer to him only as "that kid." To the *Post*'s Olga Curtis, he said: "I'm grateful I can still wander around and do stories. And I guess youth must be served. But Channel 7 stayed number one in Denver for 20 years while I was getting older, before the experts decided a young man was needed."

It was bound to happen.

Somebody was stupid enough to fight Rockies' rookie defenseman Barry Beck, who came into the league with the reputation as the most fearsome fighter in the sport—even as he played in junior hockey.

He fought Philadelphia Flyers winger Paul Holmgren, a noted heavyweight himself, in a 6-3 Colorado loss Saturday night.

If it had gone to the scorecards, Beck would have won a unanimous decision.

"There's no need to make a big deal out of it," Beck told me.

Being young and stupid, I did, anyway, running to general manager Ray Miron. "No one wanted to challenge him, and it took a guy like

Holmgren to do it," Miron told me. He added of the fight, "It's going to get around, that's definite. And it's going to get around that he won. That's even more important."

In the Broncos' 24-14 win at Houston on December 4, Craig Morton threw a pair of 13-yard touchdown passes to Riley Odoms and Rick Upchurch, and Norris Weese came on to put it away with a 5-yard fourth-quarter bootleg for a TD.

The Broncos boarded a Braniff chartered plane, and the pilot had managed to pipe the radio feed of the Raiders-Rams game over the plane intercom. If the Raiders lost, the Broncos would have clinched the AFC West championship with two games remaining. The Denver media was able to chronicle the reaction to what happened next in depth because in those days, reporters traveled aboard the team charter.

Billy Thompson recalls there was "so much noise on the plane, I went into the restroom to hear the game. I closed the door and listened to the game."

At 6:12 p.m. central time, 47 minutes after takeoff, as the plane was near Dallas, the game ended. The Rams won 20-14. The Raiders were out of the running for the AFC West title, meaning the Broncos were division champs and . . .

Thompson came out of the bathroom and joined the celebration.

Haven Moses laughingly remembers some imagined turbulence. "I think the plane just kind of went into a dive because we tore it up," he says. "We had vindicated ourselves for the year before, with that nasty situation. And then to come back and do what we did was special."

Morton looks back on the plane ride and also pantomimes mock turbulence, his hand moving up and down. "Everybody had a few beers and by the time it came on, and we had won the championship, everybody was berserk, jumping up and down, and it had to be going like this," he says, making the gesture. "It was fun, oh, God, and then we got home and all those people."

On the plane that day, Miller thanked the Broncos ownership—as he was talking, owners Gerald and Allan Phipps were wandering the aisles, hugging players—and Fred Gehrke for giving him a chance to be a head coach.

Lyle Alzado was walking around, unashamedly kissing teammates on cheeks.

Morton was spotted praying—apparently not about the turbulence.

On the plane, Thompson told reporters he was thinking about former teammates—Rich Jackson, Dave Costa, and Floyd Little—who hadn't been able to have similar celebrations. Years later, he recalls, "I knew they deserved to have been part of something like that. Those guys came to my mind, and I felt like I was their representative from that era when we were terrible. Those guys, and guys like [offensive lineman] George Goeddeke, I carried their flags with me."

Barney Chavous remembers even the usually reserved Joe Collier getting a little giggly. "Oh, man, we're back there drinking champagne and singing songs," Chavous says. "It was a feeling that we had arrived, we had achieved something and accomplished a goal that nobody ever thought we would attain."

At Stapleton International Airport, a crowd variously estimated at 3,500 to 5,000 greeted the team's arrival. On the intercom, a team official told the Broncos some of the fans at the airport had "waited 18 years to share in our celebration." After getting off the plane, Miller and many of the players walked over to the restraining ropes and shook hands with fans.

The fans were holding up many signs. One of them said: "Eat your heart out Cosell."

Miller finally got to his car. It wouldn't start. Recognizing him, some fans gave him a lift home. Many of the players headed to the Colorado Mine Company.

Despite all the pronouncements about work still to be done, Miller gave the Broncos an extra day off that week, and they didn't even meet and practice again until Wednesday.

The city still had a hangover. And, perhaps, so did some Broncos. They were expecting a more stern challenge from the Chargers on Sunday, because quarterback Dan Fouts finally had agreed to a new contract and reported at midseason, and was playing well for San Diego. His hardball agent was the same Howard Slusher who also represented John Hannah and Leon Gray.[2]

Word out of the Bay Area was that, whoa, hold on, the A's still might be sold to Marvin Davis for $12.5 million, and that one of the snags still was whether Davis could negotiate a more favorable lease than the city had outlined. A lot of us wondered if that was a smoke screen of some sort: One of the richest men in the country was going to sweat the relative nickels and dimes of lease terms?

Chicano leaders were upset that a Denver grand jury indicted only one of the three policemen involved in the summer shootings of two men in Curtis Park. David E. Neil was indicted for felony manslaughter, while the other two officers weren't indicted because the grand jury said there was evidence to corroborate their claims that the second man killed had pointed a gun at them.

On Saturday, December 10, a 15-mile-long caravan of vehicles—many of them tractors and combines—chugged through Denver and arrived at the State Capitol for a rally, creating a stunning scene of agricultural equipment parked downtown and through the Capitol Hill neighborhood. The drivers and passengers were farmers from Colorado and nearby states, representing the American Agriculture Movement and threatening to strike and cease farming. One banner on a vehicle read: "Farming is so poor, even [peanut farmer] Jimmy Carter has a part-time job." There were about 30 of the rallies around the country.

Something told me that none of the farmers headed over to McNichols Sports Arena to watch the Nuggets, behind Bobby Jones's 25 points, beat the Milwaukee Bucks to improve to 18-8 for the season. The major topic of discussion in the dressing rooms that night, though, remained something that had happened the night before in Inglewood, California, where Lakers forward Kermit Washington decked Houston's Rudy Tomjanovich during a melee in a game in the Fabulous Forum. Tomjanovich was hospitalized with a broken jaw and other injuries.[3]

The next day, the Broncos kept momentum, holding the Fouts-led Chargers to three field goals in a 17-9 victory in which Denver trailed 9-7 after three quarters and rallied. Denver's touchdowns came on a 41-

yard Morton screen pass to Lonnie Perrin and a Rick Upchurch 10-yard run. That sequence came after the Chargers seemed to have a legitimate beef when they argued that with the Broncos leading only 10-9 and San Diego driving, Fouts scrambled and his knee seemed to have hit the ground before he fumbled as Paul Smith tackled him. Joe Rizzo made the recovery, and—buoyed by Norris Weese's 21-yard run for a first down on a fake punt—the Broncos added an insurance touchdown on Upchurch's run.

Fouts threw for a staggering 276 yards, but couldn't get the ball in the end zone.

The downside for the Broncos was that their best special-teams player, defensive back Chris Pane, suffered torn knee ligaments and would be out the rest of the season. Also, Morton had to take himself out of the game for a long stretch because of what he said was shoulder numbness after he was sacked, and Craig Penrose came on in relief before Morton's late return. (The real problem was Morton's hip and upper leg.)

The most celebrated game in the NFL that day was in New Orleans, and I took a lot of teasing—including from Steve Cameron in his column—over it. The expansion Tampa Bay Buccaneers, including my father, their offensive line coach, won their first game ever—on their 27th try. They beat the Hank Stram–coached New Orleans Saints 23-14 in the Superdome, and they taunted the losing Saints quarterback, Archie Manning, by yelling at him: "It's disgraceful." (It's doubtful that Manning's infant son, Peyton, was there to witness the disgrace.) In the game week, Manning had said being the first team to lose to the Bucs would be . . . yes, disgraceful. At a huge rally when the Bucs arrived back in Tampa—you'd have thought they once had worn vertically striped socks and hadn't won a thing for 18 years—their coach, John McKay, pronounced it "the greatest victory in the history of the world." I suddenly didn't need to be as self-conscious about having a Buccaneers bumper sticker on my car—unless, of course, I was supposed to be sheepish for still driving the Pacer.[4]

By then, I wasn't making all the Rockies' road trips because after their promising start—after they made the *Hockey News* cover—they'd gone in the tank, and the newspaper also was sweating over the possible unbudgeted travel costs of having to send several writers and photographers to the Super Bowl.

A Super Bowl preview? Dallas (11-2) versus Denver (12-1)? That was the matchup in the final regular-season game, but neither had anything to play for—other than momentum—so the buildup wasn't anything extraordinary.

In fact, at the start of the week, the Broncos weren't even the lead story in the sports sections.

Marvin Davis and Charlie Finley met with Mayor Bill McNichols on Monday, December 10, and cleared one hurdle—with Davis reaching terms on a possible lease for Mile High Stadium if he bought the team and moved it to Denver. Frank Haraway's story in the *Post* indicated that major-league baseball officials believed Oakland would let the A's out of their lease if the San Francisco Giants agreed to play about one-third of their home games in Oakland.

That didn't seem like much of a problem, given the antipathy of many baseball folks for windswept Candlestick Park.

The Air Force Academy announced its choice as Ben Martin's successor, going with the young Texas Tech assistant, Bill Parcells. He was 36. "The coaching fraternity is a small group and I consider it a great honor to replace a man of Ben Martin's stature," Parcells said at his introductory news conference. "I consider this to be a real challenge and I hope I always will reflect the dignity that already has been built into this program."

Parcells previously had been an assistant at Army. "I've been on the field against Notre Dame with [Army]," he said. "I know that size in players will get you eventually when all things are equal. But you also can do things with superior quickness and speed."[5]

The hottest record in town wasn't a 33 rpm album, such as Earth Wind and Fire's "All 'N All" or "Chicago XI," but was a 45 rpm disc from Cartay Records.

The single was "Make Those Miracles Happen."

Inspired by Broncomania as he chatted with friends at his High Chaparral restaurant, Broncos fullback Jon Keyworth hit on the idea of recording an ode to the team and its ambitions. Mary Ruth and Don Weyand wrote the song, and Keyworth sang it with his house band and recorded it, and about 50,000 copies of the record were pressed. In Colorado, they were flying out of the stores.

The lyrics included:

Nobody does it alone
But if you're down and you want to be up
You want a drink from the winner's cup
You gotta make those miracles happen on your own.

The B-side was "Dance with Me, Baby."

After a year of buildup and advertising, *Close Encounters of the Third Kind*[6] was filling Denver theaters—and theaters everywhere—and drawing mixed reviews from both the public and critics. After seeing it early in its release, I had the same question many did: How come, if these aliens were so darned brilliant, they couldn't figure out a way to communicate with earthlings—instead of the other way around? It wasn't particularly fashionable to admit this, but I did enjoy another new release—*Saturday Night Fever*—a lot more. I even thought of buying a white suit.

Take Me Out to the Ballgame!

On December 14, in a news conference at his downtown Denver office, Marvin Davis announced he had closed the deal with Finley to buy the A's and move them to Denver.

Davis said that in the final conversation, he and Finley "hassled a little bit—about 10 minutes back and forth," Davis said. "I said, 'What will it take?' He said, 'If you give me this price, you've got a deal.' And I said, 'Deal.'"

It was going to be a challenge to fill the seats, he knew, especially because the A's were coming off a 63-win season and had just unloaded star pitcher Vida Blue. "In life, you get stereotyped in business," Davis said. "You do everything motivated for business. Sometimes, you want to do something for fun when you're 52 years old."

I was excited, too. Frank Haraway certainly had earned the chance to cover a major-league team, but the baseball "beat" generally was considered a two-person operation. Baseball had been my best sport; I understood it and loved reading about it. I knew I was going to toss my hat into sports editor Bick Lucas's office, saying I was interested in moving to the baseball beat.

Denver was going to just be plugged into the existing 1978 American League schedule, meaning the A's—or Bears, or whatever Davis decided to call them—would open at Anaheim on April 7, then have their first home game on April 10 against the Seattle Mariners.

Another AP story said that an attorney representing the Oakland Coliseum said he was awaiting the final details of the sale "so we'll know who to sue along with Mr. Finley." The lease at the Coliseum ran through 1987. Aw, it was all posturing. The *Rocky Mountain News* ran the team's 40-man winter roster.

The news meant the papers didn't splash the news that five Broncos—Lyle Alzado, Randy Gradishar, Tom Jackson, Billy Thompson, and Louis Wright—had been named to the AFC Pro Bowl roster. Alzado, Thompson, and Gradishar were selected as starters.

Morton's hip still was sore, and though this wasn't publicized, he was trying a different treatment regimen. That wasn't as startling as the identity of who was providing much of the treatment.

"Dolbin was giving me some treatments on the side," Morton says.

Yes, that was Jack Dolbin, one of his receivers.

The prospective chiropractor had a makeshift treatment center in his Arvada home. "In anticipation of someday practicing chiropractic, I was acquiring some physical therapy equipment," Dolbin recalls.

Dolbin says he noticed that Morton "was going to the training room every day and they were icing it down, and iced and iced and iced." Dolbin remembers approaching Steve Antonopulos, then the assistant trainer. "I called Steve aside and said, 'Steve. I don't have an ego and you don't have an ego, so let me try something.'"

Dolbin says he first suggested they try heat instead of cold, and so Antonopulos gave Morton a diathermy heat treatment.

"Craig said, 'Hey, it feels a lot better,'" Dolbin says. "So I said, 'Craig, I'm not going to practice chiropractic in the training room. First of all,

I'm not licensed.' I was only about halfway through school. I said, 'You come out to my house in Arvada, and let me work on it.' He came out to the house and I took him into the basement where I had this galvanic machine. I did some deep muscle massage on him and tried to stretch him out a little bit. Then I put the high volt machine on him, and that was a muscle stimulator. It would cause the muscle to contract with the pulsating current and he got up and said, 'Man, that feels good.'"

The treatments quietly would continue, off and on, through the next month.

Tom Jackson made a scheduled two-hour autograph-signing appearance at the May D&F store in University Hills. He showed up a half hour early and kept signing as virtually all the hundreds of orange T-shirts disappeared off the racks, as did just about all the Bronco paraphernalia the store could put out. Jackson kept signing anything and everything, and after he got up and was walking out, he signed one more autograph for a woman and her two sons. Dick Connor, watching all of this, heard the woman ask Jackson if Sunday's Cowboys game was a Super Bowl preview.

"It could be," Jackson told the family. "It could be Denver and any-body."

Oakland Coliseum officials were granted a restraining order from a U.S. district court judge in San Francisco, preventing the A's from breaking their lease and throwing a huge monkey wrench into the team's move to Denver. Also, Jerome Holtzman of the Chicago *Sun-Times* wrote that American League owners were telling him there was no way a move of the franchise would be approved until Finley bought his way out of the lease. But there still was some speculation that if the Giants agreed to play in the Coliseum at least part-time, the problem would go away. Davis said the lease issues were Finley's "problem, not ours. When he gets his release in Oakland, he will deliver us a team free and clear."

The Nuggets retired Byron Beck's number 40 before a game against the Washington Bullets. The team presented him with a new Mazda station wagon and other gifts. Nuggets cocaptains Dan Issel and David Thompson stood with him during the ceremony.[7]

After the game that followed the ceremony, Larry Brown—Beck's onetime ABA roommate—had to be restrained as he charged after referee Wally Rooney, holding him culpable for a 117-112 Denver loss in overtime. "I wanted to go up and wish him a Merry Christmas," Brown said later.

The next night, Barry Beck—no relation—had a hat trick in the Rockies' 5-1 victory over Minnesota. That was quite a feat for a defenseman, and a rookie one at that.

———

On the day before the regular-season finale, the Denver Marriott—at Hampden and Interstate 25[8]—held an "Orange Rally" in its parking lot. Several fans showed up in orange cars and orange vans. One of the attractions was a huge orange cake, decorated with orange stripes and orange goalposts. Mayor McNichols and Broncos co-owner Gerry Phipps christened an orange RTD bus with a bottle of Orange Crush. Channel 9 newscaster John Rayburn and sportscaster Gary Cruz were the masters of ceremonies, and the congenial Rayburn was funny when he addressed the issue of whether broadcast journalists should try to be objective. "The hell with that," he said. "We've been getting letters saying we're not giving big-city sports coverage. Whoever said a big-city attitude always had to be presented? The fact is, we have a neighborliness, like in small towns. I don't see a damn thing wrong with that."

In keeping with the season, Santa Claus also was there—in an orange suit.

———

The Broncos lost 14-6 to the Cowboys on Sunday.

So what? After feeling better following his treatment from Dolbin, Morton started, but threw only one pass and was in for only one series before leaving the game for good. This didn't get much notice at the time, in part because Morton shrugged off the suggestion that he had been injured, but his last play was when he was sacked on a safety blitz. At the time, he said the plan was for him to only play a series, anyway, and that was true.

Years later, though, he says he believes playing at all was a mistake because of his physical setback.

"I was hurt," he says. "Red came to me and said, 'What do you think, does it mean anything to you to play?' I said no. He said, 'You probably should just play a series, just so we don't . . .' And I just said, 'All right.'"

But, he says, "They nailed me again. My leg just ballooned up again. I was just getting to feel better and it started again."

It would become a major issue in the coming weeks. Miller's decision to play him for a series certainly is defensible because of rust and appearance issues.

Otis Armstrong didn't play at all that day because he was hurting.

Cowboys quarterback Roger Staubach threw touchdown passes of 22 yards to Preston Pearson and 7 yards to Robert Newhouse, and the Broncos—with Norris Weese and Craig Penrose sharing the quarterback duties—managed only 178 yards of total offense.

Most of the Broncos shrugged off the loss as meaningless, and still do, but Bob Swenson has a different take. "That was the most disappointing part of the season," he says. "In football, you just know when all conditions are perfect. You know it. You play hurt. You heal faster, you're hungry, you haven't been there. Things happen, you just know that all the conditions are perfect. You could just see it in the Cowboys' eyes, they knew they were going to go all the way. It was pretty amazing because they wanted to establish right there at the end of the season who was the better team. They went full speed; we went three-quarters speed. We didn't want to show them anything, they wanted to show us everything."

Another potential major problem was that Randy Gradishar suffered a twisted ankle. "Some big fat offensive lineman rolled on my ankle," Gradishar recalls.

The Broncos had finished 12-2, by far the best record in franchise history.

They had allowed only 148 points in 14 games, by far a franchise-record low.

They were the AFC West champions, beating out the $%# Raiders.

They had the home-field advantage for both playoff games, if they made it that far.

And they had the still-powerful Steelers coming up on Saturday, Christmas Eve.

Notes

1. In 2007, George Karl is the Denver Nuggets' head coach and Doug Moe—brought out of his retirement—is one of his assistants.

2. Later, Howard Slusher also was a Nike executive, and I got to know him a bit when I was working at the *Oregonian*. Notorious for never returning calls from the media, he called me out of the blue, and he laughed when it was clear I didn't believe it really was Howard Slusher. "Hang up, call Nike, and ask for me," he said. I did. He was asking me if I thought media members would show up if Nike held a party at its suburban Portland world headquarters during the NBA Finals, should the Trail Blazers make them. The Blazers did, Nike held the party, and some sportswriters didn't sober up for a month.

3. Also when I was in Portland, I appeared several times on a show Washington cohosted with Mychal Thompson. I found Washington to be thoughtful and likable, convincing me even further that he was a good guy who just snapped.

4. My father's two-season stay with the Bucs—he left to join the Chicago Bears staff—wasn't as troubling to him as you might think. He mostly loved his group of offensive linemen, in many cases smart players who gave it their all under trying circumstances.

5. As it turned out, Bill Parcells was the Falcons' coach for one season before joining the New York Giants as an assistant coach.

6. Years later, when I was told the producers of *Close Encounters* had expressed tentative interest in *The Witch's Season*, I rented the film and watched it again. I "got it" even less the second time around.

7. Among the numbers hanging in the rafters at the Pepsi Center in 2007 are Beck's 40, Thompson's 33, and Issel's 44.

8. There are many other Marriotts in the area in 2007, but that hotel on Hampden now is a Sheraton.

CHAPTER 11

Mardi Gras

He looked like he had been in a car wreck.

—ANDY MAURER

First Round: December 19–24

Saturday, December 24 vs. Pittsburgh Steelers, Mile High Stadium

On Monday, Craig Morton had just come from a hospital visit to have blood drained—or at least to have the doctors *try* to drain blood—from his bruised hip when he told Dick Connor he was going to do interviews that day with the scribes, with NBC, even with *People*, but that was going to be it. The rest of the week was going to be football. "I've been in the playoffs many, many times," he said. "Some guys try to please everybody, and it's nice to do that, but it's wrong."

Looking back, Morton remembers the injury as a hip pointer that developed into something far worse. "It kept bleeding and it wouldn't stop," he says. He had just about given up on the doctors being able to do much for him, but he kept trying. Jack Dolbin, the chiropractic student, continued to work on him, too.

It didn't rate much play in Denver, but it was noted that Steve Spurrier, cut in the exhibition season, was going into coaching. He agreed to join Doug Dickey's staff at Florida, Spurrier's alma mater.

A week after Marvin Davis's the-A's-are-coming news conference in his tower, I checked in with Jack Vickers again at his own high-rise office to ask about the state of the Rockies.

The Rockies' average home attendance was 7,659, and Vickers said the break-even point was about 10,500 a night. "I think things are coming on," Vickers said. "And you've got to take into consideration that the Broncos have had a hot year and people are stirred up there. They've enlarged the stadium and there's football fever in the air now."

But Vickers said he would be paying close attention to the sort of lease the A's ended up with in Denver, if they came, and he said one of his alternatives was to build his own arena. "If we decide to stay in town and go forward with the hockey team, and if the city continues to take the stand they have on the arena, don't think for a minute that we can't go out and build a new arena."

Scalpers were having a field day. Brazenly placing "make-an-offer" ads for Broncos tickets in the papers, ticket holders were getting between $25 and $35 for the tickets, or at least twice face value.

At midweek, Miller said the Broncos were looking good in closed practices and that Morton's bruised hip "looks a lot better. I think the soreness has gone out of it."

Morton was sticking to his plan, and not speaking to reporters himself. He also was getting treatment on the side from Jack Dolbin all week.

The Broncos also were worried about Randy Gradishar, whose sprained ankle hadn't allowed him to practice.

"I was focused on this, and the whole state and everybody else is going to parties and having a great time," Gradishar recalls with a laugh. "I knew from college I could get through this, and I was saying, 'Coach, I'll be ready,' but I was questioning myself."

As a new sportscaster in town, Ron Zappolo had walked into a hurricane.

"Every night we're doing stories on guys who paint their houses orange, people who paint their toilets orange," he recalls. "I wish I could say I'm making this stuff up! I'm not! We did this stuff. To me, it all went hand in hand with an area of the country that for whatever reason, had a little bit of a complex that 'people around the country don't view us as big-time, people back east think we're not legit.' This was the first thing that really put Denver on the map, and people celebrated that. It was just a crazy, crazy time. The term 'predominantly orange'[1] hadn't been born yet. Are you kidding me? *Predominantly* orange? *Everything* was orange. For about four or five months, the Orange Crush consumed us in this town. People sent me the most amazing crap every week. The pictures! People would send me pictures of them painting themselves orange and told me, 'Put this on the air.' People sent me so much orange stuff, I gave it away to people at Channel 4 because we didn't have room for it. Orange napkin holders, orange gloves, orange this, orange that . . ."

The newspapers and even fans whimsically were beginning to call Denver's new major-league team the "Orange Sox." But on Thursday, Marvin Davis said in a deposition taken for court proceedings that if the deal for the A's hadn't closed and the lease issue cleared up within 30 days, the deal might be off.

The next day, the restraining order against Davis and Charlie Finley was dissolved in San Francisco, and Coliseum officials announced they would meet with Finley after Christmas. The ominous part of the news was that as part of the deal to dissolve the temporary restraining order, Finley agreed he couldn't sell the team without the Coliseum's approval. It sounded as if negotiations were on, and it all came down to how much Finley was willing to pay to keep the Coliseum folks from fighting the move any further.

One more and the Broncos were Super Bowl–bound.

Outplayed for much of the first half, yet hanging in a 14-14 tie at the break, the Broncos stormed off to a 34-21 win over the Steelers on Christmas Eve—and were facing a New Year's Day rematch for the AFC championship at Denver against the Raiders.

The Steelers played stupid football, including when Mean Joe Greene punched Broncos guard Paul Howard in the stomach, leaving him on the field for several minutes and bringing Red Miller charging toward the Steelers' camp when the second quarter ended a few minutes later. He got into shouting matches with, first, Pittsburgh assistant George Perles, and then with head coach Chuck Noll. At least it wasn't as bad as Greene's tactic in a previous meeting, when the star defensive tackle nailed Howard in the groin.

Miller still was angry, if satisfied, after the game.

"I told him I didn't want any more of that bullshit, and I hope you quote me," Miller told reporters.[2] "The way you take care of that kind of thing is you go out and put more points on the board than they do. We did just that, and they're flying home tonight as losers."

Tom Jackson was the star, making many big plays and helping seal it with a late interception.

Louis Wright, who still occasionally shook his head about being beaten by Lynn Swann for two touchdowns in his first game as a starting cornerback, was the major reason Swann had only one catch all day.

Although the Broncos had 14 points in the first half, the offense had struggled. John Schultz's block of a Steeler punt set up the first TD, a Rob Lytle 7-yard run.

"It was just a quick trap, and it opened up like anything," Lytle says. In the end zone, Lytle leaped in the air to celebrate, the ball held overhead, and Claudie Minor, who caught up to him just at that moment, also leaped and enveloped Lytle in his arms. Lytle later would get a copy of a picture that recorded the moment, and send it to Minor. His inscription to Claudie: "Thanks for the ride!"

Jackson's fumble return to the Steelers 10 put the Broncos in business again, and Otis Armstrong scored from there. Terry Bradshaw and Franco Harris each went 1 yard for Pittsburgh scores in the half.

In the second half, Morton was protected well—he was sacked only once all day—and threw touchdown passes of 30 yards to Riley Odoms and 34 yards to Dolbin as Denver pulled it out.

Odoms was the third receiver on his scoring play, and Morton had the time to wait for the big tight end to get open.

The Broncos pulled out of a 21-21 tie and into a 27-21 lead on consecutive Jim Turner field goals. The first, a 44-yarder, was a prodigious kick in the cold conditions. The second came after Tom Jackson's acrobatic interception of a Bradshaw pass—he knocked the ball in the air, then corralled it—and his 33-yard return to the 9.

Morton's pass to Dolbin put it away. The veteran quarterback had lobbied the coaches to allow him to try to hit Dolbin on a home-run ball rather than simply play conservative and run the ball and perhaps accept a field goal on the drive.

"Red said, 'No, no,'" Morton recalls. "I said, 'No, we have a touchdown here. I know it's a touchdown.'"

And it was.

"We got in the huddle and I remember Craig looked at me and said, 'Can you get him?'" Dolbin says. "Well, Mel Blount had gotten hurt, he had pulled a hamstring. Mel wasn't there, a guy named [Jimmy] Allen was there in his place, and I said I can get *him*. Mel Blount, I'm not so sure about, but I can get him."

Even the play Morton called was designed to go to the strong side, or Haven Moses's side, but Morton had played out his hunch. This time, the magic words were "Doc, be alert."

Dolbin says, "I beat the guy and Craig threw a perfect strike, right over the outside shoulder. I didn't beat him by a whole lot but I made the catch."

Instead of holding on to a tenuous 27-21 lead or accepting a field goal to make it 30-21, the Broncos were up 34-21—and that's the way it stayed.

But the Broncos had some injury issues, and not just Morton's soreness.

Rick Upchurch suffered a leg injury on a first-half kickoff return. "There was a hole there and I could see the goalposts," Upchurch recalls. "That hole closed *so* fast. As I was getting through it, I got leg whipped. I got hit between the knee pads and thigh pads and it was like somebody shot me in the leg."

Lytle, who had 12 carries for 26 yards, hadn't been available late after taking a head-on hit from the Steelers' L.C. Greenwood. "I knocked myself out," Lytle says. "I was out. I was walking around and they said I was heading over to the Steeler huddle. I had the standing 10 count."

That concussion would become an issue the next week.

Gradishar knocked down a crucial pass, but he was hobbled on his bad ankle. "I did the treatment, but I wasn't close to 100 percent," he recalls. (In fact, in the dressing room that day, he called it "the worst game of my career," and refused to blame it on the ankle. But it was obvious that was the problem, and he was taking the high road.) Looking back, Gradishar remembers two major things about the game: One, his pain; and, two, the uncharacteristic giddiness of co-owner Gerald Phipps on the sideline after Dolbin's catch clinched the win. Like all the players, he has fond memories of Phipps and always calls him "Mr. Phipps." But other than that? "All I wanted to do was get back in the locker room and start putting ice on my ankle," Gradishar says.

Morton finished 11 for 23, for 164 yards.

Otis Armstrong was the Broncos' leading rusher, but had only 11 carries for 44 yards. "They were trying to intimidate us, but we weren't falling for it," he recalls.

Tom Jackson had brought his father in for the game. When the younger Tom got in the car, his father reached over, touched his son's arm, and told him he had played a "pretty good game." To Tom, it meant more than the cheers in the stadium.

Both AFC playoff games were on Christmas Eve, while the NFC games were set for Monday, with the NFL showing some respect for the Sunday Christmas holiday. The thinking made sense: This way both teams in the NFC title game would be coming off a short week, while both AFC teams would have an extra day to prepare.

The Raiders had survived against Baltimore, winning 37-31 in the second overtime.

As things wound down in the dressing room, Morton again approached "Doc" Dolbin. Both were planning to head to the Colorado Mine Company for the informal team gathering and celebration.

Dolbin says Morton asked if they could go back out to Dolbin's home first. He wanted another treatment. After that session, Dolbins says, they both went to the Mine Company for dinner.

A family gathering on Christmas Eve, with all the children and their families returning, was a tradition in the Foley family home, the former Saint Rita convent in New Orleans.

Although the AFC championship game didn't end until late afternoon, Steve Foley was determined to come through. He talked two policemen into giving him a motorcycle escort to Stapleton International Airport and caught a flight to New Orleans.

When he walked into the house later that night, he still was wearing his eyeblack.

AFC Championship: December 25–January 1
Sunday, January 1, 1978 vs. Oakland Raiders, Mile High Stadium

Red Miller told the reporters on Monday—the day after Christmas, the day after he had to spend part of his morning taking down a "Broncos Are No. 1" banner fans had strung between trees in his front yard—that Craig Morton indeed had received treatment at St. Luke's for his sore hip and leg, but the coach was adamant that Morton would practice during the week and play.

Morton still was black and blue and in pain. He had visited the hospital Sunday, and then checked in as a patient on Monday. It was a miracle the *extent* of his plight and his continued hospitalization remained secret, and closed practices couldn't completely account for the successful subterfuge.

The Broncos had to have a lot of luck, closed mouths, and—most likely—an outsider or two who figured it out going along with it and not spilling the news. Maybe the "smart money" got wind of Morton's status, though: The Raiders opened as 3½-point favorites in the Nevada sports books, and the line stayed there.

"We've been underdogs before," Miller said when the issue came up on Tuesday. "I think we've proved that we don't buckle under to that kind of thing."

At the time, Tom Jackson put it this way: "Everybody and anybody who's ever been an underdog will be rooting for us. They want to see Cinderella get her slipper back. They want to see the sheriff come in and clean up the town. Ever since I learned we were going to play Oakland, I've been wondering where the edge was going to come from. The edge came from the bookies."

Actually, of course, if the number seemed out of line, serious players and large bets would have forced it to move. It didn't. So it wasn't the bookies. It was the bettors. There was a tendency to wonder how the Broncos, in their first-ever trip to the playoffs, could handle the pressure and whether the defending champion Raiders' karma—with things such as phantom roughing-the-passer penalties tipping the balance—could win out over the franchise that still sometimes seemed like an intruder on the national stage.

Plus . . .

Pssssst! Hear about Morton?

Looking back, Morton says, "My leg was like two, three inches bigger, full of blood. It was red and purple. It was huge. So they came in all the time at the hospital and tried to drain blood from it."

That didn't do much good.

When the Broncos went back to work Wednesday, it wasn't much of a shock that Miller closed practice to the media. "We want to be accommodating, but we want to be able to keep our concentration, too," he said. "It's not that we would try to hide anything in the way of gimmicks or anything like that."

Note: He avoided addressing the issue of hiding injuries.

Miller did say that Morton was held out of practice but added the quarterback would be back in pads on Thursday.

He didn't mention that Morton still was in St. Luke's, or that he had visited him that morning. "He brought me the game plan," Morton recalls. "So I studied the game plan. There were some wrinkles in there, some things with Haven."

Morton couldn't do much else, except study.

On Thursday, Miller again reported that Morton hadn't participated in pads, but at least implied that the quarterback at least had been present, in shorts, and had thrown the ball.

Thirty years later, Morton's recollection is that he remained in the hospital all week. He also tried heat, or "the Dolbin treatment." "It helped a little bit, probably more than the doctors did," Morton says. "They couldn't get that stuff out of there."

The good news was that Randy Gradishar, while still not being able to go full speed in practice because of his bad ankle, was getting better. Rick Upchurch was undergoing therapy, too, for his leg contusion, but was making more progress than Morton.

Charlie Goldberg, long one of the team's most visible boosters and a Quarterback Club mogul, owned a demolition company. The week of the AFC championship game, he draped an "OAKLAND" sign on a building he was supposed to tear down, painted the wrecking ball orange—and let the ball beat the hell out of Oakland, so to speak.

And the walls came tumbling down.

The Nuggets finally had snapped a losing streak at five games with a victory over Phoenix, and star guard David Thompson was tired of hearing talk that the locker room was divided and dissension was a major problem. "Nobody ever expects us to lose," he told the *Post*'s Irv Moss. "That's one of the problems. Every time we lose some games, everyone thinks there's some sinister reason."

Thompson also was excited about the Broncos' run, plus the likely arrival of the A's. "If the baseball team comes here it will put Denver right up there with New York and Los Angeles," he said. "I've talked with a lot of players who would love to play for a team in Denver."

Well, that still was on hold after a three-and-a-half-hour meeting Friday in Oakland attended by Bowie Kuhn, Charlie Finley, and Coliseum representatives didn't resolve the lease issue, and all agreed to meet again the next week.

The irony was that the A's cotenants, the Raiders, indeed were on their way to Denver, arriving Friday night.

To reporters, including many from around the country, Miller acknowledged Morton didn't join in the nonpads workout on Friday.

"His injury hasn't responded to treatment as well as we'd hoped," Miller said. "It's not the first time he's missed a whole week of practice before a game this year."

The quarterback wasn't quoted in the media all week.

The serious gamblers probably noticed.

Years later, Miller has a hard time feeling guilty for the deception. "I feel bad because it was a lie, but for no other reason. Craig wasn't only black and blue. He was *black*, not black and blue, from here to here," Miller says, making a gesture that covers about his entire side. "He had some blood in there coagulating. So we took him to the hospital and I closed practice. . . . We got through the week and we got ready. Norris took almost every snap in practice." And, actually, Miller saying that Morton hadn't been involved in major practice work was a significant admission. Haven Moses says the players didn't talk about it much. "Nobody asked," he recalls. "It was 'don't ask, don't tell,' because we were trying to keep it away from Oakland that Craig hadn't practiced all week. We didn't realize how bad he had been hurt, or how bad his leg was."

But with Morton in the hospital, the Broncos practiced plays designed for Weese, including bootlegs and drags across the middle by Riley Odoms and other receivers. "We really didn't know what we were going to do, other than we were going to depend on the defense," Moses says.

The Broncos would have been well advised not to breathe too deeply at practice. The pollution index reached the disgusting level of 247, and a state official said that it had the same effect on us as smoking a half pack of cigarettes a day. One proposal being tossed out, and being taken seriously, was a ban of one-passenger cars in downtown Denver.

As game time approached Sunday, authorities were on the lookout for accused murderer Ted Bundy, who escaped from his jail cell in Glenwood Springs, shoving a ceiling light fixture out of the way and making it out through a crawl space. He was in Colorado to be tried for the 1975 murder of a vacationing nurse in Aspen.

The suspicion was that Bundy already was out of the area before his absence was discovered.

Morton hadn't done anything all week—except rest, undergo treatment, and try to get better.

A former California teammate of Morton's, Loren Hawley, was staying at Morton's house. "He came and got me," Morton recalls. "He said,

'What do you think?' I said, 'I don't know. I can't even walk.' He said, 'You've worked too hard not to play.'"

Assist, Hawley. Morton says Hawley took him straight from the hospital to the stadium, where he first spent a long stint in the whirlpool. He adds, "I went out and walked around with sweats on. I found I could back up fairly well, but I couldn't move forward, couldn't plant. So I went in and started getting dressed. I wanted everybody to see that if I was going to play, they can't hit me. It looked like it was gangrene."

His teammates marveled that he was even going to give it a try. "We'd heard all the rumors, and he hadn't practiced," says Tom Glassic. "But I didn't know how bad he really was until I saw him with his clothes off, and I saw him with all his bruises."

Moses says: "When I saw his leg, I said to myself, 'Man, I'm surprised they didn't cut that sucker off.' I had never seen anything like that. Deep, dark black."

Andy Maurer, who played the left side and would protect Morton's blind side, was banged up himself, still nursing a sore knee. He says a lot of his teammates were bruised and battered by then, but seeing Morton made them realize maybe they weren't that bad. "He looked like he had been in a car wreck," Maurer says.

Morton was standing, in uniform, with his shoes untied.

Miller recalls approaching him and asking: "Well, Craig, what do you think?"

"I said, 'Coach, you tie my shoes, I'll play,'" Morton recalls. "So he got down in front of everybody and tied my shoes. I said, 'You have to tell the line that if they don't touch me, we'll win this game.'"

The coach watched Morton make his first throw in warm-up. It was a labored, slow-motion, wincing toss. Miller says he turned to backup Norris Weese and told him: "Norris, get ready.'" Yet the coach noticed that Morton started to loosen up, wasn't wincing quite as much, and he was throwing the ball with a little more authority.

Miller says he then approached Morton. "How do you want to do it?" he asked.

This was the moment of truth—and *for* truth. A quarterback unable to move or do anything at all would hurt his team more than help. Miller recalls the subsequent exchange this way:

"Well, let me start and I'll tell you if I can't go," Morton said.

"That's good enough for me," Miller said.

But he also told Weese to warm up as if he were going to play.

Gradishar was wondering how his ankle would hold up. "I don't think I practiced on Wednesday, and it still was swollen," he recalls. "But it wasn't as bad. I was heavily taped." On the first series, he shot through and made a tackle against Clarence Davis and decided he was going to be all right. Or at least be able to get by.

Morton made it through the game, though one solid hit on his hip might have sent him back to the hospital—immediately.

"I still think that when we went out on the field and went into the huddle for the first time, we really didn't know who was going to be the quarterback," Andy Maurer says. "And then he came running out there on the field. But that's the warrior mentality that we all had. Craig had it, too."

Morton didn't get off to a promising start.

"I think the first pass I threw hit Jack Tatum right in the chest and he dropped it, which was very unfortunate," Morton recalls. "He couldn't hold onto it."

Ultimately, Morton connected with Haven Moses five times, for 168 yards and two touchdowns, in the 20-17 Broncos victory that sent Denver into Super Bowl XII against Dallas.

"That was the validation of my career," Moses recalls. "I had been solid up to that point, but didn't have an opportunity to really showcase talent and I didn't really expect to. I guess I had become the kind of ballplayer by then with a mentality that whatever I could do to make a contribution was what I wanted to do. I never had the opportunity to play with a quarterback any more than two years. I'd never been in a scheme that featured the offense, running or passing, so to me that game was totally unexpected. He hadn't worked out that whole week, but we really had a bond on the field, and it was like we were on each other's wavelength. He knew what I was going to do and I anticipated what he was going to do. I think our careers came together right there."

The first touchdown went for 74 yards in the first quarter, and it held up for a 7-3 Denver halftime lead. Morton recalls that it came after he told himself not to throw over the middle, or toward Tatum, again, and after he pretended not to understand the play sent in from the sideline and called something else. "I said, 'Don't go in there any more, Haven, go to the corner,'" Morton says. "So he did and when I saw Haven running down the sideline I said, *This is going to be our day.*"

Recalls Moses: "I was on the east side, coming in motion toward the formation. Halfway through the motion, they snapped the ball and I went upfield. Skip Rogers was the cornerback and I felt I had him beat. I wanted to hold him on my hip as long as I could, and when I got to that mark where I wanted to go [toward the sideline], I gave him the hip fake because we had been running in patterns against Oakland the whole year. So he was anticipating the in pattern, and I gave him the hip fake and broke out to the corner. I didn't know where the ball was, but I looked up and here it was coming. I said, *OK, catch it*, and I was heading straight out of bounds. But when I caught it and I looked down, I was a long ways from being out of bounds. Skip was reaching for me and he thought he was going to push me out. Just as I got to the sideline, I said, *OK, turn up*, and momentum got me going up and I started hauling ass for the end zone. I looked back and I'm thinking, *OK, OK, there's a flag somewhere.* I think the last three yards I backed into the end zone and I didn't see a flag.

"We had a long way to go. But if you think about a game plan, with him not being a part of practice the whole week, for him to call that play, there was a confidence factor there between him and me."

Moses had three more catches, all for first downs, and one in spectacular one-handed fashion along the sideline. His fifth catch, and his second touchdown, came on a diving catch that went for 12 yards in the fourth quarter, pushing the Broncos up 20-10. "Craig had read from right to left, from that side through Riley and then to me," Moses says. "He was just standing in the pocket, just trying to buy some time, and he came back to me. He threw the ball low, and I was stumbling in the end zone and couldn't get traction. Lester Hayes was on my butt and Craig threw it the only place he could throw it—down low. I was stumbling, my knees were going down, my feet were going down and I looked like the Roadrunner, with everything spinning and getting no traction. It came right in the basket and I caught it, and the only regret I have from that game is that I threw that damn ball up in the stands. Somebody's got that ball! Nobody's come forward and said they have that ball from the last touchdown!"

The most controversial play of the game came between those two Morton-to-Moses touchdowns. With Denver holding that 7-3 lead in the third quarter, Oakland's Clarence Davis fumbled at the Raider 17, and Broncos defensive end Brison Manor recovered. Moments later, Morton hit Riley Odoms for 13 yards to put the ball on the 2. On first down from there, Rob Lytle went off the left side, was hit by Jack Tatum, lost the ball, and Oakland's Mike McCoy recovered and took off the other way with the ball.

But hold on . . .

Linesman Ed Marion ruled that Lytle's forward motion was stopped and the whistle had blown before he fumbled. Replays, though, seemed to show he fumbled the second he was hit, before he was knocked back.

There's a story here, and it didn't come out after the game.

First of all, when I ask him to go through the "fumble," Lytle asks, "What fumble?"

We both laugh, and then he explains.

"Honest to God, I don't even remember the play," he says. "I told you what happened to me the week before. So I must have had a bad concussion. I had headaches and stuff, but those were the days that you didn't . . . well, it was a different era. You didn't think anything of it. I didn't play after that in the Pittsburgh game. They must have known enough to do that. I was out.

"But the following week, we're down on the goal line again and we run pretty much the same play again I scored on [against Pittsburgh]. I went over the top and Tatum hit me. I can't tell you other than what I see on film, because I was out. You get one hit, and another good hit to knock you out is that much easier, you know. I was out.

"The only thing I know that happened is that when you're out, you go loose. The ball just stayed on my stomach. If they have instant replay, it's their ball. But in that day there's no way those referees could have seen that. I ended up landing on it but I was out cold. I wasn't grabbing after it. As soon as I hit, it probably squirted out a little bit and they were able to recover."

More on this later.

After an unsportsmanlike conduct penalty on the irate Raiders put the ball on the 1, Jon Keyworth scored on the next play, and the Turner conversion made it 14-3.

It was 14-10 after Ken Stabler's 7-yard TD pass to Dave Casper early in the fourth quarter. And Oakland had the ball again when Bob Swenson, who had been having a great game already, made a crucial interception.

"Dave Casper kind of does a little delay and I had seen it on film before, so I stayed right there and Stabler hits me right in the chest," he recalls. "I run back but Gene Upshaw hits me and I fumble it and nobody knows I'm laying on the ground and nobody's moving. Nobody's scrambling and I don't have the ball. Then I kind of looked over and there it was, nobody saw it, so I got it back. I went to the sideline and I was so happy to have made this critical play and I was just hoping that we make a play so it counted."

That set up the 12-yarder from Morton to Moses that got the lead back to 20-10. "I missed the extra point, and it broke my heart," Jim Turner recalls. "I missed it. It couldn't have been pressure; I was used to pressure. Lack of concentration, whatever. It hurt my feelings. Every point counts and it could have really counted that game."

Stabler made it close with another TD pass to Casper, this time for 17 yards with 3:17 left.

The Raiders had two time-outs remaining and decided against trying an onside kick. The strategy made sense. It also didn't work.

Morton says he had a simple speech in the huddle before the first play of the possession: "If we get two first downs, we go to the Super Bowl."

They got them on a couple of clutch runs by Lonnie Perrin and Otis Armstrong and ate up the rest of the clock. On some of the plays in the drive, the Broncos put Riley Odoms outside Claudie Minor to the right, and ran that way. Regardless of the strength of the formation, Minor had lobbied with Morton to have the Broncos run inside Minor's left shoulder.

He was working against John Matuszak, and he told Morton he could ride Matuszak outside.

It was power football, and it worked, culminating with Armstrong's run for the first down.

"I remember Otis sticking his hand out of that pile of people. It just came out of nowhere. He was holding one finger, the number one, in the air."

Swenson watched that from the sideline.

"You've never seen a party from the second Otis's hand went up," Swenson says. "A whole city came out and had to be a party. It was like Bobby Thomson in our own little world, a shot heard around the world."

As the clock was winding down, co-owner Gerry Phipps approached Billy Thompson, one of the Ralston Revolt's leaders.

"I'll never forget this," Thompson recalls. "He said, 'You're the greatest . . . and you were right.'"

Joe Collier—the reserved Joe Collier—walked over and hugged his longtime friend, Red Miller.

Fans stormed the field and tore down the goalposts. Normally, you'd think when that happened, the revelers were taking their parts of the posts back to the fraternity house. This was the NFL!

Minor remembers "crying on the field, right then and there. We'd achieved something I always wanted to achieve. I wanted to be a champion. That's why I ran into people with my face, to be a champion."

The Broncos were going to the Super Bowl.

"The plane ride from Houston was for the coaches and the players," Barney Chavous says. "The AFC championship was for the city of Denver. It was for everybody."

Ron Zappolo remembers Tom Jackson talking with him on the air, and repeatedly (and very loudly) asking: "DO THEY BELIEVE NOW?"

Zappolo talked with Morton alone and was amazed. "I looked at him and thought, *I don't see how he played. I don't know how he did it*," Zappolo says.

Morton acknowledged that he had been in the hospital and hadn't practiced. The official version became that Morton left St. Luke's on Thursday.

The Broncos team physician, Richard Talbott, said Morton wasn't shot up with medication. "He just played on guts," Talbott said.

Years later, Morton says that's correct, that he didn't take any pain-killing or numbing injections.

"No," he says, shaking his head. "I used to do that a lot when I was with the Cowboys. But I found shooting up is not good. I did it for a while. I remember a game where I said, 'Naw, I don't want you to do that.' You don't feel anything. So I stopped doing that."

The Raiders were bitter about Lytle's nonfumble.

"Hell, yes, it was a fumble," John Madden, the man who once sat in young Haven Moses's Compton living room, told reporters. "Are there two balls in there? There's only one god-damned ball and we ended up with it." He did add, "When you lose, you bitch. It sounds like sour grapes. I don't like to be in that position. I chalk it up to human error."

Jack Tatum groused that "there was no whistle. I'd rather get beat by the other team than the officials."

Lytle didn't help matters with his honesty. But what everyone missed was that when he said he didn't know what happened, it was because he had been knocked woozy—and perhaps out cold—on the carry.

After the game on national television, Dick Schaap interviewed Lytle and asked the Broncos running back about the play. Lytle said something noncommittal. "So he [Schaap] said, 'Let's watch the replay,'" Lytle recalls. "And then he said, 'Now what do you think?' I said, 'Well, you win some and you lose some.'"

Lytle also recalls that the interview took place at the far end of the dressing room, just on the other side of the wall from the visiting quarters. And there, he could hear John Madden yelling.

In the next few minutes, Lytle told writers: "At the time, I didn't think I had fumbled. Now that I've seen the replays, I feel very lucky. Somebody up there likes me. I was stopped, the ball started to come loose, and it slid down my body. The referees couldn't see it."

The Broncos countered that the zebras also had disallowed a Jack Dolbin touchdown catch, saying he had trapped the ball. In fact, he made the catch cleanly.

"I caught a slant pass, dove out, laid out, caught the ball, rolled up, and got into the end zone," Dolbin recalls. "I'm looking at the official, waiting for the sign and he's just standing there looking at me. Then he's looking at the guy standing upfield looking at him. Nobody wants to make the call. Finally they said incomplete. It was the greatest catch of my career. But it didn't count. After the game I was interviewed [on television] and I said I guess things balance out. I said Rob's fumble wasn't called a fumble, and my catch wasn't called a catch. I said, 'This is the way the game goes.'"

Dolbin's running mate, Upchurch, wasn't 100 percent because of his leg contusion. But he made it through the game. "It was one I wasn't going to miss," he recalls. "This was the game of a lifetime."

In the Super Bowl at New Orleans on January 15, the Broncos were going to face the Cowboys, who had routed Minnesota 23-6 in the NFC championship game.

My brother, Dave, the assistant public relations director, was giddy, too. At age 28, he was going to get to work at a Super Bowl. "We were just sort of cleaning things up in the press box a few hours after the game, and the phone rang," he says. "I picked it up, and it was a guy who claimed to be Lyle Alzado's father and he was trying to reach Lyle. I didn't know anything about Lyle's relationship with his father at that point in time, other than to know that he hadn't been around when Lyle was growing up. I was thinking that who knows, maybe Lyle's had some kind of contact with this guy through the years and maybe it's legitimate, and maybe not."

Dave wrote down the man's phone number.

Then he went to the Colorado Mine Company and, as he knew probably was going to be the case, spotted a table with Alzado and several other Broncos, plus their girlfriends or wives.

Morton believes he was there, too. "It didn't hurt after the game," he says, and then catches himself. "Well, it probably did, but you're so elated . . ."

My brother told Alzado someone who said he was Alzado's father had called the press box and said he was trying get in touch with the Broncos star.

"Lyle just kind of went silent," Dave says. "He just stopped dead, for a minute, and then kind of nodded and said, 'Oh, okay.'"

Alzado folded up the sheet of paper handed him and put it in his pocket.

Dave remembers him then saying, "I'll talk to you about this later." And he made it clear it wouldn't be that night.

And then the celebration continued.

Super Bowl XII: January 2–15

Sunday, January 15, 1978, vs. Dallas Cowboys at New Orleans

On the Tuesday after the AFC championship game, Dick Lamm and Bill McNichols announced that the next Friday would be a city and state holiday—meaning workers got the day off, or extra salary or a compensating day off if they did work—in honor of the Broncos.

The newspapers protested, adding up the costs for the state and city. How could we have things that far out of perspective? At the time, of course, the newspapers were planning their pages and pages of coverage, and the advertising department was doing bang-up business selling Super Bowl–oriented ads.

The next day, responding to a public outcry from a few politicians and members of the public, the governor and mayor reversed their fields—and canceled the holidays. This after House Speaker Ron Strahle, a Fort Collins Republican, said the holiday would have been "an informal $2 million campaign contribution by the taxpayers of Colorado" to Lamm's reelection campaign.

"That was a mistake," Lamm says with a laugh. He remembers a business leader bringing the idea into the office, and that it sounded good to him. "You know, you have all these things coming at you, and it's like drinking from a fire hydrant," he says. "Everybody's euphoric with the Bronco victory. That, like a number of other things, should have been better thought out."

Lamm says he genuinely was a fan at that point. "And it was helped along by the fact that I had a 10-year-old son," he says. "I went to all the games. I was not a natural football fan, but I got caught up in the Broncos."

Despite the cancellation of the holiday, a planned parade through downtown to give the Broncos a "sendoff" still was on for Friday, despite heated protests from Councilman Sal Carpio about the cost to the city. Carpio reasonably pointed out that parades on weekdays and on 16th and 17th streets were illegal under the city charter. City officials responded: This isn't a parade; it's a motorcade, with players riding in cars and no silly things like floats involved.

Michael Balfe Howard, the editor of the *Rocky Mountain News*, was found guilty of charges of flourishing his handgun and interfering with the police during the August 2 disturbance at Trader Vic's. Denver County Court Judge Edward Carelli fined him $150 and sentenced him to 30 days in jail, but the jail sentence was suspended and would go away if he stayed out of trouble for the next year.

———

Lyle Alzado came to my brother's office.

He told Dave he hadn't heard from his father in years.

Dave never pinned him down, but he got the impression that it didn't really matter if the caller was Alzado's father or an imposter—and it didn't matter because Alzado didn't care to call the number and find out.

———

Getting in the spirit, the papers were whimsically calling the new baseball team the Orange Sox, and Marvin Davis said he was optimistic that Charlie Finley would wiggle out of his Oakland Coliseum lease and we could be buying tickets by the end of the week.

Oakland didn't want to lose another one to Denver, though. Coliseum officials told Finley at midweek that they weren't even going to negotiate with him. Finley called it "poker."

———

Red Miller scoffed at the notion that the Broncos would be at a disadvantage because the Cowboys had been in the Super Bowl before. Only four Broncos—Craig Morton, Andy Maurer, Jim Turner, and Randy Poltl—had played in the NFL championship game. "That's what they were saying about us in these two playoff games we won—that we hadn't been there before, either," Miller said.

And what of the continuing complaining about Lytle's "fumble"?

"If you give them the ball, they still got it at their own 1," Miller said. "And if you give them that call, you have to give us Jack Dolbin's touchdown they nullified. So it's a wash."

When the Broncos players reported back after a couple of days off, Miller cracked them up by pulling out a Spanish-language newspaper featuring a huge picture of the player his teammates called "Gomez"— Lyle Alzado.

Meanwhile, ticket manager Gail Stuckey was hoping there wouldn't be a riot when season ticket holders with priority numbers of 3,000 or lower could start buying Super Bowl tickets at the stadium. The Broncos had 10,410 tickets to sell at $30 apiece, and each customer could buy one for every season ticket he or she had, up to four. Although the Broncos were saying they could just about guarantee all the fans with the low priority numbers could buy as many as they were eligible to buy, some were taking no chances and began camping out outside the ticket office early in the week.

Season ticket holders in the 3,001 to 5,000 priority number range were told they would get second crack, and some of them began lining up in a separate queue. At one point, the Broncos announced it now looked as if all tickets would be gone to the original group, but then the team ended up with 347 tickets still left and sold them to the fans who had decided to stay in line, just in case. It made a lot of folks mad, but it wasn't as if the Broncos had a lot of practice at this.

———

Jack Dolbin, who still was giving Morton treatments, remembers opening an envelope postmarked Oakland—against his better judgment—about four days after the victory over the Raiders. The letter ranted about his statement that Lytle's nonfumble and his noncatch were examples of how the breaks even out.

The letter opened with: "Dear Stupid . . ."

———

The Rockies played an exhibition game against a touring team from the Soviet Union, Spartak. Most of the USSR's top players were on the Soviet Red Army team, so this essentially was the second-string national team, yet it beat the Rockies 8-3. By the end of the game, the Colorado players were so mad at the "commies," they were taking cheap shots and runs and becoming even more frustrated when the Soviets—except for one brief fight when a Spartak player went along with Rockies captain Wilf Paiement's challenge—didn't respond. Robert Cherenkov, Spartak's coach, told me through an interpreter: "Those kinds of things where you throw down your gloves and throw your stick at the other players have no place in hockey. That is a sign of weakness. To the Russians, strong hockey is a thinking game. You win with your wits."

The Rockies were witless.

The 29-car parade . . . oops, motorcade, went off as scheduled on Friday, January 6. Police said about 100,000 watched the winding proceedings along 14th, 15th, and 16th streets. Owners Gerald and Allan Phipps were in the first car; Miller, who had just been named Associated Press NFL coach of the year, in the second—an orange Corvette.

The players wore their jerseys, just in case the fans couldn't figure out who they were.

"I felt like MacArthur," says Tom Glassic, the toy soldier fan and military historian.

Jim Turner, for one, decided it all was a little much.

"The fans got a little exuberant," he recalls. "When they stuck their pens out, I got stabbed a couple of times. I just told the driver, 'Home, James, we're out of here.' Fans are fans and they get excited. What a wonderful crowd, though."

The car carrying Craig Morton and Haven Moses also left the motorcade before it had completed the two-mile route. If someone had bumped Morton in the hip, of course, he might have been bumped right out of the lineup.

The motorcade took so long, practice started late.

At the Broncos' headquarters, Morton wanted to assure Denver fans that an IRS lien of $34,000 filed against him and also a $38,000 lawsuit filed against him by a New York brokerage weren't diverting his attention. He told reporters that he had made a payment of roughly twice that $34,000 to the IRS in December, but that he was told he still owed that balance, and the lien was just a formality while he worked out arrangements. "Everybody's going to be paid," he told reporters, "but I don't want to interfere with my concentration until after the Super Bowl." It turned out that he had received about $125,000 from the Broncos in advance salary, but that was far from unprecedented in the NFL.

And now we had an orange building. Apartment building owners Larry Fuller and Mike Moore had their brick property at 1650 Pearl Street painted the most garish orange they could find, notified the press—and got their pictures in the paper. They also renamed the apartment house the "Broncos Building," christening the paint job and the name change with a bottle of Orange Crush, and none of the tenants seemed to mind.

The Broncos traveled to New Orleans on Monday, January 9, and when they checked into their hotel near the airport, the Sheraton in Kenner, they found they had more roommates than usual.

"There were roaches everywhere," remembers Otis Armstrong.

Miller and a few players, including Morton, went to the Superdome to talk with reporters, and the *Post* was agog that "several dozen" surrounded and grilled the Broncos quarterback. Morton went on the offensive, attempting to head off talk about him playing a "grudge" game against his former team. "Tom Landry taught me everything I know about professional football," he told the reporters. "He's a great coach, but time moves along, and it was time I left Dallas." As reporters rotated, Morton was asked several times to compare Landry and Miller. "Let's see," he told the writers. "Write this down so we'll have it and we can pass it out. Everybody's going to ask."

A writer pointed out that it was "only Monday."

Morton's response: "I won't be very good by Wednesday."

The next day, at picture day, he answered the "tax question" once, saying this was the one time he would address it, and again spelling out that all would be taken care of soon, that the IRS knew that, and that it wasn't a problem and wasn't affecting his concentration.

Within a few minutes, a reporter who had just wandered over to the "Morton Group" asked the same question.

Morton didn't answer it.

When the Broncos tried to shower at the hotel before going to Tulane Stadium for Picture Day on Tuesday morning, they didn't have any hot water.

The Broncos also practiced at Tulane, and only one player thought that was great—former Green Wave star quarterback Steve Foley.

The whole experience was becoming a nightmare for Morton.

"We had horrible practice conditions," Morton recalls. "It wasn't like a Super Bowl. It was just the worst! The worst! They were taking down the Sugar Bowl and it was muddy and terrible, and it was the worst. We had to dress at the hotel and go back and forth and it was like a high school game. It was not a Super Bowl. They had cockroaches at the hotel and everybody was screaming, and wives came in, in the middle of the night, it was horrible."

Foley tried to make up for it by having a huge group of his teammates, including his fellow defensive backs, over to his parents' home for dinner—the one at which they were so astounded to see the locks on the refrigerator and freezer.

Jack Dolbin visited with a friend, Cowboys kicker Efren Herrera, and compared notes.

"He said that every time a plane took off, the hotel shook. I told him we were on the other side and that every time one landed, our hotel shook."

And wait, there was more . . .

"The food was so bad, about midweek we sent back to Denver and brought Daddy Bruce down," Dolbin recalls. "Daddy Bruce cooked for us the rest of the time we were there."

"Daddy Bruce" Randolph was Denver's barbeque king.

Jon Keyworth was booked for the *Tonight Show* for the next Monday, to sing "Make Those Miracles Happen."

There was one catch.

He would be on only if the Broncos won.

The downside of his musical fame, apparently: Bronco officials had lined up extra security for Keyworth. It all was very vague, but reports said the FBI had been told of a death threat made against Keyworth. It eventually was traced back to a woman, unhappy with her husband, claiming that he had threatened to kill Keyworth. Later in the week, Keyworth posed with his assigned security guard, John Smith, outside his hotel room. The FBI had questioned a suspect and the U.S. attorney's office decided not to file charges.

Also, by Thursday, there was a minor crack in the Broncos' season-long united front.

"The King Tut exhibit was in New Orleans," Dolbin says. "We were all told they were going to take the team and the wives to see the King Tut exhibit. So as the week goes on we're waiting and waiting and waiting. And all of a sudden we found out that a 'select group' of players and wives went to see the King Tut exhibit on like a Wednesday and this was Thursday. We had a close-knit team, so we played well together. Our Super Bowl ring says, 'Togetherness.' And then we go to find out that the Denver Broncos leadership selected maybe a half-dozen of what they called the high-profile players and their wives to go see King Tut and left the rest of us back there. I tell you, there was a little bit of anarchy that day at the evening meal. There was a lot of people upset."

He laughs and admits he's indulging in hyperbole, but says he sometimes blames King Tut for what happened in the game.

Back in North Denver, the kids at Holy Family School—adjacent to the church Elvis Presley had visited while attending Eugene Kennedy's funeral in early 1976—were immersed in Broncomania.

"We were *required* to wear orange," recalls Vic Lombardi, who was 8 years old at the time and 30 years later is the sports anchor at KCNC/ Channel 4. "I'll never forget that. We had a dress code at school. We had to wear specific clothes, but during that year, there were days we had to wear orange. So my mom went out and bought me this Orange Crush shirt, and I wore that thing all week long the week before the Super Bowl."

Actually, the Broncos of that season were part of the Lombardi family's Americanization. His parents, Ezio and Bambina, came from Italy to Denver in 1966.

"I was in second grade that season, and I still was struggling to speak English," Vic says. "We didn't speak English at home. We spoke all Italian. I remember going to Holy Family and my sister Rita had to teach me how to speak English. I remember specifically all the ceremonial stuff we did at school. The school took on the Broncos as part of the school day. We did the Pledge of Allegiance and then we did the Pledge to the Broncos. And the drink—Orange Crush—was part of our family. I took full advantage of that. And it came not only in the cans, but those little glass bottles. My parents were trying to assimilate to the culture as much as they could. It was almost expected that we were Bronco fans. Everyone else was a Bronco fan, so under our roof, we better be Bronco fans."

By then, Lombardi says, "the M&M Connection was everything to me."

In the French Quarter, Tom Glassic came across nirvana. No, he didn't find beignets or the perfect hurricane or the best jambalaya in town. "I found *Le Petit Soldier* Shop on Rue Royal," he says. "What a great shop! He had all kinds of hand-painted stuff and Britain's toy soldier sets."

Keyworth's song still was getting major airplay and selling well in Colorado. Meanwhile, several others had come up with musical tributes to the Broncos, and another record on the market was John Chandler's "Denver into Dallas." Popular KHOW-AM disc jockey Hal Moore was playing a tape of a reworked and Broncos-oriented version of the "Battle of New Orleans." It was the brainchild of two attorneys—Bob Kapelke, who wrote it, and Jim Cunningham, the lead singer. There was no word whether they billed Moore every time he played it.

Out in Oakland, Charlie Finley said he had made his "final" offer to buy his way out of the Coliseum lease.

In Denver, prospective Orange Sox owner Marvin Davis told Frank Haraway it was a "hell of an offer. It's something around $2 million, and the Giants will play 33 games in the Oakland Coliseum. If they don't take it, I don't know what the hell he's going to do."

Time was running out.

Miller went out to dinner with his wife, Nancy, plus son Steve and daughter Lana, in the French Quarter on Thursday night. To the reporters, he said listening to the jazz reminded him of his days at Western Illinois, when he would play the piano, Lou Saban played the bass—and Joe Collier hummed along.

At another restaurant, the Broncos' seven linebackers dined, and the owner went on the street to brag about it and entice other customers to come in, ask for autographs—and spend money. He gave the players T-shirts with his restaurant name on them, and when the bill came, the tab was about $150—and nearly half of it came because he had charged them $9.50 for each of the T-shirts.

They threw them at him.

By then, Bob Swenson had a bad feeling.

"To me, New Orleans was one of the worst experiences I've ever had," Swenson recalls. "I'm a dreamer, right? So you have this dream that the Super Bowl is this all-time, all-time sporting event in the world, and in a way it is the pinnacle of everything. Rings and world champs and all that kind of stuff, and here you are, a Cinderella story. . . . So we get to New Orleans and I don't even invite my parents. Maybe it's foresight.

"You would think you'd bring your parents to see this. I'm from a small town and Tracy High, where football is like the biggest thing and now one of their high school kids is in the Super Bowl. They had Bronco day and all this stuff and it's Raider country. All of that is going on.

"So we go to the Super Bowl and I was shocked. *Wait a second, we don't get invited to the party? The Super Bowl party, the media party? We're not invited?* And there are cockroaches in the hotel. I remember that. I remember the elevator getting stuck and the practice facilities. I remember I was like, *This is it?* It was kind of like a spiritual defining moment for me."

Ah, it made me proud to be a Wheat Ridge Farmer. Among the many Bronco-related activities at local schools that week, WRHS held an Orange Crush "chug-a-lug" contest.

Think of the teeth that might have been ruined!

It wasn't just Wheat Ridge. All around the state, many young fans—and some older ones—were throwing down Orange Crush as if it was water, hoping it would help the Broncos. It replaced Coke or Pepsi as the soft drink of choice. Teenage girls, some of whom still would be able to say 30 years later that Steve Foley's birthday was November 11 as they tried to remember where they put their car keys, replaced their Bobby Sherman or Shaun Cassidy posters with Bronco team pictures.

At Northeast Elementary in Parker, teacher Bill Bloom told his students they could paint his truck—and paint it orange, as some fans had done with their cars.

An Albertson's store in Billy Thompson's Green Mountain neighborhood ordered and displayed a one-ton block of Wisconsin cheese. It was orange, of course. And it was a good thing the Broncos weren't playing the Packers. (Actually, a Packers-Broncos Super Bowl was unimaginable.)

In maternity wards, babies were wrapped in orange.

Everywhere you turned, there was orange.

State treasurer Roy Romer's proposal that the state try to buy the 22,000-acre Highlands Ranch property to forestall development, thus helping discourage further sprawl and pollution, was barely noticed. After all, it seemed a little silly to think of homes actually going up on the distant ranch property.[3]

The Dallas and Denver newspapers again showed that while we always were lectured about maintaining professionalism and objectivity, everything went out the window when others in the building got involved with sports. The *Post* had an orange front page and an editorial asking the question whether the Broncos would win, and closing with: "Of course." And the *Dallas Times-Herald* ran an ad in the *Post* declaring: "In Dallas, Cowboys Bust Broncos All Year Round!!!" The *Post*'s ad in the *Herald* was just as bad.

The Cowboys had opened as 5-point favorites, and that's where the line stayed most places.

Among the television counterprogramming in Denver was a two-hour *Firing Line* debate on the Panama Canal Treaties between pundit William F. Buckley Jr. and former actor and ex-California governor Ronald Reagan, who adamantly opposed the "giveaway." If you wanted to see both the game and debate, you could try to take advantage of a new product, a videocassette, and tape the debate. The recorders-players were selling as fast as manufacturers could make them, but there still were some problems—variances in the tapes used, meaning tapes made on one manufacturer's machines often couldn't be shown on another company's machine. And MCA had filed a lawsuit against Sony, manufacturer of the Betamax, arguing that the machines would lead to repeated violations of copyright laws.

To a lot of us, still preferring records to 8-track tapes, it sounded like a fad.

The Super Bowl kickoff was scheduled for 5 p.m. in New Orleans, and guard Tom Glassic—despite having lost considerable weight because of allergies and fatigue—was pumped all day. He says he was down to about 230, but some teammates remember him weighing in at 223 that week. His roster weight was 254.

"My family's all at the same hotel," he recalls. "There were three buses going to the stadium as usual. Fifteen minutes before we have to leave, I went to my parents' room to say goodbye and they wished me luck. You know when the adrenaline's pumping? My adrenaline's pumping, and I can't use it. So I laid down on the bed, for just a minute, and I must have dozed off because next thing I know, my father's standing at my window."

John Glassic was excited, pointing and saying, "Tommy, isn't that the last bus leaving?"

"Dad, don't screw around with me now," Tom said. "I'm too nervous."

"No, really, Tommy . . ."

Tom jumped out of bed.

The last bus had left.

Glassic spotted a policeman in the parking lot, one who obviously had been there to watch over the buses before they left.

"Excuse me, officer," Tom said, "think you can give me a ride to the game?" When the officer gave him a look, Tom added: "I'm playing today."

The officer consented, and Glassic calls him "a good guy. But he didn't put his siren on, his lights on. It's game-day traffic to the Superdome, bumper to bumper, and game time is coming up and I'm sitting in the car. I see the Superdome way in the distance and I'm looking at my watch! We finally get there, and the guy dropped me off and left. So I'm standing outside the Superdome on Super Bowl Sunday, and how the hell do I get in here?

"I walked up to the gate and said, 'I'm playing today,' and the guy says, 'Playing what, the tuba? Get out of here!' So I was walking around, trying to find the place where the players come in. When I got there, I said who I was and pleaded with the security guard. I said, 'Talk to somebody, go send somebody to the locker room. I know they're looking for me . . . at least I hope so.' So he said, 'Hey, aren't you the guy playing Randy White today? You sure you want to go in there?'

"Now," Glassic adds, shaking his head, "everybody's a comedian. I was just about to push the guy aside and go running down the hall and yelling, 'I'm here!' They were going to grab me and put me in a strait jacket. I pleaded with this guy to go send somebody to the locker room and ask."

Finally, an assistant trainer came out and vouched for him, adding: "We were wondering if he was going to show up."

As the Broncos were in the tunnel and about to take the field for kickoff, Billy Thompson looked over at Tom Jackson. Jackson was crying. Thompson understood.

"We both looked out and it was a sea of orange," Thompson recalls. "I said, 'Hey, man, we're here. We're gonna get this one.'"

They didn't.

Morton threw four interceptions among the eight Denver turnovers, and the Broncos didn't do a good job of protecting him. Although the defense hung in, it wore down and was on the field too long. Dallas had a short field all day, thanks to the turnovers. Plus, Randy Gradishar reinjured his ankle, was hobbled, and in the fourth quarter finally had to admit he couldn't go any longer.

Jim Turner drilled a 47-yard field goal in the third quarter to close it to 13-3, but the Cowboys came back with Roger Staubach's 45-yard touchdown pass to Butch Johnson, who made a terrific diving catch in the end zone that would make every "Super Bowl over the years" highlight segment for years to come.

The Broncos got back within 10 after Rick Upchurch's 67-yard punt return—a Super Bowl record at the time—set his team up at the Dallas 10. Miller sent Norris Weese on for Morton—recognizing both that it wasn't Morton's day and that mobility would give a Broncos quarterback a shot against the withering rush—and Lytle scored from 1 yard out. But then Dallas fullback Robert Newhouse's pass went for a 29-yard touchdown to Golden Richards. That was it. Game, set, match. The miracle wouldn't happen, and it didn't have the feel of a fluke at all.

Otis Armstrong says, "I think we were too star-struck to play. We were in over our heads. The Cowboys had been there before and had done that. They knew what to do."

The Broncos ended up with only 156 yards of total offense. Morton was a miserable 4 for 14, for 39 yards, with the four interceptions. Armstrong had only 7 carries, for 27 yards, and Lytle was the leading ground-gainer, with 35 yards on 10 rushes.

Glassic struggled with Randy White, but to attribute the pass rush only to him is unfair. Teammate after teammate goes out of his way to give him credit, marveling that he even was on the field at all, given his illness and weight loss. "I'm proud of him staying in there for every down and doing the best he could," Red Miller says. Glassic concedes, "I could have done better," and he says the Broncos had formulated a much better offensive line game plan to combat the flex defense by the time they next played the Cowboys.[4]

When Denver got behind and stayed behind, the Cowboys could tee off, and it all was a formula for disaster.

Miller remembers it as a "tough matchup" up front. "It's hard for a team to overcome one area like that," he says. But he also means that as a sort of compliment—that his patched-together offensive line, with two starters who weren't even with the team at the start of training camp and a third that was getting fined for being underweight, *finally* hit a wall against the Cowboys.

So did Morton, for whatever reason. A bad day? Pressures of several kinds? The cumulative effect of his unquestioned physical problems—the ones he had been so courageous to combat as he kept keep playing? The Cowboys? It almost certainly was a combination of all of the above and a whirlwind of factors. Inevitably, his performance, coupled with his well-publicized financial problems at the time and gamblers' focus on the Super Bowl, gave rise to ridiculous rumors that he had thrown the game. No credible evidence to back that up has ever surfaced, and the team had advanced him the $125,000 in future salary to help cover debts.

"We couldn't do anything right," Morton recalls. "There was no reason to think we'd play that bad. We just gave the ball away too many times. They played well and they knew we couldn't run against them. They pulled the safeties up and blitzed all the time, and we didn't protect enough. I did call audibles and that was a mistake. The depressing thing is when you look back on the game, I don't know what you do. What you do is run the ball, and we couldn't do that. When we got in passing situations, they just came after us, and they beat me to death."

He pauses.

"I've never watched that game," he says.

The game took a dark turn of a different sort in the third quarter, when the defensive coaches were told that there had been a telephoned death threat made against Rubin Carter.

They didn't tell Carter and he stayed in the game.

Carter says he was informed later that the call came early in the game, after he hit Roger Staubach a couple of times. He muses that it probably was a nervous gambler who had a lot of money riding on the Cowboys.

"Stan Jones was walking back and forth with me on the sideline because I was always a walker," Carter says. He laughs and adds, "I probably wore him out."

It was a 27-10 loss on the international stage. But as the clock wound down with the Denver defense on the field, Tom Jackson again turned to Billy Thompson as the orange-clad fans gave the Broncos a standing ovation and chanted: "WE LOVE THE BRONCOS."

"I don't know if we won or lost," Jackson said, dumbfounded.

Thompson understood. Again. Years later, he still has a tone of wonderment in his voice as he tells that story.

Barney Chavous says the Broncos "didn't play the kind of football that got us there. I don't know if we were overwhelmed, but whatever the reason, we didn't click on all cylinders. I definitely think we could have beaten the Cowboys, but we had to play like we did against the Raiders, like we played against Baltimore, like we played against Houston."

Chavous says he has talked with other players since who agree with him when he tosses out the possibility that the parade—or motorcade—sendoff might not have been a good idea. "Maybe we should have kept that thing in perspective," he says. "We hadn't won the championship yet."

When the game ended, NFL security personnel told Carter he had to get off the field. Now.

Carter protested that he knew some of the Cowboys from all-star games and, anyway, he thought it was only right to shake his opponents' hands.

The NFL men said no. They told him what was going on when he got to the locker room.

In the game, Carter had six tackles, two assists, two sacks, and a fumble recovery.

After the rest of the team filed back in, Billy Thompson—who had been having shoulder pains the entire game and didn't ever feel comfortable—finally figured out what the problem was.

He had been wearing Steve Foley's shoulder pads—and vice versa.

John Ralston, the man who was instrumental in assembling the roster, was in the Superdome that day. "I was so pleased with what they had done," he says. "I went down to New Orleans by myself and watched the game. Nobody [in the media] was around, though I saw a lot of Denver people and they saw me. Gee, I would have liked to see them win, but to see them in the game was something."

The Broncos came back home to a changed Denver.

"When we landed here," Claudie Minor says, "they had an area on the concourse over by the electric cars, roped off, and there were a lot of fans there. I don't know how many thousands of fans. We were just blown away. They cured our wounds, mended us emotionally."

It hurt Miller to lose, but he soon could allow himself to think about the overall picture and the difference from when he was with the Broncos as an assistant.

"What was great for me was I had coached games in Denver when there were 9,000 people there, maybe, and a lot of those were Boy Scouts with free tickets," he says. "I've been there with the Quonset huts, where I bumped my head every time I got up to go to the bathroom or something. I'd been there when the offense would meet in a room that was meant for maybe 10 to 15 guys, max. Some guys would have to stand up to watch film, it was that crowded. I've been here when we didn't have proper dressing facilities and proper training facilities, and we didn't have weights. I thought the people so much yearned for this, that somebody had to be the first, and that was a thrill for me."

The market was in transformation, and it never could be the same.

"Denver should have gotten the Nobel Peace Prize that year," Haven Moses says. "There was more done that year to bring people together than I've ever seen in my life. It transformed the attitudes of this city. This is a beautiful town and a beautiful place and things were starting to happen here. There was something needed to kick it off. And this brought attention to what Denver was about to become."

Notes

1. "Predominantly orange" became the Broncos' color scheme when they went to (truly predominantly) blue uniforms in the late 1990s.

2. Well, the extremely religious Dick Connor did quote Miller—as much as he could. The word came out "b---s---" in the paper.

3. In 2007, many of my friends live in Highlands Ranch, Colorado.

4. The Broncos beat the Cowboys 41-20 in Denver in the second game of the 1980 season.

CHAPTER 12

Aftermath

Louis Wright was as good a cornerback as I ever saw.
Gradishar, Tommy Jackson, Billy Thompson. None of
them are in the Hall of Fame? That's just a joke.

—CRAIG MORTON

Ownership and Staff

Red Miller, Head Coach

In the next three seasons under Miller, the Broncos went 10-6, 10-6, and
8-8. They lost their opening playoff games to Pittsburgh in 1978 and
Houston in 1979. In 1980, Denver was in playoff contention until a three-
game losing streak—a pair of losses to Oakland sandwiched around a
defeat at Kansas City—derailed them.

Suddenly, in early 1981, the Phipps brothers sold the team to industri-
alist Edgar Kaiser. At the time, young Dallas assistant Dan Reeves—the
former Cowboys running back—was considered the bright prospect. Although he had interviewed for a couple of jobs and hadn't gotten them,
it was considered a matter of time, and Kaiser decided that he was snatching up Reeves. He brought him to Canada for talks, hired him, and fired
Miller.

Ultimately, Miller had to retain a lawyer to ensure that he was paid
the settlement he was due under the terms of his contract.

Although this was in the late winter and coaching staffs for the next season were set around the league, he was approached about joining other staffs, but—because of his settlement—he didn't need to be in a hurry and Nancy Miller was reluctant to leave Denver again. So Red swallowed hard, said no to overtures from the Raiders—the *Raiders!*—and took what he thought might be a temporary job as vice president of marketing for Denver-based Kirkwood Oil.

When the spring-season United States Football League opened shop for the 1983 season, the new Denver Gold hired Miller, who wanted back into football and was also trying to save his marriage by staying in Denver. (That didn't work; he and Nancy were divorced after 32 years as husband and wife.)

The Gold was a small-time operation in a small-time spring league, but that's what the league was supposed to be as drawn up and discussed at the initial news conference in New York—a news conference I attended while covering the 1982 Stanley Cup Finals between the Islanders and Canucks. Yet the Gold drew over 40,000 a game at home that first season and made original owner Ron Blanding a lot of money. Miller, though, didn't last through the 1983 season, in part because of on-field struggles, but primarily because of his open enmity for Blanding, whom he believed didn't deliver on his promises and treated those working for him shabbily. The Gold was 4-7 when Blanding fired him, and defensive coordinator Charley Armey took over for one game before Blanding, with an eye on maintaining a high profile, hired Craig Morton to replace Miller.

Miller was back out of football, but still in Denver. "Each day that went on," he says, "my enthusiasm to turn back the clock lessened. Coaching is a real tough racket. It is mentally hard and you have to devote your whole life to it, and you can mess up other parts of your life by doing it. And for me to stick with it for 33 years, I gave it everything I had. And I achieved most of my goals."

He did some television and radio commentary work, and then finally decided to change careers. He had loved dabbling in the stock market, and he plowed ahead, trained to become a broker, passed the tests, and went to work for Dean Witter Reynolds. His prominence and popularity helped him land major clients, and he did well—both for himself and for his clients. He moved to Paine Webber in 1994. Along the way, he also met his second wife, Nan. Finally, he retired in 1999.

He and Nan live in South Denver, and Miller is one of those neighbors you hate because of the example they set—he's always working in the yard or constructing something—and love because of how they make the street look great.

Kaiser sold the franchise long ago, and Miller became a Broncos fan, in part because of how longtime owner Pat Bowlen acknowledges and embraces the franchise's past.

Joe Collier, Defensive Coordinator

The architect of the Orange Crush remained on the Denver staff through the 1988 season under Dan Reeves, going to two more Super Bowls.

At the end, Collier wasn't getting along with Reeves and was thinking of retiring, but had a year left on his contract and decided to see what would happen.

Reeves fired him, which at that point didn't break his heart.

He turned down several offers to get back into coaching before coming out of retirement to coach for two seasons under old friend Dick MacPherson with the New England Patriots in 1991 and '92. He never gave up his home in Littleton and didn't particularly enjoy the coaching experience because of the Patriots' continuing ownership problems at the time. He returned to Littleton and has been active in retirement, working out and volunteering for Meals on Wheels and other programs.

He was the top defensive coordinator in NFL history.

Myrel Moore, Linebackers Coach

In part because his father had died recently and his mother was fighting cancer, and he wanted to be close to her in northern California, Moore went over to the "Dark Side" the next season, joining the Raiders staff.

The first day he walked into his new office, he found a huge blown-up picture on his desk. It showed Rob Lytle fumbling against the Raiders the previous January 1. He left the Raiders after two years, worked for the Broncos as a scout, then returned to the Denver coaching staff for 1983 and was fired in Reeves's 1988 defensive purge.

He went with Joe Collier for the two-year stint on Dick MacPherson's staff with the Patriots, then bought and ran the landmark and old-fashioned King Chef Diner in Colorado Springs for three years. He came back to football to serve as defensive coordinator for the Scotland entry in NFL Europe for three years ("I had a ball," he says) and retired again in 2000. He lives in Wellington, Colorado.

Stan Jones, Defensive Line Coach

Like Collier, Jones remained on the Denver staff until the 1988 staff overhaul. He served as a strength and conditioning coach at Cleveland, considering it winding down before retirement, but was convinced to join Collier and Moore for the brief run at New England. The onetime All-Pro lineman was inducted into the Pro Football Hall of Fame in 1991. He is retired and lives in Fraser, Colorado.

Gerald Phipps and Allan Phipps, Co-owners

They and their minority partners sold the franchise to Kaiser in 1981 for $40 million. Gerald died of liver cancer at age 78 in 1993. Allan died four years later, at age 85. Both were well known for their philanthropy and for their continued involvement in the community.

Fred Gehrke, General Manager

Fired in the Kaiser purge that also claimed Red Miller, Gehrke retired and continued to live in Arvada until moving to Palm Springs in the late 1990s. He died in 2002.

John Ralston, Former GM-Coach

The architect of the roster came close to getting the Chicago Bears' head-coaching job in 1978, but he never did get another chance. He worked as an assistant with the Philadelphia Eagles that year and then was in the San Francisco 49ers front office during Bill Walsh's early years as head coach. He says he could have returned to college coaching at Iowa, but decided to stay in pro football. In 1982, he was one of the founding fathers of the United States Football League, and if the league had stuck to his spring-football, cost-contained model, it would have succeeded. He briefly served as head coach of the league's Oakland Invaders in 1983–84. He also coached in Europe. Eventually, he was the head coach at San Jose State from 1993 to 1996, a period where the Spartans had few resources and his work was important in keeping the program alive. Rubin Carter was one of his assistants. At age 80, he still was serving as a consultant and fund-raiser for the Spartans athletic department.

Defense

Note: * indicates Member of Broncos Ring of Fame (induction year)

Lyle Alzado, DE

By 1979, Alzado had turned off many of his teammates with his mercurial behavior and what they came to believe was his opportunism in doing everything from falling on the piles to dealing with the media. But he continued to work tirelessly with children and young people. While arguing with the Broncos over his contract, he and promoter Lyle Pedersen set up an Alzado exhibition boxing match with Muhammad Ali for Mile High Stadium on July 14, 1979. I covered both it and the buildup.

As the fight approached, it was obvious it wasn't going to do well enough at the box office for the promotion to break even. Alzado was posturing about whether he would quit football and become a boxer full-time if he did okay with Ali, but as delusional as he could be, he mainly considered this an economic venture and getting contract leverage. When Denver writers belittled the exhibition and ripped him for saying he could lose his house—which he had put up for collateral for the promotion costs—if Denver fans didn't step up and buy tickets, that was unfair. It was true. His restaurant was in huge trouble, and he was on the way to financial oblivion.

The exhibition was not nearly as bad as it has become in lore. The eight-rounder with huge gloves wasn't scored, and Ali was focused on being just serious enough to not get hurt, because Alzado clearly was trying. He didn't look any worse than a lot of palookas on nationally televised fights, and Ali was in the gray area between disinterested and passionate. After the fight, Ali tried to help Alzado get more leverage by saying he could be a decent pro fighter if he decided to take that route. "If you don't think what he did was superhuman," he told us, "try to get in the ring with him and go one round."

Alzado told me to call him that night. I assumed he thought he might be able to work something out with the Broncos that day, but he didn't. Here's what he told me: "It's under negotiation right now. Believe me, I'm not looking to pressure them for more money through this. They've been so wonderful to me. It isn't that at all."

He reported to training camp without a contract, but soon walked out, and the Broncos sent him to Cleveland. He spent three seasons with the Browns, who sent him to the Raiders in 1982. Near the end of that season, he told the *Post's* Michael Knisley that his teammates on the '77 Broncos had been jealous of him and he said he wasn't invited to some parties "because I would not do some of the things they were doing."

That didn't thrill his former teammates, either.

He retired after the 1985 season, though he made a brief comeback attempt with the Raiders in 1990. He continued to try to get an acting career off the ground, but his roles were few and demeaning.

He was diagnosed with brain cancer in April 1991. He said in a July 8, 1991, *Sports Illustrated* story—"as told to" writer Shelley Smith, my fellow Wheat Ridge High graduate—that he had been using steroids since 1969, since his days at Yankton. He said that the steroids—he cited a stunning array—and the human growth hormone he turned to in his attempted comeback had cost him as much as $30,000 a year. He also said this in the story: "We had such a defense in Denver, especially that Super Bowl year, 1977. I can't say if anybody else on the Broncos was on the stuff, but because I was, I have to think some of the others were. But I wasn't liked on the team, so I really didn't know what was going on."

He was wrong. He wasn't *disliked.* He was understood. And his implication was a cheap shot at that point, especially because he couldn't back it up.

His second wife, Cindy, said Alzado had been abusive and violent. He spent the next year saying that the steroids caused his cancer—a claim that couldn't be substantiated or disproved—and campaigning and making speeches, preaching the antisteroid message.

When the Broncos played the Raiders in Los Angeles in September 1991, Alzado was on the Raiders bench, with actor James Garner. Before the game, Barney Chavous, then a Bronco assistant, and Billy Thompson, then a Bronco scout, spotted Alzado and approached him separately.

They both told Alzado they loved him.

They meant it.

He said it back.

He died on May 14, 1992, in the Portland area, where he had gone for radical treatment.

Rubin Carter, DT

His 12-season career with the Broncos ran through Super Bowl XXI in Pasadena, and when he retired, his 152 games were the most of any nose tackle in NFL history. (The position, while not a universal one in a league of even-man fronts, takes its toll.) He was on the Broncos' staff as a defensive line and strength and conditioning coach in 1978–88, then moved on to the staffs of Howard University (1989–1993), San Jose State (under John Ralston in 1995–96), and Maryland (1997–98). He moved back to the NFL with Washington and the Jets from 1999 to 2003 before serving one year on the Temple staff and then becoming head coach at Florida A&M in 2005.

Barney Chavous, DE

Quietly walking away during the 1986 training camp after it was clear the Broncos were planning to replace him in the starting lineup with Andre Townsend, Chavous took a year off from football. On a pheasant-hunting trip with then-coach Dan Reeves, he told Reeves he would like to return to the game, and Reeves brought him back to the organization in an internship program, and he eventually became an assistant on the defensive staff, helping out with the defensive line and in the conditioning program. When Mike Shanahan took over, Chavous moved to help out on the offensive side. "That was great, I learned so much," he says. He also helped out my father, who had returned to the Broncos and was the director of college scouting, and Jack Elway, the director of pro scouting. Chavous often put players through workouts and told Jerry Frei and/ or Jack what he thought of them. After being part of two Super Bowl championship teams, but ultimately feeling he wasn't making any progress in the organization and sensing it was time to go home, Chavous walked away—again—and returned with his wife, Odessa, to the family land outside Aiken. He is a farmer, raising both crops and cattle. "But don't call me a gentleman farmer, though," he says, laughing. "I'm trying to make money at it." He also teaches and is the head football coach at Josey High School in Augusta. One of his former players, defensive end Lawrence Marsh, was a freshman on Florida's 2006 national championship team.

Steve Foley, CB

Foley switched from cornerback to free safety in 1980. His last game for the Broncos was the Super Bowl XXI loss to the New York Giants in Pasadena. By then, he had been married to the former Cindy Foto for nearly seven years, was the father of two, and decided it was time to walk away. He finished with 44 career interceptions.

He hadn't made tons of money, but he had deferred a lot of his salary, looking ahead to retirement and a planned career in business. Late in his career, he had dabbled in some construction projects and wanted to get into construction and real estate development full-time.

He and Cindy, plus children David and Natalie, moved back to New Orleans for about 18 months, and Foley was involved in building a dry-cleaning building and getting the business started.

He hated it.

"I'll never forget my best friend [Mark Olivari] said, 'What in the world are you doing back here?' If you don't have old money or you're not in the tourism business or a restaurant, it doesn't work," he says. "There's not a lot of subdivision or building, and I looked here."

"Here" was back in Denver. The family moved back to Colorado and Foley got into building houses on speculation and other aspects of real estate development. In 1999, he went into a partnership with former teammate Bob Swenson. "We've had hard times together in this business, too," Foley says. "It's a hard-nosed business. But our football background has helped out tremendously. We know we can go through some tough times."

Back in New Orleans, Foley's younger brother, Richie, purchased the family home—the former convent—from his mother and still lives there.

Hurricane Katrina left three feet of water in the home, but the Foleys battled back.

*Randy Gradishar, LB (1989)

Gradishar still was one of the top linebackers in the NFL when he retired after the 1983 season, at age 31 and having *never* missed a game in his 10 seasons. That he isn't in the Hall of Fame highlights the ridiculous crony-ism and maneuvering involved in the voting among media members at the Super Bowl site the day before the game.

But that's another story.

He quit on his own terms, announcing his decision before his final season and proving wrong those who thought he wanted the Broncos to entice him to stay with a new contract or that he might be positioning himself to take advantage of competition from the United States Football League.

That season, John Elway's first, he counted down the number of prac-tices remaining aloud, not so much out of glee, but to prove he was serious.

"I had worked 7 out of 10 years in the off-seasons, with Coors and a couple of residential alarm companies," he says. "I wasn't trying to figure out specifically what I was going to do, but I wanted to gain experience. My dad had said, 'You can do all this fun stuff, but man, you have to go to work pretty soon.' "

When he retired, Woody Hayes came to Denver for the tribute dinner put on by the Quarterback Club, and the quotes from Hayes about Gradi-shar in an earlier chapter came from Shelby Strother's interview with Hayes during that visit.

Gradishar ran the Broncos Youth Foundation until 1992, worked with Bill McCartney's Promise Keepers men's organization, and then joined the Phil Long automobile dealership group in 1997. He is the group's corporate communications director and is highly visible at the company's dealerships in Denver, Colorado Springs, and Pueblo, and also spearheads and takes part in the company's extensive community involvement. He also has visited U.S. troops in the Middle East several times.

Did I mention he should be in the Hall of Fame?

Bernard Jackson, FS

The talkative little safety played through 1980, leaving the Broncos that season and finishing up with the Chargers. He lived in Denver, doing research work for a law firm, worked as a legislative aide to State Senator Regis Groff, and then served a stint as the running backs coach at Western State in Gunnison. He was diagnosed with liver cancer in early 1997 and died in May of that year.

*Tom Jackson, LB (1992)

Like Steve Foley and Louis Wright, Jackson also retired after the 1986 season. When he walked away, his 191 games were the most of any player in Broncos history. He is a longtime and popular ESPN commentator. He lives in Cincinnati.

Joe Rizzo, LB

Rizzo's tenure with the Broncos coincided with Red Miller's. He suffered another major knee injury when he was clipped in the fourth game of the 1980 season, underwent surgery, and was released before the next season. He owns Rizzo Realty and lives in Wilmington, North Carolina.

*Paul Smith, DT (1986)

The senior member of the Orange Crush's defensive line, whose 11-season stay with the Broncos lasted through 1978, finished up with Washington in 1979–80. He died in March 2000 of pancreatic cancer. He was living in Aurora.

Bob Swenson, LB

The *Is that it?* feeling that Swenson had at the Super Bowl contributed to a spiritual reawakening, and he recommitted himself to Christianity. He was an All-Pro in 1981, and then was beset by contract disagreements with the short-pocketed new owner, Edgar Kaiser, and by injuries. He was on the injured list for both the 1983 and '84 seasons with knee problems, and then retired.

Always fascinated by real estate, he tried that business but didn't do well for years. But after he hooked up with Steve Foley as a business partner, they became spectacularly successful in the 21st century, and as of 2007, they owned or controlled over 1,000 acres of prime real estate in the Erie and Dacono areas north of Denver.

"That's pretty amazing for two little guys, one from Louisiana and one from Tracy, California," Swenson says. "I would say this: There's no way I'd be doing what I'm doing today if it weren't for the Broncos. No way would I have the audacity or the confidence to do what we're doing."

In one of their first developments, an entrance road leading into an office park is called Joe Collier Drive. Nearby, in a subdivision, one of the most prominent streets is Rubin Carter Drive. "Every subdivision, we're going to try to sneak in one of the Broncos who isn't in the Ring of Fame," Swenson says. He pauses, then adds, "Aw, maybe we'll put a couple of Ring of Fame guys in there."

*Billy Thompson, S (1987)

"B.T." played 4 more seasons. He finished with 40 interceptions in his 13-season career, and ended up being an All-NFL choice twice and an All-AFC pick four times.

After retiring, he owned and operated a McDonald's in Castle Rock for 12 years.

"I enjoyed it and I learned a lot," he says. "I also learned I didn't want to do it for 20 more years. I was on call all the time, and in that situation, you have labor problems and all sorts of things. Then Dan Reeves asked me to come back and scout. I got back in the organization and did that for two years."

He next became the team's director of player relations and alumni coordinator, and remains one of the Broncos' most popular liaisons with the community.

*Louis Wright, CB (1993)

Wright's final game also was Super Bowl XXI against the Giants. Although he had turned 34 a few days after the loss in Pasadena—and that was long-of-tooth for a cornerback—Wright still was one of the top players at the position in the game. But he resisted the organization's lobbying and indeed announced his retirement in the summer of 1987 in a letter to owner Pat Bowlen. One of the reasons he waited that long was because of his unhappiness with Dan Reeves over the way some other veterans had been treated in their final days. He also had butted heads with Reeves while serving as the player representative and at one point had a heart-to-heart with the coach that Reeves said helped him become more of a player's coach.

But Wright says that he was set to retire that year, regardless.

"I know I could have played a couple more years," he says. "Why did I retire? Because I had the phobia of the number 13. The next year was going to be my 13th year. Plus, I had kind of made up my mind that I would rather leave too early than too late. I had seen some guys who were dragging it out, getting cut or traded, and it wasn't a pretty picture. The players would say they disrespected me and the team would say he didn't have it anymore, and they ended up with a bad relationship because you just played too long."

His friends asked him, "You're coming home, aren't you?"

They meant Bakersfield or San Jose.

He laughs now, recalling his initial revulsion to Denver. But his reaction to his friends was, "I *am* home. Denver is home now."

He and Vicki had three children by then, and Louis went back to school, attending the University of Denver, and got his business management degree in 1989. He and a friend formed a business that did seismic surveys. "I made some money at that, but I was gone all the time," he says. He went into accounting, and also began coaching part-time in the Denver Public Schools. He loved coaching, but didn't like having to leave his job in midafternoon to do it and decided he wanted to become a full-time educator. After obtaining his teaching certificate, he taught various classes—business, social studies, math, and P.E.—in Denver middle schools while coaching, and he was hired as the head football coach at Montbello High School in 1994. That year, he and Vicki were divorced. He coached at Montbello through 2002, moved into the Aurora school system and now teaches physical education at Mrachek Middle School while helping coach the football team at the adjacent Rangeview High School and staying in touch with his three children. His oldest daughter, Summer, is a Northwestern graduate; daughter Kyla is a Bradley University graduate; and his son, Evan, is attending Texas Christian University on a track scholarship.

Every once in a while, a Mrachek student will come up to Wright and say: "Coach Wright, my (dad, uncle, grandfather) says you used to play for the Broncos!" And Coach Wright will nod. Or a kid will tell him: "Coach, I saw you on ESPN Classic last night!" And Coach Wright will nod. Or the butcher at King Soopers will wait for his next visit, then pop out of the back with a '77 team picture for him to sign and rattle off all kinds of things about that team and that season. "Thanks for telling me," Wright will say. "I had forgotten all about that!"

Man after man from that team joins Morton in saying that if anyone didn't get enough credit—then and later—it was Wright.

"I think he's one of the greatest corners who ever played the game," Red Miller says, decisively. "You couldn't say that he *wasn't* the greatest. Know what? He might have been. He wasn't flashy and he was in Denver, where you don't get as much media, but he was a shutdown corner before they named them shutdown corners. We'd give him one guy and then we could shade with everyone else. We didn't ever double over there."

They didn't need to.

Offense

Note: * indicates Member of Broncos Ring of Fame (induction year)

Otis Armstrong, RB

The night a Jack Tatum hit in an August 1978 exhibition game in Oakland left Darryl Stingley paralyzed for life, Otis and his wife, Yvonne, got a call from Stingley's wife, Martine. Otis tried to be reassuring, saying players get "stingers" all the time. He recalls, "But she said, 'He can't move! They say his neck is broken.'"

Armstrong couldn't sleep all night, and when he showed up at the Broncos' practice facility the next morning, Red Miller—who knew Stingley from Miller's stint as New England's offensive coordinator—said if Armstrong wanted to leave the team to go see Stingley, he would understand.

Armstrong checked and was told visitors were being strictly limited, and he decided to stay, but he always would appreciate Miller's gesture.

Yvonne Armstrong went out to the Oakland-area hospital to be with Martine. In the first week of October, after Stingley was moved to a Chicago rehabilitation hospital, Armstrong visited him.

"Darryl had a halo on and he was laying on a metal slab," Armstrong says. "They flipped him over while I was there so I was like on the floor looking up at him trying to talk to him."

The Broncos played at San Diego the next Sunday.

"I was in a fog," Armstrong says. "I forgot to get in the huddle. I couldn't believe that something like that could happen playing football. I think I carried the ball four or five times in the first quarter and Red took me out of the game. He knew what had happened to me. I wasn't ready and couldn't get focused for football after seeing Darryl like that."

After the season, he went to Super Bowl XIII—Pittsburgh's 35-31 victory over Dallas in Miami—with Stingley as guests of Patriots owner Billy Sullivan. "That was the first time I had to work with Darryl that way— pick him up, make sure he got something to eat," Armstrong says. "One night I just cracked up. He asked me to help him get out of the chair and wanted to lay down, and I was trying to fix my eyes and pretend like I wasn't crying. It just hit me at that moment and I broke up. But then I knew I had to be strong for him, and after that I was better."

Armstrong pauses, and then adds: "He was smiling and laughing and joking around all the time, and there was no way any of us could have handled it like Darryl did. It's impossible."

For the rest of his career, Armstrong looked for Tatum when the Broncos played the Raiders. "I tried to run over Jack Tatum, every single game we played against them. My buddies knew how I felt, and they were helping me out. We didn't do anything dirty, we didn't go blindside, but instead of doing a cut against Jack Tatum, I'd try to run over him. He'd get up and laugh. That's just the way he is. He's a rugged customer and he played the game recklessly."

Armstrong played only through 1980, retiring at age 30. All along, he didn't like the frequent intimations that he wasn't tough enough and was unwilling to play hurt. In his final season, when he had 470 yards on 106 carries, he started only six games because of various injuries, including a neck and back problem.

"Every time I got hit, even when I made sharp cuts, it hurt," he says. "It was like an awareness of where your limbs are in space. It was like my body's over here but I'm trying to go here, and I was having a lot of problems. It was scary because I didn't know what it was. When I told the doctors, I could see the concern on their faces. They said I was through. They said your spinal cord doesn't have much space in there and every time you wiggle around, it's a problem. I sneaked back in the game when we played against Houston, and I could see those doctors waving to the quarterback, 'Get him out of there!' Well, I carried it for a 3-yard loss and they took me out. The doctors said, 'What were you doing in the game?' The coaches were saying, 'You should have gone outside!'"

The Broncos said his spine problem was congenital. Armstrong maintained it was because of the wear and tear of football. He eventually received injury and contract settlements from the Broncos, plus disability benefits from the NFL.

He was a partner in some businesses with Jon Keyworth. He and Yvonne still live in the Greenwood Village house they moved into in 1977, and Otis is a doting grandfather who monitors his investments.

When we first talked for this book, he was worried about Stingley's deteriorating health. He and Yvonne always visited Stingley and his family when the Armstrongs were in Chicago. They went out to restaurants, and the Armstrongs called ahead to make sure all was ready for Stingley and that the establishment was handicap-accessible. Otis continued to talk with Darryl often on the phone.

In the early morning hours of April 5, 2007, Yvonne Armstrong answered the telephone.

The caller was Stingley's wife, Martine.

"I remember Yvonne looking at me with that horror on her face," Armstrong says. "She started crying and I grabbed the phone and I could hear that Martine was screaming, and I could hear the paramedics trying to revive him."

Stingley was pronounced dead at Northwestern Memorial Hospital.

He was 55.

Eighteen years—eighteen years!—after Stingley's paralysis, Tatum finally planned to visit Stingley in 1996. Stingley canceled that after he decided Tatum was doing it to publicize his book.

Armstrong still hasn't forgiven Tatum.

"I'm very disappointed in Jack," he says. "Football's a game and we are all human beings. I just wish he had had the love in his heart to at least make Darryl feel it wasn't intentional. You don't have to apologize. But he could go to him and say, 'Look, I didn't intend for that.' He could have gone to the hospital to visit him. None of that took place."

At Oak Hill Cemetery in the Chicago suburb of Hillside, Otis walked up at the end of the ceremony and took one final look at Darryl's casket. He stood there and thought of racing on a sidewalk and wrestling in a dorm room and maneuvering up a ramp into a restaurant. He thought of Darryl's laughter and his strength. And then he walked away.

"A part of me went in the ground with him," Otis says.

Jack Dolbin, WR

"Doc" had undergone major knee surgery while at Wake Forest, but it didn't slow him down. But he was noticing the knee becoming more unstable when he hurt it again. He got tangled up with running back Jim Jensen in a game at Seattle in 1979 and underwent major surgery. Doctors told him he probably ought to think about his next career, and that wasn't a problem for him. Finally a graduate of chiropractic school, he retired and had a practice in Denver before returning to Pottsville and opening a practice there.

"I have no complaints about football and professional life out there in Denver, but I just wanted to get back into this area," he says. "It's home."

Married in 1970, he and Jane have four children who all attended college on athletic scholarships: Son Joshua as a receiver at Villanova; daughter Jill as a diver at Pittsburgh; daughter Rachel as a Maryland gymnast; and daughter Christian as a runner at Auburn.

Tom Glassic, G

Glassic remained a bit of a rebel for the rest of his career, which lasted through 1983—meaning in his final season, he helped protect John Elway. His biggest problems continued to be keeping weight on and injuries, including a troublesome back, and he was in even more pain that the typical offensive lineman when he was in the lineup.

In Elway's rookie season, Glassic missed the first four games after undergoing knee surgery, and when he came back, he didn't like his role. "I had to be a shuttle guard," he recalls. "I had to stand next to Dan [Reeves] on the sideline and bring in plays. I used to lean over his clipboard and sweat on it."

In retirement, Glassic first turned his toy soldier hobby into a business, traveling to conventions and trade shows around the country and selling his soldiers and other historical artifacts. Then he decided it was better as a hobby, bought a rustic home in the mountains west of Denver, and retreated—in many ways.

"I went to work for the Girl Scouts," he says. Noting my quizzical look, he adds, "The Girl Scouts had the Tomahawk Ranch, a valley over. I was assistant caretaker." Now he's smiling. "I had to join the Girl Scouts to get the job. I went through the candlelight ceremony with the other girls."

After working for the Girl Scouts for three and a half years—I don't ask how he did at selling cookies—his back got so painful, he couldn't do even the light manual labor that was part of the job. At that point, he had been fighting the NFL for years, attempting to get disability benefits, and he finally won that battle, as had Otis Armstrong. "There are a lot of guys who should be getting it who are not," Glassic says.

And in retirement?

"I play with my toy soldiers," he says. "I paint them, have war games with my friends. I just dropped a bundle at a toy auction. You remember when you were a kid, you remember Marx play sets? Fort Apache, Civil War? That's what I collect. I also collect tiny war figures and have battles. I never leave the house unless I have to. I don't go anywhere. I love this place. I'm right here in this chair 90 percent of the time, everything's within reach, and I can't be on my feet much anyway."

Glassic has his soldiers on display both in his house and in a fireproof metal storage shed, which he put on his property after several fires threatened the area in the 1990s. He is a hermit, and although he is in constant pain, he is happy.

Paul Howard, G

One of the great ironies: The Bronco who was the most physically suspect going into the '77 season ended up sticking around the longest. He announced his retirement in a letter addressed to the team and its fans.

It read:

As a 37th birthday present to myself and my family, I have retired from pro football as of Sept. 12, 1987. I wish the team good luck and would like to thank the fans for their loyal support during the last 14 years. . . . I have requested a fishing pole for my birthday and if my wish is granted, my first goal is to make it a very used pole.

> *Gone fishing,*
> *Paul Howard*

At the time, his 187 games for the Broncos were second only to Tom Jackson's 191.

He lives in Craig, Colorado.

Jon Keyworth, FB

Keyworth was out of the game by 1981. His band made many appearances locally and in Las Vegas during his career, and his 1979 album was controversial because of the cover. He was shown wearing a tuxedo in the showers, with a nude "teammate" behind him. Target, for example, displayed the album only after stickers were placed over the "teammate's" rear end. Keyworth's third son, Scott, died of Sudden Infant Death Syndrome in 1980, and he became a tireless spokesman to raise awareness and funds to fight it. He got out of the restaurant business and by the late 1990s was a national sales representative for an insurance company. Eventually, he moved to North Carolina, where he ran a company that sold natural health and injury recovery products.

Rob Lytle, RB

Lytle, who had the distinction of becoming the first player to score a touchdown in both the Rose Bowl and Super Bowl, was a versatile Broncos back, playing until 1983. Battling both injuries and the lack of opportunity to be the featured back, his rookie rushing total—408 yards—was his top season, and he finished with 1,451 yards in his career. He says that after the 1980 season, when he had been productive playing both fullback and tailback down the stretch, Miller told him he would be given a chance as the every-down tailback the next season (Otis Armstrong was retiring)—but that went out the window when Edgar Kaiser bought the team and changed coaches. Lytle liked Dan Reeves and accepted being a utility player, but says he now is somewhat "embarrassed" that he didn't accomplish more. "I had a good career, but it wasn't what I envisioned it to be," he says.

He and Tracy returned to his native Fremont, Ohio, and poured a lot of sweat and money into the family clothing business until 1990. The store was back on its feet when a fire in an adjacent business totaled the Lytle store, too, and Rob decided it was time to close the doors for good. He worked from 1990 to 1997 for a trucking company and from 1997 to 2004 for Turner Construction, which was involved with the construction of stadiums around the country, including Invesco Field and Detroit's Comerica Park. After walking away from an accident in which his car was totaled and deciding the constant travel was getting old, he became a vice president and commercial loan officer at Fremont's Old Fort Bank.

Bobby Maples, C

The peerless long snapper and pseudo–assistant coach retired after the 1978 season. He was 48 when he died of Hodgkin's disease in 1991.

Andy Maurer, T

The Broncos cut Maurer the next year and he retired. After a 10-year journeyman's career, he says, "I'd had enough."

Back in southern Oregon, he tried construction and development and, he says, "went broke" before turning to a ministry, founding and running Christian Financial Management in Medford. On the side, he was helping coach at South Medford High when he was asked to coach the new football program at Cascade Christian High. In 2006, Cascade won the Oregon Class 2A State Championship.

Along the way, Maurer nearly died after ballooning to around 500 pounds.

"I had heart problems and I couldn't breathe and they said I needed to lose some weight," he says. "I cleaned up my diet and got on some medication and lost 100 pounds. They said, 'You're doing really good, and we're really proud of you, but the only thing is you're going to die before you lose enough weight.'" He underwent bariatric bypass surgery—stomach stapling—and at last check was down to "290-something. I got my life back."

Claudie Minor, T

Once, when Bobby Maples told Minor he could play for 15 seasons in the league, as Maples did, Minor recoiled. "Absolutely not!" he snapped.

"In those days," he says, "hitting people with your face as an offensive lineman was worse than it is now. I ended up playing nine years. I remember something Barney Chavous said at a Bible study at camp. He said, 'You prayed to get in the game, you ought to pray to leave the game.' That made sense, but it just took me some time to leave."

Minor switched to left tackle in 1978 and played through 1982. Ever since, he has said he didn't retire, but "put the Broncos on waivers." By then, he was making more money away from football than he was in it. He had started a business while playing, Premier Drilling Fluids, providing drilling fluid for oil and gas companies. Later, he bought and sold natural gas, overseeing the building of pipeline systems and being more directly involved in the discovery process; he also sold heating oil and diesel fuel. Then he and his wife got into the development business, and they have been heavily involved in the redevelopment of the old Stapleton International Airport area.

His playing days, he says, "were the best of the highs and the worst of the lows. The game and those who participate learn more about themselves while they're associated with the game.

"As I taught football to kids the last 20-some years, and as I teach it to my son, it's funny how fathers will tell their 10-year-olds to be a man, and their 12-years-olds to be tough and to be a man. I tell their sons that if your dad was tough, he would come down and go one-on-one with me, and we would define tough. Or I would say to them, 'Be 10, be 10 all day today, and be 10 right up until you're 11, and then be 11. Don't rush into being a man.'"

He and Vicki have four children—Maisha, Keesha, ShaRinn, and Claudie D. Minor III, known to almost everyone as "D."

Mike Montler, C

With second-year center Billy Bryan—who missed the entire '77 season—healthy and considered a bright prospect, Montler turned out to be a transitional soldier for Red Miller. The Broncos traded Montler to the Detroit Lions during the '78 exhibition season.

Montler wasn't particularly bitter, thanked Miller, and said he probably would retire. His family was in Boulder, his children were in school, and maybe it was time.

Lions coach Monte Clark called Montler and successfully begged him to report, saying he needed Montler for only one year. Montler quickly considered Clark to be a petty tyrant, with stupid rules and a lack of concern for his players.

Worse, the Lions tried to make Montler the long snapper and he considered himself no better than an emergency snapper.

After the fourth game of the season, a crushing loss at Seattle, the Lions were going through what everyone thought were silly and punitive drills on Monday when Montler had enough. He walked off the field. The next day, he loaded up the station wagon with Suzy and the kids, drove to the stadium, and went into the offices to see if there was anything he needed to do to "check out." Clark's secretary buzzed the coach and told him Montler was there. Montler says he heard Clark say, "Well, tell him to have a seat, I'll be with him in a minute." Montler assumes Clark thought he was there to beg for forgiveness. He responded to Clark's secretary: "Really. Well, you tell him I'm gone, I'm out of here."

He walked out and drove his family back to Boulder.

He was in construction and development for about six years. "I was really not cut out for the business world," he says. "I was too volatile and too easily taken advantage of."

He went to work for NationsWay Transport, the trucking company owned by Jerry McMorris. He was considered a management candidate and told he should go to the loading dock to learn some of the basics of the business. He's proud to say he loved the labor on the loading dock, found it paid well, and stayed at it until the company went under in 1999.

He and Suzy moved to Grand Junction in 2000, in part so they could be closer to their children in California.

*Craig Morton, QB (1988)

Although Morton was the AFC offensive player of the year, he actually had more statistically productive seasons during the remainder of his tenure with the Broncos, three more seasons under Miller and then two seasons under his former Dallas teammate Dan Reeves. At the end of Miller's tenure, he says he and Miller often were disagreeing and having "horrible arguments," a not-uncommon phenomenon between coaches and quarterbacks that would repeat itself with Reeves and John Elway. That said, Morton emphasizes, "I loved Red Miller." After the Broncos traded for Matt Robinson, Morton shared the starting job with him in Miller's final season, 1980. Under Reeves in 1981, he regained the number one spot and had his best season ever statistically, throwing for 3,195 yards and 21 touchdowns, completing 59 percent of his passes, and tying with Dan Fouts for second in NFL passing rating, behind Cincinnati's Ken Anderson.

After the strike-shortened 1982 season, he pondered trying to play one more year, to perhaps help mentor John Elway, but wasn't up to it physically.

His business partner was former state senator Arch Decker, and he says they "made a lot of money" with their ownership of Cottonwood Hill, an alcohol rehabilitation center. Then Decker suggested they try the restaurant business, and Morton went along grudgingly. They had two restaurants and both closed. He also was in the oil business and did some broadcasting work.

When Morton succeeded Red Miller as the head coach of Denver Gold in the middle of the 1983 season, that certainly didn't help mend their rift. Morton got along better with team owner Ron Blanding than did Miller. "The Denver Gold was great," Morton says. "I loved that. I had a great staff and a pretty good team. We didn't spend a lot of money, but we created some things I wanted to put in."

He installed a more wide-open offense and convinced buddy Craig Penrose to end his football retirement and play for the Gold. He also made no apologies for an unconventional and low-key coaching style, saying the marathon hours many coaches spent working often were more for show or the result of conformity than they were necessary or efficient. The team was off to a terrific 7-1 start in the 1984 season when a new owner, automobile dealer Doug Spedding, took control of the team. "I should have walked away," says Morton, who calls Spedding "the worst person I've ever known."

He says Spedding poisoned the atmosphere, demoralizing the players and staff with petty and intrusive policies. The Gold won its first game after the sale to get to 8-1, but then collapsed and finished 9-9. Morton's Gold record was 12-12 and his parting with Spedding was a mutual decision—and mutual hatred.

He briefly was on Reeves's Broncos staff on a temporary basis in 1988, working with Elway.

Later, he moved to the Portland area to help get a team there in a proposed Professional Spring Football League off the ground, but the league—designed to stick with the original USFL concept—never did play a game. Morton stayed in Oregon for about five years, serving as president of Safety Operating Systems, before moving with his wife and two children to Scottsdale, Arizona.

In 2003, he returned to his alma mater, Cal–Berkeley, as the athletic director's major gift officer. When I visited him in his office in Haas Pavilion, the Bears' basketball arena, he had just returned to work after undergoing his third knee replacement—the second on his left knee.

He and Susan divorced after 23 years of marriage. "It's not like I would have liked to have it, but it's the way it is," he says.

In 2005, Morton went through a prostate cancer scare, but it was caught early and after he underwent radiation treatment, he was pronounced cancer-free.

For the record, Morton went out of his way—at the outset—to say there is something he regrets about that '77 team.

"The defense was our team," he says. "We had some great offensive talent and we did our jobs and sometimes we did it really well, but overall, that defense was just amazing. Not having any of those guys in the Hall of Fame is just pathetic. Louis Wright was as good a cornerback as I ever saw. Gradishar, Tommy Jackson, Billy Thompson. None of them are in the Hall of Fame? That's just a joke. I'm glad John Elway got in the Hall of Fame, but he shouldn't have been the first one."

*Haven Moses, WR (1988)

Haven had decided to retire after the 1980 season, but he says the incoming Dan Reeves talked him into playing for one more year. He didn't enjoy it and didn't get along with the new coach, especially after he was put on waivers and recalled in a procedural move before the first game. He considered that demeaning, especially since Reeves had asked him to return. It got worse when he was essentially benched after about a month and Reeves said he wanted to go with the young receivers. Fittingly, his last touchdown reception came at San Diego in the 11th game.

He ended with 406 career catches for an average of 18 yards per reception, with 54 touchdowns. But 1977 remained the high-water mark.

He was a Coors Brewery executive from 1981 to 1995, both in Colorado and for four years in North Carolina. He went to work for the Archdiocese of Denver as executive director for the Seeds of Hope program to help inner-city schools and was content when his world changed in January 2003.

He attended a function at Holy Family High School's new building in Broomfield, then returned to the archdiocese offices. He walked up to the third floor and felt disoriented. His office neighbor tried to strike up a conversation. "I couldn't understand what I was saying," Moses says. "I was mumbling and I said, 'John, I don't feel like talking, I don't feel good.' I sat down and tried to turn my computer on and I couldn't do anything with the keys."

Eventually, he went home, to the family's condo in Denver's Golden Triangle, southwest of the State Capitol. Joyce was at work at a jewelry store. "I lay down, but I got up to use the restroom about 30 minutes later and I fell down," he says. "My left side just went out. I crawled to the restroom, used the bathroom, and got back in bed."

When Joyce got home, Haven got up and fell again, and Joyce told him they were going to the hospital. No, Haven pleaded, just let him sleep and he would be all right in the morning. "She finally convinced me, got me dressed, took me out to the car and we went right over to [nearby] Denver Health. They wheeled me in and in no time were telling me I had suffered a stroke. If I had slept that night, I'd probably still be sleeping."

The road back has been long and hard. "Joyce became the provider and caregiver," he says, with great emotion. His speech isn't affected, though, and as he sits, there is no noticeable toll. He still is weakened on his left side and struggles as he walks, but has made major physical progress and is often seen taking strolls around his neighborhood and in downtown Denver. He gets a lot of thumbs up and smiles and words of encouragement, whether they have recognized him as number 25 or not.

Has he felt sorry for himself or questioned his faith? "Not one time," he says. "Faith was the foundation. Family was the cornerstone. Friends were the roof. My whole life has been a blessing."

Riley Odoms, TE

The "Judge" lives in Missouri City, Texas.

*Jim Turner, K (1988)

The Redskins' Mark Moseley was the NFL's final straight-on kicker, but Turner was one of the last of the breed. He kicked two more seasons for the Broncos before Fred Steinfort, a British soccer-style kicker, took over the duties and Turner retired at age 39. He finished his career with 304 field goals in 488 attempts, for what then was a highly impressive 62 percent success rate.

Turner did radio work as a talk show host and also was a sports anchor and sportscaster before winding down and beginning a praiseworthy stint working with young athletes in the Jefferson County Schools as an academic coach. He has worked at Jefferson High and Alameda High, and the athletic complex at Jefferson High is called Jim Turner Field. He has done a terrific job as a mentor and surrogate father, getting athletes on track to get into college, whether they participate in sports or otherwise, while fighting significant health problems.

He has had heart surgery and has trouble getting his breath because of reduced lung capacity, but several foot surgeries—including one in which the doctor placed a titanium plate and three screws in the big toe on his kicking foot—have helped. He and Mary Kay still live in the Arvada home they moved into in 1973.

Rick Upchurch, WR-KR

The speedy Upchurch ended up making the Pro Bowl four times in his nine-season career, and when he retired in 1984 because of neck problems, he held or shared seven NFL punt-return records. He also caught

John Elway's first-ever completion, in the 1983 opener against the Steelers.

Upchurch had taken a lot of heat for his marijuana use, which caused the Broncos to send him to a rehabilitation center in 1983, and his initial candor that he didn't consider it a major problem was refreshing, but offended many. (Truth was, he was far from the only athlete or Bronco smoking dope, and Denver journalism had a significant drug problem—involving substances other than marijuana—at the time Upchurch's marijuana use was being made a major issue in the Denver dailies.) He worked in several businesses before getting into coaching and the sports camp business, first as the associate head football coach and co–head track coach for four years at Tabor College in Hillsboro, Kansas. He ran Rare Breed Youth Sports in Pueblo for nine years, and became a highly visible and respected leader in the Pueblo area. He served a two-season stint as the head football coach at Pueblo East High before resigning following the 2006 season. He moved to Mesquite, Nevada, and is still active in youth foundation work while having a co-ownership stake in a home-construction consulting firm.

Norris Weese, QB

The backup quarterback who threw the touchdown pass to Turner against the Raiders and came on in relief of Morton in the Super Bowl played through 1979 with the Broncos. He became an accountant and broadcaster in Denver, working as an analyst with play-by-play man Ron Zappolo on Broncos' exhibition game telecasts. After being diagnosed with cancer, he underwent extensive surgery to remove a tumor in his back in 1993. He died in 1995, at age 43.

Denver, Colorado

The Nuggets finished 48-34 in the 1977–78 regular season and again won the NBA's Midwest Division. They beat Milwaukee in seven games in the first round of the playoffs and then fell to eventual league champion Seattle 4-2 in the second round. Larry Brown coached the team until late in the 1978–79 season before moving on to UCLA. The franchise has been through many ups and downs since, including having me as the beat writer for two seasons in the 1980s.

The Colorado Rockies, meanwhile, finished 19-40-21 in 1977–78—I resorted to many bad "tie" puns in my stories—and were the 12th seed among the 12 teams that made the playoffs in the 17-team NHL. They lost a two-game miniseries to the Philadelphia Flyers, but were competitive and played in a sold-out McNichols Sports Arena in the second game. They heard predictions that they had a young team on the way to giving Denver a foothold in the NHL. However, Pat Kelly was fired early the next season. All three of the touted young stars—Wilf Paiement, Paul Gardner, and Barry Beck—eventually were traded. The team went through several coaches in the remainder of its tenure in Denver, including Don Cherry. It also went through three owners. Jack Vickers sold the team to New Jersey trucking company owner Arthur Imperatore and moved on to something he was more passionate about—golf, founding "The International" golf tournament at Castle Pines. Imperatore sold it to Buffalo cable television magnate Peter Gilbert. Gilbert eventually sold to John McMullen, who moved the franchise to New Jersey in 1982. It would be 13 years before Denver got another chance in the NHL, and then the Avalanche put together the longest recorded sellout streak in NHL history and won the Stanley Cup in 1996 and 2001.

The Denver Orange Sox never materialized. The A's couldn't get out of the Oakland Coliseum lease and remained in Oakland. To this day, I believe that if Marvin Davis had been 100 percent sold on the wisdom of acquiring the team, he would have stepped in and bought Charlie Finley out of the lease. He didn't. After many more false starts—the A's were rumored to be moving to Denver several times—Denver obtained an expansion team in the National League for 1993. The Colorado Rockies— some thought that was a curious choice for a name, given the hockey franchise's failures—played two seasons in Mile High Stadium before moving to Coors Field.

Governor Richard Lamm overcame his contentious start in office and twice was reelected, serving until 1987. His comment in this book about our emphasis on cures rather than prevention is consistent with his controversial "we have a duty to die" stand. He was an unsuccessful candidate for the Reform Party's presidential nomination in 1996. He has been a novelist and otherwise a prolific writer since leaving office, and his book

Two Wands, One Nation outlines views on illegal immigration and other issues that are—if anyone would bother to read or listen—reasonable and realistic evolutions of 1960s and 1970s liberal stands.

With C-470 and E-470 helping encourage the expansion, Denver's metro-area population has continued to grow.

Elitch's amusement park has moved to near downtown, on the banks of the South Platte. The old Elitch grounds, though, are somewhat being preserved as part of a new development, and the old theater is still standing.

One thing hasn't changed.

The Broncos still are the kings.

Their status as the number-one team in the market never has been in danger, not even when the Avalanche won the Stanley Cup or the Rockies were selling out Mile High Stadium and Coors Field. But as I alluded to in the opening chapter, the attitudes—as so much has in Denver—have been transformed.

By 1983, when John and Jack Elway were so disdainful of Baltimore Colts coach Frank Kush and also owner Robert Irsay that they tried and failed to talk the Colts out of drafting John, all vestiges of those vertically striped socks, bargain-basement, perennial-loser days had been shoved into the history books. The '77 Broncos had a lot to do with that. The Elways knew John hadn't escaped Kush only to be presented with football Siberia as the alternative. Denver and the Broncos were big-time. It was virtually automatic that after winning the battle of wills with the Colts that he would sign with the Broncos—and cease using his baseball talents and his minor-league tenure with the Yankees as leverage.

The Broncos, of course, lost the Super Bowl three times under Elway—after the 1986, '87 and '89 seasons—before winning two straight, over the Packers after the '97 season and the Falcons after the '98 season. During the run of Super Bowl losses, when the Broncos and the Minnesota Vikings were considered the always-a-bridesmaid examples, it even became fashionable to say Denver would be better off if the Broncos didn't make the NFL's bacchanal game rather than go and be embarrassed again. By then, we were deep into the contrived controversy era of sports journalism in Denver, so that view never was as widespread as some portrayed it to be. But the fact that it even could be broached—both in newspapers and on barstools—and not be considered ludicrous shows how much the landscape had changed since 1977.

The only time during the run of Super Bowl losses when the sort of wide-eyed enthusiasm we saw so often in '77 was reprised was when the Broncos staged the legendary last-minute drive to tie the Browns in the January 1987 AFC championship game and won in overtime. Other than that, for the most part, we were jaded. Denver was excited and passionate, and the coverage was ridiculously voluminous—and I say that because we cranked out pieces on short-term trivia and missed far more interesting stories and angles. Yet it all was just different. Absolutely, '77 was a bandwagon and many fans climbed aboard because the franchise—for the first time—was among the league's elite. The Broncos, even after the stadium expansion, still were selling out. Still, after that season, it was different. We were harder to impress, harder to excite, harder to unite. That's not a value judgment. There's nothing wrong with realism. Orange cupcakes get stale after a while. Denver "grew up." When the Broncos won those back-to-back titles, the celebrations were fervent, and the numbers certainly impressive, and it all led to the construction of a new state-of-the-art stadium with luxury boxes suited for wine sipping. By then Denver had established that its passion was conditional.

I'm not embarrassed to admit it: I miss the Denver of '77.

Appendix

ROSTER AND COACHING STAFF

1977 BRONCOS
OFFENSE

Starting Lineup

Position	Number	Name	Height	Weight	Season	College
WR	25	**Haven Moses**	6-3	200	10th	San Diego State
TE	88	**Riley Odoms**	6-4	230	6th	Houston
RT	71	**Claudie Minor**	6-4	282	4th	San Diego State
RG	60	**Paul Howard**	6-3	260	5th	Brigham Young
C	52	**Mike Montler**	6-5	254	9th	Colorado
LG	62	**Tom Glassic**	6-2	254	2nd	Virginia
LT	74	**Andy Maurer**	6-3	265	9th	Oregon
WR	82	**Jack Dolbin**	5-10	180	3rd	Wake Forest
QB	7	**Craig Morton**	6-4	210	13th	California
TB	24	**Otis Armstrong**	5-10	196	5th	Purdue
FB	32	**Jon Keyworth**	6-3	230	4th	Colorado
or						
FB	35	**Lonnie Perrin**	6-1	222	2nd	Illinois

Reserves

Position	Number	Name	Height	Weight	Season	College
QB	12	**Craig Penrose**	6-3	222	2nd	San Diego State
QB	14	**Norris Weese**	6-1	195	2nd	Mississippi
FB	30	**Jim Jensen**	6-3	230	2nd	Iowa
RB	33	**Jim Kiick**	5-11	215	9th	Wyoming
TB	41	**Rob Lytle**	5-11	195	1st	Michigan
C	50	**Bobby Maples**	6-3	250	13th	Baylor
G-T	65	**Glenn Hyde**	6-3	253	2nd	Pittsburgh
G	67	**Steve Schindler**	6-3	260	1st	Boston College
T	72	**Henry Allison**	6-3	255	7th	San Diego State
WR	80	**Rick Upchurch**	5-10	170	3rd	Minnesota
TE	85	**Ron Egloff**	6-5	238	1st	Wisconsin
WR	86	**John Schultz**	5-10	182	2nd	Maryland

Injured, didn't play in regular season

C	**Billy Bryan**
T	**Bill Bain**

DEFENSE

Starting Lineup

Position	Number	Name	Height	Weight	Season	College
DE	79	**Barney Chavous**	6-3	252	5th	South Carolina St.
NT	62	**Rubin Carter**	6-0	256	3rd	Miami
DE	77	**Lyle Alzado**	6-3	260	7th	Yankton College
OLB	51	**Bob Swenson**	6-3	215	3rd	California
ILB	59	**Joe Rizzo**	6-1	220	4th	Merchant Marine Academy
ILB	53	**Randy Gradishar**	6-3	233	4th	Ohio State
OLB	57	**Tom Jackson**	5-11	220	5th	Louisville
LCB	20	**Louis Wright**	6-2	195	3rd	San Jose State
RCB	43	**Steve Foley**	5-11	189	2nd	Tulane
SS	36	**Billy Thompson**	6-1	201	9th	Maryland State
FS	29	**Bernard Jackson**	6-0	178	6th	Washington State

Reserves

Position	Number	Name	Height	Weight	Season	College
DB	21	**Randy Poltl**	6-3	190	4th	Stanford
DB	23	**Chris Pane**	5-11	180	2nd	Chico State
DB	26	**Larry Riley**	5-10	192	1st	Salem College
DB	40	**Randy Rich**	5-10	178	1st	New Mexico
LB	55	**Godwin Turk**	6-2	230	4th	Southern U.
LB	56	**Larry Evans**	6-2	216	2nd	Miss. College
LB	58	**Rob Nairne**	6-4	220	1st	Oregon State
DT	63	**John Grant**	6-3	241	5th	So. California
DE	66	**Brison Manor**	6-4	248	1st	Arkansas
DE	70	**Paul Smith**	6-3	256	10th	New Mexico

COACHING STAFF

Red Miller, head coach: Played at Western Illinois. Coached at high schools in Astoria and Canton, Illinois; then was an assistant at Carthage College and Western Illinois. Assistant with Boston Patriots 1960–1961, Buffalo Bills 1962, Denver Broncos 1963–1965, St. Louis Cardinals 1966–1970, Baltimore Colts 1971–1972, New England Patriots 1973–1976. Joined Denver staff for 1977.

Joe Collier, defensive coordinator: Played at Northwestern, then was assistant at Western Illinois 1957–1959, Boston Patriots 1960–1961, Buffalo Bills 1962–1965. Head coach of Bills 1966–1968. Joined Denver staff in 1969.

Stan Jones, defensive line: Played at Maryland, then 12 seasons with the

Chicago Bears and 1 with the Washington Redskins. Coached at Denver 1967–1971, Buffalo 1972–1975, Denver, 1976–.

Myrel Moore, linebackers: Played at California–Davis, then briefly with the Washington Redskins. Coached at Santa Ana Junior College 1963, California 1964–1971, Denver, 1972–.

Bob Gambold, defensive backs: Played at Washington State, then with the Philadelphia Eagles in 1953 and the Chicago Cardinals in 1954. Head coach at Everett Junior College, assistant at Washington State and Oregon State before serving on John Ralston's Stanford staff, 1963–1971, Denver 1972–.

Babe Parilli, quarterbacks: Played at Kentucky, then with six teams in the All-America Football Conference, the NFL, and the AFL. Joined Denver staff for 1977.

Paul Roach, offensive backs: Assistant at Wyoming 1964–1971, Oakland 1972–1974, and Green Bay 1975–1976. Joined Denver staff for 1977.

Ken Gray, offensive line: Played at Howard Payne, then with the St. Louis Cardinals in 1958–1969 and Houston in 1970, and was in the Pro Bowl five times. Joined Denver staff for 1977.

Fran Polsfoot, receivers: Played at Washington State. Assistant at St. Louis 1962–1967, Houston 1968–1971 and 1975–1976, Cleveland 1972–1974. Joined Denver staff for 1977.

Marv Braden, special teams: Head coach at Southwest Missouri State 1967–1968 and United States International 1969–1972. Assistant at Iowa State 1973, Southern Methodist 1974–1975, Michigan State 1976. Joined Denver staff for 1977.

OWNERSHIP/STAFF

Gerald Phipps, Chairman of the Board
Allan Phipps, President
Jim Burris, Vice President
Richard Kitchen, Secretary
Fred Gehrke, General Manager
Carroll Hardy, Director of Player Personnel
Doc Urich, Director of Pro Scouting
Larry Elliott, Equipment Manager
Allen Hurst, Trainer
Steve Antonopulos, Assistant Trainer
Ronnie Bill, Assistant Equipment Manager
Bob Peck, Director of Public Relations
David Frei, Assistant Director of Public Relations
Gail Stuckey, Ticket Manager
Betty Combs, Assistant Ticket Manager
Bill Goldy, Assistant to the General Manager
Joanne Parker, Administrative Assistant
Yolanda Saltus, Administrative Assistant

SEASON SCORES, STATISTICS, AND HONORS

PREVIOUS BRONCO RECORDS

Season	Coach	Record
1960	Frank Filchock	4-9-1
1961	Frank Filchock	3-11
1962	Jack Faulkner	7-7
1963	Jack Faulkner	2-11-1
1964	Jack Faulkner and Mac Speedie	2-11-1
1965	Mac Speedie	4-10
1966	Mac Speedie and Ray Malavasi	4-10
1967	Lou Saban	3-11
1968	Lou Saban	5-9
1969	Lou Saban	5-8-1
1970	Lou Saban	5-8-1
1971	Lou Saban and Jerry Smith	4-9-1
1972	John Ralston	5-9
1973	John Ralston	7-5-2
1974	John Ralston	7-6-1
1975	John Ralston	6-8
1976	John Ralston	9-5

1977 BRONCOS RESULTS

Exhibitions

August 5	Mile High Stadium	Broncos 14, Baltimore Colts 8
August 13	Mile High Stadium	Broncos 15, St. Louis Cardinals 7
August 20	Atlanta	Broncos 10, Atlanta Falcons 2
August 28	Philadelphia	Philadelphia Eagles 28, Broncos 24
September 2	Seattle	Broncos 27, Seattle Seahawks 10
September 10	San Francisco	Broncos 20, San Francisco 49ers 0

Regular Season

September 7 at Mile High Stadium
BRONCOS 7, ST. LOUIS CARDINALS 0

St. Louis	0	0	0	0—0
Denver	0	0	7	0—7

Denver: Armstrong 10 run (Turner kick)

TEAM STATISTICS
Cardinals: 69 yards rushing, 196 passing, 265 total offense.
Broncos: 136 rushing, 122 passing, 258 total offense.

RUSHING

Cardinals: Otis 12 carries / 34 yards, Latin 10-23, Metcalf 3-9, Jones 4-3.

Broncos: Armstrong 17-55, Lytle 6-31, Morton 6-15, Dolbin 1-14, Perrin 4-9, Keyworth 6-2.

PASSING

Cardinals: Hart 18 completions / 35 attempts / 1 interception, 221 yards.

Broncos: Morton 12-20-1, 144.

RECEIVING

Cardinals: Metcalf 6 catches / 35 yards; Tilley 3-49, Jones 3-16, Cain 3-26, Gray 2-55, Stone 1-40, Morris 1-1.

Broncos: Upchurch 3-71, Lytle 3-21, Odoms 2-17, Dolbin 2-17, Moses 1-12, Keyworth 1-6.

September 14 at Mile High Stadium
BRONCOS 26, BUFFALO BILLS 6

Buffalo	0	6	0	0—6
Denver	3	7	13	3—26

Denver: Turner 48 FG
Buffalo: Cornell 22 fumble recovery return (kick failed)
Denver: Morton 5 run (Turner kick)
Denver: Armstrong 1 run (kick failed)
Denver: Odoms 1 pass from Morton (Turner kick)
Denver: Turner 26 FG

TEAM STATISTICS

Bills: 66 yards rushing, 63 passing, 129 total offense.

Broncos: 203 rushing, 93 passing, 296 total offense.

RUSHING

Bills: Simpson 15-43, Brown 2-14, Braxton 5-7, Ferguson 1-4, Hooks 1-(-3).

Broncos: Armstrong 20-96, Lytle 8-31, Morton 1-5, Perrin 9-34, Keyworth 7-36, Moses 1-1.

PASSING

Bills: Ferguson 13-28-3, 111.

Broncos: Morton 8-18-0, 96; Penrose 1-2-0, 35.

RECEIVING

Bills: Braxton 3-13, Gant 3-24, Hooks 3-17, Holland 2-24,Simpson 1-18, Chandler 1-15.

Broncos: Odoms 2-18, Perrin 1-37, Moses 1-35, Dolbin 1-9, Armstrong 1-2, Keyworth 1-6, Upchurch 1-4, Egloff 1-20.

October 2 at Seattle
BRONCOS 24, SEATTLE SEAHAWKS 13

Denver	10	0	14	0—24
Seattle	7	0	6	0—13

Denver: Perrin 1 run (Turner kick)
Seattle: Howard 7 pass from Myer (Leypoldt kick)
Denver: Turner 36 FG
Denver: Lytle 47 pass from Morton (Turner kick)
Seattle: Largent 43 pass from Sims (kick failed)
Denver: Morton 1 run (Turner kick)

TEAM STATISTICS
Broncos: 153 rushing, 177 passing, 330 total offense.
Seahawks: 81 rushing, 191 passing, 272 total offense.

RUSHING
Broncos: Perrin 14-55, Morton 5-35, Armstrong 11-29, Keyworth 6-23, Lytle 3-11.
Seahawks: Smith 13-47, Testerman 10-16, Sims 6-14, Hunter 2-4, Myer 1-0.

PASSING
Broncos: Morton 12-21-1, 191.
Seahawks: Myer 20-29-1, 165; Sims 1-1-0, 43; Preece 0-1-0, 0.

RECEIVING
Broncos: Moses 5-92, Armstrong 3-7, Odoms 2-24, Lytle 1-47, Kiick 1-11.
Seahawks: Ferguson 6-68, Testerman 5-19, Largent 3-71, Smith 3-37, Howard 2-10, McCullum 1-8, Hunter 1-(-5).

October 9 at Mile High Stadium
BRONCOS 23, KANSAS CITY CHIEFS 7

Kansas City	0	0	0	7—7
Denver	10	6	7	0—23

Denver: Turner 25 FG
Denver: Morton 7 run (Turner kick)
Denver: Turner 33 FG
Denver: Turner 33 FG
Denver: Armstrong 1 run (Turner kick)
Kansas City: Podolak 2 run (Stenerud kick)

TEAM STATISTICS
Chiefs: 86 rushing, 80 passing, 166 total offense.
Broncos: 124 rushing, 188 passing, 312 total offense.

Rushing

Chiefs: Bailey 8-30, Podolak 11-20, Reed 3-4, Livingston 1-3, Morgado 3-12, McKnight 3-17.

Broncos: Keyworth 13-59, Armstrong 11-29, Morton 3-7, Perrin 4-5, Kiick 1-1, Lytle 6-23.

Passing

Chiefs: Livingston 5-9-2, 51; Adams 10-18-2, 81.

Broncos: Morton 13-21-0, 189; Penrose 5-9-0, 30.

Receiving

Chiefs: White 6-49, Williams 1-8, Podolak 5-40, Morgado 2-21, Marshall 1-14.

Broncos: Armstrong 4-25, Moses 2-36, Lytle 2-24, Upchurch 2-64, Keyworth 2-27, Dolbin 3-28, Odoms 1-12, Kiick 1-3.

October 16 at Oakland
BRONCOS 30, OAKLAND RAIDERS 7

Denver	7	14	6	3—30
Oakland	7	0	0	0—7

Oakland: Casper 9 pass from Stabler (Mann kick)
Denver: Odoms 10 pass from Morton (Turner kick)
Denver: Perrin 16 run (Turner kick)
Denver: Turner 25 pass from Weese (Turner kick)
Denver: Wright 18 interception return (kick failed)
Denver: Turner 32 FG

Team Statistics

Broncos: 107 rushing, 93 passing, 200 total offense.
Raiders: 86 rushing, 239 passing, 325 total offense.

Rushing

Broncos: Perrin 13-37, Keyworth 7-26, Armstrong 12-24, Lytle 4-11, Morton 1-4, Moses 1-4, Weese 1-1.

Raiders: van Eeghen 20-61, Davis 6-17, Robiskie 1-9, Banaszak 2-0, Rae 1-(-1).

Passing

Broncos: Morton 7-16-0, 93; Weese 1-1-0, 25.
Raiders: Stabler 20-40-7, 274.

Receiving

Broncos: Odoms 2-24, Lytle 2-18, Dolbin 1-24, Turner 1-25, Armstrong 1-12, Keyworth 1-5.

Raiders: Casper 6-58, Branch 4-92, Davis 4-27, Biletnikoff 3-33, Bradshaw 2-45, Van Eeghen 2-21, Siani 1-14.

October 23 at Cincinnati
BRONCOS 24, CINCINNATI BENGALS 13

Denver	7	10	0	7—24
Cincinnati	7	3	0	3—13

Cincinnati: Johnson 1 run (Bahr kick)
Denver: Keyworth 9 run (Turner kick)
Cincinnati: Bahr 19 FG
Denver: Turner 41 FG
Denver: Dolbin 41 pass from Morton (Turner kick)
Cincinnati: Bahr 24 FG
Denver: Jensen 1 run (Turner kick)

TEAM STATISTICS
Broncos: 180 rushing, 155 passing, 335 total offense.
Bengals: 177 rushing, 159 passing, 336 total offense.

RUSHING
Broncos: Keyworth 12-58, Armstrong 11-38, Jensen 8-30, Lytle 7-30, Penrose 4-24.
Bengals: Johnson 16-108, Griffin 11-36, Casanova 1-20, Davis 3-13.

PASSING
Broncos: Morton 5-10-0, 108; Penrose 4-5-0, 47.
Bengals: Anderson 9-17-1, 67; Reeves 6-11-0, 92.

RECEIVING
Broncos: Moses 1-18, Lytle 2-29, Odoms 1-7, Keyworth 1-(-5), Dolbin 2-91, Armstrong 2-15.
Bengals: Davis 6-42, Griffin 4-39, Curtis 1-5, Trumpy 1-16, Brooks 3-37.

October 30 at Mile High Stadium
OAKLAND RAIDERS 24, BRONCOS 14

Oakland	7	10	7	0—24
Denver	0	0	0	14—14

Oakland: Branch 27 pass from Stabler (Mann kick)
Oakland: Mann 42 FG
Oakland: Davis 8 run (Mann kick)
Oakland: van Eeghen 1 run (Mann kick)

Denver: Dolbin 11 pass from Morton (Turner kick)
Denver: Armstrong 7 run (Turner kick)

TEAM STATISTICS

Raiders: 200 rushing, 70 passing, 270 total offense.
Broncos: 98 rushing, 180 passing, 278 total offense.

RUSHING

Raiders: van Eeghen 30-82, Davis 20-105, Garrett 5-7, Banaszak 1-6.
Broncos: Armstrong 9-37, Perrin 11-58, Dolbin 1-(-2), Jensen 1-4, Lytle 1-1.

PASSING

Raiders: Stabler 7-14-0, 70.
Broncos: Morton 19-32-1, 242.

RECEIVING

Raiders: Biletnikoff 2-20, Davis 1-4, Branch 2-25, Casper 2-21.
Broncos: Armstrong 3-25, Odoms 5-60, Moses 2-45, Lytle 4-35, Perrin 2-21,
Dolbin 3-56.

November 6 at Mile High Stadium
BRONCOS 21, PITTSBURGH STEELERS 7

Pittsburgh	0	0	0	7—7
Denver	14	7	0	0—21

Denver: Lytle 1 run (Turner kick)
Denver: Upchurch 87 punt return (Turner kick)
Denver: Moses 20 pass from Morton (Turner kick)
Pittsburgh: Stallworth 4 pass from Bradshaw (Gerela kick)

TEAM STATISTICS

Steelers: 119 rushing, 97 passing, 216 total offense.
Broncos: 99 rushing, 75 passing, 174 total offense.

RUSHING

Steelers: Harris 23-82, Bleier 10-38, Graff 1-4, Stallworth 1-15.
Broncos: Armstrong 12-28, Perrin 13-34, Lytle 9-25, Weese 1-1, Morton 1-2,
Jensen 2-9.

PASSING

Steelers: Bradshaw 13-26-0, 146; Graff 0-1-0, 0.
Broncos: Morton 5-12-0, 101; Penrose 1-2-0, 12.

RECEIVING

Steelers: Bleier 4-29, Swann 3-32, Lewis 1-19, Stallworth 4-57, Harris 1-9.
Broncos: Odoms 2-33, Lytle 1-14, Jensen 2-46, Moses 1-20.

November 13 at San Diego
BRONCOS 17, SAN DIEGO CHARGERS 14

Denver	3	0	7	7—17
San Diego	7	7	0	0—14

San Diego: Dean 11 fumble return (Benirschke kick)
Denver: Turner 35 FG
San Diego: Joiner 32 pass from Washington (Benirschke kick)
Denver: Moses 33 pass from Morton (Turner kick)
Denver: Moses 8 pass from Morton (Turner kick)

TEAM STATISTICS
Broncos: 102 rushing, 120 passing, 222 total offense.
Chargers: 128 rushing, 192 passing, 320 total offense.

RUSHING
Broncos: Armstrong 6-33, Perrin 9-33, Jensen 7-23, Lytle 6-12, Morton 3-10, Moses 1-(-9).
Chargers: Woods 6-24, Young 12-27, Washington 16-26, Matthews 5-18, Rodgers 1-33, Williams 2-0.

PASSING
Broncos: Morton 12-32-1, 149.
Chargers: Harris 13-31-0, 166; Washington 1-1-0, 32; Munson 0-1-0, 0.

RECEIVING
Broncos: Dolbin 2-30, Moses 3-66, Lytle 1-4, Odoms 3-28, Armstrong 3-23.
Chargers: Young 3-4, Joiner 4-79, Rodgers 3-26, Woods 2-12, Washington 2-12, Matthews 1-12.

November 20 at Kansas City
BRONCOS 14, KANSAS CITY CHIEFS 7

Denver	0	7	0	7—14
Kansas City	0	7	0	0—7

Denver: Perrin 2 run (Turner kick)
Kansas City: Marshall 16 pass from Livingston (Stenerud kick)
Denver: Moses 23 pass from Morton (Turner kick)

TEAM STATISTICS
Broncos: 249 rushing, 127 passing, 376 total offense.
Chiefs: 139 rushing, 160 passing, 299 total offense.

RUSHING
Broncos: Armstrong 21-120, Keyworth 6-20, Perrin 5-9, Lytle 12-68, Jensen 5-20, Morton 4-12.
Chiefs: Podolak 15-39, Bailey 6-43, Livingston 1-(-1), Brockington 3-0, Reed 3-9, Marshall 1-4, Burks 1-51, White 1-(-6).

Broncos: Morton 8-18-2, 135.
Chiefs: Livingston 20-33-1, 180.

RECEIVING
Broncos: Moses 4-80, Odoms 2-33, Armstrong 1-10, Jensen 1-12.
Chiefs: Brunson 5-51, White 2-9, Marshall 3-31, Bailey 2-17, Brockington
4-43, Podolak 4-29.

November 27 at Mile High Stadium
BRONCOS 27, BALTIMORE COLTS 13

Baltimore	0	3	10	0—13
Denver	7	7	0	13—27

Denver: Upchurch 41 pass from Morton (Turner kick)
Denver: Dolbin 19 pass from Morton (Turner kick)
Baltimore: Linhart 40 FG
Baltimore: Linhart 43 FG
Baltimore: Mitchell 15 pass from Jones (Linhart kick)
Denver: T. Jackson 73 interception return (Turner kick)
Denver: Morton 6 run (kick failed)

TEAM STATISTICS
Colts: 90 rushing, 236 passing, 326 total offense.
Broncos: 174 rushing, 147 passing, 321 total offense.

RUSHING
Colts: Mitchell 7-14, Leaks 5-16, McCauley 13-46, Doughty 1-(-5), Jones 1-2,
R. Lee 6-17.
Broncos: Lytle 19-71, Keyworth 3-5, Perrin 7-83, Morton 3-12, Jensen 1-3.

PASSING
Colts: Jones 27-46-3, 252.
Broncos: Morton 8-14-1, 171.

RECEIVING
Colts: Mitchell 9-74, Scott 1-4, Doughty 4-39, Chester 2-23, McCauley
11-112.
Broncos: Upchurch 3-79, Moses 1-35, Dolbin 2-35, Odoms 1-18, Perrin 1-4.

December 4 at Houston
BRONCOS 24, HOUSTON OILERS 14

Denver	0	14	3	7—24
Houston	0	7	7	0—14

Houston: Coleman 2 run (Fritsch kick)
Denver: Odoms 13 pass from Morton (Turner kick)

Denver: Upchurch 13 pass from Morton (Turner kick)
Denver: Turner 42 FG
Houston: Burrough 29 pass from Pastorini (Fritsch kick)
Denver: Weese 5 run (Turner kick)

TEAM STATISTICS

Broncos: 169 rushing, 163 passing, 332 total offense.
Oilers: 112 rushing, 139 passing, 251 total offense.

RUSHING

Broncos: Jensen 14-40, Lytle 11-39, Perrin 10-38, Keyworth 6-22, Morton
2-17, Moses 1-8, Weese 1-5.
Oilers: Carpenter 20-64, Coleman 4-16, Wilson 3-15, Pastorini 2-15,
Burrough 1-2.

PASSING

Broncos: Morton 13-22-1, 187; Penrose 2-4-0, 26.
Oilers: Pastorini 10-19-0, 152; Burrough 0-1-0, 0.

RECEIVING

Broncos: Moses 6-86, Moses 4-77, Keyworth 1-14, Upchurch 1-13, Dolbin
1-12, Lytle 1-6, Jensen 1-5.
Oilers: Carpenter 3-4, Burrough 2-80, Coleman 2-34, Barber 2-28, Giles 1-6.

December 11 at Mile High Stadium
BRONCOS 17, SAN DIEGO CHARGERS 9

San Diego	3	3	3	0—9
Denver	7	0	0	10—17

Denver: Perrin 41 pass from Morton (Turner kick)
San Diego: Benirschke 46 FG
San Diego: Benirschke 32 FG
San Diego: Benirschke 27 FG
Denver: Turner 36 FG
Denver: Upchurch 19 run (Turner kick)

TEAM STATISTICS

Chargers: 64 rushing, 260 passing, 324 total offense.
Broncos: 156 rushing, 142 passing, 298 total offense.

RUSHING

Chargers: Young 8-30, Rodgers 4-35, Williams 2-6, Matthews 3-8,
Washington 5-12, Rodgers 1-7, Fouts 1-0.

Broncos: Perrin 8-40, Keyworth 12-41, Morton 2-6, Lytle 8-29, Weese 1-21, Upchurch 1-10.

PASSING

Chargers: Fouts 24-41-2, 276.
Broncos: Morton 9-17-0, 133; Penrose 6-10-3, 49.

RECEIVING

Chargers: Joiner 4-67, Rodgers 4-35, Young 6-62, McDonald 1-7, Klein 2-13, Washington 4-36, Williams 1-5, Curran 2-40, Woods 1-11.
Broncos: Dolbin 4-46, Perrin 2-44, Moses 1-16, Egloff 1-7, Odoms 6-69, Keyworth 1-0.

December 18 at Dallas
DALLAS COWBOYS 14, BRONCOS 6

Denver	0	0	3	3—6
Dallas	7	0	7	0—14

Dallas: P. Pearson 22 pass from Staubach (Herrera kick)
Dallas: Newhouse 7 pass from Staubach (Herrera kick)
Denver: Turner 22 FG
Denver: Turner 37 FG

TEAM STATISTICS

Broncos: 98 rushing, 80 passing, 178 total offense.
Chargers: 112 rushing, 150 passing, 262 total offense.

RUSHING

Broncos: Weese 6-33, Perrin 6-21, Keyworth 5-19, Lytle 4-16, Jensen 2-14, Moses 1-(-5).
Cowboys: Dorsett 17-50, Newhouse 13-45, P. Pearson 4-15, Staubach 7-4, Brinson 1-(-2).

PASSING

Broncos: Morton 0-1-0, 0; Weese 10-19-0, 94; Penrose 2-8-1, 18.
Cowboys: Staubach 15-20-1, 160.

RECEIVING

Broncos: Dolbin 5-85, Upchurch 2-14, Odoms 2-11, Moses 1-7, Keyworth 2-(-5).
Cowboys: P. Pearson 6-48, DuPree 3-47, D. Pearson 2-38, Dorsett 3-20, Newhouse 1-7.

FINAL REGULAR SEASON RECORD: 12-2, first place in AFC West.

DIVISIONAL PLAYOFF: December 24 at Mile High Stadium
BRONCOS 34, PITTSBURGH STEELERS 21

Pittsburgh   0   14   0   7—21
Denver   7   7   7   13—34

   Denver: Lytle 1 run (Turner kick)
   Pittsburgh: Bradshaw 1 run (Gerela kick)
   Denver: Armstrong 10 run (Turner kick)
   Pittsburgh: Harris 1 run (Gerela kick)
   Denver: Odoms 30 pass from Morton (Turner kick)
   Pittsburgh: Brown 1 pass from Bradshaw (Gerela kick)
   Denver: Turner 44 FG
   Denver: Turner 44 FG
   Pittsburgh: Dolbin 34 pass from Morton (Turner kick)

TEAM STATISTICS
Steelers: 127 rushing, 177 passing, 304 total offense.
Broncos: 103 rushing, 155 passing, 258 total offense.

RUSHING
Steelers: Harris 28-92, Bradshaw 4-21, Bleier 7-14.
Broncos: Armstrong 11-44, Lytle 12-26, Keyworth 5-20, Jensen 4-13, Morton 5-0.

PASSING
Steelers: Bradshaw 19-37-3, 177.
Broncos: Morton 11-23-0, 164.

RECEIVING
Steelers: Stallworth 4-80, Harris 4-20, Cunningham 3-42, Maxson 3-11, Bleier 2-10, Grossman 1-7, Swann 1-6, Brown 1-1.
Broncos: Odoms 5-43, Moses 2-45, Jensen 2-33, Dolbin 1-34, Armstrong 1-9.

AFC CHAMPIONSHIP: January 1, 1978, at Mile High Stadium
BRONCOS 20, OAKLAND RAIDERS 17

Oakland   3   0   0   14—17
Denver   7   0   7   6—20

   Oakland: Mann 20 FG
   Denver: Moses 74 pass from Morton (Turner kick)
   Denver: Keyworth 1 run (Turner kick)
   Oakland: Casper 7 pass from Stabler (Mann kick)
   Denver: Moses 12 pass from Morton (kick failed)
   Oakland: Casper 17 pass from Stabler (Mann kick)

TEAM STATISTICS

Raiders: 94 rushing, 204 passing, 298 total offense.

Broncos: 91 rushing, 217 passing, 308 total offense

RUSHING

Raiders: van Eeghen 20-71, Banaszak 7-22, Davis 9-1.

Broncos: Perrin 11-42, Lytle 7-26, Keyworth 8-19, Armstrong 7-16, Jensen 1-2, Morton 2-(-4), Moses 1-(-10).

PASSING

Raiders: Stabler 17-35-1, 215.

Broncos: Morton 10-20-1, 224.

RECEIVING

Raiders: Casper 5-71, Biletnikoff 4-38, Branch 3-59, van Eeghen 2-8, Bradshaw 1-25, Siani 1-12, Banaszak 1-2.

Broncos: Moses 5-168, Perrin 2-20, Jensen 1-20, Odoms 1-13, Keyworth 1-3.

SUPER BOWL XII: January 15, 1978, at New Orleans
DALLAS COWBOYS 27, BRONCOS 10

Dallas	10	3	7	7—27
Denver	0	0	10	0—10

Dallas: Dorsett 3 run (Herrera kick)

Dallas: Herrera 35 FG

Dallas: Herrera 43 FG

Denver: Turner 47 FG

Dallas: Johnson 45 pass from Staubach (Herrera kick)

Denver: Lytle 1 run (Turner kick)

Dallas: Richards 29 pass from Newhouse (Herrera kick)

TEAM STATISTICS

Cowboys: 143 rushing, 182 passing, 325 total offense.

Broncos: 121 rushing, 35 passing, 156 total offense.

RUSHING

Cowboys: Dorsett 15-66, Newhouse 14-55, White 1-13, P. Pearson 3-11, Staubach 3-6, Laidlaw 1-1, Johnson 1-(-9).

Broncos: Lytle 10-35, Armstrong 7-27, Weese 3-26, Jensen 1-16, Keyworth 5-9, Perrin 3-8.

PASSING

Cowboys: Staubach 17-25-0, 183; White 1-2-0, 5; Newhouse 1-1-0, 29.

Broncos: Morton 4-15-4, 39; Weese 4-10-0, 22.

RECEIVING

Cowboys: P. Pearson 5-37, DuPree 4-66, Newhouse 3-(-1), Johnson 2-53, Richards 2-38, Dorsett 2-11, D. Pearson 1-13.

Broncos: Dolbin 2-24, Odoms 2-9, Moses 1-21, Upchurch 1-9, Jensen 1-5, Perrin 1-(-7).

FINAL REGULAR SEASON STATISTICS

RUSHING

Armstrong 130-498, Perrin 110-456, Lytle 104-408, Keyworth 83-311, Jensen 40-143, Morton 31-125, Weese 11-56, Penrose 4-24, Upchurch 1-19, Dolbin 2-12, Kiick 1-1, Dilts 1-0, Moses 5-(-1).

PASSING

Morton 131-254, 1,929 yards, 8 interceptions, 14 touchdowns; Penrose 21-40, 217 yards, 4 interceptions, 0 touchdowns; Weese 11-20, 119 yards, 0 interceptions, 1 touchdown.

RECEIVING

Odoms 37-429, 3 touchdowns; Moses 27-539, 4; Dolbin 26-443, 3; Armstrong 18-128, 0; Lytle 17-198, 1; Upchurch 12-245, 2; Keyworth 11-48, 0; Perrin 6-106, 1; Jensen 4-63, 0; Egloff 2-27, 0; Kiick 2-14, 0; Turner 1-25, 1.

INDIVIDUAL HONORS

Pro Bowl: Lyle Alzado, Randy Gradishar, Tom Jackson, Billy Thompson, Louis Wright.

All-NFL: Alzado, Gradishar, T. Jackson, Thompson.

NFL Coach of the Year: Red Miller.

Notes and Sources

Post signifies the *Denver Post*
News signifies *Rocky Mountain News*
All dates are in 1977 unless otherwise noted

Introduction: The Young Sportswriter, a Different Denver ... and a Player Revolt

"tighter control over the operation is needed in the area of expenditures . . .": *News*, December 19, 1976

"We don't believe that it's possible to win a championship . . ." and "verified as in agreement with what we are doing . . .": *News*, December 22, 1976

"Now I think it is up to those players to prove . . ." and "In my 26 years of coaching and working with young people . . .": *News*, December 24, 1976

Chapter 2: Defenders of the Realm
It All Stops Here: Randy Gradishar

Woody Hayes's comments on Gradishar: *Post*, December 18, 1983

Commentator: Tom Jackson

"I wasn't really trying to hide it . . .": *Post*, November 30, 1973

Jackson background from various *News* and *Post* stories; also *Blitz: An Autobiography*, Tom Jackson with Woodrow Paige (Chicago: Contemporary Books, 1987).

Abandoned Ship: Joe Rizzo

". . . will be able to push a couple of vets in camp.": *Post*, June 2, 1981

Chapter 3: M&M Connection
Prelude

"It's incredible to see 16 and 17 year old kids who are so bright . . .":
Post, July 8

". . . deprive Denver fans of their Sunday afternoon football . . .": *Post*,
September 11

Chapter 4: Campers
Fort Collins: July 15–August 4

"It would be nice if we had a group here . . .": *Post*, July 18

"I felt like Rocky out there this afternoon . . .": *News*, July 24

"Everybody was broke . . .": *News*, July 25

". . . final chapter.": *News*, July 30

Chapter 5: Runners
Exhibitions: August 5–20

"I'm the most qualified . . ." and "The *News* editor waved a gun . . .":
Post, August 7

"Ciancio has always been against . . .": *Post*, August 14

"Police say bomb try . . .": *News*, August 9, 1997

"We're going to use that ground . . ." and "They just lit 'em up . . .":
News, August 5

"They want to go down to see shows like *Shenandoah* . . .": *Post*, August
11

"Where do you guys get that . . .": *Post*, August 13

Chapter 6: United Front

Yet More Exhibitions: August 21–September 10

"We have to teach our young children . . .": *Post*, August 24

"We've all got to get together . . .": *Post*, August 31

"I notice a very positive mental attitude . . .": *Post*, September 1

On the Nose: Rubin Carter

"It took four football players to subdue . . .": *Post*, February 26

". . . one of the highlights of this league as a person.": *Post*, March 29

". . . a fine young man.": *Post*, February 27

In the Clearing Stands a Boxer: Lyle Alzado

"Our nickname was the Golden Tornadoes . . ." and "I remember when the draft was . . .": *Post*, April 3

"I wanted to go real badly to New Mexico State but I didn't have the grades . . ." and "John Ralston is the finest thing . . .": *Post*, December 6, 1973

"I was in the Dirty Dozen. We've . . ." and "In some ways, Coach Ralston was . . .": *Mile High: The Story of Lyle Alzado and the Amazing Denver Broncos*. New York: Atheneum, 1978.

Chapter 7: Paving the Way

From the Gate: September 11–25

". . . media is downgrading us"; "The child should be taught in the language . . ."; "We can't park in front of our own . . ." and other quotes from stadium-area residents: *Post*, September 17

"The future of Denver is untold . . ." and "Each city has only one moment in history . . .": *Post*, September 18

"Every team has problems . . .": *Post*, September 20

"What'll you give me . . .": *Post*, September 23

"There are times when I'm filling out a form . . .": *Post*, September 24

"Oooh, bad dudes.": *News*, September 25

Still Unbeaten: September 26–October 9

"People are going to continue . . ."; "Most people can't work a 20-hour . . ."; and "I've met the big stars . . .": *Post*, September 28

"absolutely no interest . . .": *Post*, September 29

"Enough is whatever it takes to win the game . . .": *Post*, October 3

"emotions flared and several isolated . . .": *Post*, October 4

"This is the best country to get sick in . . .": *Post*, October 9

Chapter 8: Raiders, Raiders

"Ol' Hightops": Jim Turner

"I've always looked upon Ralston . . .": *News*, December 24, 1976

In Their House: October 10–16

"We've got to become more consistent . . .": *Post*, October 10

"I was just kind of disturbed about . . .": *Post*, October 13

"Seven NFL teams now use the 3-4 . . .": *Sports Illustrated*, October 17

"We have failed to challenge the people . . .": *Post*, October 14

"It's all over, fat man!": *Blitz*

Rematch: October 17–30

"fleabag joint of a bar" . . . : *Post*, October 17, 1978

"Clearly it hasn't yet gotten so bad . . ." and "Our players found out how much . . .": *Post*, October 22

"I'm worried, and I urge Coloradans to become aware of an emerging pattern of using . . .": *Post*, July 10

Carter and Lamm comments: *Post*, October 23

"We played one game a week . . .": *Post*, October 26

"We can't get it out fast enough . . .": *Post*, October 29

"We must hear from the farmers . . .": *Post*, October 30

"We're not ashamed of anything . . .": *Post*, October 31

Chapter 9: Rebounding and Receiving

Back on Track: October 31–November 13

"they better have the muscle . . .": *Post*, November 1

"I go hunting every year . . .": *Post*, November 4

"That cloud out there . . .": *Post*, November 5

"un-American . . ." and ". . . an important date to make.": *Post*, November 7

"consumer fraud" and "Service academy football is . . .": *Post*, November 11

"Judge": Riley Odoms

News conference comments: *Post*, February 29, 1972

Chapter 10: Standing Their Ground

First and Goal from the 1: November 14–27

". . . a 12-hour whirlpool day" and "the distinct impression that Denver would be competing very favorably . . .": *Post*, November 15

"I saw him every day, but I had no confrontations . . .": *News*, November 18

"I want you to learn what it is like . . .": *Post*, November 18 "something good at the end . . .": *Post*, November 26

"It was like a hockey game . . .": *Post*, November 27

"I had all the gears open . . .": *News*, November 28

"I just thought that something like that . . .": *Post*, November 28

Arabian Bar incident: *News*, November 28.

Down the Stretch: November 28–December 18

"This is the only way we can make certain . . ." and "We've got three more . . .": *Post*, November 29

"We're number one!": *News*, November 29

"I don't think that the lease . . .": *Post*, December 3

"I'm grateful I can still wander around . . .": *Post*, December 4

"Farming is so poor . . .": *Post*, December 11

". . . the greatest victory in the history of the world.": *Post*, December 12

"I consider this to be a real challenge . . .": *Post*, December 14

"hassled a little bit . . .": *Post*, December 15

"It could be . . ." and "I wanted to go up and wish him . . .": *Post*, December 17

"When he gets his release in Oakland . . .": *Post*, December 16

"The hell with that . . .": *News*, December 18

Chapter 11: Mardi Gras
First Round: December 19–24

"I've been in the playoffs many . . .": *Post*, December 19

"looks a lot better . . .": *Post*, December 22

"I told him I didn't want . . ." and "the worst game of my career . . .": *Post*, December 25

"pretty good game . . .": *Blitz*

AFC Championship: December 25–January 1

"We've been underdogs . . ." and "Nobody ever expects . . .": *Post*, December 28

"Everybody and anybody who's ever been an underdog . . ." and "We want to be accommodating . . .": *Post*, December 29

"His injury hasn't responded . . .": *Post*, December 31

"At the time, I didn't think I had . . ." and "Are there two balls . . .": *News*, January 2, 1978

"He just played on . . ."; "Hell, yes, it was . . ."; and "When you lose, you . . .": *Post*, January 2

Super Bowl XII: January 2–15

"an informal $2-million campaign . . .": *Post*, January 4, 1978

"poker.": *Post*, January 6, 1978

"That's what they were saying about us . . .": *Post*, January 3, 1978

"Everybody's going to be paid . . .": *Post*, January 7, 1978

"Tom Landry taught me . . .": *Post*, January 10, 1978

"hell of an offer . . .": *Post*, January 16, 1978

Chapter 12: Aftermath

Defense

"because I would not do some . . .": *Post*, December 23, 1982

Index